Guide to Manuscript Revision

ab .... Spell out abbreviation (M7b)

adv .... Use adverb form (U2c)

agr .... Make verb agree with subject
or pronoun with antecedent (U3a, U2d)

ap .... Use apostrophe (M2b)

cap .... Capitalize (M2a)

coll .... Use less colloquial word (U2a)

CS .... Revise comma splice (M4a)

d .... Improve diction (W3)

dev .... Develop your point (C1b, C2b)

div .... Revise word division (M7a)

DM .... Revise dangling modifier (U3c)

frag .... Revise sentence fragment (M3a)

FP .... Revise faulty parallelism (U3f)

awk .... Rewrite awkward sentence (U4)

lc .... Use lower case (M2a)

MM .... Shift misplaced modifier (U3c)

p .... Improve punctuation (M3-6)

¶ .... New paragraph (C1)

no¶ .... Take out paragraph break (C1)

ref .... Improve pronoun reference (U3b)

rep .... Avoid repetition (U3d)

shift .... Avoid shift in perspective (U3e)

sl .... Use less slangy word (U2a)

sp .... Revise misspelled word (M1)

st .... Improve sentence structure (U3, U4)

t .... Change tense of verb (U1a)

trans .... Provide better transition (C2e)

w .... Reduce wordiness (U4)

American English Today

American English Today

General Editor and Senior Author: **Hans P. Guth**

Complete Course and Reference Handbook

Third Edition

WEBSTER DIVISION/McGRAW-HILL BOOK COMPANY
New York   St. Louis   San Francisco   Dallas   Atlanta

Editorial Development: *John A. Rothermich*
Managing Editor: *Hester Eggert Weeden*
Design: *Bennie Arrington*
Production: *Judith Tisdale*

Acknowledgments—see page 482

Library of Congress Cataloging in Publication Data

Guth, Hans Paul, date
    Our changing language.

    (His American English today; [6])
    SUMMARY: A 12th grade text offering instruction in composition, word study, grammar, usage, mechanics, and speech.
    1. English language—Composition and exercises.
    2. English language—Grammar—1950–
    [1. English language—Composition and exercises.
    2. English language—Grammar] I. Title.
[PE1408.G933 1980 vol. 6] [PE1413] 808'.042s [808'.042] 79–13967
ISBN: 0-07-025022-7

THE AUTHOR

HANS P. GUTH

General Editor and Senior Author

Dr. Guth is a widely published teacher-scholar who writes about effective communication with the authority that comes from successful practice. He is widely known for his work in workshops and in-service meetings for teachers of language and composition. His first book on the teaching of English, *English Today and Tomorrow,* was widely praised and hailed as a "milestone" and as a book "with no equal in its field." His recent book for teachers, *English for a New Generation,* has been called "a book that every teacher of the language arts should read." Through his college textbooks—especially the widely used rhetoric handbook, *Words and Ideas* (Wadsworth)—Dr. Guth has become known as a leading authority on teaching composition to today's students. He has spoken at numerous regional and national conferences and has taught in institutes sponsored by Stanford University, University of Illinois, and University of Hawaii.

Consultants and Contributors

Student Writing	**Gabriele Rico,** *San Jose State University*
Cultural Minorities	**Carol Kizine,** *Kansas City Public Schools*
Linguistics	**Edgar H. Schuster,** *Allentown (Pa.) Public Schools*
Teaching Suggestions	**Barbara Johnston,** *San Jose, California*
Testing and Measurement	**William Kline,** *California Test Bureau*
Graphics	**Herbert Zettl,** *San Francisco State University*

The Authors and the Publishers also thank the following teachers who evaluated manuscript, provided hundreds of examples of student writing, and tried out *American English Today* in their classrooms:

Marge Archer, Lawrenceville, New Jersey
James Conway, St. Louis, Missouri
Jeanne Irwin, Los Angeles, California
Cherry Mallory, Kansas City, Missouri
Donald Mayfield, San Diego, California
Virginia McCormick, Allentown, Pennsylvania
Jane McGill, Chula Vista, California
Janet Minesinger, Columbia, Maryland
Nancy Mitchell, Lakewood, California
Richard E. Roberts, Clinton Corners, New York
Margaret Timm, Bay City, Michigan
Marilyn Walker, Salem, Oregon

To the Teacher

American English Today, Third Edition, offers solid productive work in the basic areas of language and composition. Its aim is to provide materials that are intelligible, workable, and motivating for today's students. The following are key features of the new Third Edition:

1. More varied, effective, and interesting exercises than any competing series.

2. A functional, plain-English approach designed to help students defeated by awkward, elaborate terminology or theory.

3. Streamlined, compact presentation for efficient study and reference.

4. A positive, constructive teaching program systematically developing the students' skills and proficiencies.

5. Frequent provision for measurement of student achievement, with new unit review exercises, diagnostic tests, and achievement tests. A new section on how to take tests, complete with sample tests, appears in the resource chapter of each volume.

6. High-interest materials designed to help teachers overcome students' resistance to English as a subject.

7. Effective use of charts and other visuals designed to help students take things in at a glance.

8. A positive, habit-building program for teaching standard English.

9. Proven step-by-step instruction in the process of composition.

10. Special attention to familiar trouble spots and problem areas for students.

Chapter Table of Contents

TABLE OF CONTENTS

Chapter   3

COMPOSITION   Writing for a Purpose

Chapter 4

USAGE Using Standard English   263

Chapter 5

MECHANICS   Words on a Page   333

Chapter 6

ORAL LANGUAGE   Public Speech   413

Chapter 7

RESOURCES   Special Helps for Writers   433

PROSE MODELS

To the Student

Language is our greatest invention. Without it, trade, government, family life, religion, and the arts would be either impossible or very different. How we use language, and how well, has much to do with what kind of people we are. Much of education in one way or another helps us extend our understanding and mastery of language.

As you extend your own understanding and mastery of language, remember these basic points:

(1) *Language has a history*. Language is the way it is for the same reason a mountain or a giant redwood is the way it is. The forces working on it from time immemorial have shaped it over the centuries.

(2) *Language is a system*. Just as the study of anatomy impresses us with the marvelous complexity of the human body, so the study of language impresses us with the complexity of human speech. The parts of a sentence work together in intricate ways.

(3) *Language is everywhere a part of our lives*. One of the most noticeable things about people is the way they talk. Schools teach standard English for two major reasons: Before radio and television helped to level speech differences, regional dialects could drift apart until they became a real barrier to communication. Speakers or writers who want to be heard outside their families and neighborhoods must be able to use the kind of language that is current everywhere. In the United States, as in other countries, the standard language has become the badge of the educated person and a symbol of social and economic status. It is essential for success in school and office.

The purpose of this book is to help you become more aware of how language works all around you in the real world. Its purpose is to help you hold your own when your turn comes to make yourself heard—in speaking or in writing.

Chapter 1

Words
Building Your Vocabulary

Chapter Preview 1

IN THIS CHAPTER:

- How to learn from language history.

- How to broaden your vocabulary for serious discussion and serious reading.

- How to master and use technical terms.

- How to use words that are clear and accurate.

- How to make effective use of connotative and figurative words.

Learn more about the rich vocabulary resources of English and put them to good use.

How can you best develop your knowledge of words? How can you expand your vocabulary?

The hard way to build up your word power is to study words as separate words. When we study words on word lists, we soon become discouraged by how many there are. A big dictionary lists many thousands of words. To make new words come to life for us, we ask questions like the following: Where do they come from? How are they related to other words? How do people use them? What role do they play in our lives?

Find the answers to these and similar questions about the words in the following preview exercises.

PREVIEW EXERCISE 1

How has our language developed its rich vocabulary resources? Throughout its history, words have come into English from *other languages*. Study the examples given in the five following sets. For each language, select three of the sample words. In your own words, explain briefly in a sentence or two what each word means and how it is used.

1. GREEK: ethnic, hypocrite, emphasis, anarchy, tyranny
2. LATIN: per capita, erroneous, emancipation, custody, authoritarian
3. FRENCH: élite, avant-garde, coup, deluxe, nonchalant
4. SPANISH: aficionado, padre, junta, Chicano, mariachi
5. ITALIAN: forte, soprano, finale, crescendo, bravura

Some words have played a special role in the American experience. They stand for something special in our history or *way of life*. Some of these words have become known around the world. Choose five of the following. For each, sum up briefly the role it has played in the American way of life.

1. blue jeans
2. dating
3. cowboy
4. dixie
5. drugstore
6. musical
7. vaudeville
8. slapstick
9. gangster
10. pioneer
11. sundae
12. drive-in
13. Model T
14. vigilante
15. Western
16. sheriff
17. jazz
18. posse
19. Mormons
20. Rotarians

Modern science, modern technology, and modern advertising constantly need *new words*. Often, they take an old word and give it a new meaning. Can you explain why each of the following new words (or old words with new meanings) is a recent addition to our vocabulary? Choose *ten* of these. In one sentence for each word you choose, explain what each means or how it is used.

1. minisub
2. flashcube
3. holding pattern
4. helipad
5. videotape
6. replay
7. hardware
8. hydrofoil
9. splashdown
10. closed circuit
11. feedback
12. rotary engine
13. voice-over
14. input
15. transplant
16. antibiotic
17. supersonic
18. microfilm
19. telephoto
20. transfusion

Study some of the major changes that have made English what it is today.

The story of English is the story of how a language spoken by small tribes of peasant-warriors became the national language of several major nations in the modern world. It is a story of words from many sources coming into our language since it was first spoken in the British Isles.

Words

A good dictionary includes a brief history of many of the words listed. We call this history of a word its **etymology**—the study of its origins, or roots. Dictionaries usually give etymological information in square brackets at the beginning or end of an entry:

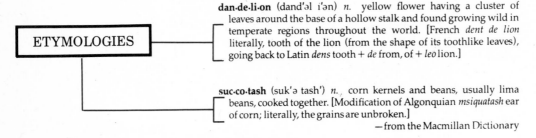

dan·de·li·on (dand'əl i'ən) *n.* yellow flower having a cluster of leaves around the base of a hollow stalk and found growing wild in temperate regions throughout the world. [French *dent de lion* literally, tooth of the lion (from the shape of its toothlike leaves), going back to Latin *dens* tooth + *de* from, of + *leo* lion.]

suc·co·tash (suk'ə tash') *n.* corn kernels and beans, usually lima beans, cooked together. [Modification of Algonquian *msiquatash* ear of corn; literally, the grains are unbroken.]

—from the Macmillan Dictionary

Here are some sample etymologies from the same dictionary:

con·sid·er ... [Old French *considerer* to observe closely, from Latin *considerare* originally, to observe the stars, from *con-* with + *sidus* star; from the ancient astrological practice of consulting the stars when trying to make a decision.]

hol·ster ... [Dutch *holster.*]

vi·a·ble ... [French *viable* capable of living, from *vie* life, from Latin *vita.*]

(Many dictionaries use abbreviations in their accounts of word history: *L* for Latin, *F* for French, *OE* for Old English, *G* for German, and the like.)

W1a
Language History

Study the major stages in the development of Modern English.

English, like most European languages, goes back to a *common Indo-European parent language.* English, German, and Russian, like Latin and Greek, all go back to a common language spoken (but never written down) about three thousand years before the birth of Christ. These languages are cousins, belonging to the same language family. To judge from words found in most Indo-European languages, the people who spoke the common parent language

- lived in an area where birch, beech, oak, and willow grew; where wolf, bear, beaver, eagle, and owl were found (perhaps an area along the Baltic coast of Germany and Poland).
- had dogs; raised pigs, cattle, and goats; raised grain crops.
- lived before the discovery of iron but after the invention of the wheel.

ENGLISH AND THE INDO-EUROPEAN FAMILY
(A Simplified Family Tree)

POLISH
CZECH
SERBO-CROATIAN
RUSSIAN
SLAVIC

BRETON
WELSH
GAELIC
CELTIC

PERSIAN
IRANIAN

SPANISH
PORTUGUESE
LATIN
FRENCH
ITALIAN

ARMENIAN

GREEK

LITHUANIAN
LATVIAN
BALTIC

NORWEGIAN
SWEDISH
DANISH
GERMAN
ENGLISH
DUTCH
Germanic

BENGALI

SANSKRIT

HINDI
INDIC

FOR DISCUSSION: Which other languages are the closest relatives of English? What other languages represented here have you heard spoken? When and where? Which have played a role in the history of your family or your community? How?

Words

As these people spread over a larger area, different groups developed their own dialects. These later became separate languages. Major subdivisions of the original Indo-European language include the following:

CELTIC: at one time, the language of England and France; surviving only in areas like Brittany and Wales;

GERMANIC: splitting up later into English. Dutch, German, Danish, Swedish, and Norwegian;

LATIN: splitting up into Italian, French, Spanish, and Portuguese;

GREEK: parent of modern Greek;

SLAVIC: splitting up into Czech, Polish, Russian, and Serbo-Croatian (the language of modern Yugoslavia);

PERSIAN: the language of modern Iran;

SANSKRIT: an ancient language once spoken in India and still preserved in religious writings.

Some languages *not* derived from Indo-European are Hungarian and Finnish (related to Turkish); the Hebrew of the Old Testament (related to Arabic); the languages of Africa, the Pacific, and the Far East.

Here are some words shared by many Indo-European languages:

ENGLISH	GERMAN	LATIN
father	Vater	pater
mother	Mutter	mater
brother	Bruder	frater
heart	Herz	cord-

The basic number words in many of the Indo-European languages go back to a common root:

ENGLISH	GERMAN	LATIN
two	zwei	duo
three	drei	tres
seven	sieben	septem
nine	neun	novem

Here are the major stages in the development of English from its ancient roots:

(1) The oldest form of English was brought to England by Germanic invaders, the **Anglo-Saxons.** Toward the end of the fifth century A.D., Germanic tribes from the Continent invaded Britain. Over a period of two hundred years, they gradually took over most of the country. These tribes spoke **Old English,** a close cousin of Dutch and

German. Even today, many English and German words are very similar:

| ENGLISH: | hand | finger | water | house | drink |
| GERMAN: | Hand | Finger | Wasser | Haus | trinken |

The Old English period stretches roughly from A.D. 450 to 1100. Much of the basic vocabulary of English to this day is of Old English stock. In the eighth century, a second wave of Germanic invaders began to raid the coast of England: the Vikings from Denmark and Norway. After much fighting, they settled in the northeastern part of England and gradually blended with the Anglo-Saxon population. Many words from their Scandinavian dialects, called **Norse** in most dictionaries, reinforced the common Germanic stock of English. Here are some everyday words they brought to England:

| cast | egg | hit | skin | take |
| cut | fellow | leg | sky | wing |

(2) *As the result of the Norman conquest, thousands of French words came into English.* The Normans were originally Viking raiders who had settled in northern France. They had gradually adopted the language of their French neighbors. After the Battle of Hastings in 1066, the Normans conquered all of England. Norman nobles took over the land. Norman priests took over the highest posts in the church. The language of the king's court, of government, law, and literature, for several centuries was French.

Meanwhile, English was still spoken by the common people. In their dealings with their French-speaking rulers, they learned thousands of French words. These gradually became a permanent part of the language during the **Middle English** period (roughly from A.D. 1100 to 1500). Many of the words taken over were related to the political and military role of the new rulers:

| court | army | treasure | peace | messenger |
| castle | servant | tower | treason | privilege |

To this day, our language of government and law includes many words that came from French:

impeach   ratify   sovereign   revenue   statute

Many of the new French words provided doubles for English words that survived. We call such words with roughly the same meaning **synonyms:**

| ENGLISH: | might | wish | bough | help | begin |
| FRENCH: | power | desire | branch | aid | commence |

(3) English took over thousands of Latin and Greek words. For centuries, Latin was the language of religion, education, and science. Latin was the language of the medieval (Roman Catholic) church. The authorized Roman Catholic version of the Bible was in Latin. Schools and universities taught Latin (and, to a lesser extent, Greek) to all students. Most books printed in Europe before 1500 were in Latin. Early modern science used Latin as an international language. Latin was the language of educated people throughout Europe.

When the Anglo-Saxons converted to Christianity, they took over many Latin and Greek words related to the teachings and ceremonies of the church:

apostle   creed   disciple   martyr   shrine

Here are some Latin words that came into our language during the early stages of Modern English—the time when the King James Version of the Bible was written, and when the plays of Shakespeare were first performed. Can you give a one-sentence definition for each of these words?

agile   confederate   infinite   genius   rational

For many familiar English words, Latin provided synonyms—words very close to them in meaning:

ENGLISH:	breakable	sunder	feeling	onlooker
LATIN:	fragile	separate	emotion	spectator

(4) Modern English took over words from several of England's neighbors on the Continent. Much of the language of music came into English from Italy. Words like *solo, tenor, opera, aria,* and *violin* were Italian. For a time, Holland was a great naval power, rivaling England. Many Dutch sailors' words were taken into English. How many of the following examples of maritime vocabulary do you and your classmates know?

boom	buoy	keel	scow
bowsprit	dock	lighter	skipper

EXERCISE 1

Study the italicized word in each of the following sentences. Each word has come into English from one of the major outside sources of our vocabulary: Latin, Greek, or French. Of the three possible meanings, choose the one that best fits the sentence. Put the letter for the right meaning after the number of the sentence.

EXAMPLE: 7. Many *ethnic* groups have made this country great.
            a. moral   b. national   c. socioeconomic

(Answer)   *7b*

1. Town meetings provided a *forum* for the exchange of ideas.
   a. door   b. marketplace   c. prison
2. The senator had an upright bearing and *patrician* manners.
   a. aristocratic   b. commonplace   c. unusual
3. People used *barbaric* methods in treating the mentally ill.
   a. simple   b. tried and true   c. very cruel
4. The government expected considerable *revenue* from the tax.
   a. opposition   b. income   c. support
5. The missionaries taught the *creed* in schools and churches.
   a. beliefs   b. letters   c. regulations
6. The struggle was continued by the *disciples* of the leader.
   a. star pupils   b. relatives   c. enemies
7. The quarrel had been only an *episode* in our journey to the West.
   a. high point   b. short event   c. obituary
8. The newspapers were full of *homage* to the new conductor.
   a. sly barbs   b. good wishes   c. highest praise
9. Our friends accepted the king as their true *sovereign*.
   a. counselor   b. friend   c. ruler
10. She merely *paraphrased* the contents of the letter for us.
    a. questioned   b. restated   c. forgot
11. A *panic* broke out in the building when the rumor spread.
    a. blind rush   b. apprehension   c. applause
12. The President put strong *emphasis* on the need for unity.
    a. refusal   b. stress   c. resistance
13. Lawyers were still trying to interpret the new *statute*.
    a. sculpture   b. government   c. law
14. The Senate refused to *ratify* the treaty.
    a. approve   b. debate   c. change
15. The investigators faced an *infinite* number of possibilities.
    a. unchanged   b. unlimited   c. large
16. The burglar who entered the window must have been *agile*.
    a. quick-moving   b. desperate   c. unknown
17. The suspect and her *confederate* had left the country.
    a. classmate   b. admirer   c. partner
18. We were all too excited to make a *rational* decision.
    a. sudden   b. right   c. intelligent
19. Isak Dinesen took her readers to the *realm* of fantasy.
    a. kingdom   b. excitement   c. realism
20. The new material was much less *fragile* than glass.
    a. expensive   b. breakable   c. transparent

Words that have come into our language from Latin and French often provide *close synonyms* for older English words. Look at the original English words in the column on the left. In the column on

EXERCISE 2

the right, find a close synonym that came into the language later. Put the letter for the synonym after the number of the word.

1. hearty	A. conceal
2. dear	B. sacred
3. childhood	C. infancy
4. trip	D. expensive
5. make bigger	E. malignant
6. understanding	F. cordial
7. hallowed	G. boil
8. evil	H. magnify
9. reckon	I. labor
10. hide	J. count
11. feed	K. pursue
12. follow	L. excursion
13. folk	M. people
14. mankind	N. intelligence
15. shun	O. branch
16. work	P. nourish
17. seethe	Q. rage
18. bough	R. humble
19. wrath	S. avoid
20. meek	T. humanity

EXERCISE 3

Some words that have come into English were once close synonyms of other earlier words. But the words have come to serve somewhat different purposes. For *five* of the following pairs, explain briefly what the two words have in common and what sets them apart.

1. fear—terror	6. frail—fragile
2. stool—chair	7. luck—fortune
3. sickness—disease	8. deep—profound
4. house—mansion	9. ask—demand
5. ask—interrogate	10. appease—pacify

EXERCISE 4

After the number of each of the following words, write the name of the *language from which it came into English.* Be prepared to explain in class what you could find out about the etymological background of the word. (Use a college dictionary if one is available.)

1. alphabet	6. caravan	11. etiquette	16. pundit
2. bamboo	7. clan	12. ghoul	17. shibboleth
3. banana	8. coffee	13. honcho	18. ski
4. buccaneer	9. coolie	14. matinee	19. sloop
5. budget	10. czar	15. patio	20. trek

Study the history of a word to understand its range of meaning and its changing uses.

Words do not stand still. They shift in meaning, lose some of their old uses, and find new applications. *Hound* once stood for any kind of dog but later came to stand for a special kind of hunting dog. A good dictionary gives us the original meaning of a word and shows how it has changed or branched out.

The following entry shows how the meaning of *nice* shifted gradually from "ignorant" through "finicky" to "respectable":

> **nice** \ 'nɪs \ *adj* [ME, foolish, wanton, fr. OF, fr. L *nescias* ignorant, fr. *nescire* not to know, fr. *ne-* not + *scire* to know] **1:** showing fastidious or finicky tastes : REFINED **2:** marked by or demanding delicate discrimination or treatment *nice* distinction **3a:** PLEASING, AGREEABLE < *nice* time > < *nice* person > **b:** well-executed < *nice* shot > **4a:** socially acceptable : WELL-BRED < offensive to *nice* people > **b:** VIRTUOUS, RESPECTABLE < *nice* girl >

> *—Webster's New Students Dictionary*

Remember:

(1) Old words adapt to new experience. As our way of life changes, we stretch the meaning of an old word to fit the new facts:

shoot	originally "hurl" or "throw"; it came to mean "fire a gun" after firearms replaced spears and other thrown weapons
broadcast	originally "scatter seed with a wide circular motion," the way a farmer used to at sowing time, walking down the field; it came to mean "transmit (and thus spread widely) by radio"

(2) Often, words shift gradually by small logical steps, sometimes traveling far from their original meaning. Here is a rough outline tracing the gradual shifts in the history of some familiar words. What is the missing modern meaning in the spaces left blank?

meal	time > time for eating > food
pretty	tricky > clever > comely > beautiful
curious	careful > inquisitive > strange
weird	fateful > supernatural > _____
wit	the mind > good sense > _____
cunning	knowing > skillful > _____

(3) Almost all of our more common words have branched out from a common core to develop several meanings and applications. For the verb *run*, a widely used high school dictionary lists fifty-five meanings. Can you explain how the following words branched out

into several related meanings? What major current meaning is missing in the spaces left blank?

shop	1. workshop 2. store 3. factory
hand	1. part of body 2. handwriting 3. applause 4. cards dealt a player 5. laborer
magazine	1. storehouse 2. storehouse for powder or ammunition 3. _____
fraternity	1. brotherhood by blood 2. brotherly feeling for all people 3. _____
short	1. short circuit 2. short _____

(4) Change in meaning often moves in familiar directions. Here are some kinds of change that we encounter frequently:

• A word may *narrow* its range. *Ill,* originally "bad" or "evil" in a more general sense, has come to mean primarily "sick." The broader meaning survives in *ill-bred* and *ill-advised.* Here are some examples of such narrowing:

captain	originally the same word as *chieftain:* generally a "leader"; then narrowed to the commander of a ship or a company
starve	originally "die"; then narrowed to "die of hunger"

• Words that stand for something good or indifferent may shift to express *disapproval.* The word *accident* originally meant any accidental or chance happening. It has come to stand for unfortunate accidents, mishaps, mischances. Other examples:

gossip	godparent > idle, malicious talker
knave	boy > rascal

• A name may be transferred from one thing to another by some process of *association.* Here is the development of *stogy:*

> *Stogy,* for instance, calls to mind the Conestoga wagon and the part it played in the amazing westward push early in the nineteenth century. . . . *Conestoga* was the name of an Iroquoian tribe, now long extinct. The tribal designation was applied to a valley in Lancaster County, Pennsylvania, where the large covered wagon which was the principal means of westward transportation before the introduction of railroads seems to have originated. The early Conestoga wagoners rolled long cigars for smoking on their trips, and such a cigar was called a *conestogy* (which is merely the earlier pronunciation of *Conestoga,* like *Iowy* for Iowa). This was subsequently clipped to *stogy.* —Thomas Pyles, *Words and Ways of American English*

WHAT'S NEW IN DICTIONARIES?

economy-size, applied *attrib.,* esp. in *Advertising,* to objects which are sold in a size that is said to be economically advantageous to the customer; also *economy-sized* adj.; also in extended uses. orig. *U.S.*

In practice freq. but not always the largest packet, etc., in a series.
1950 R. P. BISSELL *Stretch on River* xix. 185 The only trouble with the economy size tube of shaving cream is that it takes up more room in the valise than a pair of rubber boots.

cope, *v.²* Add: **4. b.** *absol.* To manage, deal (competently) with, a situation or problem. *colloq.*

1934 E. BOWEN *Cat Jumps* 248 Angela rang the bell wildly for someone to come and cope. 1955 *Essays in Criticism* V. 62 More confidence might be placed in the writer did we not find on the same page a typical shift of tone to this, on Romeo and Juliet: 'the kids get involved in a lively way, but then they cannot cope.'

Frisbee, frisbee (fri·zbi). Also **frisby.** [See quot. 1970.] A concave plastic disc which spins when thrown into the air and is used in a catching game.

The word *Frisbee* is a proprietary name in the U.S. (see quot. 1959).
1957 *Newsweek* 8 July 85 The object of the game is simply for one player to toss the Frisbee, or disk, into the air and try to keep it from his opponent's grasp.

brai·nwashing. orig. *U.S.* [f. BRAIN *sb.* + WASHING *vbl. sb.* 1. *fig.*] The systematic and often forcible elimination from a person's mind of all established ideas, esp. political ones, so that another set of ideas may take their place; this process regarded as the kind of coercive conversion practised by certain totalitarian states on political dissidents. Also *attrib.* and *transf.* Hence, by back-formation, **brainwash** *v. trans.,* to practise brainwashing on; **brainwashed** *ppl. a.;* **brainwasher,** one who practises it.

1950 E. HUNTER in *New Leader* 7 Oct. 7/2 'Brain-reform' is the objective, popularly referred to as 'brainwashing'. 1952 *Time* 26 May 41/1 Ai Tze-chi was Red China's chief indoctrinator or, as he was generally called, Brainwasher No. 1. 1953 *Manch. Guardian Weekly* 21 May 15 You refer to brainwashing. You feel ..that you have been browbeaten? 1953 *Sat. Even. Post* 31 Oct. 10/1 The anticommunist soldiers..may be blackmailed or brain-washed or third-degreed.

cat, *sb.¹* Add: **2.**
c. An expert in, or one expertly appreciative of, jazz. *slang* (orig. *U.S.*). Cf. *HEP-CAT.

[1922 J. A. CARPENTER (*title of ballet*) Krazy Kat.] 1932 *Melody Maker* Oct. 836/1 [citing L. Armstrong] All the cats were there. 1935 *Down Beat* 1 Nov. 8 The slanguage of swing-terms that 'cats' use.

A Supplement to the Oxford English Dictionary, © Oxford University Press, 1972

In 1972, the publishers of the **Oxford English Dictionary** listed new words and meanings that have come into English in modern times. To judge from these examples, *what kinds* of words does the dictionary maker have to watch out for? For each of the examples above, give a one-sentence definition in your own words.

(5) As words change, some of their older meanings go out of use. If we still occasionally encounter these meanings, we call them **archaic.** If they have gone out of use altogether, we call them **obsolete.** Here are examples of meanings no longer in common use from a book published in 1782:

We are all animated with the spirit of an *industry* which is unfettered and unrestrained. (diligent word)

A pleasing uniformity of decent *competence* appears throughout our habitations. (enough to live on)

There he sees ... a farmer who does not *riot* on the labor of others. (live luxuriously)

Words

EXERCISE 1

Check your dictionary for the *original meaning* of the following words. Answer each question in a word or phrase.

1. What was originally stored in a *barn?*
2. What was the original meaning of *wife?*
3. Does a *husband* have to be a married man?
4. What was the original occupation of a *lady?*
5. What were the original duties of a *marshal?*
6. What was the most basic privilege of a *lord?*
7. Why would it originally have been hard to "pocket" a *fee?*
8. What did the *gentle* in "gentleman" originally stand for?
9. What kind of stories did a *jester* originally tell?
10. What animal is hidden in the word *chivalry?*

EXERCISE 2

How much does your dictionary tell you about words that have an interesting history? Look up five of the following. Tell the story of each in a sentence or two.

1. master	11. psalm
2. altar	12. loyal
3. candidate	13. gerrymander
4. parliament	14. arena
5. crusade	15. ambassador
6. messiah	16. hazard
7. stevedore	17. enchantment
8. economy	18. curfew
9. senate	19. pedagogue
10. filibuster	20. savage

EXERCISE 3

Answer the questions about each of the following words in a sentence. (Your teacher may assign different parts of this exercise to different members of the class.)

1. What is the buried *original meaning* of each: *Halloween, handicap, disaster, inveigle, algebra?*
2. What are three major *different current meanings* for each of the following nouns: *foot, crown, pipe, train, paper?*
3. How does the history of each of the following illustrate a change from desirable to undesirable: *ban, casualty, censure, idiot, predicament?*
4. How does each of the following words illustrate the transfer from a proper name to a noun conveying a more general meaning: *atlas, cereal, marathon, vandalism, boycott?*
5. What is one new or modern application of each of the following older words: *screen, lobby, basket, tube, pilot?*

W2a

After the number of each word, put the letter of the choice closest to it in meaning.

1. malignant	a. evil	b. pointed	c. wandering
2. statute	a. road map	b. condition	c. law
3. cordial	a. tied up	b. heartfelt	c. very hot
4. filibuster	a. reprimand	b. excavate	c. stall
5. creed	a. credit	b. belief	c. reputation
6. shibboleth	a. hymn	b. touchstone	c. ritual meal
7. realm	a. square mile	b. joist	c. kingdom
8. infancy	a. childhood	b. poverty	c. training
9. pundit	a. wise person	b. follower	c. choirboy
10. predicament	a. long sermon	b. plight	c. experiment
11. pacify	a. make calm	b. join forces	c. antagonize
12. pedagogue	a. teacher	b. foot doctor	c. nursery
13. impeach	a. engrave	b. apologize	c. force out
14. disciple	a. letter	b. pupil	c. record
15. revenue	a. outgo	b. interest	c. income
16. interrogate	a. rainproof	b. connect	c. question
17. confederate	a. taxpayer	b. partner	c. lawyer
18. profound	a. very deep	b. spotty	c. visible
19. coolie	a. worker	b. adviser	c. pal
20. ratify	a. split up	b. give notice	c. approve

Keep learning new words.

W2
LEARNING NEW WORDS

To use language well in speaking and writing, you need to be able to choose the right word. To profit from your reading, you need a good reading vocabulary. In any occupation, you need to know the language of the trade.

Keep adding new words to your vocabulary. Know how to study new words and how to watch them in action.

To make new words your own, study what they mean and how they are used.

W2a
Words in Context

How do we learn new words? In order to make a word really your own, follow these steps:

(1) Study the definition of a word carefully. A good **definition** sums up in a sentence or two exactly what the word stands for. Sometimes writers or speakers define a difficult word. Often you have to look up a word in a good dictionary. On the following page are some typical dictionary definitions:

verdict	the finding or decision of a jury on the matter submitted to them in trial
subsidy	a grant by a government to a private person or company to assist an enterprise deemed advantageous to the public
trustee	a natural or legal person to whom property is legally committed to be administered for the benefit of a beneficiary (as a person or a charitable organization)

Try to repeat the definition *in your own words*. There is no point in memorizing a definition that you don't fully understand. Restate a dictionary definition something like this:

subsidy	money that the government gives to a business when helping that business seems in the public interest
trustee	a person or organization that is legally in charge of property to be managed for someone else's benefit

(2) Pay special attention to distinctive features. Ask: What makes this word different from others that might be similar in meaning or in use? A definition often places the word in a general category first. Then the definition shows how the word is different from other things in the same category.

The following definitions fit this general scheme:

WORD TO BE DEFINED	WHAT GENERAL CATEGORY?	HOW IS IT DIFFERENT?
A franchise	is the right to market a brand-name product,	granted by the original company for a special area.
An apprentice	is a worker	receiving systematic instruction in the craft or trade.

(3) Study unfamiliar words in context. Fix your attention not on the word alone but on how it is used. Often the statement of which the word is a part gives us important clues to its meaning. Look for familiar *context clues:*

• A *definition* or paraphrase translates the word, sometimes following the word at some distance in the same sentence or paragraph:

The influence of technology on the way we think is obvious to the *anthropologist*—the student of our human ways.

- One or more *synonyms* appear in discussion of the same idea:

Fanatics commit themselves wholeheartedly to an idea, *dogmatically* rejecting anything that might change their minds. (narrow-minded attitude that suits a fanatic)

- One or more *examples* go with a general word:

Humanity has found it hard to escape a familiar *predicament*—too much brawn with too little brain. (something undesirable that is like a trap)

- Details furnish the *elements* for a definition:

Every human being is a *paradox*—half dust, half spirit. (something mixed of contradictory elements)

- Contrasting elements point to their *opposite:*

Today, even brutal dictatorships give lip service to *humanitarian* principles. (the opposite of brutal)

(4) *Fix the meaning of a word in your mind by an example.* Dictionaries often provide an example of the word's use in a sample sentence or phrase:

reciprocal	mutual; shared or felt equally by both sides; returned in kind (They feared the *reciprocal* devastation of nuclear war) (The countries extended *reciprocal* rights to each other's citizens)
temporize	to draw out discussions or negotiations in order to gain time (We *temporized* until we could tell what they wanted us to say)

Check each italicized word in your dictionary. Find the meaning that fits the context. Restate the meaning *in your own words* and write it after the number of the sentence.

EXERCISE 1

1. The course was designed to help students develop their *potential.*
2. The sales representatives of the computer corporation received all their income from *commissions.*
3. The lawyer showed the judge the *affidavit.*
4. The expression on their faces showed that Uncle Joe was playing the *martyr* again.
5. His aunt and uncle had joined a group of *pacifists* during the war.
6. The school had completely changed its *curriculum.*
7. It took the passengers forty minutes to go through *customs.*
8. *Erosion* has destroyed areas that used to feed many people.
9. Doctors were expecting a flu *epidemic* during the coming winter.
10. The author thoroughly enjoyed the free *publicity.*
11. The television station canceled the *controversial* program.

12. The employees were used to the employer's *paternalism.*
13. This company needs better *rapport* between management and the workers on the assembly line.
14. The story of their trek through the desert is an *epic* of endurance and determination.
15. The President's decision served as a *catalyst.*

After the number of each sentence, put the letter for the choice closest in meaning to the italicized word. Be prepared to explain in class how the *context of the word* helps you to understand and remember its meaning.

1. Everyone in the room smiled at my little brother's *ingenuous* remark.
   a. naïve   b. casual   c. remembered
2. The government's already stiff requirements were becoming more *stringent.*
   a. lax   b. demanding   c. delayed
3. *Militant* workers refused to settle the strike.
   a. up in arms   b. overworked   c. well-paid
4. The defense lawyer *refuted* the charges point by point.
   a. repeated   b. knocked out   c. discussed
5. She did not say so, but the *implication* was that we had failed.
   a. news   b. reason   c. hint
6. After centuries of *despotism,* the nation gained its freedom.
   a. complaints   b. taxation   c. tyranny
7. After six months, Margot was still a *probationary* employee.
   a. on trial basis   b. in good standing   c. efficient
8. There had never been a fire, and our fire drills were *perfunctory.*
   a. thorough   b. out of date   c. halfhearted
9. My father tried to *intimidate* us by stern looks, but he never actually punished anyone.
   a. scare   b. penalize   c. reward
10. Each person is a *unique* individual and contributes to the group in a different way.
    a. alone   b. one of a kind   c. part of a whole
11. In the era of the hydrogen bomb, politics is as *obsolete* as oxcarts on Broadway.
    a. dangerous   b. outdated   c. familiar
12. Countless patriotic speeches had made many people suspicious of *grandiloquent* words.
    a. bombastic   b. new   c. indecisive
13. The visiting diplomats were friendly at the banquet but very *truculent* at the conference table.
    a. friendly   b. talkative   c. stubborn

14. The founder of the firm had been motivated not by just ordinary greed but by a monumental *rapacity*.
    a. kindness   b. pride   c. extreme greed

15. Former friends had turned into *implacable* enemies, rejecting all thought of compromise.
    a. unforgiving   b. unexpected   c. blameworthy

16. Centuries of sun, wind, and rain had finally *obliterated* all traces of human habitation.
    a. erased   b. changed   c. accentuated

17. The listeners looked at the speaker with a *rapt* expression, absorbed in the vision of a better tomorrow.
    a. bored   b. doubtful   c. entranced

18. The suspect was beginning to show the effects of lack of sleep and *incessant* questioning.
    a. unceasing   b. occasional   c. infrequent

19. The pilot gingerly guided the boat through the *treacherous* waters.
    a. dangerous   b. quiet   c. deep

20. Scientific research proves previous findings false as often as it *corroborates* them and proves them true.
    a. contradicts   b. bears out   c. records

EXERCISE 3

Choose five of the following words. Explain briefly *where and how* you have found each used.

1. technicality	6. motivate	11. overt
2. photogenic	7. distortion	12. ostensible
3. satellite	8. subsistence	13. compulsive
4. assess	9. intervention	14. intuition
5. concept	10. nostalgia	15. alienated

W2b
Synonyms and Antonyms

Expand your knowledge of words by studying synonyms and antonyms.

The quickest and briefest way to show the meaning of a word is to give another word that has almost the same meaning. We call such words **synonyms.** Dictionaries give *order* as a synonym of *command.* Sometimes we can pinpoint a word by giving another word that is almost its exact opposite. We call such words **antonyms.** *Eager* is an antonym of *reluctant.*

Look at the way synonyms can help us with unfamiliar words:

exorbitant	excessive, extravagant, unreasonable
rustic	rural, simple, rough, uncouth

Look at the way antonyms can help us understand the meaning of an unfamiliar word:

sophisticated | crude, naïve, simple

Remember:

(1) We usually have a choice of several words that mean roughly but not quite the same thing. As the result of constant additions over the centuries, our language offers us a wealth of resources. When we travel, the result may be a *trip,* a *journey,* a *voyage,* an *excursion,* a *jaunt,* or a *tour.* It may even be an *expedition,* a *cruise,* or a *safari.* A "word hoard" like *Roget's Thesaurus* lists key ideas and then provides dozens of closely related words. How do the following words overlap in meaning? How do they differ?

food	nourishment, sustenance, nurture, provender, provisions, rations, diet, victuals, edibles, viands
repetition	reiteration, duplication, recurrence, echo, encore, refrain, recapitulation
freedom	liberty, independence, autonomy, emancipation, elbowroom, laissez-faire

(2) Learn to choose the synonym with the right shade of meaning. No two words are simply interchangeable. **Synonyms** are words that mean almost the same—but not quite. *Discard* and *spurn* are synonyms of *reject.* But we discard things rather casually. We reject something more deliberately. We spurn something with indignation.

A good dictionary shows such differences, often in synonymies following the regular dictionary entry. Restate in your own words the differences that set apart the words in the following sets:

Syn. *v.* **1. Roam, rove, ramble** mean to wander. **Roam** means to go about here and there as one pleases over a wide area, with no special plan or aim: *The photographer roamed about the world.* **Rove** usually adds the suggestion of a definite purpose, though not of a settled destination: *Submarines roved the ocean.* **Ramble** particularly suggests straying from a regular path or plan and wandering about aimlessly for one's own pleasure: *We rambled through the shopping district.*

—*Thorndike Barnhart Dictionary*

syn LONG, YEARN, HANKER, PINE, HUNGER, THIRST mean to have a strong desire for something. LONG implies a wishing with one's whole heart and often a striving to attain; YEARN suggests an eager, restless, or painful longing; HANKER suggests the uneasy promptings of unsatisfied appetite or desire; PINE implies a languishing or a fruitless longing for what is impossible; HUNGER and THIRST imply an insistent or impatient craving or a compelling need

—*Webster's Seventh New Collegiate Dictionary*

W2b

A. Of the three words that follow each listed word, two mean roughly the same as the original word. Find the word that is *not* a synonym. Put its number after the letter of the original word.

EXERCISE 1

EXAMPLE: 7. **apathetic** a. lifeless b. sluggish c. brilliant
(Answer) *7c*

1. **agile**	a. spry	b. very dry	c. nimble
2. **enterprise**	a. combat	b. undertaking	c. venture
3. **loaf**	a. loiter	b. dawdle	c. pry
4. **abridge**	a. connect	b. abbreviate	c. curtail
5. **punctual**	a. prompt	b. pointed	c. timely
6. **exertion**	a. hostility	b. effort	c. endeavor
7. **interfere**	a. meddle	b. intrude	c. bypass
8. **covetous**	a. transparent	b. avaricious	c. greedy
9. **postpone**	a. set up	b. defer	c. suspend
10. **convenient**	a. suitable	b. appropriate	c. hospitable

B. Of the three words that follow each listed word, two mean roughly the opposite of the original word. Find the word that is *not* an antonym. Put its number after the letter of the original word.

EXAMPLE: 5. **indifferent** a. eager b. similar c. interested
(Answer) *5b*

1. **active**	a. rotating	b. passive	c. stagnant
2. **encourage**	a. deter	b. promote	c. dissuade
3. **deliberate**	a. inadvertent	b. regular	c. unintentional
4. **stingy**	a. lavish	b. generous	c. unusual
5. **obstinate**	a. diagonal	b. flexible	c. pliable
6. **extravagant**	a. colorful	b. moderate	c. restrained
7. **concentrate**	a. disperse	b. examine	c. scatter
8. **respect**	a. contempt	b. scorn	c. attendance
9. **immune**	a. vulnerable	b. experimental	c. susceptible
10. **authoritarian**	a. traditional	b. liberal	c. permissive

For each of the following ideas, find *two* or more synonyms. Write them after the number of each idea.

EXERCISE 2

EXAMPLE: work
(Answer) *labor, toil, drudgery, task*

1. line of work	6. unexpected or unusual benefit or reward
2. payment for work	7. tight with money
3. time off from work	8. trying something out
4. group of workers	9. plan for work to be done
5. person directing work	10. something that has been done well

Words

EXERCISE 3

Choose *five* of the following groups of words. Explain briefly the differences in meaning that set the synonyms in each group apart. (Your teacher may ask you to use a dictionary in working this exercise.)

1. calm—serene—placid
2. enthusiasm—gusto—fervor
3. bias—predisposition—prejudice
4. emotion—passion—affection
5. grotesque—bizarre—fantastic
6. tradition—convention—custom
7. instruct—educate—train
8. cryptic—secretive—mysterious
9. pretend—dissemble—simulate
10. hesitate—vacillate—procrastinate
11. revolution—insurrection—mutiny
12. regret—remorse—contrition
13. vindicate—rehabilitate—reinstate
14. pardon—parole—amnesty
15. practical—feasible—expedient

W2c

Latin and Greek Roots

Expand your knowledge of words by studying Latin and Greek roots.

Knowledge of familiar building blocks often helps us understand and remember a new word. We have many words in our language in which the syllable *noc–* means "harm." It appears in words like *noxious* ("harmful"), *innocuous* ("harmless"), and *innocent* ("not meaning any harm"). *Inter–* often means "between." We find it in words like *interval* ("pause between two events") and *intervene* ("come between two quarreling parties").

Do the following to help you build up your vocabulary:

(1) Relate unfamiliar words to familiar Latin roots. The meaning of *innate* is "inborn." The same root is used in *prenatal* ("before birth") and in *native* ("someone who was born here"). Such cross-references help us get from the familiar to the new.

Here is a review of some of the more helpful Latin roots. Choose one of the three groups of ten on the next page. Translate each word given as an example in such a way that *the meaning of the root* shows. For each sample word, try to give a rough translation like the following:

flor–	*flower*	florist: "flower seller"
		flora: "flowers and plants of a region"
		florid: "flowery (language or style)"

ROOT	MEANING	EXAMPLES
ann–, enn–	*year*	annual, centennial, perennial
aqu–	*water*	aquarium, aquatic, aqueduct
audi–	*hear*	audition, auditorium, inaudible
capit–	*head*	capital, decapitate, per capita
carn–	*flesh*	carnal, incarnation, carnivorous
cred–	*believe*	credible, credulous, credo
culp–	*guilt*	culpable, culprit, exculpate
curr–	*run*	current, concurrent, precursor
doc–	*teach*	doctor, docile, doctrine
duc–	*lead*	duct, conducive, conductor

GROUP A

ROOT	MEANING	EXAMPLES
gress–	*march*	progress, aggressive, retrogression
jur–	*swear*	juror, perjure, conjure
laps–	*fall*	relapse, collapse, elapse
loqu–	*talk*	eloquent, colloquial, colloquium
magn–	*large*	magnitude, magnify, magnificent
man–	*hand*	manual, manuscript, manicure
meter–	*measure*	barometer, chronometer, thermometer
min–	*small*	minimum, diminutive, diminish
pos–	*put*	compose, depose, impose
port–	*carry*	portage, deport, transport

GROUP B

ROOT	MEANING	EXAMPLES
rupt–	*break*	rupture, disrupt, interrupt
sanct–	*holy*	sanctuary, sanctify, sanctity
sci–	*know*	science, prescient, omniscience
scrib–, scrip–	*write*	inscribe, proscribe, prescription
sec–, sequ–	*follow*	consecutive, sequel, consequence
temp–	*time*	temporary, temporal, contemporary
ten–	*hold*	tenant, tenet, tenure
tract–	*draw*	extract, protracted, distract
verb–	*word*	verbal, verbatim, verbiage
vit–	*life*	vitality, revitalize, vitamin

GROUP C

Words

(2) Learn to recognize Greek roots, especially in the words of science and technology. For each of the sample words in the following list, give a rough translation that makes *the meaning of the root* show:

ROOT	MEANING	EXAMPLES
bio–	*life*	biology, biographer, antibiotic
chron–	*time*	anachronistic, synchronized, chronological
cosm–	*universe*	cosmos, cosmic, cosmopolitan
geo–	*earth*	geography, geology, geocentric
graph–	*write*	stenographer, orthography, graph
hydr–	*water*	dehydrate, hydraulic, hydroelectric
path–	*feel*	sympathy, empathy, antipathy
phil–	*love*	philanthropy, anglophile, philosophy
phob–	*fear*	phobia, xenophobia, anglophobe
pyr–	*fire*	pyre, pyromaniac, pyrotechnics

(3) Pay attention to how familiar Latin and Greek prefixes and suffixes change the meaning of different roots. Group together words like the following:

*pre*cursor (forerunner), *pre*dict (foretell), *pre*monition (foreboding)

Here is a review of some Latin and Greek prefixes. Choose five prefixes from each of the following two groups. Do a rough translation of the sample words to show how the prefix works.

	PREFIX	MEANING	EXAMPLES
LATIN	ab–	*away*	absent, abduct, abstain
	ante–	*before*	antedate, antebellum, anterior
	circum–	*around*	circumvent, circumnavigate, circumspect
	co–, con–	*together*	concord, conspire, convene
	contra–	*against*	contradict, contravene, contraband
	de–	*down*	depose, deject, detract
	dis–	*apart*	dissent, disperse, dismember
	ex–, e–	*out of*	extract, exhume, eject
	post–	*after*	posterity, postscript, postmortem
	pro–	*forward*	progress, projection, provident
	re–	*back*	reject, recede, regenerate
	sub–	*under*	submerge, subjugate, subterranean
	trans–	*beyond*	transcend, transfuse, transitory

GREEK

PREFIX	MEANING	EXAMPLES
a–	*without*	ahistorical, amoral, anonymous
anti–	*against*	antipathy, antidote, antithesis
auto–	*self*	automatic, autograph, autonomy
eu–	*beautiful*	euphony, eulogy, euphemism
hetero–	*different*	heterogeneous, heterodox, heterosexual
hyper–	*excessive*	hypercritical, hypersensitive, hyperbole
mon–	*one*	monarch, monogamy, monotone
ortho–	*right*	orthodox, orthography, orthodontics
poly–	*many*	polygon, polygamy, polytheism
syn–, sym–	*together*	synchronize, synthesis, symposium

Some Latin and Greek *suffixes* have meanings that help us master new words:

SUFFIX	MEANING	EXAMPLES
–cide	*killer*	parricide, fratricide, suicide
–esce	*grow, become*	coalesce, convalesce, putrescent
–fy	*make*	magnify, glorify, vilify
–lateral	*sided*	unilateral, bilateral, multilateral
–logy	*study*	meteorology, zoology, biology
–meter	*measure*	altimeter, millimeter, thermometer

NOTE: The common prefix *in–* has two very different meanings:

in, into: *inter* (put in the ground), *inflammable* (easily bursts into flames)
not: *inedible* (cannot be eaten), *incoherent* (not hanging together)

Prefixes like *in–* and *ad–* often blend with the word that follows by changing spelling:

in–: *illegible, irresponsible, irrational*
ad–: *attach, ascend, affirm*

Can you relate unfamiliar words to familiar Greek and Latin roots? Test your knowledge of Latin and Greek roots. After the number of each word in the following list, put the letter for the choice closest to it in meaning.

EXERCISE 1

1. carnivorous   a. flesh-eating   b. open-ended   c. flexible
2. pyrotechnics   a. water duct   b. fireworks   c. leathercraft

3. **credulous** a. believing b. doubting c. faithful
4. **docile** a. hard to do b. teachable c. forgetful
5. **antipathy** a. remedy b. hostility c. friendship
6. **protracted** a. pushed out b. fertile c. drawn out
7. **omniscient** a. powerful b. knows all c. fatigued
8. **biography** a. life story b. contract c. false promise
9. **precursor** a. supervisor b. forerunner c. generator
10. **diminutive** a. very small b. outside c. contagious
11. **sequel** a. peer group b. follow-up c. detour
12. **tenure** a. reworking b. fertilizer c. lasting hold
13. **dehydration** a. fire fighting b. water loss c. rehabilitation
14. **eloquent** a. speaks well b. outdated c. dried out
15. **anachronistic** a. multicolored b. hostile c. wrong in time
16. **geocentric** a. symmetrical b. circular c. earth-centered
17. **verbatim** a. for a time b. illegally c. word for word
18. **sanctuary** a. holy place b. reward c. cemetery
19. **vital** a. expensive b. life-giving c. chemical
20. **retrogression** a. going back b. doubling c. infiltration

EXERCISE 2

Test your knowledge of common prefixes and suffixes. After the number of each word in the following list, put the letter for the choice closest to it in meaning. How does familiarity with Greek and Latin prefixes and suffixes help expand your vocabulary?

1. **circumvent** a. get around b. put down c. bring inside
2. **orthodox** a. long-lasting b. accidental c. right-thinking
3. **dismember** a. take apart b. bar c. pull backward
4. **eject** a. plan before b. throw out c. march back
5. **submerge** a. count back b. replace c. put under
6. **convalesce** a. travel far b. get better c. think about
7. **autonomy** a. self-rule b. prohibition c. outside help
8. **hypersensitive** a. farfetched b. too touchy c. not smart
9. **monarch** a. single ruler b. deputy c. next in line
10. **vilify** a. grow older b. grow solid c. make seem bad
11. **convene** a. count out b. apologize c. come together
12. **anonymous** a. well trained b. healthy c. unnamed
13. **abstain** a. keep from b. turn c. explore
14. **contraband** a. auxiliary b. illegal c. inside story
15. **postscript** a. invitation b. certificate c. written last
16. **provident** a. looks ahead b. turns c. holds back
17. **recede** a. swell up b. ask in c. go back
18. **heterogeneous** a. well-born b. mixed c. harmless
19. **polytheistic** a. of many gods b. one-piece c. transparent
20. **conspire** a. hurry away b. omit c. plot together

Look at the italicized root in each of the following words. What does the root mean? For each, find one additional word that uses the same root.

(Latin)	(Greek)
1. *san*itation	6. *psych*ology
2. in*fall*ible	7. sym*phony*
3. *pac*ify	8. *thermo*stat
4. *cresc*endo	9. stetho*scope*
5. re*fuge*	10. atmo*sphere*

What is the meaning of the italicized word in each of the following sentences? After the number of the sentence, write the letter of the choice closest in meaning to that of the italicized word.

1. The contract called for *reciprocal* services and obligations.
   a. continued   b. mutual   c. expensive
2. There is less *rapport* now between management and employees.
   a. conflict   b. gap   c. good feeling
3. The new government seemed *immune* to corruption.
   a. sealed off   b. vulnerable   c. used
4. She checked the word in an *unabridged* dictionary.
   a. full-length   b. up-to-date   c. pocket-size
5. He was sitting in the corner with a *placid* look on his face.
   a. worried   b. angry   c. very calm
6. The investigation had *vindicated* the senator.
   a. second-guessed b. damaged   c. cleared
7. The shouts from the sidelines had *distracted* me.
   a. unsettled   b. encouraged   c. angered
8. The area had a high *per capita* income.
   a. on capital   b. before taxes   c. per head
9. A judge may decide on *concurrent* terms.
   a. suspended   b. running together c. spread apart
10. They were angered by my *innocuous* remark.
    a. insulting   b. harmless   c. ill-advised
11. Several people who were unknown to us *disrupted* the meeting.
    a. broke up   b. attended   c. boycotted
12. The brochure *conjured up* visions of tropical island beaches.
    a. discouraged   b. brought by magic c. recalled
13. The author was writing her books for *posterity*.
    a. quick income b. future generations c. book lovers
14. The article *refuted* my basic beliefs about diet.
    a. proved wrong b. confirmed   c. changed
15. He called the dress of the actors *anachronistic*.
    a. gaudy   b. elaborate   c. wrong in time

16. Her parents had always had very *orthodox* beliefs.
    a. right-thinking   b. unconventional   c. imaginative
17. He wanted people to believe that he was *infallible*.
    a. very kind   b. always right   c. in perfect health
18. She repeated the operator's message *verbatim*.
    a. approximately   b. incompletely   c. word for word
19. The novel takes place in a *subterranean* city.
    a. deteriorating   b. underground   c. spread out
20. The manager called our demands *exorbitant*.
    a. extravagant   b. reasonable   c. unexpected

W3
EFFECTIVE WORDS

Choose the words that are right for your purpose.

Effective speakers and writers know how to put language to work. They know how to choose the words that will do the job. Use the advice in the following sections as a guide to effective **diction,** that is, effective word choice.

W3a
Accurate Words

Use words that carry clear and accurate information.

Language carries information. It is like a map that points to people, things, and places all around us. Often our main concern is that the map should be clear. When we assemble a model engine, we want the instructions to point clearly to parts that are actually there. When we assign someone to summarize all laws and ordinances that apply to bicycles, we want the straight up-to-date facts.

Do the following to help make your use of language clear and accurate:

(1) Look for specific words. General words are convenient because they cover much ground: "Birds fly." But specific words carry more information. They set one thing apart from the other. We come closer to the *real* bird when we do not simply call it a bird but a robin, a hummingbird, a sparrow, a buzzard, a bluejay, or a quail.

GENERAL: tool
SPECIFIC: drill, wrench, gauge, chisel, plane, lever, wedge

GENERAL: fish
SPECIFIC: trout, salmon, cod, haddock, shad

(2) Look for words that make expression concrete. Some words appeal strongly to our senses. They conjure up shapes and colors. They make us hear sounds or feel textures. Such words with a

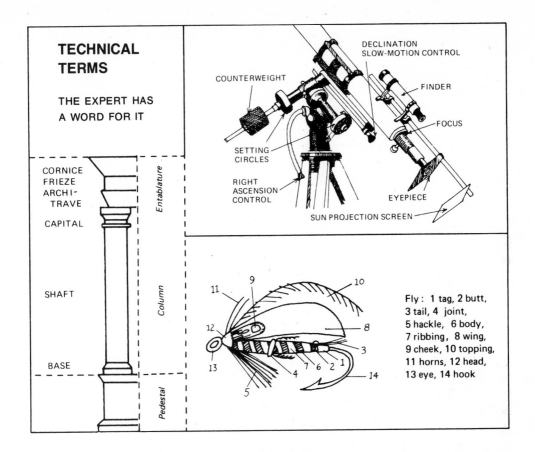

TECHNICAL
TERMS

THE EXPERT HAS
A WORD FOR IT

CORNICE
FRIEZE
ARCHI-
TRAVE

CAPITAL

SHAFT

BASE

Entablature

Column

Pedestal

DECLINATION
SLOW-MOTION CONTROL

COUNTERWEIGHT

FINDER

FOCUS

SETTING
CIRCLES

RIGHT
ASCENSION
CONTROL

EYEPIECE

SUN PROJECTION SCREEN

Fly: 1 tag, 2 butt,
3 tail, 4 joint,
5 hackle, 6 body,
7 ribbing, 8 wing,
9 cheek, 10 topping,
11 horns, 12 head,
13 eye, 14 hook

strong **sensory** dimension help us create the actual feel of concrete experience. A colorless word like *drink* provides basic information. But a concrete word like *guzzle, sip,* or *slurp* makes us see the person taking a drink.

COLORLESS: eat
CONCRETE: swallow, nibble, gobble, bolt, munch, gnaw, devour

COLORLESS: shout
CONCRETE: bellow, bawl, halloo, whoop, scream, screech, shriek, bark, growl

(3) Learn how to master and use technical terms. Few people can work or study profitably without exact technical terms. A mechanic who wants to order parts must know their exact technical names. A cardiologist cannot simply say, "There is something wrong with your heart." He or she must have a large and exact vocabulary for different heart conditions.

Words

The technical terms used in the following dictionary entry enable us to talk exactly about how a fluorescent lamp operates and is put together:

fluorescent lamp *n* : a tubular electric lamp having a coating of fluorescent material on its inner surface and containing mercury vapor whose bombardment by electrons from the cathode provides ultraviolet light which causes the material to emit visible light

fluorescent lamp: *1* anode, *2* stem press, *3* base pins, *4* exhaust tubes, *5* cathode

—*Webster's Seventh New Collegiate Dictionary*

Whenever you deal with a technical or scholarly field, take note of important terms and get their exact bearings. Here are some technical terms that you might encounter in two different fields of study:

MECHANICS: flywheel, inertia, fulcrum, ratchet, caliper, filament, gyroscope, crankshaft, sprocket

ARCHITECTURE: cloister, portico, nave, apse, colonnade, pediment, cornice, cantilever, clerestory

EXERCISE 1

For each of the following, write down as quickly as possible as many different specific words as you can:

1. shrub
2. furniture
3. engine part
4. reptile
5. bird
6. carpenter's tool
7. jewelry
8. wind instrument
9. musical composition
10. vehicle

EXERCISE 2

For each of the numbered statements, supply five specific or concrete words that could fill the blank.

1. Crowd noises that a listener might hear at a game include _____ .
2. When people are unhappy, we might hear them _____ .
3. To describe different ways people walk, we can say they _____ .
4. To describe different ways people run, we can say they _____ .
5. We can describe people who are the opposite of plump as _____ .
6. To describe different ways people speak, we can say they _____ .
7. To describe different ways vehicles move, we can say they _____ .
8. When we use our voices for musical purposes, we _____ .
9. When people use different kinds of gestures, we can see them _____ .
10. A line that we draw on a piece of paper may _____ .

Examine the use of technical terms in the following passages. Explain all italicized terms briefly in your own words.

1. In much of the *temperate* zone, the trees are *deciduous,* providing an appearance of dense *foliage* during the warm months and barren twigs the rest of the year.
2. The Taj Mahal is a *mausoleum* in India erected by Shah Jehan to the memory of his favorite queen. It is *octagonal* in form. The gilt *crescent* at the *apex* of its dome is two hundred and seventy feet from the ground level.
3. In the ordinary *combustion* engine, a *carburetor* is needed to mix gasoline and air. This mixture is then *ignited* in the *cylinder.*
4. The force of *inertia* helps a *flywheel* maintain an even speed. The flywheel in turn helps even out the *velocity* of *revolutions* of the engine shaft.
5. Precious metals do not *oxidize* or *corrode.* Copper forms a *patina.* Some *alloys* resist corrosion better than others.
6. *Net* profits were down, and *dividends* were lower than they had been in previous years.
7. Only a small part of the sum was the *principal* and all the rest *compound interest.*
8. A brief *epilogue* followed the final *curtain* after the unexpected *denouement* of the play.
9. Because of *erosion* and extremely difficult *terrain, reforestation* was proceeding very slowly.
10. Two witnesses had ignored their *subpoenas,* and a third had gone abroad and was fighting *extradition.*

Exploit the resources of figurative language.

Words often have a strong imaginative element. The word *helicopter* points directly to the thing. *Whirlybird* points to the thing but at the same time makes us see it as a huge bird with whirling wings. We call language that uses such imaginative comparisons **figurative** language. Literally, we uproot trees. Figuratively, we uproot people or traditions.

The following kinds of figurative language work in somewhat different ways:

SIMILE: a short comparison that *explicitly* compares one thing to another. It often uses words like *like, as,* or *as though:*

> The evening air was pale and chilly, and after every charge and thud of the footballers the greasy leather orb flew *like a heavy bird* through the grey light.   (James Joyce)

METAPHOR: a compressed comparison actually *substituting* one thing for another. It lets readers or listeners make the necessary translation from the figurative to the literal:

> In the changing *skies* of our republic some *stars* will set, while other *lights* seen as *planets* will glow more brightly as the heavens become bare around them.   (literally not about *stars* but about political *leaders*)

ALLUSION: a capsule reference to something in *history, legend,* or *mythology.* It asks listeners or readers to work out for themselves the implied parallel:

> After years of wheeling and dealing, the governor finally *met his Waterloo.* (was finally and decisively defeated after a great career, like the Emperor Napoleon at the Battle of Waterloo in 1815)

SYMBOL: something specific that acquires a more *general significance.* It stands as one representative example for many similar cases:

> Expect poison from the *standing water.*   (William Blake)

To make figurative language serve you well, remember the following guidelines:

(1) For figurative language to be effective, the implied analogy must fit:

APPROPRIATE: *Beneath the thick crust of our actions,* the heart of the child remains unchanged. (A crust may build up gradually without destroying what is underneath.)

APPROPRIATE: Inflation had *turned into a wild river, sweeping away all dams* built hastily by the government. (A wild river is a good example of something that keeps going in spite of our human efforts.)

INAPPROPRIATE: Education provides the *foundation upon which an individual is to be built.* (Education *develops* an individual who already exists, who is not really built *after* education provides a foundation.)

(2) Make sure several comparisons reinforce each other. In a **mixed metaphor,** they tend to cancel each other out:

CONSISTENT: Legends are the slowly perfected *fruit from a shoot of imagination grafted onto a tree of fact.* (The tree, the shoot, and the fruit are all part of the same comparison.)

MIXED: He decided not to *fall for the bait of easy money* the way his father had. (Fish do not *fall* for bait but *rise* to it.)

(3) Use fresh analogies to get attention. **Clichés** have lost their original humorous or dramatic quality as the result of too much repetition:

TRITE: With the President in trouble, other members of the party tried to *save their skins*.

TRITE: With inflation continuing, it became harder to *keep the wolf from the door*.

TRITE: She always used to come to work, even on Monday mornings, *fresh as a daisy*.

Effective authors make use of striking fresh analogies:

FRESH: His son spent money as if he were trying to *see the bottom of the mint*. (Alice Walker)

FRESH: All poetry is *dipped in the dyes of the heart*. (Edith Sitwell)

FRESH: A riot is the *language of the unheard*. (Martin Luther King)

Evaluate the use of figurative language in the following passages. After the number of each passage, put the appropriate abbreviations: *E* for effective; *M* for mixed metaphor; *T* for trite. (Be prepared to defend your choices in class.)

EXERCISE 1

1. The support from students and parents gave the team a real shot in the arm.
2. A diver should not just plop and hit the water like a baby whale.
3. Individualism is the belief that we should all paddle our own canoes, especially on the high seas.
4. On how to cut the crime rate, the candidates talked out of both sides of their mouths.
5. The medical field has climbed from the very bottom to make it what it is today.
6. At first the mayor denied that the school would be closed, but she finally let the cat out of the bag.
7. Wit is a lean creature with a sharp nose, whereas humor has a kindly eye.
8. Wealthy people must be careful, because money makes it easy for them to step on other people's toes.
9. Young people will have to roll up their sleeves if they want to take their place at life's banquet.
10. Only once do I remember my father having breathed a word of complaint about his fortunes to me, and that for a passing moment. Only once did he lift his visor in my sight.   (Sir Winston Churchill)
11. A theme topic that might die on its feet in the wrong circumstances may catch fire when assigned at the right time.
12. There are some students who are content with an assembly-line education, with the student at the end stamped "B.A., certified fit for corporate consumption."
13. Any student who really wants to succeed will have to burn the midnight oil regularly.

14. Teachers who rely on classic comics to acquaint students with great writers are using a sugar-coated crutch.
15. Satirists frequently prick the balloon of a politician's self-inflation.
16. She plunged into the course with vigor and interest as the portal to a life's career.
17. His campaign speech warned that the long arm of federal tyranny is reaching out to crush us under its boot.
18. These new safety devices are about as useful as a screen door on a submarine.
19. Poems are peculiar plants, and nobody knows much about what makes them germinate.
20. The person I love will have to realize that life is more than peaches and cream.

EXERCISE 2

Find a fresher or more striking comparison for each of the following clichés. After the number of the sentence, write a figurative expression that would fill the blank.

1. He knew he *came from the wrong side of the tracks.*
   He knew he _____ .

2. The governor looked at the proposed law *with a jaundiced eye.*
   The governor _____ .

3. The senator came into office *on the President's coattails.*
   The senator came into office _____ .

4. The new director *was a wolf in sheep's clothing.*
   The new director _____ .

5. Marcia was horrified to discover that her new friend *was a real snake in the grass.*
   Marcia was horrified to discover that _____ .

6. To survive, a professional athlete *has to roll with the punches.*
   To survive, a professional athlete _____ .

7. In recent years, minorities have *asked for their place in the sun.*
   In recent years, minorities have _____ .

8. When we travel, we plan to *stay off the beaten track.*
   When we travel, we plan to _____ .

9. My aunt Letitia was one of those people who *always land on their feet.*
   My aunt Letitia was one of those people who _____ .

10. Building a bigger stadium to get a better team is *putting the cart before the horse.*
    Building a bigger stadium to get a better team is _____ .

Your teacher will ask you to investigate one or more of the following categories:

A. In one sentence each, explain the origin of *five* of the following figurative expressions:

1. backlog
2. dark horse
3. a jerkwater town
4. jackpot
5. hue and cry

6. give short shift
7. hamstring someone
8. a sounding board
9. in the doldrums
10. get the hang of it

B. Modern American English uses many sports metaphors from football or baseball: *fumble the ball, be off base, strike out.* Which older or less familiar sports and games are represented by the following figurative expressions? What is their meaning?

1. allure
2. there's the rub
3. retrieve
4. worry
5. foible

6. checkmate
7. crestfallen
8. gambit
9. pawn
10. haggard

C. The following names often appear in allusions to Greek mythology. Choose *five*. Tell the story of each in a sentence or two.

1. Cupid
2. Hercules
3. Ulysses
4. Cassandra
5. Circe

6. Procrustes
7. Prometheus
8. Tantalus
9. Sisyphus
10. Bacchus

D. Investigate the metaphorical uses made in *everyday language* of one major area of experience. Investigate expressions making metaphorical use of animals (to strain at a *gnat*), of sailing (be on an even *keel*), or of parts of the body (be all *ears*).

E. What are the *symbolic associations* of common colors? Collect as many common expressions using major colors as you can; for instance, *white lie, white elephant, blue mood, greenhorn, see red.* Present your findings.

Take into account the overtones and connotations of words.

Information is not all there is to language. Words often reflect personal preference. Language is often less like an impersonal map than like a guide with strong personal feelings. When a person calls a house a "shack," we learn something about how the person feels about the house.

THE STRAIGHT NEWS, PLEASE

Suppose you read the following letter to the editor in a newsmagazine. What are the connotations of each of the words that the writer objected to? What associations or reactions does each produce?

> I'm not active in politics, but I recognize a loaded adjective when I see one. Your article on one of the candidates for senator contains the words: go to almost any lengths, gregarious, accosting, loquacity, verbosity, ambiguous, eroded, hedges, mouthing, cant, unctuousness, bombast, bully, artificial, cajole, ingratiate, and many more. Every word carries its load, besides the tone of the entire article. Opposition is one thing; unfair assault is another.

BONUS: Check a recent issue of a newsmagazine for an article about a prominent public figure. How much use of loaded language (favorable or unfavorable) is there in the article?

We can often divide the meaning of a word into two major parts: The part of the meaning that gives us factual information is the **denotation** of the word. The part of the meaning that shows our attitude is the **connotation** of the word. The factual information in the word *guzzle* is that someone is drinking quickly and copiously. The attitude expressed is that the person is greedy and careless.

A good dictionary shows that a word often reveals the attitude or feelings of the speaker. The most important distinction is between approval and disapproval, between favorable and unfavorable connotations. *Project*, as a synonym of *plan*, often implies approval or admiration. Other synonyms, like *scheme*, imply disapproval or opposition:

> SYN.—**plan** refers to any detailed method, formulated beforehand, for doing or making something (vacation *plans*); **design** stresses the final outcome of a plan and implies the use of skill or craft, sometimes in an unfavorable sense, in executing or arranging this (it was his *design* to separate us); **project** implies the use of enterprise or imagination in formulating an ambitious or extensive plan (they've begun work on the housing *project*); **scheme,** a less definite term than the preceding, often connotes either an impractical, visionary plan or an underhand intrigue (a *scheme* to embezzle the funds)
>
> —*Webster's New World Dictionary*

Of a whole set of synonyms, few may turn out to be neutral:

FAVORABLE: chuckle, smile, guffaw
UNFAVORABLE: snicker, cackle, smirk

FAVORABLE: lad, youngster, youth
UNFAVORABLE: brat, juvenile, punk

FAVORABLE: firm, resolute, resolved, determined
UNFAVORABLE: stubborn, dogmatic, obstinate, doctrinaire

An effective speaker or writer has to be sensitive to connotations. Remember:

(1) The same word may have different connotations in different contexts. The word *wise* is favorable in "wise man" but unfavorable in the slang term "wise guy." The word *style* suggests admiration in some contexts but not in others:

NEUTRAL: American cars are known for their frequently changing *styles*.
FAVORABLE: This car really has *style*.

(2) The connotations of a word may differ for different audiences. To the ordinary city dweller, *primitive* implies a deplorable lack of modern conveniences and refinements. But to many lovers of modern art, and to many nature lovers, *primitive* implies something powerful, genuine, or unspoiled.

(3) Words with the wrong connotations cause confusing double takes. In sentences like the following, why do the connotations of important words clash with the intended meaning?

In the past, I always *looked forward* to my English classes with regret.
He has *subjected* us to many profitable hours of lecture and discussion.

NOTE: A word with offensive connotations, thoughtlessly used, can undo the good done by an eloquent speech. Contemptuous terms for nationalities or races alienate not only the groups involved but also outsiders of goodwill.

Examine each italicized word for possible connotations. What connotations does it have *in the context of its sentence?* After the number of the sentence, write *F* if a word seems favorable, *U* if it seems unfavorable, *N* if it seems neutral. (Be prepared to discuss the connotations of these words.)

EXERCISE 1

1. The new computer is the *heart* of a sophisticated communications network.
2. He once *concocted* a story about a girl surviving for months in an uncharted wilderness.

3. Bud was the kind of dog who would bark up a storm and then *slink off* without a fight.
4. Water *cascaded* from the top of the mountain to the valley below.
5. "Human engineering" is an attempt to treat the worker and employee like a *machine*.
6. Boys and girls were dressing in *unisex* fashions.
7. He had grown up on the East Side and was always *bad-mouthing* his family and his old neighborhood.
8. The railroad had just developed a *piggyback* system for shipping loaded trucks on railroad cars.
9. The private club facing the avenue was a *cocoon* of luxury and privilege.
10. Our lives are being regulated by *anonymous* office workers.
11. Development of the new center has been *obstructed* by a group of former tenants.
12. Parents and students contributed many *constructive* suggestions.
13. The meeting strengthened the *enduring* ties between the countries.
14. The article told the story of *immigration* to this country from the Orient.
15. Because of improved ticket sales, our athletic program had become entirely *self-supporting*.
16. The authors of this plan for providing more student loans live in a *fantasy* world.
17. The cost of going to college has risen *astronomically*.
18. Apart from economic self-interest, other more *intangible* factors influence a voter's choice.
19. Our English teacher was always *drubbing* into us the structure of the paragraph and of the sentence.
20. The change in the situation resulted from the *vigilance* of our law enforcement officers.

EXERCISE 2

In each of the following pairs, one word clearly implies an unfavorable judgment. After the number of each pair, put the letter for the more *negative* term. (Be prepared to discuss the full implications of both terms in class.)

1. (a) colorful   (b) gaudy
2. (a) impetuous   (b) rash
3. (a) gloat   (b) rejoice
4. (a) worship   (b) idolatry
5. (a) appeasing   (b) conciliatory
6. (a) blustering   (b) assertive
7. (a) obedient   (b) obsequious
8. (a) do-gooder   (b) humanitarian
9. (a) attentive   (b) officious
10. (a) ogle   (b) stare

In each of the following pairs, which is the *stronger* word? After the number of the pair, put the letter for the stronger or more emphatic term. Be prepared to explain in class what the stronger word adds to the meaning it shares with the weaker one. (Your classmates may disagree with you on the connotations of some of these terms.)

1. (a) suffering   (b) agony
2. (a) threat   (b) menace
3. (a) triumph   (b) victory
4. (a) savage   (b) wild
5. (a) old   (b) ancient
6. (a) gigantic   (b) big
7. (a) terror   (b) fear
8. (a) dried out   (b) parched
9. (a) fertile   (b) prolific
10. (a) warped   (b) twisted

How do the synonyms in each of the following groups *differ in connotation?* Be prepared to discuss fully the reactions people might typically have to the different words in each group. (Your teacher may ask you to select *three* of these groups and write a paragraph about each.)

1. intelligent—clever—shrewd—sly
2. vagrant—drifter—wanderer—bum
3. secret—furtive—discreet
4. coddle—spoil—pamper
5. gossip—chatterbox—tattletale—blabbermouth
6. eccentric—character—oddball—crank
7. forthright—blunt—brazen
8. filch—steal—pilfer—loot
9. gang—peer group—clique—club
10. fad—vogue—craze—fashion

Know how to be brief, blunt, and direct.

W3d

Plain English

The effective speaker and writer knows how to put language to work. He or she knows how to choose the words that will do the job. Use the following advice as a guide to effective diction, that is, effective word choice:

(1) Use words economically. One accurate word is better than two woolly ones. Much wordiness is the result of **padding,** of words

used without conviction in hopes of filling an empty space. Try to be concise and straightforward.

Verbs greatly contribute to the meaning of the English language.
The automobile is here to stay.

Unnecessary duplication of words is **redundancy:** "Forward progress" is redundant, because it is not possible to make *backward* progress. "Basic essentials" is redundant, because what is basic is *always* essential.

REDUNDANT: *All of a sudden* it happened *overnight*.
REDUNDANT: The *average* voter is *usually* not interested in economics.
REDUNDANT: Physical education develops one's *physical body* control and coordination.

(2) Use words no bigger than your subject. The use of big words for trivial things is **jargon.** Jargon results when someone tries to impress us by always using the longer, more technical, or more scholarly word. Use technical words only where they are necessary. Fight the temptation to use a fancy word when a plain one will do instead:

FANCY	PLAIN	FANCY	PLAIN
conceptualize	think	methodology	method
anomalous	strange	hypothesize	guess
implement	put into effect	effectuate	bring about
escalate	step up	ambivalent	contradictory
dichotomy	split	epiphany	revelation

Trim pretentious statements by translating them into plain English:

JARGON: Debating *polarizes* a class into *dichotomized* groups for the exploration of *discussible* issues.
PLAIN ENGLISH: Debating splits a class into opposing groups for discussion.

JARGON: It is *imperative* that nursing *personnel* be offered improved *monetary incentives*.
PLAIN ENGLISH: We should give nurses more money.

(3) When necessary, be blunt and direct. Sometimes we have to gloss things over in order to be tactful. But we merely trick ourselves and others if we always use beautiful words for ugly things. Pretty words used instead of direct ones to gloss over not-so-pretty things are **euphemisms:**

EUPHEMISM	BLUNT
low-income group	poor
senior citizens	old people
long illness	cancer
problem child	troublemaker
be ill	vomit
financial trouble	bankruptcy

When· language becomes too fancy or too roundabout, it becomes a barrier between you and your audience. Learn to ask yourself: What exactly am I trying to say?

Rewrite each sentence in plain English. Be prepared to explain what made the sentence wordy, pretentious, or roundabout.

EXERCISE 1

1. The amount of exercise engaged in by an individual is determined by the cultural group with which the individual is associated.
2. John is inclined to take the property of others without permission and tends to stretch the truth.
3. Modern mountain climbers plan walks that are not commensurate with their stamina.
4. Bad behavior pertaining to hospitality was shown against Odysseus.
5. During my childhood years, I was not physically well coordinated.
6. A youth may feel severity of depression at being scorned because his tie is not of the latest fashion.
7. After a smoke, I usually berate myself for having so indulged.
8. The purpose of taking the life of a criminal is aimed at deterring others from the commission of the crime.
9. My projected employment as a gardener did not materialize, as we could not agree on a suitable remuneration.
10. Children in compacted urban areas are in dire need of improved educational opportunities.
11. In planning for the first year at an institution of higher education, we consider money a vital constituent.
12. The personnel officer implements the acquisition of human resources to realize specific institutional goals.
13. A crucial area for concern centers on the selection of teaching materials, which have been the catalyst for many community uproars.
14. All members of the community should become knowledgeable about information pertinent to decision making.
15. In this day of clashing opinions, it is imperative that logical debate become a part of the resolution of confusions.

Words

There are various ways in which language can come between writers and their audience. In each of the following passages, what *distracts* the reader from the subject at hand? Be prepared to discuss each passage in detail.

1. I finally left my boon companions to return to my humble abode, for I had to rise bright and early the next A.M. to return to the pursuit of filthy lucre, earning the coin of the realm necessary to the obtaining of life's necessities.

2. From angels through witches, women have been at home in the air for millenniums! And now, for milady's eyes only, X Airlines offers Plane & Fancy—62 pages of timely travel information for women on the go, written by women in the know! Here you'll find travel bits and tidbits ranging from dreams to schemes, tots to tipping, weights to wardrobes—plus pertinent pointers on planning, packing, proposals, pets, and palate pampering.

3. The last chapter of the book is an illogical finale to a story whose whole modus operandi was tragedy. The hero's outcome could not possibly reach so blissful a conclusion. He was a member of the quintuplet whose fate could end in nothing less than despair.

Which would be the more effective choice for the blank in each of the following sentences? After the number of the sentence, put the letter for the choice that is more specific, more concrete, more imaginative, or more appropriate.

1. After much delay, he finally _____ the whole story.
   a. told us   b. blurted out
2. The familiar lecture about traffic safety was as dull as _____.
   a. dishwater   b. a commercial seen the third time
3. My sister and brother used to spend hours sitting in front of the set, happily _____ peanuts.
   a. munching   b. eating
4. Everyone should support our mayor's new _____ for a downtown convention center.
   a. scheme   b. plan
5. The new borough president was ideally suited for difficult negotiations because of her _____ manner.
   a. conciliatory   b. appeasing
6. Ignoring the insistent shouts of the irate coach, my tired friends and I were _____ around the field.
   a. running   b. trotting
7. The sculptor kept using the _____ with quick, firm taps.
   a. cutting tool   b. chisel

8. Pursued by the tacklers, the runner _____ across the field.
   a. zigzagged   b. ran this way and that
9. What I earned that summer was hardly enough to keep _____ .
   a. my head above water   b. our cats in pet food
10. We can no longer afford _____ opposition to new ideas.
    a. determined   b. dogmatic
11. Swallows were _____ across the evening sky.
    a. darting   b. flying
12. His ankle had healed, but the injury left him with a slight _____ .
    a. impediment   b. limp
13. The pep talk by the trainer _____ .
    a. gave us a shot in the arm   b. put bounce in our step
14. He had down-to-earth humor that made audiences _____ .
    a. laugh   b. guffaw
15. My little brother had _____ away an apple and several candy bars.
    a. squirreled   b. saved and hidden
16. We welcome especially a labor union _____ from upstate.
    a. boss   b. leader
17. Every young person should have a _____ of friends.
    a. group   b. clique
18. The car _____ sharply to the right to avoid hitting the cat.
    a. moved   b. swerved
19. Writing a research paper without notes is _____ .
    a. doing things the hard way   b. like going up the down escalator
20. They met us at the door, fresh as _____ .
    a. a daisy   b. dew

FOR FURTHER STUDY

OUR DICTIONARY RESOURCES

A dictionary is a very practical tool. But it is also a book for browsing. By looking up interesting words, we learn much about our changing language and the way it mirrors our changing way of life.

Little of the ancient *Celtic* language of Britain survives in Modern English. What is the history and meaning of the following Celtic words?

ACTIVITY 1

1. bard	6. banshee
2. cairn	7. colleen
3. druid	8. pibroch
4. shamrock	9. bryn mawr
5. loch	10. Llewellyn

ACTIVITY 2

What is the original meaning of the following terms from *Greek and Roman history and literature?* How does the origin of the word help explain its current meaning? (Your teacher may ask you to write a sentence or two about *five* of these words.)

1. apotheosis
2. barbarian
3. mentor
4. ostracize
5. panic
6. laconic
7. lethargic
8. patrician
9. plebeian
10. Spartan

ACTIVITY 3

French was the language of the *age of chivalry,* of knighthood and romance. Select *ten* of the following words and explain them briefly.

1. chevalier
2. dalliance
3. damsel
4. fealty
5. fief
6. goblet
7. homage
8. joust
9. lute
10. mastiff
11. minstrel
12. palfrey
13. paramour
14. plume
15. prowess
16. puissance
17. realm
18. stratagem
19. travail
20. turret

ACTIVITY 4

The following is the beginning of the Book of Psalms in the *Early Modern English* of the King James Version. Check the origin of the italicized words. How many go back to Old English? How many came into English from French? How many from Latin? (Use a college dictionary if you can.)

1 *Blessed* is the *man* that *walketh* not in the *counsel* of the *ungodly,* nor *standeth* in the *way* of *sinners,* nor *sitteth* in the *seat* of the *scornful.*

2 But his *delight* is in the *law* of the *Lord;* and in his law doth he *meditate day* and *night.*

3 And he shall be like a *tree planted* by the *rivers* of *water,* that *bringeth* forth his *fruit* in his *season;* his *leaf* also shall not *wither;* and whatsoever he doeth shall *prosper.*

4 The ungodly are not so: but are like the *chaff* which the *wind driveth* away.

5 Therefore the ungodly shall not stand in the *judgment,* nor sinners in the *congregation* of the *righteous.*

6 For the Lord *knoweth* the way of the righteous: but the way of the ungodly shall *perish.*

In each of the following sets of three, the first word is from *Old English,* the second from *French,* and the third from *Latin.* What are the differences in meaning or in use? Does your dictionary show that the French and Latin words go back to the same root? (Select *five* of these sets.)

1. deem—judge—adjudicate
2. folk—people—population
3. follow—pursue—prosecute
4. hallowed—sacred—consecrated
5. evil—malign—malignant
6. evildoer—malfeasance—malefactor
7. want—poverty—pauperism
8. leaf—foil—folio
9. reckon—count—compute
10. draw out—portray—protract

Each of the words italicized in the following passages illustrates a *meaning no longer in common use.* Write down the word and after it the meaning that fits the context.

1. Bless you, fair *dame!* I am not to you known,
   Though in your state of honor I am *perfect.*
   I *doubt,* some danger does approach you nearly:
   If you will take a *homely* man's advice,
   Be not found here; *hence,* with your little ones. (*Macbeth,* Act IV, Sc. 2)

2.   Say from whence
   You owe this strange *intelligence?* or why
   Upon this *blasted* heath you stop our way
   With such prophetic greeting? (*Macbeth,* Act I, Sc. 3)

3. Let the gods so *speed* me as I love
   The name of honor more than I fear death. (*Julius Caesar,* Act I, Sc. 2)

4.   I am as constant as the Northern Star
   Of whose true-fixed and resting quality
   There is no *fellow* in the firmament. (*Julius Caesar,* Act III, Sc. 1)

5.   Were I so minded
   I here could pluck his highness' frown upon you
   And *justify* you traitors. (*Tempest.* Act V. Sc. 1)

6. If I forget thee, O Jerusalem, let my right hand forget her *cunning.* (Psalms)

7. He is a gentleman that is very *singular* in his behavior. . . . He has all his life dressed very well, and remembered *habits* as others do men. (Sir Richard Steele)

8. Let us raise a *standard* to which the wise and honest can *repair.* (George Washington)

9. He was fitted neither by abilities nor disposition to *answer* the wishes of his mother and sister. (Jane Austen)

10. The butler's pantry, the servants' hall, and the entrance hall were equally alive; and the *saloons* only were left void and still. (Charlotte Brontë)

ACTIVITY 7

An **idiom** is a characteristic way of saying things; typically its meaning is more than the sum of its parts. What is the difference between "doing good" and "doing well"? These are idiomatic phrases whose meanings we cannot piece together by just looking at the separate words. A good dictionary lists some of the common idioms in which a word is used. Help a dictionary maker pin down the meaning of the following idioms using the word *head.* Explain each briefly in your own words:

1. The horse won by a head.
2. Matters were coming to a head.
3. Her promotion had gone to her head.
4. He was head and shoulders above the competition.
5. The principal headed off the investigation just in time.
6. He fell head over heels in love.
7. She always kept her head in an emergency.
8. The passenger lost his head completely.
9. I can't make head or tail of it.
10. The explanation was completely over the customer's head.

How well does your dictionary cover idioms? For each of the following, find three familiar idioms using the word:

1. heart
2. mind
3. hand
4. foot
5. finger

Have you ever investigated the origin of *first names?* Can you find a dictionary that gives the source and original meaning of the following? (Select *ten.* Your teacher may ask you to write a sentence or two about each.)

Abdul	Edgar	Harold	Manuel	Natalie
Catherine	Edith	Jack	Margery	Pablo
Cecily	Elizabeth	John	Matthew	Theresa
Charles	Fred	Joseph	Michael	Walter
Donna	Gregory	Judith	Muhammad	William

Chapter 2

Sentences
Writing Better Sentences

Chapter Preview 2

IN THIS CHAPTER:

● How to recognize basic sentence parts and simple patterns of the complete sentence.

● How to expand and adapt the basic patterns.

● How to make full use of modifying words and phrases.

● How to use the full range of coordination and subordination in sentence combining.

● How to use verbals and absolute constructions in advanced sentence work.

Know the resources of the English sentence and put them to good use.

How can you learn to write better sentences? How can you learn to use the full resources of the English sentence?

Know the resources you are working with, and learn to put them to good use. Know the basic sentence parts and how we put them together. Know the different ways we put together and expand a complete English sentence. Practice putting the English sentence through its paces: Study the sentence resources used by speakers and writers who know how. Then practice putting these resources to good use in your own speaking and writing.

As you start on a program of sentence study and sentence practice, remember the following basic facts:

(1) When we put an English sentence together, we put the right words in the right order. **Word order** helps give our words their full meaning in a sentence. Look at the following examples:

DOER	ACTION VERB	TARGET	
The batter	hit	the ball.	

SENDER	ACTION VERB	ADDRESS	MISSIVE
The boy	sent	his mother	a letter.

PERSON	LINKING VERB	LABEL	
Red	looked	happy.	

DOER	ACTION VERB	TARGET	LABEL
Mary	called	Jean	a bumbler.

THE ENGLISH SENTENCE
A Summary

KINDS OF WORDS

Nouns	*The driver* asked *a question.*
Pronouns	*Somebody* gave *us your* name.
Verbs	The guests *danced* and *sang.*
Adjectives	He grew *beautiful* flowers.
Adverbs	She explained it *clearly.*
Prepositions	We parked *in* the driveway.
Connectives	Food *and* water had run out.

SEVEN SENTENCE PATTERNS

S–V	Speed kills.
S–V–O	Lincoln freed the slaves.
S–LV–N	Benedict Arnold was a traitor.
S–LV–Adj	Advice is cheap.
S–V–IO–O	My uncle showed Juan the way.
S–V–O–OC	Mary called Jean her friend.
S–V–O–Adj	Her help made the work easy.

THREE KINDS OF SENTENCES

Statements	The price has gone up.
Questions	Did he notify you?
Requests	Help us fight smog.

KINDS OF CLAUSES

Independent	She called, *but* I kept walking.
Adverbial	We stay indoors *when* it rains.
Relative	He looked for people *who* cared.
Noun Clause	Tell me *that* you love me.

SPECIAL SENTENCE RESOURCES

Appositive	Gonzalez, *a senior,* won the award.
Present Participle	*Barking* dogs don't bite.
Past Participle	She raked up the *fallen* leaves.
Verbal Noun	*Seeing* is *believing.*
Infinitive	*To err* is human.

Sentences

In the first example in the chart on page 50, when we come to the word *ball,* we know: "This is what is being hit." In the second sentence, when we come to the word *mother,* we know: "This is to whom it was sent." Arranged in a different order, the same words would mean something completely different:

The ball hit the batter.
His mother sent the boy a letter.
Happy looked red.
A bumbler called Mary Jean.

(2) We often change the form of a word to fit it into a sentence. Notice how the word *I* changes in the following sentences depending on how it fits in:

DOER: *I* watched the police officer.
TARGET: The police officer watched *me.*
OWNER: The police officer checked *my* motorcycle.

When we "bend" words this way to make them fit into a sentence, we call the result **inflected** forms. In many languages that are close cousins to English, words have a great variety of inflected forms. In English, the use of separate word forms has become streamlined over the centuries. We use different word forms mainly to show differences in number and in time:

ONE: Their *car* blocked the driveway.
SEVERAL: Their *cars* blocked the driveway.

PRESENT: People *write* angry letters to the editor.
PAST: Pamela *wrote* a thank-you letter to her assistant.
RECENT PAST: She has already *written* the letter.

(3) **Function words** *help hold the different parts of a sentence together.* Function words are needed to help turn the following strings of words into complete English sentences:

WORDS: I—meet—you—three o'clock—station
SENTENCE: I *will* meet you *at* three o'clock *behind the* station.

WORDS: Car—stopped—roadblock—police.
SENTENCE: *Their* car *was* stopped *at a* roadblock *by the* police.

Four important categories of function words are:

DETERMINERS: *the, a, an; my, your, his, her; this, that*
AUXILIARIES: *be, have, will, may, can, shall*
PREPOSITIONS: *at, in, by, on, during, under, about, through, with, without, from*
CONNECTIVES: *and, but, if, though, because, however, therefore*

From each of the following sentences, construct a *new sentence* using the same words in a different order. (Do not change the *form* of any of the words.)

1. The car turned right at the corner.
2. The criminal called the lawyer a liar.
3. My friend called his sister brilliant.
4. Her new friend looked handsome.
5. Police stopped the car.
6. The word spread.
7. The owner had the roof fixed.
8. I remember the joke that you told.
9. The reporter had the mistake corrected.
10. Jim ate only the fish.

Change the form of the word in the left column to make it fit into the blank space in the sentence. Write the changed form after the number of the sentence.

1. **be**   Modern English _____ a member of the Indo-European family of languages.

2. **speak**   Indo-European languages are _____ today by half of the world's population.

3. **million**   But _____ of people speak languages not related to our own.

4. **live**   Sometimes only a few speakers of a language are still _____ in isolated communities.

5. **man**   But a language like Chinese is the native tongue of many millions of _____ and women.

6. **identify**   Linguists have _____ several major language families besides the Indo-European.

7. **include**   The Semitic family _____ Hebrew and Arabic.

8. **choose**   Hebrew was _____ as the national language of Israel.

9. **be**   For many centuries, Arabic has _____ the national language of Egypt.

10. **African**   The language of many _____ belongs to the Bantu family.

11. **resemble**   Chinese _____ the languages of Tibet and Vietnam.

12. **we**   It surprises most of _____ that Chinese and Japanese are not related.

13. **use**   The Japanese are _____ a writing system borrowed from the Chinese.

14. **bring**   The Europeans _____ English and Spanish to America.

15. **language**   The original inhabitants spoke many different _____.

Sentences

PREVIEW
EXERCISE 3

Rewrite each of the following groups of words as an English sentence. Use one or more *function words* to fill in each blank space.

1. _____ tenants discovered _____ hole _____ roof _____ accident.
2. Guests _____ shoes _____ barred _____ club.
3. Philip _____ written _____ parents _____ money.
4. _____ sinking _____ *Titanic* came _____ surprise _____ experts.
5. Computers _____ not swayed _____ prejudice.
6. Lisa went _____ Egypt _____ studying Arabic _____ years.
7. _____ traffic jam _____ called monumental _____ chief _____ police.
8. _____ beginning _____ World War II _____ last commercial airship _____ gone down _____ flames.
9. _____ teacher _____ not treat _____ students _____ drill sergeant _____ army.
10. _____ bird _____ hand is worth two _____ bush.

S1

WORDS IN A SENTENCE

Know the basic building blocks that help us make up the English sentence.

Word order, word forms, and function words are the major sentence signals that help us find our way in a sentence. Several major **word classes,** or "parts of speech," furnish the basic sentence parts that we put together in speaking and writing. We can tell them apart by how they are used in a sentence—by the sentence signals that go with them.

S1a

Recognizing Nouns and Pronouns

Know the signals that help us identify nouns.

Nouns are label words. They help us identify countless things that are part of our lives: *car, match, chair, door, belt, glass.* They enable us to label people, places, and ideas: *attendant, citizen, lake, park, freedom, justice.* We call nouns **proper** nouns when they name one particular person, place, or institution: *Juan, Canada, Kremlin.*

Know the signals that help us identify nouns in a sentence:

(1) English nouns have forms that show differences in number. Most nouns have a separate form for **plural,** giving us the signal for "several of a kind":

SINGULAR:	bird	house	man	tooth	child	mouse
PLURAL:	birds	houses	men	teeth	children	mice

Normally, the plural form adds to the plain noun the ending spelled *–s* or *–es: trucks, tourists, birds, hoboes, families, stories.* Other ways of forming the plural were common during earlier stages in the history of the language. Here are a few modern survivals:

–en PLURAL:	ox*en*, child*ren*
VOWEL CHANGE:	m*i*ce, t*ee*th, m*e*n, g*ee*se, f*ee*t
NO ENDING:	deer, sheep, fish

When foreign words are imported, they sometimes bring inflected forms along with them. For instance, the following words preserve their original *Latin or Greek plural forms.* For some of them, Anglicized, or "Englished," plurals are now coming into standard use:

	ORIGINAL PLURAL	ANGLICIZED PLURAL
appendix	appendices	appendixes
crisis	crises	
formula	formulae	formulas
medium	media	
memorandum	memoranda	memorandums

NOTE: English *no longer* uses separate word forms to indicate differences in **gender.** In many languages, these show differences in sex. In Spanish, *Roberto* is a boy, *Roberta* a girl. In English, we have separate forms for male and female for a few nouns borrowed from Latin or French:

MASCULINE:	alumnus (plural: alumni)	fiancé
FEMININE:	alumna (plural: alumnae)	fiancée

(2) Nouns often come after **determiners.** These are "noun markers," giving us the signal that a noun will shortly follow. There are three major kinds:

ARTICLES:	*the, a, an*
POSSESSIVE PRONOUNS:	*my, your, his, hers, its, our, their*
DEMONSTRATIVE PRONOUNS:	*this, these; that, those*

Notice that proper names, with a few exceptions, are not preceded by determiners. We say "*My country* won," but "*America* entered the war." We say "*Her brother* left," but "*John* ran away."

Other words may come between the determiner and the noun:

the tinted *glass*
a marvelous *opportunity*
an in-depth *study*
these unforgettable *holidays*
our first *anniversary*

(3) Many nouns show familiar noun-forming endings. People speaking English have always been able to make new nouns by starting with some other word and attaching a noun-making **suffix** like *–er* or *–dom:*

–er: speaker, singer, ruler, fighter, examiner
–dom: kingdom, wisdom, serfdom, martyrdom

Other familiar noun-making endings are *–hood* (womanhood), *–ment* (government), *–ness* (likeness), *–ship* (friendship), and *–tion* (devotion). A few noun-forming suffixes are especially active in contemporary American English. They appear in many new words first used by journalists or advertisers. For instance, we use the ending *–ism* for many new (and old) attitudes, movements, and the like: *optimism, extremism, terrorism.*

(4) The place of a noun may be taken by a **pronoun.** Pronouns are shortcut words. We use **personal pronouns** like *he, she,* or *it* when who or what they point to is already clear.

NOUN: *Martha* took flying lessons.
PRONOUN: *She* got her license.

NOUN: *The storm* destroyed their crops.
PRONOUN: *It* was very sudden.

The personal pronouns are *I, you, he, she, it, we,* and *they.* They have additional forms for use as **object** forms: *me, him, her, us, them.* Other kinds of pronouns can also take the place of a noun. For a complete listing, see the pronoun chart on the next page.

See **U2b** for object forms.

INDEFINITE PRONOUNS HELP US
TALK ABOUT THINGS IN GENERAL:

There is more space where nobody is than where anybody is.

A WISE PERSON KNOWS EVERYTHING;
A SHREWD ONE, EVERYBODY.

If EVERYBODY became SOMEBODY, there wouldn't be ANYBODY left to be NOBODY .

THE ENGLISH PRONOUN
A Summary

PERSONAL PRONOUNS
They replace nouns *already mentioned* or understood as part of the situation: *I, you, he, she, it, we, they.*

First Mention: *Jim* called *Bertha* on the phone.
Second Mention: *He* asked *her* about the exam.

POSSESSIVE PRONOUNS
One set is used as determiners: *my, your, his, her, its, our, their.*
The other set is used alone: *mine, yours, his, hers, its, ours, theirs.*

Determiner: *Her* audition was yesterday.
Noun Substitute: *Mine* will be today.

Determiner: *Your* application has been approved.
Noun Substitute: *Ours* was rejected.

DEMONSTRATIVE
("POINTING") PRONOUNS
The *same* form is used alone and as a determiner: *this, these; that, those.*

Introduces Noun: *That* man is my brother.
Replaces Noun: *That* is the man.

Introduces Noun: *These* seats are reserved.
Replaces Noun: *These* are available.

INDEFINITE PRONOUNS
They do not point to any specific person or thing: *one; somebody (someone), anybody (anyone), everybody (everyone), nobody (no one or none); something, anything, everything, nothing.*

   Everybody was late for the party.
   Nobody had mentioned a fee.
   Nothing was said about her trip.

INTERROGATIVE PRONOUNS
They ask questions to be *answered* by nouns: *who, whom, what, which.*

   Who furnished the money? *My aunt* did.
   What are you eating? *A snack.*

See **S4c** for relative pronouns.

Sentences

EXERCISE 1

What missing word or words would you use to fill in the blanks in the following sayings? Each word you fill in will be a noun. (Notice that there may be other words that come between each noun and its determiner).

1. Love me, love my _____.
2. When the _____ is away, the _____ have a ball.
3. A _____ and his _____ are soon parted.
4. The _____ that squeaks loudest gets the _____.
5. He was running around like a _____ with its _____ cut off.
6. The early _____ gets the _____.
7. A liar needs a good _____.
8. She was caught between the _____ and the deep blue _____.
9. A good _____ shines like a _____ in a dark _____.
10. It takes a _____ to build a barn, but a _____ can kick one down.

EXERCISE 2

After the number of each sentence, write down every noun that meets at least one of the following requirements:

(1) It has an –s ending that shows it is a plural form.
(2) It follows *the, a, an,* or another determiner.
(3) It has a noun-forming suffix like *–ment, –hood,* or *–tion.*
(4) Its place can be taken by one of the personal pronouns *he (him), she (her), it, they (them).*

1. Applicants for employment usually fill in a questionnaire.
2. The new appliances needed constant repairs.
3. The authorities monitored the level of noise at the airport.
4. Judges may suspend the licenses of reckless drivers.
5. Treaties had promised the tribe protection of its rights.
6. Students often need transcripts of their grades.
7. An apprentice often earned only room and board.
8. The government took precautions to prevent nuclear accidents.
9. The candidate for the job had passed an examination.
10. The association needed a permit for the parade.
11. Governments collect taxes from their citizens.
12. Taxpayers may forget to file a return.
13. Employers dislike employees who constantly watch the clock.
14. Local ordinances regulate construction.
15. Vandalism has cost our schools millions of dollars.
16. These workers pay dues to their organizations.
17. New laws were passed to protect the wilderness.
18. The way to hell is paved with good intentions.
19. A happy crowd watched the troupe perform.
20. Volunteers battled the flames for hours.

What is the *imported plural* of each of the following nouns? (Choose *ten* from this list.)

1. analysis
2. nebula
3. fungus
4. index
5. thesis
6. cherub
7. antenna
8. virtuoso
9. phenomenon
10. criterion
11. beau
12. hypothesis
13. synthesis
14. tempo
15. cactus
16. curriculum
17. stigma
18. larva
19. nucleus
20. stimulus

A. For each of the following noun-making suffixes, provide two additional examples. (Write on a separate sheet.)

1. –hood womanhood, _____ , _____
2. –ment government, _____ , _____
3. –ness likeness, _____ , _____
4. –ship apprenticeship, _____ , _____
5. –tion determination, _____ , _____

B. For each of the following currently active noun-making suffixes, find two additional examples:

6. –ee draftee, _____ , _____
7. –eer pamphleteer, _____ , _____
8. –ette dinette, _____ , _____
9. –or interceptor, _____ , _____
10. –ster mobster, _____ , _____

C. Find an *–ism* word for each of the following:

11. a movement that fights for equal rights for women
12. a movement that protects the rights of consumers
13. the practice of giving political appointments to relatives
14. a "we-can't-win" attitude
15. overvaluing the standards of a small elite

Know the signals that help us identify verbs.

Verbs are words that help us set things in motion. They enable us to talk about things happening and things being done. When we want people to do something, we can draw on hundreds of verbs like *eat, drink, enter, knock, wait, try, investigate, ask, write, confess, apply, hide,* and *prepare.*

S1b

Recognizing Verbs

Sentences

Know the signals that help us identify verbs in a sentence:

(1) English verbs have a built-in reference to time. They tell us about actions or events as they happen (or could happen) in time. Verbs are the only words that can show a change in time by a change in form. We call this difference a difference in **tense:**

PRESENT:	I *ask*	we *help*	I *see*	they *teach*
PAST:	I *asked*	we *helped*	I *saw*	they *taught*

Originally, verbs changed their form to show not only *when* something was done but also *who* was doing it. Today, only the verb *be* still has this double system of word forms. Here is a rough scheme:

FORMS OF *BE*	PRESENT	SINGULAR	PLURAL
	First person (speaking)	I *am*	we *are*
	Second person (spoken *to*)	you *are*	you *are*
	Third person (spoken *about*)	he *is*	they *are*
	PAST		
	First person	I *was*	we *were*
	Second person	you *were*	you *were*
	Third person	he *was*	they *were*

Modern English verbs have four or five basic forms:

• Verbs have different forms for present and past. For many modern English verbs (but not all), the ending that signals past tense is *–ed:*

PRESENT TENSE:	walk	slip	retreat	write	bring
PAST TENSE:	walked	slipped	retreated	wrote	brought

• A form with the ending *–s* sets apart the **third person singular** from other uses of the present tense. This is the form for "one third party—action now":

PLAIN:	(I, you, we, they)	run	walk	sing	decide
THIRD PERSON:	(he, she, it)	*runs*	*walks*	*sings*	*decides*

• Many verbs have a form for use after *have* (and *has* and *had*). We call the combinations with *have* the **perfect** tenses. They usually point to the recent past: I have already *eaten.* She had *driven* the car. Many of these forms, but not all, have the *–en* endings:

PRESENT	PAST	PERFECT
fall	fell	have *fallen*
write	wrote	have *written*
sing	sang	have *sung*
take	took	have *taken*

- All verbs have the *–ing* form: *walking, slipping, singing.* Here are typical verbs with five different forms:

PLAIN	THIRD PERSON	PAST	PERFECT	*–ing*
break	breaks	broke	(have) broken	breaking
fall	falls	fell	(have) fallen	falling
take	takes	took	(have) taken	taking
sing	sings	sang	(have) sung	singing
know	knows	knew	(have) known	knowing

NOTE: With many other verbs, the past form does double duty. They do not have a separate form to correspond to *broken* or *fallen:*

PAST: They *helped* us.
PERFECT: They *have helped* us.

PAST: He *apologized* to the guests.
PERFECT: He *had apologized* to the guests.

For standard and nonstandard verb forms, see **U1a.**

For formal and informal verb forms, see **U2d.**

(2) *Verbs often come after auxiliaries.*   Some forms of a verb can serve as a complete verb without further help. All of the following make a complete statement:

Birds *sing.*	The bird *sings.*	Birds *sang.*
Dogs *bark.*	The dog *barks.*	Dogs *barked.*

Other forms of verbs need a form of *have (has, had)* or *be (am, are, is, was, were, has been,* and so on). *Have* and *be* are then used as helping verbs, or **auxiliaries:**

Snow *has fallen.*	Sarah *is driving.*
Jim *had known.*	Birds *were singing.*
Cars *are driven.*	I *am eating.*
A leader *had been chosen.*	Fred *has been working.*

THE ENGLISH VERB
A Summary

Verb forms and auxiliaries together give us our inventory of possible *time distinctions,* or **tenses.** The names of the tenses may call attention to only *one* possible use out of several, as shown in the following examples:

PRESENT:
I *concede.* (now)
I *exercise* regularly. (past, present, and future)
I *leave* tomorrow. (future)
Suddenly I *see* this man. . . . (vivid past)

PAST:
He *left.* (past and done with)
If he *left* us tomorrow. . . . (possibility)

PERFECT:
She *has applied.* (recently completed, with bearing on the past)

PAST PERFECT:
He *had resigned.* (in the more distant past)

FUTURE:
She *will preside.*

For all five of these tenses we have alternate forms for *action in progress:*

PROGRESSIVE —
PRESENT: He *is talking.*
PAST: They *were quarreling.*
PERFECT: It *has been raining.*
PAST PERFECT: We *had been talking.*
FUTURE: She *will be waiting.*

Familiar combinations come before verbs to add meanings similar to those shown by auxiliaries:

FUTURE:
He *will leave.*
She *is going to* leave.
He *is about to* leave.

OBLIGATION:
We *must* go.
We *ought to* go.
We *have to* go.

HABITUAL PAST:
They *would* sit around a fire and sing.
They *used to* sit around a fire and sing.

The plain form of a verb often combines with one of the **modal** auxiliaries: *can (could), may (might), will (would), shall (should), must:*

Birds *fly*.	Times *change*.
Birds *can fly*.	Times *may change*.
Birds *must fly*.	Times *will change*.
Birds *should fly*.	Times *might change*.

By using one or more auxiliaries before the main verb, we can put together many different combinations. These follow a fairly simple pattern: Modal (if any) first; form of *have* (if any) second; form of *be* (if only *one*) third; *being* (if two forms of *be* are present) immediately before the main verb.

MODAL	HAVE	BE	(BEING)	MAIN VERB
	has			arrived
will				succeed
		was		condemned
		is		changing
		is	being	changed
can		be		improved
	had	been		postponed
might	have	been		overlooked
should	have	been		corrected
		was	being	rebuilt

> **VERB AND AUXILIARIES**

(3) *Many verbs show familiar verb-making endings.* Familiar verb-making suffixes are *–ize, –fy,* and *–ate:*

- **–ize:** organize, neutralize, realize
- **–fy:** liquefy, amplify, rectify, certify
- **–ate:** contaminate, nominate, illuminate

After the number of each sentence, write down the complete verb, including any auxiliaries.

EXERCISE 1

1. The wind was blowing with tremendous force.
2. The immigrants from Ireland never forgot the past.
3. The police will investigate the crime.
4. Juanita has been studying in the public library.
5. The railroad should indemnify the victims of the accident.
6. In the old days, weavers made cloth by hand.
7. The newspapers had accused the mayor of corruption.

8. Faith moves mountains.
9. The guard opened the gate for us.
10. The whales were traveling south along the California coast.

EXERCISE 2

Which verb would best describe what is happening or what is being done in each of the following sentences? After the number of the sentence, write a form that would fit into the blank space. Each time, choose a single word.

1. When we make exact copies of a letter, we _____ it.
2. When sick people are getting better, they are _____ .
3. Blood returns to the heart after it _____ through the body.
4. To make two watches show exactly the same time, we _____ them.
5. After using surgical instruments, doctors _____ them.
6. To get to know applicants personally, an employer _____ them.
7. National party conventions _____ Presidential candidates.
8. People who accuse someone by sly hints are _____ something.
9. We can cash a check after we have _____ it.
10. To protect us against shock, electricians _____ wires.
11. People who moonlight are _____ their income.
12. When people meet all the requirements, they _____ for a job.
13. An employer often _____ taxes and dues from a paycheck.
14. To give many people a chance, companies _____ their top jobs.
15. When accused people clear their names, they _____ themselves.
16. Landlords have often _____ tenants unable to pay their rent.
17. Tenants sometimes _____ part of their apartments to someone else.
18. When income matches spending, we have _____ our budget.
19. A director hiring actors usually _____ many people.
20. A doctor who pinpoints what is wrong _____ the patient's illness.

EXERCISE 3

The following words can be used either as nouns or as verbs. For each word, make up a pair of short sentences. In the first sentence, use the word as a *plural* noun. In the second sentence use the word as a verb in the *past* tense.

EXAMPLE: hand
(Answer)   His *hands* were chapped.
           She *handed* me the photograph.

1. table
2. structure
3. author
4. position
5. voice
6. vacation
7. thumb
8. service
9. style
10. engineer

Know the signals that help us recognize adjectives and adverbs.

Adjectives are words like *short, strong, heavy, blue, washable, real, imaginary,* and *wonderful.* They tell us which one or what kind. Their most typical position in a sentence is in front of a noun: the *blue* sweater, a *real* treat, *washable* fabrics, a *wonderful* vacation. **Adverbs** are words like *slowly, eagerly, frequently, recklessly, often, here, upstairs,* and *tomorrow.* They tell us how, when, and where. They often appear close to a verb to tell us how, when, or where something is done:

He ran *upstairs eagerly.*
The car *slowly* backed out of the garage.

Remember the following points:

(1) Adjectives often refer to qualities that can change in degree. Most true adjectives have special forms for use in comparisons. They have a **comparative** form with the ending *–er* or the word *more.* They have a **superlative** form with the ending *–est* or the word *most:*

PLAIN	COMPARATIVE	SUPERLATIVE
thin	thinner	thinnest
heavy	heavier	heaviest
mean	meaner	meanest
valuable	more valuable	most valuable
humorous	more humorous	most humorous

Like most adjectives, many adverbs have forms with *–er/–est* or *more/most* for comparative and superlative:

ADVERB: I can run *faster* than you can.
ADVERB: Pete ate the pie *more quickly* than Juan.
ADVERB: We can buy it *more cheaply* next door.

Adjectives and adverbs that show degree fit in after words like *very, fairly, rather, exceptionally,* and *extremely:* very warm, fairly valuable, rather thin, exceptionally bright, extremely often. We call such degree words **intensifiers.**

(2) Many adjectives show familiar adjective-making endings. Many adjectives end in *–ous, –able, –ible, –ful,* or *–less:*

–ous: marvelous, numerous, courageous, poisonous
–able: manageable, retractable, negotiable
–ible: edible, contemptible, incorrigible
–ful: wonderful, hopeful, powerful
–less: hopeless, luckless, penniless

(3) Many adverbs have the typical –ly *ending.* We can often make up an adverb by adding the *–ly* ending to an adjective:

ADJECTIVE: *Eager* listeners crowded the hall.
ADVERB: The audience listened *eagerly.*

ADJECTIVE: The *frequent* stops annoyed us.
ADVERB: The train stopped *frequently.*

When both adjective and adverb use the same root word, the adverb is typically the form with *–ly.* But many adverbs, especially those telling us where and when, lack the typical adverb ending: *here, there, away, abroad, now, soon, today, yesterday, tomorrow.* And some adjectives also have an *–ly* ending:

ADVERB: rapidly, similarly, regularly, speedily, successfully, incredibly
ADJECTIVE: a *friendly* smile, a *leisurely* walk, the *early* train

In some cases, adjective and adverb are *identical:*

ADJECTIVE: a *fast* train, *early* notice, the *right* answer, a *forward* movement
ADVERB: ran *fast,* rose *early,* did it *right,* moved *forward*

NOTE: A few adverbs show adverb endings other than *–ly:* length*wise,* other*wise,* cross*wise.*

See **U2c** for adverb forms in formal written English.

(4) Adjectives modify nouns. Adverbs modify verbs, adjectives, and other adverbs. Adjectives tell us which one or what kind. They add to or narrow down the meaning of a noun. We say they **modify** the noun. When adverbs tell us how, when, or where, they modify a verb. They may also tell us how much or in what way when they appear next to an adjective or *other* adverb:

ADVERB + ADJECTIVE: The tickets were *surprisingly cheap.*

ADVERB + ADJECTIVE: We have had an *extremely cold* winter.

ADVERB + ADVERB: We arrived *incredibly late.*

ADVERB + ADVERB: They had worked *extremely hard.*

NOTE: Adverbs telling us when and where sometimes modify a noun:

our arrival *here*   the conference *tomorrow*
Americans *abroad*   the room *upstairs*

(5) Adjectives usually come before the nouns they modify. However, adjectives *follow* nouns in many set expressions:

court-*martial*	the voters *present*
attorney *general*	the funds *available*
heir *apparent*	the only solution *possible*
notary *public*	God *Almighty*

**ADJECTIVES TELL US WHICH ONE
OR WHAT KIND**
Find all the adjectives in these phrases.

Marvelous
Sales

The Final Touch

My Supreme Effort

An Ideal Vacation

Get the Whole Story

Adjectives frequently follow nouns when *more than one* adjective modifies the same noun or when the adjective is in turn modified by other material:

Makola, *silent and sullen,* despised the two men.
Phyllis, *proud of her new title,* smiled with pleasure.
Randy, *tall and agile,* was a natural at basketball.

Not all modifiers that come before a noun are true adjectives:

• **Number adjectives** are special kinds of adjectives. They come before any true adjective modifying the same noun: *three* blind mice, the *second* big mistake, *many* valuable paintings, *innumerable* old-time musicals. Number adjectives include actual number words and also words like *few, several, no, all, both, neither, some, much,* and *many.*

• Often a second noun comes before another noun and takes the place of an adjective. This **modifying noun** follows any true adjective: a successful *football* team, a large *discount* store, a famous *gossip* columnist, familiar *tourist* attractions.

(6) Adverbs have more freedom of movement than other sentence parts. The same adverb may appear at several different places in a sentence:

The car *suddenly* inched forward.
Suddenly the car inched forward.
The car inched forward *suddenly.*

Sentences

EXERCISE 1

A. For each of the following, write down five adjectives that would fit into the space before the noun. Each time, use an adjective that fits in after *very*.

1. a very _____ motorcycle
2. a very _____ movie
3. a very _____ leader
4. a very _____ building
5. a very _____ friend

B. For each of the following, write down five adverbs that would fit in after the verb. Each time, use the *–ly* ending.

6. talk _____ly
7. drive _____ly
8. work _____ly
9. dance _____ly
10. investigate _____ly

EXERCISE 2

Find all adjectives and adverbs in the following sentences. Write them after the number of the sentence. Add the right abbreviation in parentheses: *(Adj)* or *(Adv)*. Do *not* include determiners.

EXAMPLE: A good engine runs smoothly.
(Answer)   *good (Adj), smoothly (Adv)*

1. We should talk softly and carry a big stick.
2. The spectators looked forward eagerly to the final event.
3. The meeting took place in the hottest room.
4. The school had successfully sponsored athletic contests.
5. Soccer quickly became the favorite game of my friends.
6. A big company will soon build a new factory there.
7. The drivers frequently parked their trucks outside.
8. The device pumped oil economically from old wells.
9. We had already defeated a considerably stronger team.
10. My friend had always wanted a powerful motorcycle.
11. The article was about poor people in the richest nation in the world.
12. Divers were looking for priceless treasure in ancient ships.
13. An angry citizen suddenly seized the microphone.
14. The climb was an incredibly difficult task.
15. Dogs pulled heavy sleds across the arctic ice.
16. The train finally left after an interminable delay.
17. A courageous woman led the group to safety.
18. A conscientious official carefully measured the distance.
19. The survivors waited desperately for a hopeful sign.
20. The friendly guide rescued the thankful travelers.

Practice adding information to a simple sentence by using adjectives and adverbs. Build up each of the following sentences by adding several of these modifiers.

EXERCISE 3

EXAMPLE: The mail carrier rings.
(Answer)   The *extremely patient* mail carrier *almost always* rings *twice*.

1. My friend played a guitar.
2. The star pleased the crowd.
3. The crew finished its work.
4. A bear attacked the campers.
5. A crowd came to the picnic.
6. A customer should ask for a warranty.
7. My cousin drove a car.
8. Nations must find sources of energy.
9. Tourists visit our town.
10. Our laws protect animals.

Write down each word that is italicized in the following sentences. After each, write the abbreviation that shows how it was used: *Adj* for "true adjective"; *Num* for "number adjective"; *MN* for "modifying noun." Be prepared to explain what adjective features, if any, each word shares. (Number the words from 1 through 25.)

EXERCISE 4

1. In 1876 the *first great international* exposition was held in the United States.
2. The *Centennial* Exhibition in Philadelphia was the *greatest* fair ever held anywhere in the world.
3. It cost *six* times as much as the *famous* exposition in the *Crystal* Palace in London in 1851.
4. It was *bigger* even than the *Vienna* Exhibition of 1874 with its *fifty* acres of buildings.
5. Down on *River* Street, he could see the *harbor* lights and the light from the stars on the *calm black* water.
6. The Wright-Sherwin plant was a *grim black* shadow on River Street, with the *street* light shining on its *blind brick* façade.
7. Against the *mica* panes of the *small* window, the *early* daylight showed like fog, *silvery* and *chilly*.

Sometimes *three or more adjectives and adverbs* are closely related in origin or in meaning. Since the *–ly* ending is not a reliable guide, we have to rely on their role in a sentence to sort them out. After the number of each sentence, put *Adj* if the italicized

EXERCISE 5

word is an adjective. Put *Adv* if it is an adverb. (Be prepared to explain in class the differences in use and meaning.)

1. The *late* Senator Gordon was a friend of labor.
2. The Senate has passed few labor laws *lately*.
3. The law had been passed *late* in the year.
4. His *homely* brother had become a handsome boy.
5. The children had been sent *home*.
6. We especially enjoyed the *homelike* atmosphere.
7. We need a *good* map.
8. He studied the map *well*.
9. A *goodly* number had already arrived.
10. Turn *right* at the corner.
11. The *right* person has not yet been found.
12. The mayor handled the problem *right*.
13. She has *rightly* been called a friend of the poor.
14. His home county had been a very *backward* area.
15. Jim always did everything *backward*.
16. We considered their action a step *backward*.
17. His parents had always worked *hard*.
18. His father *hardly* ever worked.
19. Her mother had been a *hard* worker.
20. Her grandfather had been a *hardy* soul.

S1d
Recognizing Connectives and Prepositions

Recognize the connectives and prepositions that we use as links in a sentence.

Several kinds of words help us provide links between the major building blocks of a sentence. The most important of these are connectives and prepositions. Remember:

(1) Connectives help us join two or more similar elements. Even in a short sentence, **connectives** like *and* and *or* help us join two or more things of the same kind:

Condors *and* eagles are large birds of prey.
Usually, we ate in the cafeteria *or* sent someone out for snacks.

Connectives do their most important work when they help us join short sentences as parts of a longer combined sentence. There are several major kinds of connectives:

COORDINATING:	and, or, but, for, yet, so, nor
SUBORDINATING:	if, when, because, unless, although, whereas
ADVERBIAL:	however, therefore, moreover, indeed
SPECIAL:	that, whether, how, why

See **S4** for a full treatment of connectives.

(2) Prepositions help us link a noun (or pronoun) to the rest of the sentence. **Prepositions** are words like *in, at, on, of, from, to, by, like, with, without, about, around, during,* and *across*. Together with the noun that they bring into the sentence, they make up a **prepositional phrase.** Such prepositional phrases come into a sentence as modifiers. They can modify different parts of a sentence:

The driver turned *by mistake.*
The clock *over the fireplace* has stopped.
Neal waved to the girl *on the motorcycle.*

More than one prepositional phrase may come into the same sentence. Often the prepositional phrase in turn carries other modifying material with it:

In the afternoon, at Mother's request, Father took me *for a walk.* (Frank O'Connor)

Another rectangular hole *in a small cleared space among the dusty greenery* had caught Mr. Lever's eye. (Graham Greene)

PREPOSITIONS
A Checklist

The following words may all be used as prepositions. Note that many point out relationships in *time* or in *space:*

about	behind	from	since
above	below	in	through
across	beneath	inside	to
after	beside	into	toward
against	between	like	under
along	beyond	near	until
among	by	of	up
around	despite	off	upon
as	during	on	with
at	except	outside	within
before	for	over	without

The following *combinations* are also used as prepositions:

aside from	instead of
as to	in view of
as well as	on account of
because of	on behalf of
due to	out of
in spite of	regardless of

---

(3) Prepositions are part of many familiar expressions. Several words that always combine the same way to state an idea are called an **idiom.** To use language well, we have to know idiomatic prepositions. Know what preposition goes with a given noun, or verb, or adjective. Would you have used the same idiomatic preposition with each of the following?

IDIOMATIC PREPOSITIONS		
	NOUNS	anger *at* his remarks dissatisfaction *with* a solution dissent *from* an opinion surprise *at* a decision
	VERBS	abstain *from* voting agree *with* a person, *to* a proposal, *on* a solution aspire *to* high honors confide *in* somebody conform *to* specifications delight *in* mischief dissuade *from* an action infer *from* evidence interfere *with* a performance, *in* someone's business object *to* a solution persevere *in* a task refrain *from* wrongdoing rejoice *at* good news resolve *on* a course of action
	ADJECTIVES	alarmed *at* the news capable *of* an action deficient *in* strength identical *with* the original ignorant *of* the facts indifferent *to* praise inferior *to* the competition jealous *of* rivals

NOTE: When you look for prepositions in actual sentences, be prepared for some variations from the way prepositions are normally used:

• Many prepositions do *double duty as adverbs.* They modify a verb in such a way as to tell us "where." Note that the words in the chart on the top of the next page can act both as prepositions and as adverbs.

PREPOSITION	ADVERB
He fell *down the stairs.*	He fell *down.*
Jim came *in a convertible.*	Jim came *in.*
Dora came *up the path.*	The subject came *up.*
We looked *around the corner.*	We looked *around.*
The bear came *near the fire.*	The bear came *near.*

• Some former prepositions have *blended with a verb* to become the second part of a **phrasal verb.** They may then trade places with the noun they help link to the sentence:

Marilyn *turned in* her key.
Marilyn *turned* her key *in.*

We all *looked up* the word.
We all *looked* the word *up.*

What prepositions are missing in each of the following sayings? Write the missing prepositions after the number of the sentence. (Write on a separate sheet.)

EXERCISE 1

1. Don't change horses _____ the middle _____ the stream.
2. He looked _____ a sick dog _____ a thorn _____ its foot.
3. An apple never falls far _____ the tree.
4. There's many a slip _____ the cup and the lip.
5. They were as crooked _____ a barrel _____ fishhooks.
6. A person _____ debt is a swimmer _____ boots on.
7. A place _____ birds is _____ food _____ seasoning.
8. Charity begins _____ home.
9. There is nothing new _____ the sun.
10. It's only one short step _____ genius _____ madness.

What idiomatic preposition would fit into the blank space in each of the following sentences? Write the missing preposition after the number of the sentence.

EXERCISE 2

1. He had never been accused _____ a crime.
2. We promised to abide _____ the new regulations.
3. The allies did not adhere _____ the original plan.
4. She should be attending _____ her business.
5. Juvenile offenders are seldom charged _____ more than a misdemeanor.
6. They had failed to comply _____ the order.

7. The prisoners were deprived _____ all privileges for a week.
8. The lawyer concurred _____ our decision.
9. She was reluctant to part _____ the ring.
10. Maria always insisted _____ total honesty.
11. He found fault _____ everything I said.
12. His remarks did not really pertain _____ the subject.
13. We prevailed _____ the guard to let us speak to the boys.
14. A watch prevented the bullet _____ doing serious harm.
15. These actions are completely inconsistent _____ his past record.
16. The states decided to secede _____ the Union.
17. The daredevil driver did not succeed _____ his attempt.
18. Her qualifications were superior _____ those of the other applicants.
19. My mother showed her surprise _____ the news.
20. All concerned should refrain _____ aggravating the situation.

EXERCISE 3

Practice adding information to a simple sentence by using prepositional phrases. Build up each of the following sentences, using two or more of these modifiers.

EXAMPLE: The sergeant talked.
(Answer)   The sergeant *in a new uniform* talked *to the visitor from Toledo.*

1. The car stopped.
2. The girl waved.
3. The owner opened the door.
4. A delegate talked.
5. A painting was hanging.
6. My friends played soccer.
7. The competitor won.
8. People visited the house.
9. The gorilla climbed.
10. The boy was reading a book.

EXERCISE 4

Modifiers help us add specific information. Study the following examples. Then take each of the original words and add prepositional phrases and other modifiers in very much the same way as the original author did. But use your modifiers to add *different* details.

1. paper
   smooth creamy paper, *a little yellowed by age* (George Orwell)
   YOUR TURN: _____

2. a shop
   a *frowsy little junk* shop *in a slummy quarter of the town* (George Orwell)
   YOUR TURN: _____

3. a woman
   a *black* woman, *tall as a cypress* (Mari Evans)
   YOUR TURN: ————————————————————————

4. a jacket
   a *short* jacket *of brown corduroy, newer than the remainder of his suit*
   (Thomas Hardy)
   YOUR TURN: ————————————————————————

5. signs
   For-Rent signs *in the upstairs window of a building* (Alice Munro)
   YOUR TURN: ————————————————————————

In each of the following sentences, one word has been italicized. What kind of word is it? After the number of the sentence, put the right abbreviation:

UNIT REVIEW EXERCISE

N	noun
Pro	pronoun
V	verb (or part of a complete verb)
Adj	adjective
Adv	adverb
Con	connective
Prep	preposition

EXAMPLE: *Tourists* were boarding the buses.
(Answer) *N*

1. Her family had *visited* Mexico on a previous trip.
2. The lion attacked the hunters with a *ferocious* roar.
3. The metal was *cooling* slowly.
4. In the distance we could see the *lights* of the city.
5. After much discussion, *cooler* heads won out.
6. The government furnished information *to* farmers.
7. *She* ran faster than any of her competitors.
8. My brothers were celebrating *upstairs*.
9. We seldom have snow in this *part* of Texas.
10. We finally chose the *lightest* color of the three.
11. They always shared their food *freely* with their guests.
12. The Websters were painting their *house*.
13. The actors *talked* about the theater after the performance.
14. *Everyone* was talking during the intermission.
15. Blue skies *and* a light breeze made it a perfect day.
16. A blizzard had trapped the luckless *hikers*.
17. The pages had already *yellowed*.
18. The new neighbors very *seldom* talked to us.
19. The voters showed their confidence in their *government*.

20. An *audible* sigh of relief swept the stadium.
21. My grandmother always got up *extremely* early.
22. A *friendly* smile sometimes makes all the difference.
23. We knew that a rabbit's foot *brought* good luck.
24. Very few people will *pay* this price for a ticket.
25. We could not find the place *without* a map.

S2
THE COMPLETE SENTENCE

Review the basic structure of the complete English sentence.

Sometimes, a single word, or a short group of words, says what is on our minds:

Fire!   Silence!   My books!   What a story!

Usually, however, we need a complete sentence to state an idea. Know the basic parts of the complete English sentence. Know the basic patterns in which they combine.

S2a
Subject and Predicate

Recognize the subject and the predicate of a sentence.

The normal English sentence has at least two basic parts. We focus first on some thing or idea. This first part we call the **subject.** We then *make a statement* about whatever we have identified. This second part we call the **predicate.** The two-part structure that calls our attention to a subject, and then makes a statement about the subject, we call a **sentence.**

Remember:

(1) The core of the subject is typically a noun. In all of the following sentences, the subject slot is filled either by a noun standing alone or by a noun with its noun marker, or determiner:

SUBJECT	PREDICATE
Rain	falls.
A truck	had stalled.
The pavement	was wet.
Tourists	were passing by.
Your invitation	surprised us.
The conference	had begun.
These interruptions	must end.
Their politeness	was unexpected.

The Complete Sentence

The following pointers will help you find the subject of a sentence:

• The place of a noun may be taken by a *noun substitute*. Most single words that take the place of a noun are **pronouns.** In the following pairs, pronouns take the place of the original subjects in the second sentence of each pair:

NOUN: *The customer* returned the shoes.
PRONOUN: *He* returned the shoes.

NOUN: *My sister* passed the test.
PRONOUN: *Everyone* passed the test.

• Modifiers may come before and after a noun that serves as the subject:

The driver *of the red car* looked around.
The *wet* pavement was slippery.

• Several nouns, joined by *and* or *or,* may combine to serve as a **compound** subject:

The owl and *the pussycat* / went to sea.
The walrus and *the carpenter* / were walking close at hand.

• The noun that serves as subject of a sentence is *not* linked to the rest of the sentence by a preposition:

(In the afternoon) *the group* / reached a deserted village.
The first *half* (of the afternoon) / had passed.

(2) The core of the predicate is a complete verb. The verb is the part of the sentence that actually makes a statement. In all of the following sentences, the predicate slot is filled by a verb standing alone as a single word or by a verb that includes one or more auxiliaries.

SUBJECT	PREDICATE
Time	*passes.*
Your visit	*helped.*
Times	*have changed.*
Your turn	*will come.*
The results	*were announced.*
A storm	*was brewing.*
Lori	*may disagree.*
A rescue party	*is being organized.*

Sentences

Remember these points:

• Many English verbs are *two-word combinations*. A word like *at, up, on,* or *down* combines with a familiar short verb to form a new unit. Sometimes *three* words combine to take the place of some other single verb with the same meaning:

ONE WORD:	We *watched.*	I *yielded.*	He *rose.*
TWO WORDS:	We *looked on.*	I *gave in.*	He *stood up.*

ONE WORD:	She was *admired* by all.
THREE WORDS:	She was *looked up to* by all.

• Several verbs may follow the same subject. Joined by *and* or *or,* they form a **compound** predicate:

> They *laughed* and *tumbled* and *shouted* on the mountain. (William Golding)

• When the subject changes in **number,** the verb frequently changes along with it. We say it agrees with the subject.

> *The girl* selected by the group *has left.*
> *The girls* selected by the group *have left.*

See **U3a** for agreement of subject and verb.

EXERCISE 1

Which of the following could serve as the subject of a normal English sentence? After the number of each item that is eligible, write *Yes*. After the number of each item that could not normally serve as a subject, write *No*. (Your teacher may ask you to fill in a predicate for each possible subject.)

1. the deep blue sea
2. incredibly beautiful
3. liberty
4. had never been visited
5. our very successful track stars
6. everyone present
7. silent in the moonlight
8. could have prevented
9. years of heat and drought
10. a farmer and the two oldest children
11. this extreme callousness
12. with great ease
13. nobody
14. very little encouragement
15. those familiar excuses
16. may happen again

17. a young girl in a light blue cotton dress
18. on approval
19. my first and last attempt
20. a leisurely walk along the shore

Which of the following could serve as the *complete verb* of a normal English sentence? After the number of each item that is eligible, write *Yes*. After the number of each item that could not normally serve as the complete verb, write *No*. (Your teacher may ask you to fill in a subject for each possible predicate.)

1. her invincible hatred
2. might have failed
3. argue
4. pushing back his hair
5. had been ringing
6. roses and carnations
7. varies
8. fallen
9. had frozen over
10. is being repaired
11. fell
12. a sudden rain
13. theorize
14. stopped
15. being followed
16. his annoying laugh
17. has been confirmed
18. should get up
19. their insistent questions
20. will soften

One way we can make a sentence carry extra freight is to make *more than one verb* follow the same subject. Choose three of the following as model sentences. For each, fill in the same basic frame with material of your own. Imitate the structure as best you can.

1. MODEL SENTENCE: In Little Rock the people *bear*
Babes, and *comb* and *part* their hair,
And *watch* the want ads. (Gwendolyn Brooks)

   SAMPLE IMITATION: In New York City, the people ride the subway, and dodge and curse the traffic, and jostle their fellow pedestrians.

   YOUR TURN: In _____, the _____,
and _____, and _____.

2. She *ditched* her sandwich board and *rolled* her banner *up,* and *set off* through the swing doors into the cosy warmth. (Margaret Drabble)
3. He *bent down, took up* a double handful of lukewarm water, and *rubbed* the mess from his face. (William Golding)
4. Farmers *heap* hay in stacks and *bind* corn in shocks against the biting breath of frost. (Margaret Walker)
5. He *noticed* blood on his hands and *grimaced* distastefully, *looked* for something on which to clean them, then *wiped* them on his shorts and *laughed.* (William Golding)

S2b
Simple Sentence Patterns

Know the four most common short sentence patterns.

The most basic sentence model has only two basic parts: a noun and its verb. But often a third and perhaps a fourth basic part follow the verb. They are needed to complete the predicate and are called "completers," or **complements.** A completer is not linked to the rest of the sentence by a preposition or other connecting word. It is an essential part of the basic structure. It is as necessary as the third side of a triangle or the third and fourth sides of a square.

Each of the following examples would have a chopped-off effect without the added completer:

SUBJECT	VERB	COMPLETER
Dinner	is	*ready.*
The Smiths	bought	*a trailer.*
My friend	had been	*a lifeguard.*
The storm	has damaged	*the roof.*

We can sort out common sentence patterns by asking: Is a complement necessary to complete this sentence? If so, what kind?

For each of the following four simple sentence patterns, look first at the simple bare-bones models. These include only the basic sentence parts. Then look at the pattern as it might be expanded in actual sentences. In the expanded patterns, modifiers have been added to the basic parts. Sometimes, one of the basic parts has been repeated, with the two similar parts linked by *and* or *or.*

(1) PATTERN ONE: SUBJECT–VERB (S–V)

This is the bare-minimum sentence in English. The *verb alone* serves as the complete predicate. Verbs in this pattern are **intransitive.** They are not in "transit"—they are not going anywhere.

PATTERN ONE: Kites fly.
Mary nodded.
The phone was ringing.
The rain had stopped.
A replacement will arrive.

EXPANDED: *A cat may look* on a king.
He leaned forward *and listened* to us.
The faint *noise* behind the door *continued.*
The two *women stood* for a minute staring at each other in the last golden light. (Edith Wharton)

(2) PATTERN TWO: SUBJECT–VERB–OBJECT (S–V–O)

In this pattern, a **transitive** verb *carries the action of the subject across to a second noun* (or noun substitute). The difference between a transitive and an intransitive verb is like that between a through road and a dead-end street. The second noun becomes part of the basic structure of the sentence and is called the **direct object.** In many sentences, it is the target of an action. Sometimes it is the result of a process.

PATTERN TWO: Dogs chase cats.
The arrow hit the target.
Familiarity breeds contempt.
The manager will interview the candidates.
The factory manufactured bricks.

EXPANDED: *She pushed the* heavy *cart* across the concrete floor.
The new *manager had made the arrangements* for the meeting.
The people know the salt of the sea *and the strength* of the wind. (Carl Sandburg)

(3) PATTERN THREE: SUBJECT–LINKING VERB–NOUN (S–LV–N)

In this pattern, the verb *pins a label on the subject.* The label is a second noun that serves as a description of the first. The second noun in this pattern is often called a "predicate noun." The verb linking it to the subject is called a **linking verb.**

Most commonly the linking verb is a form of *be.* Other linking verbs used in this pattern are *become, remain,* and *seem:*

PATTERN THREE: Philip is a fool.
Bertha was a dispatcher.
He remained my friend.
Her parents had become citizens.
The decision seemed a mistake.

EXPANDED: *A thing* of beauty *is a joy* forever. (John Keats)
The sound must seem an echo to the sense. (Alexander Pope)
Punctuality is the thief of time. (Oscar Wilde)
Loneliness is the poverty of the self. (May Sarton)

(4) PATTERN FOUR: SUBJECT–LINKING VERB–ADJECTIVE (S–LV–Adj)

In this pattern, the linking verb again pins a label on the subject. But this time the label is *not* a second noun. It is a word from the third major word class: an adjective. Adjectives are words like *warm, slender, blue, heavy, beautiful,* and *studious.* Remember that most true adjectives fit in after **intensifiers** like *very, fairly, extremely:* very short, fairly expensive, extremely beautiful. The adjective that follows the linking verb is often called a "predicate adjective."

Verbs that may serve as linking verbs in this pattern include *be, seem, appear, become, grow, prove, feel, taste, sound,* and *look:*

PATTERN FOUR: The rooms were small.
Dinosaurs had become extinct.
The soup tasted strange.
These tires have proved reliable.
The caller sounded desperate.
My brother looked unhappy.

EXPANDED: *Vacations are* always too *short.*
The new *neighbors seemed* very *strange* to me.
No one has ever *become great* by imitation.
She was evidently far less *sure* than her companion of herself and of her rights in the world. (Edith Wharton)

EXERCISE 1

What is the basic sentence pattern in each of the following expanded sentences? After the number of the sentence, put the right abbreviation:

S–V
S–V–O
S–LV–N
S–LV–Adj

1. Her niece had found a job in Arizona.
2. Millions of immigrants became citizens.
3. Our task seemed almost impossible.
4. Malaria was a common disease in the tropics.
5. The answer sounded wrong to me.
6. Readers of the magazine were canceling their subscriptions.
7. The driver of the van signaled for a left turn.
8. American athletes were competing in the events.
9. The exhibition was a complete success.
10. Pollution was killing fish in the river.
11. Fires were burning out of control in the Alaskan National Forest.
12. An itinerary is a schedule for a traveler.
13. The ancient materials in the tomb had disintegrated.
14. Machines were now harvesting the crops.
15. The people in the town were suspicious of foreigners.
16. His grandmother had been the owner of the general store.
17. The people on the bus looked unhappy.

18. The manager had interviewed the applicants for the position.
19. The judge put the youngsters on probation.
20. The old courthouse remained an eyesore in the center of town.

Each of the following sentences illustrates one of the four simple sentence patterns. Study first the simple pattern and then the expanded version which serves as a *model sentence*. Fill in the same basic sentence frame with material of your own.

1. BASIC PATTERN: O'Brien was a man.
   EXPANDED: *O'Brien was a* large burly *man* with a thick neck and a coarse, humorous, brutal face. (George Orwell)
   YOUR TURN: My (mother) (uncle) (grandfather) (_____) was a _____ with _____ and _____.

2. BASIC PATTERN: Irene took back a feeling.
   EXPANDED: Sister *Irene took back* with her to the convent *a feeling* of betrayal and confusion. (Joyce Carol Oates)
   YOUR TURN: _____ took back with _____ to _____ a _____ and _____.

3. BASIC PATTERN: He was a boy.
   EXPANDED: *He was* only *a* little *boy,* ten years old, with hair like dusty yellow grass and with shy polite gray eyes. (John Steinbeck)
   YOUR TURN: I am a _____, _____, with _____ and with _____.

4. BASIC PATTERN: He had heard a word.
   EXPANDED: During all those years, *he had* never *heard* from any of his masters *a* flippant *word.* (James Joyce)
   YOUR TURN: During _____, I have never heard _____.

5. BASIC PATTERN: A band was playing.
   EXPANDED: In a quiet bystreet, *a* German *band* of five players in faded uniforms and with battered brass instruments *was playing* to an audience of street urchins and leisurely messenger boys. (James Joyce)
   YOUR TURN: _____, a _____ band _____ was playing to an audience of _____ and _____.

6. BASIC PATTERN: The sea remained still.
   EXPANDED: Under the sinister splendor of that sky, *the sea,* blue and profound, *remained still,* without a stir, without a ripple, without a wrinkle. (Joseph Conrad)
   YOUR TURN: _____, the _____ remained _____, _____.

S2c
Longer Sentence Patterns

Know the sentence patterns that use four basic parts.

Several common sentence patterns have four basic parts. They need *two* completers before they make a complete statement. We can add one complement after the verb and still leave the sentence incomplete. Each of the following would seem chopped off without the second completer:

SUBJECT	VERB	COMPLETER	COMPLETER
Edith	gave	the driver	*instructions.*
The critic	called	the play	*a triumph.*
Her answer	left	her friend	*speechless.*

The following patterns use four basic parts:

(1) PATTERN FIVE: SUBJECT–VERB–INDIRECT OBJECT–OBJECT (S–V–IO–O)

In this pattern, a transitive verb makes a *detour through a second complement* before carrying the action across to the direct object. The additional noun (or noun substitute) inserted between the verb and direct object is called the **indirect object.** Typically, the indirect object shows the intended *recipient or destination.*

Verbs that fit this pattern include *give, send, teach, write, buy, leave, lend, offer, show, ask:*

PATTERN FIVE: Manuel wrote *his parents* a letter.
The teachers taught *us* judo.
Dorothy gave *the motorist* directions.
My uncle lent *strangers* money.
My aunt showed *the visitors* the way.

EXPANDED: *Her* crotchety *parents* finally *gave the* young *couple their* blessing.
The grateful *owner* of the collie *offered us a* large *reward* of cake and cookies.

(2) PATTERN SIX: SUBJECT–VERB–OBJECT–OBJECT COMPLEMENT (S- V–O–OC)

In this pattern, a transitive verb first carries the action or process across to the object. We then go on to a second complement that *pins a label* on the object. In this pattern, the label pinned on the object is an additional *noun* (or noun substitute). It is called the **object complement.**

The resulting pattern looks the same as Pattern Five but is put together differently. In Pattern Five, we look at three elements: "sender—destination—missive." *What* is sent and *to whom* are different things. In Pattern Six, we have a combination of Pattern Two ("I consider John") and Pattern Three ("John is a fool"). As a result, in "I consider John a fool," John and the fool are the *same person.*

Verbs that fit this pattern include *consider, think, call, make, name, choose, elect, vote, appoint:*

PATTERN SIX: I consider John *my friend.*
                Jim called Mr. Green *his mentor.*
                The parents had named the child *Miranda.*
                The voters elected the actor *governor.*
                They nicknamed Roosevelt *the Rough Rider.*

EXPANDED: A child's *laughter makes the darkness light.*
                Coleridge called Shakespeare's *plays works* of true genius.
                The President appointed Thurgood Marshall a Supreme Court justice.

(3) PATTERN SEVEN: SUBJECT–VERB–OBJECT–ADJECTIVE S–V–O–Adj)

In this pattern we again have the verb pin a label on the object. This time, the *label is an adjective.* The result is a combination of Pattern Two ("I consider this action") and Pattern Four ("This action is premature"). Combining these two statements, we have "I consider this action premature."

Verbs that fit this pattern include some of the verbs from Pattern Six but also many others: *consider, think, call, make, find, paint, turn, keep:*

PATTERN SEVEN: I consider John *eligible.*
                Her actions made the voters *happy.*
                You will find the food *excellent.*
                We are painting the roses *red.*
                The fire kept us *warm.*
                He thought the task *dangerous.*

EXPANDED: *The* good *news* from my brother *had made my parents* very *glad.*
                An earlier *report had called the* security *arrangements unsatisfactory.*
                Soon *practice may make me* middling-*perfect.* (Adrienne Rich)

Sentences

Add a second complement to complete each of the following sentences. Make sure the complete sentence fits one of the four-part patterns. Write the completer after the number of the sentence. (Write on a separate sheet.)

EXAMPLE: The hurricane left the family _____ .
(Answer) *homeless*

1. The lawyers called the case _____ .
2. The magazine offered subscribers _____ .
3. Banks pay their depositors _____ .
4. The customer considered the refund _____ .
5. The noise was making work _____ .
6. The company granted the applicant _____ .
7. The judge will give the jurors _____ .
8. The company named the car _____ .
9. Miranda should have taught her brother _____ .
10. The physician called the operation _____ .
11. The city has kept taxes _____ .
12. The contract guaranteed employees _____ .
13. Her supervisor had offered Josephine _____ .
14. The chemical turned the water _____ .
15. Erosion had made the country _____ .
16. The voters elected her sister _____ .
17. The citation called his driving _____ .
18. A bonus gives employees _____ .
19. This law had made discounts _____ .
20. Incentives keep morale _____ .

Many English verbs *change their meaning* as they move from one basic pattern to the other. After the number of each sentence, write down the abbreviation for the basic pattern used. (Write on a separate sheet.)

S–V
S–V–O
S–LV–N
S–LV–Adj
S–V–IO–O
S–V–O–OC
S–V–O–Adj

1. The governor *stayed* in the capital.
2. The governor *stayed* the execution.

3. The speakers *rendered* tribute to her achievement.
4. The defect *rendered* the machine useless.

5. Jake *washes* his hair every night.
6. This material *washes* well.

7. Joan *walked* to work.
8. Joan *walked* her dog.

9. A relative *left* the family a fortune.
10. Uncle Simon *left* his family destitute.

11. Isabel *had made* the decision.
12. Isabel *had made* her mother happy.

13. This time the machine *worked*.
14. The new manager *worked* a miracle.

15. Smith *called* the office.
16. Smith *called* the office a madhouse.

17. George *found* his mother a taxi.
18. George *found* the party dull.

19. The sentinel *sounded* the alarm.
20. The sentinel *sounded* sleepy.

Which is the basic pattern in each of the following sentences? After the number of the sentence, write down the right abbreviation:

UNIT REVIEW EXERCISE

S–V
S–V–O
S–LV–N
S–LV–Adj
S–V–IO–O
S–V–O–OC
S–V–O–Adj

1. In India, English had long been the language of government.
2. The British made English the official language.
3. The schools taught all students English.
4. Now the government is adopting Hindi as the national language.
5. The supporters of this change consider English foreign.
6. Not all Indians speak Hindi.
7. The government recognizes fifteen major languages.
8. Now the schools teach many people Hindi.
9. A duplicate in English accompanies official documents.
10. English will remain a "link" language.

11. Also, Hindi will absorb many English words.
12. For instance, English gave the Indians the word *motor*.
13. In a modern language, many scientific words are necessary.
14. Hindi lacked many necessary terms.
15. India's translators translated all laws.
16. Publishers offered the schools Hindi textbooks.
17. Many people changed their customary ways.
18. The government called the changeover inevitable.
19. India is a proud modern nation.
20. A national language gives people a common identity.

S3
ADAPTING THE SIMPLE SENTENCE

Know the most common ways of adapting simple sentences for special uses.

If we needed language only to make simple statements, the basic sentence patterns would be sufficient. But in practice we often have to ask questions or make requests of people. We therefore have to adapt or stretch the basic patterns to make them serve our needs. In sentences that are not statements, but questions or requests, the material in the simple sentence has been reshuffled or rearranged. We may still recognize some of the basic parts. But they have been adjusted and fitted together in a different way. We call such re-adjustments and rearrangements of the basic sentence patterns **transformations.**

Study some common ways by which we adapt simple sentences for special uses.

S3a
Questions and Requests

Know how we turn statements into questions and requests.

We can turn a statement into a question or a request by changing or rearranging some of the basic sentence parts:

(1) To turn a statement into a question, put all or part of the verb in front of the subject. "He is your friend" is a statement. "*Is* he your friend?" is a question. Here we have moved the whole verb in front of the subject. This works whenever the complete verb is a single form of the verb *be:*

Time *is up.*	⟶	*Is* time *up?*
Peter *was absent.*	⟶	*Was* Peter *absent?*
You *are a member.*	⟶	*Are* you *a member?*
It *was late.*	⟶	*Was* it *late?*
They *were quick.*	⟶	*Were* they *quick?*
I *am the boss.*	⟶	*Am* I *the boss?*

STATEMENTS

Malnutrition has become a national menace.

Bromo-Seltzer Will Cure that Headache.

A Corn cost him his job.

Hall's Hair Renewer Grows Bountiful Beautiful Hair.

QUESTIONS

HAVE YOU DONE YOUR SHARE?

How Much Do You Know About Diet?

What does the future hold?

REQUESTS

PLEASE TURN OFF LIGHTS TO CONSERVE ENERGY.

Ring bell for service.

PARK HERE ANY TIME.

Keep America Beautiful.

If the verb includes one or more auxiliaries, we *switch the first auxiliary* so that it comes before the subject. The subject then splits up the verb:

Irma *was waiting*.   ⟶ *Was* Irma *waiting?*

Your friend *has finished* his work.   ⟶ *Has* your friend *finished* his work?

The road *had been paved*.   ⟶ *Had* the road *been paved?*

If there is no auxiliary that can be moved, we put a form of *do* in front of the subject:

Greene *lives* here.   ⟶ *Does* Greene *live* here?

You *collect* stamps.   ⟶ *Do* you *collect* stamps?

The team *won*.   ⟶ *Did* the team *win?*

With the addition of a question word, the same switch produces questions beginning with words like *when, where, what, why,* or *how.* "George *is happy*" becomes "Why *is* George *happy?*"

The boat *will return*.   ⟶ When *will* the boat *return?*

It *could have been avoided*.   ⟶ How *could* it *have been avoided?*

The driver *told* you her name. ⟶ When *did* the driver *tell* you her name?

You *had* tea for breakfast.   ⟶ What *did* you *have* for breakfast?

The Smiths *live* there.   ⟶ Where *do* the Smiths *live?*

These rules do *not* apply when *who, what,* or *which* asks a question about the subject:

Who took the car?

What happened?

Which road leads to Chicago?

NOTE: *Do* is also used in negative statements with *not* (or the more informal *–n't*). Here, however, the subject does not change its position:

Fred *speaks* French.   ⟶ Fred *doesn't speak* French.

The U.S. *recognized* the state. ⟶ The U.S. *did* not *recognize* the state.

The natives *like* tourists.   ⟶ The natives *do* not *like* tourists.

In questions and negative statements with *not*, the word *do* is used as an auxiliary. It adds the auxiliary missing from the basic pattern. A third use of *do* as an auxiliary is its use in the **emphatic** form of a verb: "I *do* believe you." "That *does* make a difference."

(2) To turn a statement into a request, leave out the subject and change the verb. To turn a sentence into an order or a request, we take out the subject and then change the verb to the request form, or **imperative.** The rest of the sentence remains unchanged.

SUBJECT	VERB	COMPLEMENT	COMPLEMENT
John	stopped. *Stop!*		
Jean	opened *Open*	the window. the window!	
Marcia	is *Be*	reasonable. reasonable!	
The boys	kept *Keep*	quiet. quiet!	
A friend	gave *Give*	the boy the boy	a chance. a chance!
The voters	elected *Elect*	Smith Smith	senator. senator!
The marshal	kept *Keep*	the citizens the citizens	calm. calm!

Request sentences are the major exception to the rule that the typical English sentence has at least a subject and a predicate. The subject of a request sentence is *you,* "understood." Notice that this "understood" *you* sometimes appears in spoken English. It also reappears in the **tag questions** that we can add to make a request more polite:

SPOKEN ENGLISH: Now *you be* careful.
  You tell him exactly what I said.
  You give him this key.

TAG QUESTIONS: *Give* him this key, will *you?*
  Be careful, will *you?*
  Tell him exactly what I said, will *you?*

Turn each of the following statements into a question. Use simple *Yes-or-No* questions ("Has he called?"). Use all parts of the original sentence. Change only the verb or its position as necessary. Write your question after the number of the sentence.

EXERCISE 1

1. The service has improved.
2. George Eliot was a woman.
3. You knew about the fine.
4. The bus stops here on Sundays.

5. The warning system was working.
6. A track star should train all year round.
7. Other states have tried to ban handguns.
8. Candidates for a police officer's job have to be citizens.
9. Anyone can join a fraternity.
10. Bears attack people.
11. All workers are eligible for the pension.
12. Your friend really cares.
13. The bank has been notified.
14. Bats sleep upside down.
15. The delegates paid their own way.

EXERCISE 2

Rewrite each of the following sentences to turn it into a request. Leave out the subject and change the verb to the request, or imperative, form.

1. The hikers watched out for snakes.
2. The witness told us the whole story.
3. Everyone will be there at eight o'clock.
4. You should have brought a friend.
5. Local authorities were cooperating with the federal examiners.
6. They were proud of our common heritage.
7. You should clean up the neighborhood.
8. Many people were voting for the clean-air candidate.
9. My friends are driving carefully.
10. My aunt always hoped for the best.

EXERCISE 3

The request form frequently appears in popular sayings, advertising slogans, and good advice. For five of the following, write a similar saying or slogan of your own with a more personal or a more modern touch.

1. Sue a beggar and catch a louse.
   SAMPLE IMITATION: Kick a dog and catch fleas.

2. Believe half you see and nothing you hear.
3. Drive slowly and see our town—drive fast and see our jail.
4. Take off your hat to nothing known or unknown.
5. Conserve energy—buy a horse.
6. Honk twice if you favor noise abatement.
7. Startle your parents—say "please" and "thank you."
8. Fight inflation—hibernate.
9. Love the earth and sun and the animals. (Walt Whitman)
10. Please don't litter the landscape . . . someone else may want to take a picture of it.

Know how we change sentences from active to passive.

S3b

The Passive

When we describe an action, we usually go from the "doer" to the action and from there to the target. In such sentences, the subject *does* something. We call such sentences **active** sentences:

ACTIVE: The mechanic was checking the car.

ACTIVE: The assistant manager approved my check.

Sometimes, however, we start a sentence with the target or the receiver. The subject has something *done* to it. We call such sentences **passive** sentences:

PASSIVE: The car had been checked by a first-rate mechanic.

PASSIVE: My check was returned.

Here is how we turn sentences from active to passive:

(1) To produce a passive sentence, we move an original object in front of the verb. There it becomes the *subject* of the new sentence. Then we change the verb to a passive form, using the auxiliary *be (is, was, has been, will be)*. Third, we move the original subject to a place after the verb and introduce it by the preposition *by:*

ACTIVE: The dog chases *the cat.*

PASSIVE: *The cat* is chased by the dog.

ACTIVE: The mayor called *the reporter* a liar.

PASSIVE: *The reporter* was called a liar by the mayor.

ACTIVE: The storm had swept *the streets* clean.

PASSIVE: *The streets* had been swept clean by the storm.

THE PASSIVE OFTEN SOUNDS IMPERSONAL:

Sentences

(2) The original subject often disappears from the sentence. This happens when our interest is not in who started an action but in what *result* the action produced. This use of the passive often sounds impersonal:

ACTIVE:	*Tow trucks* towed away unauthorized cars.
SHORT PASSIVE:	Unauthorized cars were towed away.

ACTIVE:	*The customer* had paid the bill in full.
SHORT PASSIVE:	The bill had been paid in full.

(3) When there are two objects, two different passives are possible:

ACTIVE:	The Browne family offered *the city the site.*
FIRST PASSIVE:	*The city* was offered *the site* by the Browne family.
SECOND PASSIVE:	*The site* was offered *the city* by the Browne family.

See **U4a** on avoiding the awkward passive.

NOTE: In some sentences the subject moves toward the end of the sentence but *remains* the subject of the sentence. We often use the word *there* as a sentence opener, followed by a form of *be:* "There is . . ."; "There are . . ."; "There was . . ."; and the like. The word *there* is not the subject in such a sentence:

	VERB	SUBJECT
There	is	a chance.
There	are	three possibilities.
There	was	no room.
There	has been	a change.

Sometimes, *there* with a postponed subject appears in sentences using other verbs:

In January, there *came* bitterly hard *weather.*

EXERCISE 1

For each of the following active sentences, write a complete passive version (with the original subject included after *by*).

1. The earthquake had destroyed the whole city.
2. The candidate for President usually chooses the future Vice-President.
3. An alert physician can diagnose cancer early.
4. Well-coordinated police work broke up the drug ring.
5. Muckraking newspapers exposed corruption in high places.
6. The mayor's press secretary emphatically denied the story.
7. The secretary should have notified all members of the commission.

94

8. A French team had once before climbed the face of the mountain.
9. The Russian authorities had denied his wife an exit visa.
10. An intoxicated tenant had mistaken the mail carrier for a burglar.

For each of the following passive sentences, write the original active version.

1. The building plans have been approved by the planning commission.
2. A lecture on solar energy will be given by a specialist.
3. The winner of the contest was announced by the judges.
4. Our humor magazine has been banned by the school board.
5. The fight was finally stopped by the referee.
6. These forms must be filled out by every applicant.
7. These parking spaces may not be used by visitors.
8. The election results were being examined by a three-judge panel.
9. The annual picnic was cut short by thunder and lightning.
10. Every friend and well-wisher of the band had been invited by the hospitality committee.

Each of the following simple sentences has been adapted. Determine how. Then put the right abbreviation after the number of the sentence:

Imp	imperative, or request
Pass	passive
Ques	question
Neg	negative statement
There	there is

EXAMPLE: Have you seen Laurence Olivier in *Hamlet?*
(Answer)   *Ques*

(Be prepared to *reconstruct* in class the original sentence as it was before it was adapted.)

1. There is only one Shakespeare in English literature.
2. He is generally considered the greatest English writer.
3. His plays have been translated into all major languages.
4. They are performed by theater groups all over the world.
5. His characters have been studied by many critics.
6. Which plays have you read?
7. Do you know any plays besides *Julius Caesar* and *Macbeth?*
8. In Shakespeare's time, there were many successful playwrights.
9. He was called an upstart by a rival.
10. Shakespeare's contemporaries did not worship him quite like later generations.

11. Except for Marlowe, his rivals have been almost forgotten.
12. Shakespeare's plays were written for the popular stage.
13. He did not give the printer carefully revised copies.
14. You should not merely read his plays.
15. Attend a live performance.
16. See them on the stage.
17. Be ready for a fast-moving spectacle.
18. There have been movie versions of several plays.
19. Have you seen the film version of *Hamlet?*
20. Did you find it different from the written play?

S4

WRITING COMBINED SENTENCES

Make several related ideas part of a larger combined sentence.

Often we need a sentence that spells out not only what but also why, when, or where. We need not just an opinion but also some of the necessary if's and but's. We then build the kind of sentence that combines several ideas and shows how they are related:

SEPARATE: She was not happy here. She would not go back East. She came from there.

COMBINED: She was not happy with those masterful women, *but* she would not go back East *where* she came from. (Dorothy M. Johnson)

SEPARATE: He talked. Her face grew stern. It seemed to grow more lean.

COMBINED: *As* he talked, Mama's face grew stern, *and* it seemed to grow more lean. (John Steinbeck)

When we use a unit with its own subject and verb as part of a larger combined sentence, we call it a **clause.** To combine clauses in the larger sentence, we use words like *and, but, until, although, who, which,* and *that.* These serve as connecting links, or **connectives.** There are five major kinds of connectives. Each group works in a somewhat different way. Each gives us a different way of joining one idea to another.

S4a

Coordination

Use coordinating and adverbial connectives to join independent clauses.

Some ways of linking two or more clauses leave them **independent,** or self-contained. Like freight cars coupled together to make up a train, they could be unhitched again to function as separate sentences. We call the combining of two independent clauses **coordination.** When we coordinate two things, we make them work together but leave them on an equal footing.

Writing Combined Sentences

We have three major ways of joining two or more independent clauses:

(1) We can join two clauses by using coordinating connectives. The true **coordinators,** or coordinating connectives, are *and, but, or, for, so, yet,* and *nor.* In writing, a comma usually shows the slight break between the two clauses. In the following examples, make sure you see the subject and the verb of both clauses:

> The crew had had little sleep, *and* they had worked hard all day.
> The host yawned several times, *but* nobody took the hint.
> Our bus had already left, *so* we walked the rest of the way.
> We should go right now, *or* the store will be closed.
> Gina knew the town, *for* her mother had worked there.
> The set was only three months old, *yet* the warranty had expired.

Nor makes all or part of the verb trade places with the subject:

> He did not apologize, *nor* did he help with the repairs.

NOTE: All the words used as coordinating connectives between clauses also serve other functions. *And, but,* and *or,* for instance, also link elements *within* a clause.

> He went down on hands *and* knees in the dust *and* opened his suitcase. He took out his wife's photograph *and* stood it on the box. (Graham Greene)

(2) We can join two clauses by more formal adverbial connectives. They are words like *however, therefore, nevertheless, consequently, instead, besides, furthermore, moreover, on the other hand, indeed,* and *in fact.* These generally make for a more noticeable break between the two clauses than do coordinating connectives. The most typical punctuation with these **adverbial connectives** is the semicolon:

> I think; *therefore,* I am.
> This kind of conduct had once been legal; *however,* the rules were changed to prohibit it.
> He had hoped for a promotion; *instead,* the company transferred him to a branch office.
> Our cousin always acted superior; we liked her *nevertheless.*

Adverbial connectives share with adverbs *freedom of movement within the second clause.* Note that one or more commas often set them off from the rest of the second clause:

> The doctor rushed in; *however,* her efforts were useless.
> The doctor rushed in; her efforts, *however,* were useless.
> The doctor rushed in; her efforts were useless, *however.*

(3) We can coordinate two clauses by merely putting them next to each other without a connective. The signal that says "sentence goes on" is the semicolon. We can show that two statements go together by simply changing the period between them to a semicolon:

The Lord is my shepherd; I shall not want. (Psalms)

The movie lot is open to the public; three times a day stunt actors act out Western scenes.

There was a bit of the magpie about Father; he expected everything to come in handy. (Frank O'Connor)

See **M4a** for punctuation with independent clauses.

KINDS OF CONNECTIVES	
COORDINATING CONNECTIVES:	and, but, for, or, nor, yet, so
ADVERBIAL CONNECTIVES:	however, therefore, moreover, furthermore, nevertheless, besides, indeed, consequently, instead, in fact
SUBORDINATING CONNECTIVES:	when, whenever, while, before, after, since, until, as, if, because, unless, provided, though, although, whereas; so that, no matter how, no matter what
RELATIVE PRONOUNS:	who, whom, whose; which, that
SPECIAL CONNECTIVES:	that, why, whether, how, who, what, whoever, whatever

---

EXERCISE 1

A connective shows how two clauses are related. It may show a contrast, a reason, or a logical result. In each of the following, choose the connective that shows the right relationship. Write it after the number of the sentence.

A. Choose one of the seven *coordinators:*

1. The place looked like a real gold rush town, _____ it was only part of a movie set.
2. Our stadium must have better parking, _____ the fans will go elsewhere.
3. Birds fluttered around the benches, _____ squirrels scurried up and down the trees.
4. Business was poor, _____ many of our old customers had moved.

5. The medication was not safe, _____ was it really necessary.

6. Television astronauts travel through time, _____ real astronauts still travel in a small part of space.

7. Humanity cannot multiply forever, _____ the resources of our planet are limited.

8. Our sewage pollutes the water, _____ our exhaust fumes pollute the air.

9. Travelers preferred their own cars, _____ railroad travel steadily declined.

10. We must work for peace, _____ our nuclear weaponry will destroy us all.

B. Choose an *adverbial connective:*

11. A letter may get lost in the mail; _____ , you should always keep a copy.

12. Computers handle much information very quickly; _____ , they do make mistakes.

13. The trek to the West was long and dangerous; many thousands undertook it, _____ .

14. We had ordered two pewter plates; _____ , we received a pewter pot.

15. The price of gasoline is high; the cost of insurance, _____ , is going up.

16. Many of the early settlers were very poor; _____ , many lived in sod houses.

17. On the one hand, the work was fascinating; _____ , the pay was poor.

18. She looked forward to the visit; _____ , she loved flying.

19. Our new coach had high hopes; the first season, _____ , has not been a success.

20. The art festival attracted many visitors; the town, _____ , made it an annual event.

Look at the italicized words in the following passages. After the number of the word, put the right abbreviation:

EXERCISE 2

In connective joining parts *inside* a clause
Co *coordinator* that joins two clauses
Ad *adverbial* connective that joins two clauses
No *not* used as a connective

A. I asked *for* (1) an application, *for* (2) I was interested in the job, *but* (3) the position had been filled.

B. Matthew was a subeditor *on* (4) a large London newspaper, *and* (5) Susan worked in an advertising firm. (Doris Lessing)

C. The tears filled his eyes; *something* (6) precious had passed away.

D. Then all the congregation stopped rustling *and* (7) was still, so (8) I turned myself to more fitting thoughts. (Alan Paton)

E. The vote count was not *yet* (9) complete; *however,* (10) the results were already clear.

F. The old woman in bed said *nothing* (11) at all, *and* (12) she did not look around. (Eudora Welty)

G. We wanted something *besides* (13) entertainment, *yet* (14) we were tired of gloomy plays.

H. Workers had been busy night *and* (15) day; the project, *nevertheless,* (16) dragged on.

I. Moths beat against his lamp, *but* (17) there were no mosquitoes; he hadn't seen *or* (18) heard one. (Graham Greene)

J. The place had neither water *nor* (19) vegetation; water and fuel, *consequently,* (20) had to be brought along.

EXERCISE 3

In each of the following model sentences, two or more ideas are worked into a larger sentence. Point out each connective used to link the separate parts. Then fill in a very similar sentence frame with material of your own choice. (Choose *five*. Write your imitation after the number of the passage.)

1. You can take the boy out of the country, but you can't take the country out of the boy.
   SAMPLE IMITATION: You can change your name, but you can't change your personality.

2. The fox provides for itself, but God provides for the lion.

3. The land sloped gracefully down through a field dotted with lavender weeds, and at the start of the rise their small yellow frame house sat primly between two giant hickory trees. (Flannery O'Connor)

4. The blade seemed to fly open in mid-air, and with a thump the point dug into the redwood post, and the black handle quivered. (John Steinbeck)

5. Children sweeten labors, but they make misfortunes more bitter. They increase the cares of life, but they mitigate the remembrance of death. (Sir Francis Bacon)

6. Everything important has already been said, but nobody ever listens; therefore, we always have to start all over again. (André Gide)

Use subordination to link a dependent clause to the main clause.

Connectives like *if, when,* and *because* subordinate the second clause to the main clause. We call them subordinating connectives, or **subordinators,** for short. Subordination makes the added clause **dependent** on the main clause. Like a shelf detached from its wall, or a two-wheel trailer detached from a car, the dependent clause alone would be incomplete. If someone says, "when she calls," we ask: "When she calls—then what?"

MAIN CLAUSE	DEPENDENT CLAUSE
The alarm goes off	*if the window is forced open.*
The crowd cheered	*when she waved.*
He helped her	*because she is a friend.*

Remember:

(1) Subordinators show many different relationships. They often help us find out how, when, or where something occurs, much as adverbs themselves do. We therefore call the kind of clause they introduce an **adverbial** clause. Here are familiar subordinators and the relationships they show:

TIME AND PLACE: when, whenever, while, before, after, since, until, as, as long as, where, wherever

REASON OR CONDITION: if, because, unless, provided, so that

CONTRAST: though, although, whereas, no matter how, no matter what

COMPARISON: as if, as though

Study these connectives at work in the following sentences:

Rita pulled the door tight *until it clicked.*
The crowd applauded Hernandez *as they marched across the arena.*
Manuel walked across the sand, *while Zurito rode out of the ring.*
A sudden breeze shook the trees, *so that the leaves tossed and fluttered.*
Everything had a battered, trampled-on look, *as though the place had just been visited by some large violent animal.* (George Orwell)
I will sing unto the Lord, *because He hath dealt bountifully with me.* (Psalms)

(2) When we use a subordinator, the dependent clause may trade places with the main clause. It may also interrupt the main clause.

(A clause that starts with a coordinator always *follows* the other clause.)

> *When he felt well,* my father recited poems.
> *If you need more time,* we will cancel the meeting.
> *Where they stood,* it was dark.

> My father, *when he felt well,* recited poems.

More than one dependent clause may go with the same main clause:

> *Although she usually had a pleasant smile,* my aunt could be quite firm *when it was necessary.*

(3) Some subordinators are combinations of two or more words. With *paired* connectives like *so that, as ... as, so ... as,* or *more ... than,* the first part of the combination often hooks back into the main clause:

> Band practice took *so* much time *that* everything else suffered.
> People with initiative make *more* opportunities *than* they find.

NOTE: *Before, after, since, until,* and *as* double as prepositions. They then introduce a noun, rather than a clause with its own subject and verb:

PREPOSITION	CONNECTIVE
after the rain	after the rain stopped
until next time	until we meet next time
as a replacement	as the replacement arrived

See **M4b** for the punctuation of adverbial clauses.

EXERCISE 1

After the number of each statement, write a dependent clause that would complete the sentence. Include the subordinator. Write on a separate sheet.

EXAMPLE: Birds travel south *when* _____ .
(Answer)   when *the weather turns cold*

1. Travelers need a visa *when* _____ .
2. People object to supersonic planes *because* _____ .
3. In some places, water is not safe to drink *unless* _____ .
4. Many Japanese students learn English, *whereas* _____ .
5. Many people drive without seat belts, *although* _____ .

6. *When* _____ , you should pull over to the side of the road.
7. *If* _____ , a candidate may ask for a recount.
8. Surgeons sterilize their instruments *before* _____ .
9. The colonists broke with England *because* _____ .
10. Public television is viewer-supported, *so that* _____ .
11. Chimpanzees sometimes behave *as if* _____ .
12. Some customers will not buy a product *no matter how* _____ .
13. The outfits made the players look *as though* _____ .
14. Most spectators stand *while* _____ .
15. Coaches usually keep their jobs *as long as* _____ .
16. People do not get a driver's license *until* _____ .
17. *Whenever* _____ , newspapers put the story on page one.
18. There are usually American consulates *wherever* _____ .
19. *Before* _____ , books had to be copied by hand.
20. The ball club reserved season tickets for faithful fans, *provided* _____ .

EXERCISE 2

In each of the following sentences, two ideas are brought together with the help of a subordinating connective. Choose five of these as *model sentences*. After the number of the sentence, write a very similar sentence of your own. Follow the structure of the original sentence as much as you can.

1. Fools rush in where angels fear to tread.
   SAMPLE IMITATION: Panic sets in when ratings begin to drop.

2. If you save one person from hunger, you work a miracle.

3. When you have had a fight with a skunk, you are bound to smell a little.

4. A new broom sweeps clean, whereas an old broom gets in the corners.

5. After I sang in the church choir, two hundred people changed their religion. (Fred Allen)

6. If you gave some people free beer, they would want an egg in it.

EXERCISE 3

In each of the following sentences, *more than two clauses* are joined by a variety of coordinating and subordinating connectives. Choose three of these as model sentences. For each, write a sentence of your own that is very similar in structure. Use the *same* connectives as the original.

1. *When* the short days of winter came, dusk fell *before* we had well eaten our dinners. (James Joyce)

2. *When* we met in the street, the cold air stung us, *and* we played *till* our bodies glowed. (James Joyce)

3. *When* he came to the canyon opening, he swung once in his saddle and looked back, *but* the houses were swallowed in the misty light. (John Steinbeck)

4. The forest protected us from the direct sun, *but* it shut out the air, *and* the occasional clearings seemed cooler than the shade *because* there was a little more air to breathe.

5. She was not happy with those masterful women, *but* she would not go back East *where* she came from. (Dorothy M. Johnson)

S4c

Relative and Noun Clauses

Use relative clauses and noun clauses to bring additional material into a sentence.

Two special kinds of dependent clauses are not simply joined to the main clause by a connective. Instead, they modify or replace a *part* of the main clause. Remember:

(1) Relative clauses modify a part of the main clause. They start with a **relative pronoun:** *who, whom, whose, which,* or *that.* These serve as connectives, because they link the added clause to the original statement. But they also act like pronouns: They have taken the place of something in the added clause. Look at how we combine two statements to produce a relative clause:

STATEMENT: Amy knew the girl.
ADDED SOURCE: The girl had left the message.
RESULT: Amy knew the girl *who had left the message.*

STATEMENT: The people never talked to anyone.
ADDED SOURCE: The people lived there.
RESULT: The people *that lived there* never talked to anyone.

We use *who* when the pronoun refers to persons. We use *which* when it refers to things or ideas. We use *that* for either. *Whose* also is now acceptable for both persons and things:

She remembered her mother, *who had died young.*
My parcel, *which had arrived the week before,* was still unopened.
We were kept awake by the wild geese, *whose wings we could hear overhead.*
The locks *that they had installed* were burglarproof.

See **U2b** for *who* and *whom.*

A relative clause modifies a noun (or noun substitute) in a sentence. It can therefore come into a sentence at several different points. More than one relative clause may come into the same sentence:

The people *who lived there* always waved at the trains *that passed by.*

NOTE: The relative pronoun *that* is often left out when it would have been the object in the relative clause:

The words *they had shouted* still echoed in my ears.
The only thing *I like about rich people* is their money. (Lady Astor)

(2) Noun clauses replace a part of the main clause. That, if, whether, and question words like *who (whoever), what (whatever), why, where,* and *how* can be used as **special connectives** to introduce a **noun clause.** Such a clause replaces one of the nouns in the main clause:

NOUN: The neighbor reported *the news.*
NOUN CLAUSE: The neighbor reported *that James had left.*

NOUN: Ann asked me *a question.*
NOUN CLAUSE: Ann asked me *how I knew.*

NOUN: *The informer* is not known.
NOUN CLAUSE: *Who told the police* is not known.

Noun clauses may appear in a variety of noun positions:

We asked *when the meeting would be held.*
What really happened may never be known.
By the late summer the news of *what had happened on Animal Farm* had spread across half the county. (George Orwell)

The word *that* is often left out at the beginning of a noun clause:

He told us *the well was dry.*

NOTE: Relative clauses are sometimes separated from the rest of the sentence by commas. These commas show that the relative clause is not part of the main point. It merely gives additional information. Noun clauses are *not* set off.

See **M4c** for punctuation of relative clauses and noun clauses.

Can you sort out the different kinds of dependent clauses? After the number of each sentence, write *Sub* for clause linked by a subordinator, *Rel* for relative clause, *NC* for noun clause.

EXERCISE 1

1. He can count to twenty when he takes his shoes off.
2. You never can tell by the looks of a cat how far it can jump.
3. The road was icy, so that the descent was slow.
4. Simon, whom they expected to find there, was not in the pool.

5. Fred adores Hilda, though she detests him.
6. I could never tell what passed through her mind.
7. He always uses my pen, which he has permanently borrowed.
8. She lived in the memory of her mother, whom she had loved.
9. As they watched the game, their jeers and cheers showed their emotions.
10. Our friends left the country, because their visas had expired.
11. The candidate claimed that many crimes are never reported.
12. Whoever gave you the information was very confused.
13. When we arrived with our bags, the counselor welcomed us.
14. We finally heard a voice we knew.
15. The evil that men do lives after them. *(Julius Caesar)*
16. An apologetic voice announced that the band was late.
17. We never found out whether he really knew the President.
18. The people who had brought the supplies were resting around the fire.
19. The neighbors my parents had helped showed their gratitude.
20. There was no life except for a few large birds whose wings creaked overhead through the invisible sky.

EXERCISE 2

Rewrite each of the following sentences *two ways*. First, add a relative clause that modifies the italicized noun. Then, add a noun clause that replaces the italicized noun.

EXAMPLE: Greg repeated *the rumor.*
(Answer)   Greg repeated the rumor *that he had heard.*
          Greg repeated *what people were saying.*

1. The driver denied *the charge.*
2. The interviewer asked the candidate *a question.*
3. *The person* meant well.
4. Few people know *the secret.*
5. My aunt did not remember *the person.*

EXERCISE 3

Study the following model sentences. They show some of the sentence variety that becomes possible when we use different kinds of relative clauses and noun clauses. Choose *five* of these as models. Fill in the sentence frame that follows each sentence with material of your own choice.

1. The person who jumps to conclusions often lands on unfirm ground.
   YOUR TURN: The person who _____ often _____ .

2. The evil that men do lives after them. *(Julius Caesar)*
   YOUR TURN: The _____ that _____ .

3. Energy is the power that drives every human being. (Germaine Greer)
   YOUR TURN: _____ is the _____ that _____ .

4. What is now proved was once only imagined. (William Blake)
   YOUR TURN: What is now _____ was once _____ .

5. What the heart knows today, the head will understand tomorrow.
   YOUR TURN: What the _____ , the _____ .

6. Death is like a loose shingle that falls on whoever is passing beneath.
   YOUR TURN: _____ is like a _____ that _____ .

7. It is about time that we realize that many women make better teachers than mothers, better actresses than wives, better diplomats than cooks. (Marya Mannes)
   YOUR TURN: It is about time that we realize that many _____ ,
   _____ , _____ .

8. Whoever wants to wear the judge's wig should be certain that she has the right-sized head.
   YOUR TURN: Whoever wants to _____ should be certain that
   _____ .

9. It's a poor road that doesn't have an inn at the end of it. (Irish saying)
   YOUR TURN: It's a poor _____ that _____ .

10. We shouldn't worry about why a black hen lays a white egg.
    YOUR TURN: We shouldn't worry about _____ .

Can you classify connectives, including some of the *less common ones,* according to how they behave in a sentence? After the number of each sentence, put the right abbreviation:

Co   coordinating (both connective and clause stay in place)
Adv   adverbial (connective may *shift* within its clause)
Sub   subordinating (*clause* may shift within the sentence)
Rel   relative pronoun (replaces a *noun* in relative clause)
Spec special (clause replaces a noun in *main* clause)

1. Many people talk about modern painters, *yet* few buy their works.
2. Some people will buy a painting, *provided* it treats familiar subjects.
3. They welcome art *as long as* it deals with flowers and sunsets.
4. Few ask *whether* the treatment is original.
5. Most prefer realistic art; *accordingly,* they distrust strange colors and shapes.
6. They neglect artists *that* prefer an abstract style.
7. Many modern painters avoid familiar objects *so that* they can experiment with lines and angles.
8. They do not reproduce familiar sights, *nor* do they tell a story.
9. They do not paint cheerful scenes, *no matter how* much the public may like optimistic art.

10. Many modern artists are impatient with popular taste; many, *in fact,* do not cater to a commercial public.
11. What are the forces *that* have shaped modern art?
12. Modern artists do not repeat *what* everyone else has done.
13. They express their own feelings; *otherwise* they feel stifled.
14. They reject convention *in order that* they may have creative freedom.
15. They know the rewards of conformity; *nevertheless,* they travel their own lonely road.
16. Not every artist is a true pioneer, *or* artists would not be human.
17. The true leaders create new styles, *whereas* lesser artists follow current fashions.
18. Some artists merely want to be different, *as if* originality were an end in itself.
19. True artists want to be themselves; *consequently,* each searches for a personal style.
20. True artists follow *wherever* their genius leads them.

S5

SPECIAL SENTENCE RESOURCES

Know and use special sentence resources.

Many of the building blocks we use in an English sentence do double duty. We do not always put familiar sentence parts to their simple and ordinary uses. We may use them for special purposes, thus adding to our sentence resources. Study these special uses of words. Make use of them to stretch your own sentence resources.

S5a
Using Appositives

Use appositives to work added information into a sentence.

An appositive is a second noun that modifies another noun. We simply put it there, next to the original noun:

ORIGINAL: *Czernik* fumbled the ball.
APPOSITIVE: Czernik, *the quarterback,* fumbled the ball.

ORIGINAL: *Crossley* had a pleasant face.
APPOSITIVE: Crossley, *a big man of forty or fifty,* had a pleasant face.

ORIGINAL: We are having a party on *Wednesday.*
APPOSITIVE: We are having a party on Wednesday, *my birthday.*

(1) The appositive usually causes an audible break. We usually use commas to set it off from the rest of the sentence. But sometimes appositives are essential for identification (and in effect become part of a name). The breaks and the commas then disappear:

Catherine *the Great*
William *the Conqueror*
my sister *Clare*

(2) Often, the appositive carries its own determiner and modifiers along with it :

She was reading a book about Billie Jean King, *the famous tennis player.*

Willa Cather wrote about her neighbors in Nebraska, *often recent immigrants from eastern Europe.*

(3) Appositives are not always locked into the same position. They may point forward or backward to the original noun from other positions in a sentence. Notice the different positions of the appositives in the following sentences:

A creature of custom, Marya read on from force of habit.

My eye was caught by a chik-chak, *a little brown house lizard with a large head,* high up on the wall. (W. Somerset Maugham)

Ralph turned involuntarily, *a black, humped figure against the lagoon.* (William Golding)

(4) More than one appositive may modify the same noun:

He was her old friend, *a second or third cousin, a Canadian.*

Check each sentence to see if it includes one or more appositives. After the number of the sentence, write the appositives, including any material each carries along with it. If there is no appositive, write *No* after the number of the sentence.

EXERCISE 1

EXAMPLE: Everyone noticed the car, a black limousine.
(Answer) *a black limousine*

1. Columbus, a sailor from Genoa, served Isabella, the queen of Spain, and Ferdinand, the king.
2. Columbus landed at San Salvador, a Caribbean island.
3. After their long voyage, his crew had almost given up hope when at last land was spotted.
4. Marco Polo, another Italian explorer, had reached China.
5. A third famous traveler was Magellan, who was Portuguese.
6. The Dutch, a seafaring people, sent colonists to the New World to establish New Amsterdam, modern New York City.
7. The *Santa Maria,* the flagship of Columbus, was a small ship by modern standards.
8. The Sandwich Islands, which are now called Hawaii, were reached by Polynesian seafarers centuries ago.
9. A world-famous traveler, Captain Cook had various places named after him.
10. Tales of brave adventurers who travel to far-off places are among the oldest-known stories.

Sentences

EXERCISE 2

Write down an appositive that would fit into the blank space in each sentence. Include any other additional material as appropriate. Write on a separate sheet of paper.

EXAMPLE: George Eliot, _____, wrote her books about everyday lives.
(Answer) *a famous Victorian novelist*

1. Eleanor Roosevelt, _____, supported many liberal causes.
2. Martin Luther King, _____, was assassinated.
3. People everywhere have heard of Hollywood, _____.
4. Groucho Marx, _____, was famous for his cigar, moustache, and biting wit.
5. Marian Anderson, _____, was born in 1908.
6. Louis Armstrong, _____, was loved by audiences at home and around the world.
7. Sigmund Freud, _____, changed the modern view of the human mind.
8. Sitting Bull, _____, defeated General Custer at the battle of Little Bighorn.
9. Helen Keller, _____, is known to every American.
10. Mark Twain, _____, said that everyone has a darker side, like the moon.
11. Not many people were on the *Mayflower*, _____.
12. A trip to Yosemite, _____, makes an ideal vacation for the average city dweller.
13. Almost every student had read *Julius Caesar*, _____.
14. Helium, _____, was needed to float the airships.
15. Amelia Earhart, _____, disappeared over the Pacific during a flight around the world.
16. Penicillin, _____, was discovered accidentally.
17. There are many ancient sculptures of the Sphinx, _____.
18. Thousands signed up for the marathon, _____.
19. The story of Robinson Crusoe, _____, has been retold and imitated many times.
20. Visitors to Egypt usually see the pyramids, _____.

EXERCISE 3

Write three simple sentences, using basic patterns with two or more nouns. Then write *two different expanded versions* of each. Make varied use of appositives.

EXAMPLE: John stopped the car.
(Answers) 1. John, *the shy rookie police officer from Buffalo,* stopped the car, *a black limousine with drawn curtains.*
2. John, *the family's trusted chauffeur,* stopped the car, *a beautiful antique with polished brass trim.*

Use participles to help build up detail in a sentence.

Verbals are verb forms that we can lift out of their usual place in a sentence. We can make them serve new or unusual purposes. Participles are verbals that we can use to replace ordinary modifiers. There are two kinds of participles. Both usually appear as part of a complete verb after an auxiliary. The *–ing* form (**present participle**) appears after *be: is crying, was waiting, are returning.* The *–en* form (**past participle**) appears after both *be* and *have: was taken, had fallen, were caught, had been helped.*

We can lift either kind of participle out of its usual place after the auxiliary. We then use it to modify a noun, or sometimes a whole sentence. Such a participle often carries with it the objects or modifiers that accompanied it when it was part of a verb. Together with such material it makes up a verbal phrase:

STATEMENT:	Mary and I looked at the leaves.
ADDED SOURCE:	The leaves were *falling.*
RESULT:	Mary and I looked at the *falling* leaves.

STATEMENT:	George went up into the gallery.
ADDED SOURCE:	He was *whistling under his breath.*
RESULT:	George went up into the gallery, *whistling under his breath.*

STATEMENT:	I was left alone with my ship.
ADDED SOURCE:	It had been *anchored in the bay.*
RESULT:	I was left alone with my ship, *anchored in the bay.*

More complicated forms of the participle carry auxiliaries along to show perfect tense or progressive:

PERFECT:	*Having discovered* radiation, Marie Curie pioneered X-ray technology.
PROGRESSIVE:	The authors *being studied* were listed on the board.

Participles alone or as part of a **verbal phrase** may appear in many different positions in a sentence. They thus make possible great variety in sentence style:

(1) The verbal may come immediately before the noun it modifies:

He was driven to his bed by a *raging* fever.
The driver showed us her *badly cut* hands.

(2) One or more verbals may appear at the end of a sentence:

The groom at the head looked back, *jerking the leading rope.*
They turned to each other, *laughing excitedly, talking, not listening.*
By midmorning the thin sun appeared, *rapidly burning away mist and cloud, warming the air and the earth.* (William Faulkner)

(3) One or more verbals may introduce a sentence:

Following the curve of the road, Boris's carriage came straight upon the main terrace and the house. (Isak Dinesen)
Sold at auction, bought for a song, the painting had then disappeared.

(4) A verbal may interrupt a sentence at various points:

Trees, *forced by the damp heat,* found too little soil for full growth, fell early, and decayed. (William Golding)

NOTE: The verbals in these examples are hybrids between adjectives and verbs. They share some features of each. Some verbals cross over completely to become true adjectives. They can follow intensifiers like *very:* a very *interesting* story, a very *charming* host.

See **M5a** for information on how to punctuate verbals.

EXERCISE 1

How is each italicized word used in the following sentences? After the number of the word, put the right abbreviation:

V used as a complete verb
P used as part of a complete verb
Vb verbal used as a modifier

A. We *looked* (1) at the bales of merchandise *stacked* (2) along the walls.

B. *Hurrying* (3) down in the staircase, she *saw* (4) the friends who were *waiting* (5) in the lobby.

C. We *hurried* (6) away, *breathing* (7) hard, *looking* (8) forward to rest.

D. One night an officer had *come* (9) to the house and had *stood* (10) in the hallway, *talking* (11) in a low voice to my parents.

E. The *cheering* (12) crowd in the *packed* (13) auditorium *encouraged* (14) the speaker.

F. The lights were now *coming* (15) on in the *surrounding* (16) houses.

G. The *injured* (17) player was *sitting* (18) up in bed, *grumbling* (19) and *picking* (20) at his food.

H. The *broken* (21) windowpane let in the wind *whistling* (22) around the corners.

I. The woman *elected* (23) to the position *remained* (24) in the room, *thanking* (25) her well-wishers.

J. The neighbors *bothered* (26) by the noise had *complained* (27) to us.

K. *Roving* (28) across the landscape, her eyes *took* (29) note of the damage *brought* (30) by the storm.

Rewrite each of the following pairs as a *single sentence*. Making use of participles, work the material from the second sentence into the first as a verbal or verbal phrase.

EXERCISE 2

EXAMPLE: The child went into the house.
It was crying bitterly.
(Answer) *Crying bitterly, the child went into the house.*

1. Many people read Charles Dickens.
They are living in all parts of the world.

2. His books have sold millions of copies.
They have been translated everywhere.

3. His stories usually have a strong moral.
They were written in Victorian England.

4. Dickens reforms his old skinflint Scrooge.
He turns him into a kindly old gentleman.

5. In *David Copperfield,* David does well.
He is leading a good life.

6. Steerforth perishes in a shipwreck.
He had strayed from the right path.

7. Dickens deals in extremes.
He puts kindness next to brutal evil.

8. The heroine of *Hard Times* is Rachel.
She bears misfortune with saintly patience.

9. *A Tale of Two Cities* describes bloodthirsty revolutionaries.
They are driven by the spirit of revenge.

10. Dickens still cherished kindness.
He knew the dark side of human nature.

Look at where and how participles bring added details into the following *model sentences.* Choose five of these as models for sentences of your own. Fill in the blank spaces in each sentence frame with material of your own choice. As much as you can, use verbals in ways similar to those of the original author. (Write on a separate sheet.)

EXERCISE 3

1. MODEL SENTENCE: Gazing up into the darkness, I saw myself as a creature driven by vanity. (James Joyce)
SAMPLE IMITATION: Looking at my wet clothes, I saw myself as a person saved by sheer luck.
YOUR TURN: —————, I saw myself as a person ————— .

2. Progress is anything turning on and off by itself. (Arthur Miller)

    YOUR TURN: _____ is anything _____.

3. Most of the children, feeling too late the smart of sunburn, had put their clothes on. (William Golding)

    YOUR TURN: Most of the students, _____, had put their (dressy) (worst) (_____) clothes on.

4. She would stand gazing at a hillside brilliant with ferns and bracken, jewelled with running water. (Doris Lessing)

    YOUR TURN: I would stand looking at _____, _____.

5. Jules was driving a truck filled with flowers around the unflowery streets of Detroit. (Joyce Carol Oates)

    YOUR TURN: _____ was driving _____.

6. The horses plunged down the bank, slipping and sliding in the wet earth, crashing through the willows and into the water.

    YOUR TURN: The crowd rushed out of the _____, _____, _____.

7. I imagined myself saving people from sinking ships, cutting away masts in a hurricane, or swimming through a surf with a line.

    YOUR TURN: I imagined myself _____, _____, or _____.

8. One evening, rambling through the house while Daddy was at choir rehearsal, looking through drawers and opening doors, we noticed a light under the door to the attic. (Lucille Clifton)

    YOUR TURN: (One day) (One night), _____, _____, we _____.

S5c
Verbal Nouns and Infinitives

Experiment with the different uses of verbal nouns and infinitives.

Verbals often take the place of nouns. One such verbal is the familiar *–ing* form: *asking, leaving, writing.* When this form replaces a noun, we call it a **verbal noun.** Another verbal is the *to* form: *to ask, to leave, to write.* We call this form the **infinitive.**

In each of the following examples, a verbal noun or an infinitive takes the place of a noun:

SUBJECT	VERB	OBJECT	OBJECT	PREP. PHRASE
Smoking	endangers	health.		
The guests	hated	*to leave.*		
Linda	had asked	me	*to write.*	
Phil	surprised	us		*by studying.*

Like other verbals, verbal nouns and infinitives often carry along their own objects or modifiers:

Watering the plants frequently is essential.
To live day by day is not *to live at all.*

The auxiliary *have* or *be* becomes part of a verbal that shows perfect tense or passive:

PERFECT: having failed, having won, having yielded, to have tried, to have loved, to have grown

PASSIVE: being wanted, being admired, being rejected, to be taught, to be accused, to be acquitted

The basic function of verbal nouns is to take the place of a noun. Infinitives have many additional uses:

(1) The infinitive appears in many extended verb phrases. Those start with *have to, ought to, am going to,* and *used to.* Very similar is the use of the infinitive after verbs like *happen, seem, need, dare, hesitate:*

His friends *had to leave.*
She *ought to pay* her own bills.
My cousin *was going to join* the army.
Big steamboats *used to travel* up the river.

She *seems to have taken* it to heart.
Her aides *hesitated to wake* her *up.*
This proposal *needs to be studied.*

VERBALS ARE EVERYWHERE
Point out all the verbals in these examples.

SURVEYING PAYS BIG

HOW TO QUIT SMOKING

LEARNING THE VIOLIN AT AGE 4

STAINED GLASS

How To Repair

Knowing the LAW

LEARN MEAT CUTTING

(2) The infinitive often takes the place of a second object. This happens after verbs like *ask, cause, want, permit, allow, enable, order,* like:

SUBJECT	VERB	OBJECT	INFINITIVE
Henry	asked	us	*to leave.*
The device	enabled	him	*to see again.*
The director	allowed	spectators	*to sit on the stage.*

The *unmarked* infinitive, with the *to* left out, appears in the same position after verbs like *see, hear, let, make, watch:*

No one	saw	her	*leave the house.*
The ending	made	everyone	*cry.*

(3) The infinitive is very versatile as a modifier. We use it to modify nouns, verbs, adjectives, or a sentence as a whole:

NOUN: a place *to live*
the point *to remember*

VERB: paused *to think*
resigned *to return to private practice*

ADJECTIVE: glad *to be back*
eager *to meet him*

SENTENCE: *To start the motor,* turn the key.
To be safe, I locked the door.

(4) The infinitive is often used in sentences that start with It:

It is impossible *to please everybody.*
It annoys me *to see such shoddy work.*

NOTE: Infinitives always preserve some of their verb features. Many verbal nouns, however, cross over completely to become true nouns. They then no longer carry objects with them. They are no longer modified by adverbs telling us how. Instead, they acquire such noun features as determiners or a plural –s. They are modified by adjectives:

The shipping of snakes is illegal.
The older dwellings were substandard.

For each sentence, write down every verbal noun and infinitive. Do not include any other part of a verbal phrase. (Do not include verb forms that are part of a complete verb.)

EXERCISE 1

EXAMPLE: We wanted to start packing.
(Answer) *to start, packing*

1. She started to show me all the plants that needed pruning.
2. To enjoy heat, you have to be really cold first.
3. Running for office is becoming too expensive.
4. Complaining and blaming others will not solve our problems.
5. After thinking it over, they consented to help us.
6. Modern methods of irrigation have made the desert bloom.
7. Being captured by the rebels was a harrowing experience.
8. I want to congratulate you on having passed the test.
9. The only thing to do was to retrace our steps.
10. An applauding crowd saw the fliers perform precision stunts.
11. He remembered hearing the order to disperse.
12. Having two teachers for parents helped Marie Curie become interested in science.
13. The new trail to the ridge has made hiking easier.
14. The company used to spray pesticides without getting clearance from the government.
15. Living in the woods had accustomed her to noticing rare plants.
16. The new coach seems to have worked a miracle.
17. Studying in the crowded library is getting difficult.
18. To be the youngest in a large family is not always easy.
19. Being elected to office was a great thrill for me.
20. The instructors were teaching beginners to paddle and to float.

Fill in the blank space in each sentence frame *three* different ways. Each time try to use a longer verbal phrase than the first one or two. Use both verbal nouns and infinitives.

EXERCISE 2

EXAMPLE: _____ is discouraging.
(Answers) *To lose three games in a row is discouraging.*
Trying to write a book report about a book you haven't really read is discouraging.
Waiting for a phone call all day and finally getting one—from Wayne—is discouraging.

1. _____ is discouraging.
2. _____ makes me happy.
3. _____ tests a person's faith in people.
4. _____ is useless.
5. My favorite daydream is _____.

By substituting for other sentence parts, verbal nouns and infinitives help us ring the changes on the ordinary English sentence. Study the variety in sentence structure made possible by the use of verbals in the following *model sentences*. Then fill in the blank spaces in the sentence frames with material of your own choice. Use verbals in the same places as the original author. (Choose *five* of these as models.)

1. MODEL SENTENCE: Cunning is the art of concealing our own defects and discovering other people's weaknesses.

   SAMPLE IMITATION: Politics is the art of making one's own record look good and making the other person's look bad.

   YOUR TURN: _____ is the art of _____ and _____ .

2. Economy is the art of making the most of life. (G. B. Shaw)

   YOUR TURN: _____ is the art of _____ .

3. To create a little flower is a labor of the ages. (William Blake)

   YOUR TURN: To _____ is _____ .

4. It is a miserable state of mind to have few things to desire and many things to fear. (Sir Francis Bacon)

   YOUR TURN: It is a _____ to _____ and _____ .

5. The roaring of lions, the howling of wolves, the raging of the stormy sea, and the destructive sword are portions of eternity, too great for the eye of man. (William Blake)

   YOUR TURN: The _____ of _____ , the _____ of _____ , and the _____ of _____ are all part of _____ .

6. Scientists have to be interested in things, not in persons. (Marie Curie)

   YOUR TURN: _____ have to be _____ , not _____ .

7. There is no greater desert or wilderness than to be without true friends. (Sir Francis Bacon)

   YOUR TURN: There is no _____ than _____ .

S5d

Absolute Constructions

Experiment with verbals that carry along their own subjects.

A verbal worked into a sentence from an added source may carry along *its own subject*. The resulting verbal phrase is less closely tied to the rest of the sentence than most other modifiers. It is called an **absolute** construction:

STATEMENT: Planes were waiting in line.

ADDED SOURCE: *Their lights* were blinking.

RESULT: Planes were waiting in line, *their lights blinking.*

STATEMENT:	The customer repeated his complaint.
ADDED SOURCE:	*His voice* was rising.
RESULT:	*His voice rising,* the customer repeated his complaint.

STATEMENT:	He walked on.
ADDED SOURCE:	*His arms* were scarcely swinging at all.
ADDED SOURCE:	*His body* was bent forward a little from the waist.
RESULT:	He walked on, *his arms scarcely swinging at all, his body bent forward a little from the waist.*

Absolute constructions sometimes appear in a shortened form. When the verb in the source statement is a form of *be,* the verbal is often *omitted:*

STATEMENT:	The director stood at the window.
ADDED SOURCE:	Her back *was* to the light.
RESULT:	The director stood at the window, *her back to the light.*

Absolute constructions may appear at various points in a sentence. They thus add further to our resources for *sentence variety:*

(1) The most typical position for the absolute construction is at the end:

He turned uneasily aside, *the retreating steps of the horses echoing in his ears.* (D. H. Lawrence)

(2) One or more absolute constructions may appear at the beginning:

My head bursting with stories and schemes, I stumbled in next door. (Frank O'Connor)

Eyes shining, mouths open, we watched the magician perform.

(3) One or more absolute constructions may interrupt a sentence:

Kayerts, *his round eyes suffused with tears, his fat cheeks quivering,* rubbed his bald head and declared, "This is a splendid book." (Joseph Conrad)

EXERCISE 1

Identify and write down any absolute construction in each of the following sentences. Write *No* if there is no such construction in a sentence.

EXAMPLE: Her eyes twinkling, she told us the story.
(Answer) *her eyes twinkling*

1. The boat sped along, its sails stretched taut by the gale.
2. Visibly shaken, the witness asked for time to think.

3. The teams left the court, the winners smiling, the losers fighting tears.
4. His patience wearing thin, he repeated the instructions.
5. Having nothing else to do, we watched the passing cars.
6. We found an abandoned cabin, its windows broken, the door gone.
7. Spring being our favorite season, we spent much time outdoors.
8. We found old arrowheads, left there centuries earlier.
9. The picture showed the new champion, her hands raised in victory.
10. My father, his face flushed, was trying to remain calm.
11. We huddled on the ledge, our stomachs empty, our clothes wet.
12. The audience sat spellbound, listening to the choir.
13. Having grown up there, Willa Cather wrote about Nebraska.
14. The price having been raised, we decided not to buy the set.
15. She was unable to register, the deadline having passed.
16. Its engines belching smoke, the big plane rose into the sky.
17. Encouraged by the polls, the incumbent decided to run again.
18. The picture showed my grandfather, a fur cap on his head, mittens on his hands.
19. The tanker ran aground close to the shore, its oil fouling the beaches.
20. Humming a happy tune, she was leaving for a well-earned vacation.

EXERCISE 2

Study the way absolute constructions are worked into the following *model sentences*. Read each sentence out loud. After the number of each sentence, write similar absolute constructions that could fill the blank space or spaces in each sentence frame. (Choose five. Write on a separate sheet.)

EXAMPLE: She reached the church unseen, and, *the door being only latched,* she entered.

SENTENCE FRAME: I reached the school, and _____, I entered.

(Answer)   *the bell having rung*

1. Another car, traveling slowly by, hesitated opposite, *its red dome light blinking.* (Hortense Calisher)

   SENTENCE FRAME: A big truck, coming the other way, slowed down, _____.

2. The band came marching down the street, *the trumpets blaring, the banners flying.*

   SENTENCE FRAME: Our band marched onto the field, _____, _____.

3. *The bank being closed,* we could do nothing but wait.

   SENTENCE FRAME: _____, we had no choice but to go home.

4. She went out of the room with the tray, *her face impassive and unchanged.* (D. H. Lawrence)

   SENTENCE FRAME: The boy came to our table with his tray, _____.

Special Sentence Resources

5. Davies' white, indoor face was hard with his intensity, *his young-looking eyes shining, his big mouth drawn down to be firm.* (Walter V. T. Clark)
   SENTENCE FRAME: The runners were coming down the stretch, _____ ,
   _____ .

6. *The choice made,* she could surrender her will to the strange, the exhilarating, the gigantic event. (Graham Greene)
   SENTENCE FRAME: _____ , we could lean back and enjoy the show.

Study the use of special sentence resources in the following sentences. After the number of each sentence, put the right abbreviation:

App	appositive
Part	participle
VN	verbal noun
Inf	infinitive
Abs	absolute construction.

(Do not include any forms used as parts of a complete verb.)

1. Willa Cather is an author admired by many readers.
2. Reading her stories takes us back to an earlier America.
3. At the age of eight, she moved to Nebraska, pioneer territory.
4. She spent much time outdoors, riding the prairie.
5. She learned to kill rattlesnakes.
6. She later wrote about her neighbors, recent immigrants from various countries in Europe.
7. One of her characters helps a Czech girl learn English.
8. These newcomers just barely survived, each member of a family helping in the fields.
9. Some of them had been city people, their skills now useless.
10. Willa Cather attended the University of Nebraska, working at the same time as a newspaper correspondent.
11. Her education finished, she moved to Pittsburgh.
12. She later became managing editor of a magazine in New York.
13. By 1912 she had saved enough money to quit her job.
14. She had always wanted to be a full-time writer.
15. She did not believe in drawing up lists of rules or goals.
16. Writers should learn by living close to people and places they love.
17. Many readers remember *My Ántonia,* her best-known book.
18. Willa Cather loved writing about young people.
19. Her best stories take place in her favorite region, the prairie country of south-central Nebraska.
20. Readers who like real people and places enjoy reading many of Willa Cather's books.

FOR FURTHER STUDY

OUR CHANGING LANGUAGE

Through the centuries, as the English language evolved into its present form, there were many changes in the way words work together in a sentence. Often these changes were slow and sometimes incomplete. Sometimes older ways of doing things survive in special situations. Study the following examples of earlier English.

ACTIVITY 1

For each of the following inflected forms, dictionaries list a *double,* serving the same function in a sentence. On a separate sheet, write down this alternative form after the number of the word. (Be prepared to report in class what you can find out about differences in the history, meaning, or use of the two forms in each pair.)

1. brothers
2. dived
3. sank
4. cows
5. waked
6. shone
7. pennies
8. hung
9. proven
10. thrived

ACTIVITY 2

The following lines are taken from the Psalms in the King James Version of the Bible (1611). They illustrate possibilities of word order in *Early Modern English.* Rewrite each line to make it follow normal or typical modern word order. Modernize archaic forms.

1. In the Lord put I my trust.
2. In the net which they hid is their own foot taken.
3. With our tongue will we prevail.
4. In thy presence is fullness of joy.
5. By them is thy servant warned.
6. Good and upright is the Lord.
7. Him shall he teach in the way that he shall choose.
8. Eyes have they, but they see not.
9. One thing have I desired of the Lord.
10. Thou knowest my downsitting and mine uprising, thou understandest my thought afar off.

ACTIVITY 3

The use of *do* to fill in for a missing auxiliary is relatively new. In Shakespeare's plays and in the King James Version of the Bible, the *do* is missing from many questions where it would be required today. Using *do,* modernize each of the following examples:

1. What ring gave you, my Lord?
2. How goes the night, boy?
3. Live you? Or are you aught
   That man may question?
4. What means this shouting? I do fear the people
   choose Caesar for their king.
5. Wherefore then serveth the law?
6. Why, what care I? If thou canst nod, speak too.

What are some of the other features of Early Modern English that are illustrated in Shakespeare's plays? Look at the features that make each of the following passages different from current American English. Pay special attention to pronoun and verb forms. Rewrite each passage to fit modern standards of usage.

ACTIVITY 4

1. Macbeth: Thou art the best o' th' cut-throats;
   Yet he's good that did the like for Fleance:
   If thou didst it, thou art the nonpareil.

   Murderer: Most royal Sir . . . Fleance is scap'd.

   Macbeth: Then comes my fit again: I had else been perfect.

   —*Macbeth,* Act III, Sc. 4

2. Marcellus: Peace, break thee off. Look where it comes again.

   Bernardo: In the same figure like the king that's dead.

   Marcellus: Thou art a scholar; speak to it, Horatio.

   Bernardo: Looks 'a not like the king? Mark it, Horatio.

   Horatio: Most like. It harrows me with fear and wonder.

   Bernardo: It would be spoke to.

   Marcellus: Question it, Horatio.

   —*Hamlet,* Act I, Sc. 1

3. Are ye fantastical, or that indeed
   Which outwardly ye show? My noble partner
   You greet with present grace and great prediction
   Of noble having and of royal hope,
   That he seems rapt withal: to me you speak not.

   —*Macbeth,* Act I, Sc. 3

4. How far that little candle throws his beams! . . .
   A substitute shines brightly as a king
   Until a king be by.

   —*Merchant of Venice,* Act V, Sc. 1

5. I am not sick, if Brutus have in hand
   Any exploit worthy the name of honor. . . .

   Here will I stand till Caesar pass along
   And as a suitor will I give him this. . . .

   —*Julius Caesar,* Act II, Sc. 1, 3

6. Hamlet: Did you not speak to it?
   Horatio: My lord, I did;
               But answer made it none. Yet once methought
               It lifted up its head and did address
               Itself to motion like as it would speak:
               But even then the morning cock crew loud,
               And at the sound it shrunk in haste away.

   —*Hamlet,* Act I, Sc. 2

7. Brutus, I do observe you now of late;
   I have not from your eyes that gentleness
   And show of love as I was wont to have.

   —*Julius Caesar,* Act I, Sc. 1, 2

ACTIVITY 5

In the following passages from the Prologue to Chaucer's *Canterbury Tales* (1386–1400), almost all the words used survive in Modern English. (Some have changed in spelling, form, or meaning. Others have become archaic, like *lief, wend,* or *wight.*) Make sure first that you recognize all the words. Then ask: For what special features of Chaucer's English does the modern reader have to be prepared? Rewrite each passage in modern English.

1. Thanne longen folk to goon on pilgrimages.

2. And specially from every shires ende
   Of Engelond to Canterbury they wende
   The holy blisful martyr for to seeke
   That hem hath holpen whan that they were seke.

3. Me thinketh it accordant to resoun
   To telle you al the condicioun
   Of eech of hem, so as it seemed me.

4. He nevere yit no vilainye ne saide
   In al his life unto no manere wight.

5. Short was his gowne, with sleeves longe and wide,
   Wel coude he sitte on hors, and faire ride.

6. Of smale houndes hadde she that she fedde
   With rosted flesh, or milk and wastelbreed.

7. And in his harping, whan he hadde songe,
   His yën twinkled in his heed aright
   As doon the sterres in the frosty night.

8. For him was levere have at his beddes heed
   Twenty bookes, clad in blak or reed,
   Of Aristotle and his philosophye,
   Than robes riche.

Chapter 3

Composition
Writing for a Purpose

Chapter Preview 3

> **IN THIS CHAPTER:**
>
> - How to follow up a point in a well-developed paragraph.
>
> - How to organize a short paper.
>
> - How to make effective use of transitions, titles, introductions, and conclusions.
>
> - How to find and organize authentic detail in descriptive and autobiographical writing.
>
> - How to define terms and generalize effectively in convincing argument.
>
> - How to write papers about literature and prepare a full-length research paper.

Learn to write a composition that effectively serves its purpose.

Good writing serves a purpose. Suppose a reader asks you about something you have written: "Why are you telling me this? Why did you write this down?" Your writing shows a sense of purpose when your answer could be something like the following:

- "Here is something important or fascinating. People just pass it by. I want them to notice."
- "This is something that made me angry, or happy, or sad. I want someone to care."
- "Here is something that has often been misrepresented. Someone has to set the record straight."
- "Here is an obligation that many people turn their backs on. But I won't let them."
- "Here is some useful information that is not generally known. I want to share it."

The following activities give you a chance to think about what makes people write and why they write what they do.

PREVIEW EXERCISE 1

Study the writing samples on the facing page. About each sample, ask: What kind of writing is this? What seems to be its major purpose? How is it different from some of the other samples?

1. History—the "gringo" version anyway—portrays Pancho Villa as a notorious bandit and a cold-blooded terrorist.

Perhaps here lies the misconception of the man whose real name was Doroteo Arango, known in all of Mexico as General Francisco Villa, The Centurion of the North, and to the world simply as Pancho Villa.

During his administration, President of Mexico Gustavo Diaz Ordaz ordered the official placement of Francisco (Pancho) Villa's name among the heroes of the Mexican Revolution and of Mexican history. This wiped out the label of bandido, something all of Mexico had demanded for a long time. His name, therefore, has been engraved in gold in the National Congress of Mexico at the National palace.

During the unfriendly relations between the United States and Japan, the Japanese, faced with the possibility of war between the two countries, proposed alliance with Mexico against the United States. When General Villa was confronted with the proposal by Japanese officials he answered, "I do not know what resentment Japan feels over the conduct of the United States. I know my own country only. But if the American people go to war with another country, and I am in a high position in the government, the people of Mexico will refuse the United States nothing they may ask in the way of materials of war. The government in Washington is our good friend and American citizens favor our Revolutionary cause."

2. The Kryptonite Lock is unusual in that it incorporates a padlock without leaving the bolt of the padlock accessible to bolt cutters. Whereas a chain can be readily cut, the Kryptonite Lock does not lend itself to being cut with a bolt cutter or saw. Weighing about five pounds, it can be stored on the bicycle on a rack, in baskets, . . .

3. The story of a boy who lowered himself by a rope into someone else's backyard to "liberate" a small refrigerator and thus impress his girl friend appears in the yearbook of a prominent New York City high school. This form of rip-off is frequently directed against organizations that represent the system itself. A favorite steal is to enter a subway station and have a friend distract the token seller while a group of people pass in through the exit door free.

4. The field at the end of the street is gone. Small rabbits scrambled there, and sometimes we saw ducks and pheasants. Children skated on the pond, and in summer they built a tree house and played bold and splendid games. Now houses stand there, with smooth lawns and polished yews, and we are saddened and wonder where the pheasants went. . . .

5. The controversial polygraph machine, more commonly known as the lie detector, works on the simple principle of blood pressure, heartbeat and touch. With modern homes equipped with all sorts of mechanical gadgets, I think every home should also have a polygraph machine. . . .

Composition

Each of the following sample passages illustrates a familiar task often taken on by a writer. Choose one or more of these for a practice run. Write a similar passage of your own that serves the same purpose as the original. (Discuss in class how and how well each sample passage serves its purpose.)

1. We often write to explain something technical or difficult:

Light is radiation that we can see. Heat is radiation that we can feel. Radio and television waves and X-rays are electromagnetic waves of radiation we can neither see nor feel, but with whose usefulness we are well acquainted. Now we are hearing more and more about another kind of radiation as a result of continuing scientific and engineering achievements. This is nuclear radiation. Nuclear radiation consists of a stream of fast-flying particles or waves originating in and coming from the nucleus, or heart, of an atom. It is a form of energy we have come to call atomic, or nuclear energy.—U.S. Atomic Energy Commission, *Atomic Energy in Use*

2. We often write to describe a task or a job:

The checker, or researcher, for a newsmagazine makes sure that the news stories are factually accurate. The work consists of assembling research materials early in the week and then checking the writer's story at the end of the week. The checker gets no credit if the story is right but gets the blame if it is wrong. It doesn't matter if the story is slanted, if it misinterprets or misses the point of the week's news. That is the responsibility of the editors. What matters—and what seems to attract most of the hostile letters to the editors—is whether a championship poodle stands thirty-six or forty inches high, whether the eyes of Prince Juan Carlos of Spain are blue or brown, whether the population of some city in Kansas is 15,000 or 18,000.

3. We often write to describe a person:

Cecil was a small, brown-skinned man of perpetual motion and tremendous spirit. I admired the way he kept the paper going from the cramped and disordered space he called his office. He wrote the editorials, sports, news and society columns, hustled ads and kept his numerous creditors at bay with fast talk and sincere promises. And he was an honest man. His confidence in himself and his paper was more than the average person would have dared dream. He didn't have much money to offer his few employees, but the titles he handed them were of Herculean stature. If you wanted to be a correspondent instead of a reporter that was your prerogative. If you wanted to be a *foreign* correspondent, then mail back a story on your trip abroad. You could be anything from copyboy up to assistant managing editor—as long as you could afford the title and live off the pay.—Gordon Parks, *A Choice of Weapons*

4. We often write to call attention to something that is neglected or overlooked. This is what an artist did in the following letter she wrote to the editor of a newspaper:

> A few years ago, noting that post offices were sterile, dehumanized buildings, I was hired at minimum pay to paint murals for several [post offices] in Marin and Sonoma. The Novato Post Office had no windows in the back work area, but it now has some color, warmth, and art. The U.S. government can pay artists to help relieve the barren walls of these facilities where thousands of workers spend a great portion of their lives. Art is an important job. A world without artists would be a grey, sexless, claustrophobic space.

Use a well-developed paragraph to do justice to one major point at a time.

C1

WRITING A PARAGRAPH

In a sentence, we can state an opinion. We can let the reader know what we think. In a well-developed paragraph, we can explain and support our point of view. We can show why and how we reached the conclusion we did. We can show how something came about. We can supply the details needed to inform and convince the reader.

Pull together related material to support a single point.

C1a

The Topic Sentence

A well-written paragraph has a point. Often the very first sentence sums up the key idea of the paragraph. When the central point or idea of a paragraph is clearly stated, we call it the **topic sentence.**

The writer who has a point is the one who has learned how to make related material add up. Suppose you have decided to write about our disappearing native wildlife. Here is an inventory of material you could use:

- You may remember reading about the passenger pigeon. It once lived in this country in huge flocks of tens of thousands of birds. But it was hunted till it finally became extinct.
- You may recall seeing prairie dogs live where the prairie is now covered by subdivisions and parking lots.
- You may recall stories your grandfather told about shooting mountain lions in hills where such animals are no longer seen.
- You may remember magazine articles about the dangers to fish from industrial wastes in our streams and lakes.
- You may ask what small animals you still encounter: lizards, frogs, squirrels, an occasional snake.

These memories and observations all help tell the same story. The point of that story could be summed up in a single sentence. This sentence could become the key idea of a paragraph:

TOPIC SENTENCE: Unless we preserve a livable environment for our wildlife, our remaining animal species will soon be extinct.

In the following paragraph, a well-known writer has *pulled together* material about our vanishing animal species. He has put the key idea at the beginning of the paragraph as a topic sentence:

> *We need viable habitats for the species that our expansion threatens.* Some, like the passenger pigeon, are beyond our belated friendship. But there are the waterfowl whose nesting and feeding places we have drained or flooded, and the fish whose spawning grounds we have drowned or poisoned with agricultural sprays, and the robins whose decimation Rachel Carson made use of to shock a whole people. There are also the frogs, toads, newts, lizards, snakes, skunks, prairie dogs, coyotes, alligators, mountain lions, and nocturnal varmints that are apparently "useless" or "harmful," yet by their enduring in the biotic pyramid give us both the pleasure of their company and the assurance of their biological support.—Wallace Stegner, "What Ever Happened to the Great Outdoors?" *Saturday Review*

Many paragraphs follow this basic pattern of a key idea first, followed by the material that backs up or supports the key idea. Here are some common variations:

1. A *question or other introductory* sentence may come before the topic sentence.

2. A short topic sentence may be followed by one or more sentences *restating and explaining* the key idea.

3. A *clincher sentence* at the end may remind us of the key idea and help drive it home.

The following model paragraph shows all three possibilities:

(Question)   How many of the planets in our solar system were suitable for the development of life? *Among its sister*
(Topic Sentence) *planets, only Earth was right for supporting life.* Only
(Explanation)   Earth had the right size, the right kind of materials, and the right kind of temperature needed to make possible
(Support)   life as we know it. Venus, in many ways a twin to our own planet, is closer to the sun and has grown too hot. Mars is farther from the sun and smaller. The moon is very much smaller than Earth and therefore lacks the
(Clincher   gravity to hold life-sustaining gases. Only Earth is just
Sentence)   right, tilted just right, and spinning at just the right speed, to make possible the survival of the life forms we know.

Each of the following sample paragraphs starts with a topic sentence. Read each paragraph carefully. For each paragraph, do the following:

A. Restate the point made in the topic sentence.

B. Summarize the material that has been pulled together in the paragraph.

C. Show briefly that the material in the paragraph is *relevant* —that it is related to the topic sentence.

1. *Romantic love was not a major theme either in serious American literature on its highest level or in familiar American folklore.* After the first few chapters, *Moby Dick* has no female characters. There were not many women, either, in the *great cycles of myth* that dealt with the wilderness, the river, the cattle ranges, and the mining camps. All consisted of stories about men, working or wandering, hunting, fighting, enduring hardships, getting rich, or running away from civilization, but seldom or never passionately in love. *Huck Finn* was of course too young for love, but all the familiar heroes were boys at heart. *Old Leatherstocking* died a bachelor.—Malcolm Cowley, "American Myths, Old and New," *Saturday Review*

2. *Our children are given years of cultural nonparticipation in which they are permitted to live in a world of their own.* They are allowed to say what they like, when they like, how they like, to ignore many of the conventions of their adults. Those who try to stem the tide are derided as "old fogies," "old fashioned," "hide bound" and flee in confusion before these magic words of exorcism. This state of discipline is due to very real causes in American society. In an immigrant country, the children are able to make a much better adjustment than have their parents. The rapid rate of invention and change in the material side of life has also made each generation of children relatively more proficient than their parents. So the last generation use the telephone more easily than their parents. The present generation are more at home in automobiles than are their fathers and mothers. When the grandparent generation has lived through the introduction of the telegraph, telephone, wireless, radio and telephotography, automobiles and airplanes, it is not surprising that control should slip through their amazed fingers into the more readily adaptable hands of children.—Margaret Mead, *Growing Up in New Guinea*

3. *Puerto Ricans in New York are often caught in a maze of non-identities.* In the racially polarized city they are not white, though they may be referred to as "Puerto Rican white," and they are not black, at least not black enough. To some degree they are not even Latin American in the eyes of other Latins, who feel that Puerto Rico was

lost to the sisterhood of Latin-American nations when the United States took possession in 1898. In the eyes of other New Yorkers, however, Puerto Ricans are not American. Finally, New York Puerto Ricans—"Newyoricans" as they are sometimes called—who return to the Island to visit families, to study, or to live permanently must confront barriers which their language and cultural adaptation to New York has placed between them and their fellow compatriotas. —Samuel Betances, "The Latin Diaspora," *New York*

4. *In the war of sun and dryness against living things, life has its secrets of survival.* Life, no matter on what level, must be moist or it will disappear. I find most interesting the conspiracy of life in the desert to circumvent the death rays of the all-conquering sun. The beaten earth appears defeated and dead, but it only appears so. A vast and inventive organization of living matter survives by seeming to have lost. The gray and dusty sage wears oily armor to protect its inward small moistness. Some plants engorge themselves with water in the rare rainfall and store it for future use. Animal life wears a hard, dry skin or an outer skeleton to defy the desiccation. And every living thing has developed techniques for finding or creating shade. Small reptiles and rodents burrow or slide below the surface or cling to the shaded side of an outcropping. Those animals which must drink moisture get it at second hand—a rabbit from a leaf, a coyote from the blood of a rabbit.—John Steinbeck, *Travels with Charley*

EXERCISE 2

In each of the following paragraphs, related material has been brought together. About each paragraph, ask: "What is the point?" Then write a statement that could serve as the missing topic sentence for the paragraph. Write on a separate sheet of paper. (Compare your sentence with those written by your classmates.)

1. TOPIC SENTENCE: _____.
At a university in the West, administrators were charged with misusing two hundred thousand dollars of federal scholarship money to bolster their sagging football team. At the same time, in a California sailing race, the captain of the winning boat was disqualified shortly after receiving the gold cup. It was discovered that during the race he had ducked his sailboat into a cove and turned on its power motor. In a recent soap box derby, one-third of the twelve-year-old contestants were expelled for cheating.

2. TOPIC SENTENCE: _____.
A Dane and a Dutch traveler meeting in Rome will almost automatically find themselves speaking to each other in English. The

pilots of a Russian plane approaching Cairo will use English to ask for landing instructions. Malayan lecturers use English when addressing their Malayan students in Kuala Lumpur. To people in Africa, Asia, and South America, English is an important foreign language to master, not merely because it is the language of Britain or the United States, but because it provides ready access to world scholarship and world trade. It is understood more widely than any other language.

3. TOPIC SENTENCE: ——————————————————————— .
The other day I happened to look at the dog-food shelf in the local supermarket. It turns out that dog food now comes in half a dozen different flavors, including chicken, cheese, and vegetable. It comes in many different shapes and consistencies. Some cans contain little patties like hamburgers. Some make their own gravy, thus saving the dog's owner all that messy work over the hot stove. Dog food is now enriched with vitamins and extra nutrients, with your choice of bone meal and wheat germ and cod liver oil. These valuable ingredients keep your dog at top form, with a keen eye and a glossy coat. One brand of dog food contains chlorophyll to give your dog a sweeter breath.

4. TOPIC SENTENCE: ——————————————————————— .
Huck Finn's father tries to cheat him and then imprisons him. In order to get away from this drunken "mudcat," Huck must set it up so that everyone will think he has been murdered. This is a boy who, although surrounded by Aunt Sallies who want to "sivilize" him, runs off to be himself. He has to protect himself against fraudulent adults like the Duke and the Dauphin. Every time he gets off that raft he is yelped at by dogs and menaced by people.

5. TOPIC SENTENCE: ——————————————————————— .
Our churches are all private voluntary associations, and have been ever since the Revolution and its aftermath broke the connection between church and state. Our political parties are private voluntary associations. . . . Our labor unions, fraternal orders, clubs, business and professional societies—the bar associations and medical associations and chambers of commerce, the associations of scholars and of librarians, of artists and musicians, of alumni and of veterans —all are voluntary. Most of our colleges and universities are the products of such voluntary associations. Most of our reforms, too, have been carried through by just such organizations . . . almost all of them were carried to completion by associations of individuals. Thus the abolition of slavery, temperance, women's rights, prisons and penal reforms—these and a hundred others belong in this category.—Henry Steele Commager, *Freedom, Loyalty, Dissent*

6. TOPIC SENTENCE: _____.

When I was a child, I went with my grandfather when he hunted wild turkey, or quail, driving through the roadless woods under great water oaks shining as though newly washed by rain. Once on reaching a river, I jumped from the wagon. Running into the deep shade, I sat down on a large alligator, taking it for a half-buried log. I was also the child who walked out on a plank placed as a pier to reach the center of the dark pool, then knelt, plunged in her hands to scoop up a drink, and saw that fatal snake, a water moccasin, dart between her closing hands.—Florida Scott Maxwell, *The Measure of My Days*

7. TOPIC SENTENCE: _____.

In the classroom we all learned past participles, but in the streets and in our homes the Blacks learned to drop *s*'s from plurals and suffixes from past-tense verbs. We were alert to the gap separating the written word from the colloquial. We learned to slide out of one language and into another without being conscious of the effort. At school, in a given situation, we might respond with "That's not unusual." But in the street, meeting the same situation, we easily said, "It be's like that sometimes."—Maya Angelou, *I Know Why the Caged Bird Sings*

8. TOPIC SENTENCE: _____.

In a recent year, the average American child aged 2 through 11 was exposed to more than 20,000 commercials. Schoolchildren spent more time before the tube than they did in classrooms. Advertisers were spending more than $400 million a year to reach TV's young audience. About 20 percent of that was spent by the cereal makers who are, for the most part, promoting presugared products. Other heavily promoted products for children include candy, gum, cookies, crackers, fruit drinks, puddings, cakes, chocolate mixes, and toys.

EXERCISE 3

Study each of the following model paragraphs. Can you see that each writer has arrived at a topic sentence by adding up the observations listed later in the paragraph? For each topic, ask: "How would it have looked to me?" What material can *you* collect from your own experience or reading? Use the material in a paragraph of your own. Start with a topic sentence that adds up what *you* have observed.

1. TOPIC: Manners of young people today

Young people today have very little of what used to be called "manners." Young people today smoke in the presence of others, seldom

bothering to ask for permission. We seldom see a young person opening a door or surrendering a seat on a bus to an older person. Parents
of teen-agers can seldom get them to listen, let alone to give a polite
answer. Students talking to their teachers use language that would
have gotten them expelled from school not too many years ago. They
use four-letter words freely to show their disapproval of things as
they are.

2. TOPIC: The nonexpert versus the expert

*In a complicated situation, the nonexpert is helpless because noth-
ing clearly stands out.* A library, a museum, or a machine shop is
merely a maze for the newcomer. The expert sees everything in its
place and knows exactly where to turn. To the nonexpert, a cater-
pillar is just skin and squash. A biologist can dissect it and show us
the exquisite viscera. In a battle or at a fire, the nonexpert is surrounded by noise and confusion. The veteran takes in the situation
and analyzes immediately what is happening and what needs to
be done.

Select *five* of the following topics. What statement could you
make about each that you could support well in a paragraph? Write
the statement down as a possible topic sentence.

EXERCISE 4

1. Cheerleaders
2. Environmentalists
3. Foreign students
4. Television humor
5. Voter apathy
6. Dropouts
7. Modern weddings
8. Music lovers
9. Physical education
10. Science teaching

(Your teacher may ask you to write a paragraph to follow up
one or more of your possible topic sentences.)

Follow up a topic sentence with well-chosen examples.

C1b
Giving Examples

The most useful all-purpose paragraph first gives the topic sentence. It then follows up the topic sentence with several convincing
examples. It moves from the key idea to the "for example" or "for instance." How many different examples can you identify in the model
paragraph on the following page? How would you restate the key
idea they all support?

Composition

(Topic   *The Zuñi religion places great reliance upon imitative magic.*
Sentence) In the priests' retreats for rain, they roll round stones across
(Examples) the floor to produce thunder. Water is sprinkled to cause the
rain. A bowl of water is placed upon the altar that the springs
may be full. Suds are beaten up from a native plant that clouds
may pile in the heavens. Tobacco smoke is blown out that the
gods "may not withhold their misty breath." In the Masked-
God Dances, mortals clothe themselves with the "flesh" of the
supernaturals, that is, their paint and their masks, and by this
means the gods are constrained to grant their blessings.—
Ruth Benedict, *Patterns of Culture*

Remember:

(1) Make it a habit to follow up a general point with specific examples. With an effective writer, going on to the specifics has become second nature. In the following pairs, a general idea begins to come to life as the writer goes on to one or more striking examples:

GENERAL: Gang members find it hard to accept the traditional recreation offered by community agencies.

SPECIFIC: They find it more exciting to roam the streets than to play Ping-Pong at a youth center.

GENERAL: Without their creative intelligence, humans would still be at their most primitive level of development.

SPECIFIC: Humans would be no more than a species of primates living on seeds, fruit, roots, and uncooked flesh. They would be wandering naked through the woods like chimpanzees.

GENERAL: Typically, even a great artist's motives are partly disinterested and partly commercial.

SPECIFIC: As Mahalia Jackson once said, "I've been singing now for almost forty years, and most of the time I've been singing for my supper as well as for the Lord."

(2) If you use one main example, develop it in detail. Often good writers will present half a dozen or more examples to support a point. But sometimes they will rely on one especially striking or detailed example to convince the reader:

(Topic   *Often intelligence tests measure information and call it*
Sentence) *intelligence.* A child who is neither informed about inter-
(Extended national currency nor well-traveled, for example, may not
Example) be able to select the word that fits with "dollar, peso, mark,
lira" from these possibilities: "change, franc, foreign, purchase, bank." According to the test makers, the correct
answer (franc) is an indication of intelligence. And the child

who associates "dollar" with either "bank" or "purchase"
is less intelligent. . . .—Arlene Silberman, "The Tests That
Cheat Our Children," *McCall's*

*(3) Experiment with making your examples lead up to the key
point.*   Sometimes, we state the examples first and then draw a conclusion at the end. Such an **inductive** paragraph takes the reader
along to the desired conclusion. It makes the reader think along with
the writer. Here is an examples-first paragraph, with the topic sentence at the end:

(Examples)   Fran, Chris, and Sandy were students in the same class.
Fran was good at mathematics and science, but she had
trouble putting ideas down on paper. Chris wrote well but
had trouble in math. Sandy did very well in class discussions of literature, but she had trouble outlining things or
(Topic   planning a research paper. *Students differ in their aptitude
Sentence)   for different kinds of school work.*

*(4) Use the directional signals that help readers see where they
are going.*   The following **transitional expressions** are common
in paragraphs that give examples:

- for example, for instance, to illustrate;
- moreover, similarly, furthermore;
- also, besides, thus.

Each of the following is the beginning of a paragraph that gives
examples. Each starts with a topic sentence and then gives the first
example. For each, write the next sentence in the paragraph. Use
it to give *a second example* that would continue the paragraph. (Write
on a separate sheet.)

EXERCISE 1

1.   *In different areas of the world, quite different animals have been used
as major means of transportation and as beasts of burden.* In Europe
and North America, the horse was for a long time the major means of
moving people and loads. _____
_____ .

2.   *Human beings have long exploited the power of the wind as a source
of self-renewing natural energy.* Wind powered the windmills that people used for centuries to grind grain. _____
_____ .

3.   *Many kinds of folk music that were at first strictly regional have spread
around the world.* The polka started as a Czech folk dance; it is now
known everywhere. _____
_____ .

4. *Immigrants have often remained bilingual.* They have continued to speak their native language with their families and their friends. Spanish-speaking Americans still often use Spanish as the language of the family and the neighborhood. _____

    _____ .

5. *Though the U.S. is a leading industrial nation, it is also a leading producer of basic foodstuffs.* Large areas of the Midwest and the West grow the wheat that helps feed people around the world. _____

    _____ .

6. *Our language still mirrors the roles people played when business and politics were largely reserved for men.* Politicians and journalists were used to talking about "businessmen" rather than "people in business."

    _____ .

7. *Nations that were at one time our enemies have since become allies or friends.* The War of Independence was fought against Britain, which later was America's staunchest ally in two world wars. _____

    _____ .

8. *Many of the ancient tribal names are now forgotten, but some will be long remembered.* The Sioux fought some of their last battles under leaders like Sitting Bull. _____

    _____ .

9. *In our mechanized and automated society, home building still requires much old-fashioned manual work.* Carpenters still put up the frame of the house, hammering in one nail at a time. _____

    _____ .

10. *Some of the sports growing in popularity are not mainly spectator sports but sports for participation.* Thousands of people have taken up running—reading about it, making it part of their routine, participating in events. _____

    _____ .

EXERCISE 2

Sometimes a writer will concentrate on one single example that seems especially typical. In each of the following paragraphs, the writer concentrates on a single incident or a single case that illustrates a more general point. The single incident discussed seemed to the writer a part of a larger pattern. What is that more general pattern in each case? What was the writer's point?

1. On a crowded bus, a mother sat by quietly while her five-year-old in various ways disturbed the other passengers—squeezing through the crowded aisle, stepping on people's toes, playing with their luggage. Finally, an older man, speaking carefully in a heavy foreign

accent, asked the mother to do something about the child's behavior. The mother told the man to mind his own business, whereupon several other passengers came to his defense. At the end of the somewhat heated exchange, the mother triumphantly concluded: "At least *I* am an American." At this point, the driver, who had been listening quietly so far, turned around and said: "That's a pity."

2. Some years ago, a girl crashed in a light plane in Alaska. She finally made it back to civilization after severe hardships. These were not "untold hardships," however, for newspapers and magazines all over the country immediately picked up her story. Editors and publishers' agents tried to sign her up for an "authentic first-hand account" of her "real-life adventure." When the book finally appeared, it had been thoroughly worked over by ghost writers and editors on the basis of numerous tape recordings the girl had made. When the girl appeared on a national television program, she herself seemed no longer sure of the details of what happened to her. Everything had been edited and "adapted" too many times.

Choose one or more of the following for a practice paragraph:

1. Write a paragraph in which you start with a topic sentence. Follow it up with *three or more examples*. Choose one of the following topics:

- the American love of fads or novelty;
- nostalgia for earlier periods or old styles;
- a changing neighborhood;
- the way older people are treated in our society;
- a current trend in commercials.

2. Write a paragraph about a *single case* or a single incident that to you seems part of a larger pattern. Start with a topic sentence that sums up the general pattern or the lesson to be learned from the incident. For instance, you may discuss a recent case of vandalism, censorship, individual achievement, red tape, or the like.

3. Write an *examples-first* paragraph. Show several examples of a trend or pattern that many people may not have noticed. Conclude with a topic sentence that sums up what you have shown.

Write a paragraph that traces a process or a series of events.

Not every paragraph starts with a topic sentence and goes on to examples. Often a paragraph serves a special purpose and follows a pattern of its own. The most useful kind of special-purpose paragraph traces a process or a series of events. This is the kind of paragraph we use when we want to show how something works or how it came about. Remember:

(1) We usually trace a process as it happens in time. In other words, we follow **chronological** order. Show how the following model paragraph follows chronological order through several major stages. Like many process paragraphs, this example immediately starts at the beginning and takes us along without summarizing the process in a topic sentence. If the author had wanted to start with a topic sentence, she could have added a first sentence like the following: "In A.D. 79, Mount Vesuvius erupted and buried the Roman town of Pompeii under ash and lava."

> The eruption of Mount Vesuvius in A.D. 79 was completely unexpected because no previous volcanic activity had ever been recorded. It started about 10 o'clock in the morning with an explosion that shattered the basalt "plug" of the volcano. Then the molten, churning core hurtled upward through the throat of Vesuvius and down upon the land in deadly torrents of gas and cinders. For some 30 hours, the volcano thundered, boomed and shook, spewing clouds that buried Pompeii under 12 feet of ash. The onset of rainstorms turned the ash into vast mudflows which engulfed some towns to a depth of 60 feet. This volcanic mud eventually hardened into a concretelike substance, locking everything into stony stillness.—Blanche R. Brown, "Out of the Ashes: Glowing Treasures of Pompeii," *The New York Times Magazine.*

(2) A process paragraph often shows us the causes behind the events. Like the following example, it moves **from cause to effect:**

> Whenever a significant body of black people move North, they do not escape Jim Crow. They merely encounter another, not-less-deadly variety. They do not move to Chicago, they move to the South Side. They do not move to New York, they move to Harlem. The pressure within the ghetto causes the ghetto walls to expand, and this expansion is always violent. White people hold the line as long as they can, and in as many ways as they can, from verbal intimidation to physical violence. But inevitably the border which has divided the ghetto from the rest of the world falls back.... The landlords make a tidy profit by raising the rent, chopping up the rooms, and all but dispensing with the upkeep; and what has once been a neighborhood turns into a "turf."—James Baldwin, *Nobody Knows My Name*

(3) We often use directional signals to help the reader move forward in the right direction. The **transitional** expressions in a process paragraph may include links like *first, second, now, then, next,*

later, meanwhile, finally, and others. Look at the use of such links in the following sample paragraph:

> You do not have to travel to find the sea, for the traces of its ancient stands are everywhere about. Though you may be a thousand miles inland, you can easily find reminders that will reconstruct for the eye and ear of the mind the processions of its ghostly waves and the roar of its surf, far back in time. So, on a mountain top in Pennsylvania, I have sat on rocks of whitened limestone, fashioned of the shells of billions upon billions of minute sea creatures. *Once* they had lived and died in an arm of the ocean that overlay this place, and their limy remains had settled to the bottom. *Then,* after eons of time, they had become compacted into rock and the sea had receded. *After yet* more eons the rock had been uplifted by bucklings of the earth's crust and *now* it formed the backbone of a long mountain range.—Rachel Carson, *The Sea Around Us*

Study the following examples of paragraphs that trace a process. Answer the following questions about each:

EXERCISE 1

A. Is there a topic sentence? Restate the *key idea* of the paragraph in your own words.

B. What are the *major stages* of the process, or the major changes the process brings about? Summarize the stages or changes briefly in your own words.

C. What links or expressions help us see events in their place *in time?* Point out several expressions that help us place things in time.

1. Beavers often create forest ponds that for a time become the home of insects, reptiles, fish, otter, herons, and other animals. Beavers can transform a pine forest into an entirely new habitat by damming a stream. The pond will flourish for a short time—perhaps a few decades. The pond's creatures adapt to seasonal changes. In the winter, the pace slows beneath the frozen surface. Frogs and turtles bury themselves in the mud. But soon after the ice thaws, the natural rhythms accelerate. Dragonflies breed, fish spawn, and soon all the energies begin to prepare for another winter. But when the food supply is exhausted, the beavers will leave. Without their hard work and constant maintenance, the dam falls into disrepair and the water runs out. The area reverts to a swamp, then a marsh, a meadow, and finally a forest once again in this never-ending natural cycle.

2. From 1880 to 1929, the most prominent characteristic of the American Jewish community was its phenomenal growth. Close to three million Jews arrived here during this fifty-year period, swelling the American Jewish population from 250,000 to 4,500,000, and trans-

forming it from a small, mainly native-born, upper-middle-class group to a lower-class community primarily of foreign origin. . . . The new Jewish immigrants clustered in distinct neighborhoods in major cities, and the Jewish population of the United States became, for the first time, a predominantly urban, industrial, and labor-oriented community. The streets where the immigrants lived, slum districts close to the downtown area, became all but exclusively Jewish in population. The merchandise in the stores, the Yiddish heard on the streets, and the festive atmosphere on the Jewish sabbath and holidays reflected the character of the inhabitants. Every large city had such an area between 1880 and 1920, but the largest of them was the Lower East Side of New York City. In 1915, it sheltered in less than two square miles an estimated 350,000 Jews.—Sarah Schmidt, "From Ghetto to University," *American Educator*

3.   In the "flush times" of steamboating, a race between two notoriously fleet steamers was an event of vast importance. The date was set for it several weeks in advance, and from that time forward the whole Mississippi valley was in a state of consuming excitement. Politics and the weather were dropped, and people talked only of the coming race. As the time approached, the two steamers "stripped" and got ready. Every encumbrance that added weight, or exposed a resisting surface to wind or water, was removed, if the boat could possibly do without it. The "spars," and sometimes even their supporting derricks, were sent ashore, and no means left to set the boat afloat in case she got aground. When the *Eclipse* and the *A. L. Shotwell* ran their great race many years ago, it was said that pains were taken to scrape the gilding off the fanciful device which hung between the *Eclipse's* chimneys. For that one trip the captain left off his kid gloves and had his head shaved.—Mark Twain, *Life on the Mississippi*

EXERCISE 2

Write a process paragraph that traces in detail how something *begins*. Start your practice paragraph with one of the following lead sentences:

1. "The runners (swimmers) are lining up for the race. . . ."
2. "The inning is about to begin. . . ."
3. "The teams are getting ready for the kickoff. . . ."
4. "The cook is getting things ready on the kitchen counter. . . ."
5. "The members of the orchestra are taking their seats. . . ."
6. "The bricklayer is getting ready to lay the first brick. . . ."
7. "The potter is getting ready a lump of clay. . . ."
8. "The marching band is lining up, ready to march onto the field. . . ."
9. "The announcer is announcing the first event of the rodeo. . . ."
10. "A patrol car starts out after a speeding motorist. . . ."

Choose one or more of the following for a practice paragraph:

1. Some things seem hard to do at first, but we learn to do them by habit, almost without thinking. It is only when we try to teach them to someone else that we realize they are complicated for the beginner. Write a paragraph that shows a beginner how to parallel-park a car, change a tire, dance a new or traditional dance, or the like.

2. Trace a major change that has happened to a place or to a group of people that you know well or that you have recently read about. Show the major stages or the major results.

3. Trace a natural process that is often repeated. For instance, trace the growth of a plant, or the annual cycle of a tree, or the life cycle of an insect.

Write a paragraph that traces a comparison or contrast.

A special kind of paragraph looks at two things to show in what ways they are alike and in what ways they are different. We often compare things when we have to choose among them. But we also often explain something new by comparing it with something the reader knows.

Often a comparison shows first the similarities and then the differences between two things. As a result, both things being compared then become clearer in our minds:

(Topic Sentence) (Similarities)	*To many people, jogging seems merely a fashionable revival of old-fashioned running, but the two are not really the same.* It is true that both get people out into the open air. In both the stamina of the person, the development of the leg muscles, and the right kind of breathing are important.
(Differences)	But jogging avoids the high peaks of strain and the dangerous overexertion that went with the all-out effort of much old-style running. Where old-style running was built around the triumphs and frustrations of competition, jogging is designed to produce calm and peace of mind.

Here are some special uses of comparison and contrast:

(1) We often use comparison to help something strange or different become more familiar. In the following paragraph, a long-distance swimmer uses a comparison to explain the appeal of her sport:

Marathon swimming will never be as popular as other sports for obvious reasons. Spectators can only watch the finish, not the whole process. It's like the Tour de France—the most popular cycling race in the country, and you can't see anything. But there is empathy among the spectators when the contestants stop for the night. You see their huge legs, muscular bodies dust-covered and sweaty, their power exhausted. There is the same empathy at the end of a marathon swim. People have spent the whole day waiting. From a mile out, I can hear clapping and screaming. The people realize I swam from a place they couldn't see on the clearest day. They know I may faint when I arrive. They share with me the most extreme moment of all—after the pain, the cold, the hours, the distance, after the fatigue and the loneliness.—Diana Nyad, "Mind over Water," *Esquire*

(2) We often use contrast to highlight the results of change. Look at the **then-and-now** contrast in the following model paragraph:

(Then)   *Yesterday,* African history shut out the native peoples and all their traditional cultures. The history of the continent began with the travels of the Spanish and Portuguese explorers. The heroes of the school books were white travelers and empire builders: Liv-

(Now)   ingstone, Stanley, Cecil Rhodes. *Today,* African history begins with the arts of prehistoric peoples. It traces the rise of the great African civilizations. It treats the European colonization as an alien intrusion, often disastrous for long-established cultures and ways of life.

(3) We sometimes trace similarities in very close detail as an aid to instruction or explanation. We call such a close tracing of similarities an **analogy.** Can you show all the details or expressions that help carry through the basic analogy in the following paragraph?

A true map of the Arab world would show it as an archipelago: a scattering of fertile islands through a void of sand and sea. These islands stretch from Morocco through the Algerian coastal plain and the thin periphery of Libya to the slim island valley of the Nile, then on to the oases of Syria and Arabia and, finally, the larger island of Iraq. Bahrain and Aden and the oases of Suva and Dakhla are as minute as Pacific atolls. On this map, the desert, like the sea, both divides and joins. On it the small fertile areas outweigh in importance the spaces of *sahara,* the Arab word for desert.—Desmond Stewart, *The Arab World*

NOTE: In a paragraph that compares or contrasts, a topic sentence may appear at the beginning. But often the writer will develop the comparison step by step and then *sum it up* at the end. Transitional expressions in a paragraph that stresses similarities may be *similarly, in the same way, also, furthermore,* and the like. When we stress differences, the links may be *by contrast, on the contrary, on the other hand, but,* and *however.*

WHAT IS THE POINT?

What point was made by putting the pictures in each pair next to each other? Choose one of these pairs. Write a paragraph that makes roughly the same point as the two pictures in the pair.

Composition

EXERCISE 1

Study the following sample paragraphs. Describe fully what use each makes of comparison or contrast.

1. Turn to the opening pages of some great novelist. . . . It is not merely that we are in the presence of a different person—Defoe, Jane Austen, or Thomas Hardy—but that we are living in a different world. Here, in *Robinson Crusoe,* we are trudging a plain high road. One thing happens after another; the fact and the order of the fact is enough. But if the open air and adventure mean everything to Defoe, they mean nothing to Jane Austen. Hers is the drawing-room, and people talking, and by the many mirrors of their talk revealing their characters. And if, when we have accustomed ourselves to the drawing-room and its reflections, we turn to Hardy, we are once more spun around. The moors are round us and the stars are above our heads. The other side of the mind is now exposed—the dark side that comes uppermost in solitude, not the light side that shows in company.—Virginia Woolf, "How Should One Read a Book?"

2. Today we know that within the tiny atom there are even tinier particles of matter. *Matter* is something that occupies space and has weight. Atoms, although very tiny, do have size and weight, as do the smaller particles within them. Look at an ordinary steel pin. It is made largely of iron, one of the elements found in nature. The iron atoms are so small that, if you think of a single row of them extending side by side along the length of the pin, there would be about 250 million of them in a pin one inch long. If you take into account the thickness of the pin and include the pinhead as well, you can see that there must be billions of iron atoms in the pin. You know how light the pin feels. It is not surprising then that an individual iron atom weights only $\frac{93}{1,000,000,000,000,000,000,000,000}$ of a gram. There are 28½ grams in an ounce. —Irene Jaworski and Alexander Joseph, *Atomic Energy: The Story of Nuclear Science*

3. The word *mass* simply means "the amount of matter in an object." Mass is constant, no matter where in the universe the object is located. *Weight,* on the other hand, is not constant. A ball that weighs six pounds here on earth will weigh only one pound on the moon. But its mass will not be changed by the trip to the moon. Weight changes because it measures the pull of gravity on the object. Mass does not change because it is a property of the object itself.—Sara B. Chase, *Moving to Win*

EXERCISE 2

Choose one or more of the following for a practice paragraph:

1. Show some *similarities* between two things that people do not usually think of together. For instance, write about

- football (or baseball) and ballet;
- modern skyscrapers and the pyramids, temples, or monuments of earlier civilizations;
- a school and a hospital;
- a person and a tree;
- cooking and music.

2. Show a *contrast* between two things that are in some other ways similar or related. Concentrate on showing one major difference. For instance, write about

- hunting and fishing;
- an airport and a bus station;
- a downtown shopping area and a suburban shopping center;
- football and soccer;
- a rodeo and a circus.

3. Write a paragraph to help your reader tell apart the members of one of the following pairs:

- a horse and a donkey;
- an eagle and a vulture;
- a chicken and a duck;
- a trumpet and a trombone;
- a banjo and a guitar.

Write a paragraph that defends a conclusion or argues a point.

C1e

Arguing a Point

When we present an argument, we make a special effort to defend our opinion or to convince a reader. We want the reader to see that we have thought about the matter seriously. Study the kinds of paragraphs that are often part of a serious argument:

(1) We often support a point with detailed facts and figures. We often use statistics to document the extent of a need or of a problem:

(Need)   *Schools must recognize the special needs and problems of bilingual children.* Five million American children have a non-

(Statistics)   English mother tongue. The Center for Applied Linguistics estimates that 20 million Americans do not speak English natively. Of the 3 million children whom the U.S. Office of Education estimates to still be using their native language, 1.75 million are of Spanish background, not counting 317,000 Cuban refugees. Another 144,000 are Indians enrolled in various schools. A million speak some thirty other languages like French, German, Polish, Italian, and Czech.

(2) We often explain something that might seem strange or doubtful. We try to satisfy the reader who wants to know why:

(Question)

(Reasons)

A good outfielder can toss the ball with a velocity of 100 feet per second toward, say, second base. But a fast runner can only go 30 feet per second. *Why doesn't the ball's velocity make it impossible for the runner to be safe on second?* There are two reasons: *First,* the ball coming in from the outfield has a lot farther to travel—maybe as much as 250 feet. The runner travels 90 feet from base to base, a total of 180 feet from home plate to second. *Also,* the runner can change velocity by increasing speed, but the ball cannot. Once the ball has left the fielder's hand, it can't speed up. *In fact,* air (friction) slows it down. The ball can't change its horizontal direction, either. And a very slight error in horizontal direction at the fielder's position becomes a much bigger error by the time the ball reaches second base.—Sara B. Chase, *Moving to Win*

(3) We often have to weigh conflicting evidence in order to reach a balanced conclusion. In a serious argument, we cannot simply ignore the evidence on the other side. Here are some transitional expressions we are likely to use when we weigh the **pro and con:** *on the one hand . . . on the other hand; it is true that . . . granted that; but, however, nevertheless,* and the like. Look at the transitional expressions in the following sample paragraph:

(Pro and Con)

Since only 7 percent of the earth's surface is under cultivation, it would appear that the task of expanding the world's food-producing areas would be simple. *But* no two qualified people will agree on the validity of this. Approximately half of the earth's land surface is covered with ice, tundra, mountains, or desert. It is estimated, *however,* that there are still remaining 1.3 billion acres that might be brought under cultivation. A billion of these are in the tropics. None of them would be simple to cultivate. Humanity has already plowed the easy acres. *Nevertheless,* if the human race is to survive, these unproductive wastelands must be brought into service.

(Conclusion)

Can it be done? The most brilliant of farming experts think it can; but not cheaply.

EXERCISE 1

Study the following paragraphs and answer the questions:

A. What is the point the writer is trying to defend or to support? Restate it in your own words.

B. How does the writer support the key point? Describe the means or method used as fully as you can.

C. What use does the writer make of transitional expressions?

1. The land is dying. Over vast reaches of every continent, the rainfall, soil fertility, and vegetation necessary to most forms of life are diminishing or disappearing. The result is that the world's deserts are spreading. New deserts are appearing and growing. It is estimated that fertile, productive land is being denuded and destroyed at a rate of 14 million acres a year. Already about 43 percent of the planet's land surface is desert or semidesert. Some scientists say fully one-third of today's arable land will be lost during the next twenty-five years, while the world's need for food will nearly double.

2. The curfews that some communities impose upon teenagers seem to me to do more harm than good. On the one hand, they do keep troublemakers off the streets. They do reduce the number of acts of vandalism reported by the local newspaper. They give everyone a chance to rediscover the attractions of a quiet evening spent in the family home. On the other hand, such curfews have bad psychological effects. Like the rain, they fall upon the just and the unjust. They make teenagers rebellious and contribute to a poor attitude toward adult authority.

3. Language is indispensable to human thinking, but this does not mean that mental ability is the same thing as having a large vocabulary. A limited vocabulary, it is true, restricts the range of our thinking. And this may lead us, mistakenly, to think of people as being unintelligent merely because certain words are unfamiliar to them. The children in an underprivileged neighborhood, for example, did very poorly in an intelligence test which contained questions such as this: "A hand is to an arm as a foot is to a _____." Only a few children filled the blank with "leg" and most of them scored low in intelligence. But later it was learned that the expression "is to" was unfamiliar to these children. They would have said "goes with," that is, a hand "goes with" an arm, and when "goes with" was substituted for "is to" in the same test, they did very well, and scored high in "intelligence."—Lionel Ruby, *The Art of Making Sense*

Collect some detailed statistics about a *current trend* of interest to people in your community or in your school. For instance, you may investigate growth or decline in population, in jobs, in enrollment, or the like. Present your conclusion in a paragraph and back it up with facts and figures.

EXERCISE 2

Write a paragraph in which you recommend a change in school policy. Or you may choose to defend a school policy or custom that has recently been questioned. Use a paragraph frame like the one on the following page:

EXERCISE 3

Composition

I feel that high schools should _____.
In the first place, _____.
Also, _____.
Besides, _____.
Therefore, most people would agree that _____.

EXERCISE 4

What issue has recently made you feel that there is something to be said on both sides? Write a paragraph in which you weigh the *pro and con* on an issue like the following:

- calls for "cracking down" on juvenile offenders;
- stricter requirements for driver's licenses;
- greater freedom of choice for students;
- restricted access to overcrowded recreation areas, such as campgrounds;
- laws to reduce violence in television programs or movies;
- bilingual instruction;
- use of test scores to screen students for admission to college.

UNIT REVIEW EXERCISE

Study the following paragraphs and answer the questions:

A. What kind of paragraph is it? What is its major purpose, or what is the basic procedure?

B. Is the main idea summed up in a topic sentence? Restate or sum up the key idea in your own words.

C. What material has been used? How is it organized?

D. Are there any transitional expressions used? Where and how?

1. Pompeii is marvelously intact. Exterior walls still carry shop signs and shopowners' accounts, political endorsements for municipal elections, children's schoolwork and thousands of graffiti, which say many of the same things that our graffiti do today. They proclaim the writer, his friends, his enemies, his sports heroes, his loves and would-be loves. One Pompeiian, looking at all those scratched messages, scribbled his own comment: "It is a wonder, oh wall, that you have not yet crumbled under the weight of so much written nonsense."—Blanche R. Brown, "Out of the Ashes: Glowing Treasures of Pompeii," *The New York Times Magazine*

2. The American supermarket often serves people from many different income groups. Rich people like and drive big cars, but so do people with much less money. American millionaires eat cornflakes and hot dogs. Rich and poor watch the same television shows and root for the same baseball teams. As a result, foreign visitors to our country are often surprised to see how much is alike in the lifestyles of Americans from different social classes.

3.   Visitors to Wyoming may be surprised to know that the pronghorn antelope was once in danger of extinction. When Lewis and Clark made their famous trip through the Western wilderness in 1805, they saw antelope on the plains wherever they looked. According to some estimates, there may have been 35 million. Then came the mountain men, the meat hunters, and the settlers. With no laws to protect the wildlife, within a hundred years the antelope diminished to perhaps 20,000, and was still dwindling. Then, just in time, laws were passed to protect them. Gradually their numbers built up again. They are hunted again, but this time under strict laws that protect the herds. Today the pronghorn live in much of the range they originally occupied. Travelers can often see little bands of them from the road.

4.   Schools should do everything they can to help handicapped children participate fully in ordinary instruction and ordinary school activities. It is true that many handicapped children need expert help and profit from highly specialized training. They also need to be protected from thoughtless gawking or ridicule by other students. But what many of the handicapped need most is a feeling of belonging, of being accepted. They need to see how other children play and learn. They need to be challenged to do many things that others normally do.

5.   At one time, much productive and manufacturing work was done in the home. People wove their own cloth and often made most of the clothes for members of the family. Baking, brewing, canning, and preserving were part of the household routine. Homemakers boiled fat for soap and dipped their own candles. Today, the production of light, soap, and clothes is each the work of a major industry. Giant food-processing companies have come between the farmer and the consumer. Even cooking is left more and more to the fast-food restaurant at the corner.

Gather material, organize it, and present it effectively to your reader.

C2
PLANNING A PAPER

As readers, we see only the finished product. All the words are already in place on the page. The facts, conclusions, and arguments have all been arranged for us. When we become writers ourselves, we change our point of view. We ask: How do we *get* to the finished product? How is a piece of writing produced? We ask questions like the following:

- What am I going to cover?
- Where am I going to find material?
- How am I going to sort it out?
- What do I do to attract the attention of my readers?
- How do I take them along from point to point?

Composition means "putting things together." The next few sections will help you follow a writer through the major steps in the process of composition.

C2a

Focusing on a Topic

Focus on a limited topic and do it justice.

The first thing a writer does is to *limit* the territory he or she is going to cover. An observer aboard a space satellite has a true bird's-eye view of our planet. But such an observer takes in too large a picture to say much about the forms of life that might be found here. Travelers in a plane can make out houses, schools, and highways. But they still take in a panorama. To describe well an actual house, with its weeds in the lawn and a broken toy on the stairway, we would have to get down on the ground. We would have to walk up to the house for a *close-up view*.

Much good writing is "close-up writing." As you explore possible subjects, look for a limited area that you can cover in detail. The narrowing process might go something like this:

GENERAL AREA: Cooking
LESS GENERAL: Cooking for special diets
CLOSE-UP: Cooking for vegetarians

In the following example, the large, general subject of censorship is split, first, into subject areas of intermediate size and, finally, into limited topics:

GENERAL TOPIC: CENSORSHIP

INTERMEDIATE: Moral censorship
LIMITED: Kissing in the movies
No dirty jokes on TV
Profanity in what students read

INTERMEDIATE: Political censorship
LIMITED: News magazines not in your library
What students are taught about socialism
Crime news your paper won't print

INTERMEDIATE: Religious censorship
LIMITED: Baptists and heresy
Blasphemy and the law
Equal time for atheists?

A teacher who assigns you a topic may already have done most of the narrowing down that a large subject requires. Even so, you will typically concentrate on an area *within* the larger topic and cover it in depth. Here are some ways of bringing an assigned topic into focus:

(1) Concentrate on one key term. Perhaps you have been asked to write about individualism in modern American life. If you look for examples of the self-reliant individual, you may think of the pioneers and their prominent role in American history. You might focus your paper on the way Americans *today* use the term "pioneer." What picture does the word bring to mind? Where do we find the term used? How much of the pioneering spirit actually survives in today's society?

(Jot down your own answers to these questions. What kind of material could you bring together for a paper focused on the "pioneering" spirit in America today?)

(2) Ask a "what-is-the-most" question. Focus the spotlight on one central issue by asking a question like the following:

- What is the single most serious cause of accidents?
- What is the single most serious cause of student dissatisfaction with school?
- What is the single most common misunderstanding about factory workers (or about farmers, or about artists)?
- What is the single most pressing need of black Americans (or Spanish-speaking Americans, or Chinese-Americans)?
- What is the single most disappointing trait or habit you have encountered in other people?

(If you were asked to choose one of these as a topic for a paper, which would you choose? Why? What would be some of the material you would use?)

(3) Concentrate on a test case or key example. An important test case can really make us think about what is involved in a familiar issue. We have all heard about people who "take the law into their own hands." They have lost faith in the efficiency of law enforcement, or their conscience makes them rebel against a law they consider unjust. Can you think of a recent test case that was discussed at length in the newspapers? Summarize briefly what you remember about the case.

Much has been written in recent years about the following general subjects. For each of them, write down a more limited topic that you might focus on in a paper of between 350 and 500 words. Compare

EXERCISE 1

your topics with those of your classmates. Which of them best stake out a limited territory that could be explored in detail? (Your teacher may ask you to write a short paper on one of your topics.)

1. Our vanishing open spaces
2. The students' voice in their own education
3. Our wasteful technology
4. Decay in American cities
5. Teenage marriage
6. Automation and the unskilled worker
7. Minorities asking for a place in the sun
8. The attitude of young Americans toward business
9. Reform in our churches
10. Violence and the entertainment media

EXERCISE 2

Have you ever complained that you have nothing to write about? See how many promising subjects you can discover by writing down three or four limited topics under each of the following general subjects.

1. Neighbors
2. Things I like to do
3. Movies
4. Things and people that annoy me
5. Problems
6. Fads
7. Fashions
8. Advertising
9. Job hunting
10. Serving the public

C2b

Supporting a Central Idea

Present material that supports a central idea.

When we study a topic, we notice many different things. Different ideas pass through our minds. But to produce an effective piece of writing, we try to make things add up. We work toward a general impression, or toward a key idea that most of the material supports. This way, our readers will feel that the writing was done with a purpose: There is something we want them to know. There is something we want them to remember.

We call the statement that sums up the central idea of a paper its **thesis.** The most commonly written kind of short paper presents its thesis close to the beginning—often at the end of a short introductory paragraph. It then presents three or four well-developed paragraphs with material that supports the central idea.

Suppose an interviewer has spent some time visiting an older person. Talking to the person, watching her surroundings, learning about her activities, the visitor gradually forms a strong general impression. This general impression could become the central idea of a short article. The different kinds of observations could provide the material for several separate paragraphs:

(Thesis)
> *At 75, she never for a moment either thinks she is old, or projects her age in mood or word . . . .*

(Paragraph 1: details about appearance)
> She is gradually thinning down, fading out in her body; but she shows no sign whatever of aging in her mind or emotions. . . .

(Paragraph 2: details about activities)
> Books lie on the table. The piano is open and has music on it. She is going to the library tomorrow. . . .

(Paragraph 3: details about surroundings)
> The room flowers around her: the coffee on the table; the square silver box of sugar; the plants in the window . . . . —Louis Bogan, "From the Journals of a Poet," *The New Yorker*

In the following excerpted versions of short papers, the material in several paragraphs adds up to the main point of the paper. The main point appears as a thesis toward the beginning of the paper. Restate it in your own words. Describe the material that each writer has used to support the central idea:

PAPER 1

No Time for Pranks?

(Thesis)
> *Compared with the derring-do of today's juvenile delinquents, the student pranks of years gone by seem like innocent amusement.*

(Paragraph 1)
> When my oldest brother went to college, the students showed their defiance of authority by water fights with the campus police. On a hot summer night, they would open fire hydrants, rout the local fire department, and drench the dean of students. . . .

(Paragraph 2)
> But the typical student prank used to be more elaborate. One year, five students at an Ohio university stole a corpse from an undertaking parlor, transported it a hundred miles, and placed it in front of the union building on their college campus. . . .

(Paragraph 3)
> Only rarely did the pranks of yesterday's students have any political significance. At one Southern school, a group of students once replaced a statue of General Lee with one of General Grant, shipped in a huge crate from an adjoining state. . . .

Composition

No End to Violence

(Thesis)   *New York City is rapidly becoming a place that is not fit for people to live in.*

(Paragraph 1)   Police officers, who are supposed to protect others from violence, have become the objects of mass assaults. Every week we read news stories about officers beaten, wounded, or killed in the course of their duty. Only last week an officer, age twenty-nine, died of gunshot wounds inflicted when he and another officer prevented a holdup at a grocery store. . . .

(Paragraph 2)   No woman of any age is any longer safe to go out alone at night. An old lady we know finally left her city apartment after she was robbed twice in the elevator. She found a place to stay with the Little Sisters of the Poor. . . .

(Paragraph 3)   Much of the violence is cowardly and mean. It is hard to think of anything more downright mean than a couple of young hoodlums stealing the watch and wallet left on the wharf by a passerby who is trying to rescue a man drowning in the river. . . .

EXERCISE 1   Study the following passage. Can you see that all four paragraphs support the same basic point? Sum up the central point as the thesis of the passage. Describe the supporting material the author uses. (Do you agree with her? Why or why not? Be prepared to defend your viewpoint in class.)

Boys, Girls, and Human Beings

Society says it wants people to be different but it doesn't really mean it. Parents like to believe their children are different from other children —smarter, of course, better-looking, and so forth—but most parents are secretly disturbed when their children are *really* different—not like others at all. In fact, very early they start to pigeonhole you in certain ways.

Take the difference of sex, for instance. Little girls are pink; little boys are blue. Little girls want dolls; little boys want trains.

For a long time, for instance, the word "tom-boy" to a girl held undertones of worry and disapproval. All it meant was that the girl liked to play ball, climb trees, and skin her knees instead of wearing frilly dresses and curtseying. The companion word for boys, of course, was "sissy"—meaning the kid liked music and poetry and hated fighting. These ignorant and damaging labels have now been discredited, thanks largely to the more enlightened members of our society. But there is still, alas, a large Squareland left where growing girls are told from the age of twelve onward not only by their mothers but by the mass media that marriage is the only valid female goal and that Career is a dirty word.

Even now—even when you know how silly it is (at least, I hope you do), most parents hear wedding bells the minute a girl is born. Most parents see an executive office when a boy is born. The relentless conditioning starts on its merry way. Educate a girl for the marriage market; educate a boy for success. That you, as a human being, as a separate identity, may not want or fit in with either of these goals is considered not a sign of independence but of failure.—Marya Mannes, "Who Am I?"

Write a *thesis-and-support* paper that has three or four paragraphs. Write on one of the following:

EXERCISE 2

- what parents expect of their children;
- what children expect of their parents;
- what teachers expect of their students;
- what students expect of their teachers;
- what married people expect of each other;
- what young people look for in their friends;
- what young people today look for in a job.

Work out a pattern of organization that fits your material.

C2c

Outlining a Paper

How do writers organize their material?

A good pattern of organization seems tailor-made. It makes the reader feel: "This is a good way to tackle *this particular subject.*" Even so, some common patterns of organization are frequently used because they fit many similar situations.

The following ways of organizing a paper will often help you arrange your material:

- **classification**—sorting things out into categories;
- **comparison and contrast**—tracing similarities and differences;
- **chronological order**—tracing a process or the order of events in time.

Learn how to make use of each of these:

(1) Sort things into major categories. Classification simply means putting things together that belong together. When you first jot down possible ideas for a paper, your list will be *miscellaneous*. Things will appear as they come to mind, with no obvious connection between one idea and the next. On the following page is one such miscellaneous list for a paper taking stock of what the author learned in high school:

  (1) drafting
  (2) algebra and geometry
  (3) working with other people
  (4) note-taking
  (5) when to lead and when to follow
  (6) meeting schedules, budgeting one's time
  (7) how to work hard for grades
  (8) how to overcome a bad first impression
  (9) study habits
(10) learn how to take second place

What goes with what? Obviously (1) and (2) go together as the kinds of practical courses that will be useful to someone who plans a career as a technician or engineer. What about the rest? Several points—(4), (6), (7), and (9)—deal not with subject matter but with *how* a student studies—work habits, in other words. The remaining points—(3), (5), (8), (10)—deal with the kind of education for which there are no tests and grades: working and living with other people. After you sort out the material in this list, you may arrive at an outline like the following:

```
          You Can Take It with You

     I.  Career skills
         A.  Drafting
         B.  Algebra and geometry
    II.  Study habits
         A.  Note-taking
         B.  Meeting schedules
         C.  Concentrating on a definite
             goal
   III.  Social skills
         A.  Teamwork
         B.  Being a good loser
```

Remember: A good scheme of classification serves a *purpose*. A member of Congress writing an article about the mail she receives might just **chat** amusingly about various unusual letters. At the end, though, she would realize that she has told the reader little about how a member of Congress—and Congress—works. In an organized article, she could talk about how she classifies her mail according to whether it is "lobby mail," "fan mail," or "case mail," in order to decide *what to do* with it. The following might be a rough scheme for the article:

I. "Lobby mail" urges the special cause of some organized group, with numerous letters almost identical in content and wording. Such letters can be tabulated to provide a rough guide to public opinion.

II. "Fan mail" requests autographs or photographs and applauds stands taken by the member of Congress. Most of these should receive a pleasant reply that may look personalized but is often typed on an automatic typewriter.

III. "Case mail" asks for assistance in dealing with government agencies or for support for important projects. Letters in this category, if they are considered justified or important, are acted upon by the legislator's staff.

(2) Select several key points for comparison and contrast. Suppose a first-year college student were to write a paper on the differences between high school and college. The writer might decide to concentrate on one key point: Though beginning college courses often cover areas similar to those covered in high school, the *work* expected of the student may be more demanding. The outline of the finished paper might look as follows:

THESIS: In college, former high school students are expected to work and think on their own.

 I. Material assigned
    A. In high schools, materials for study are often carefully screened to eliminate controversial treatments of sex or political ideology
    B. In college, courses in literature or the social sciences may concentrate heavily on "taboo" subjects

 II. Preparation expected
    A. In high school, students may have become used to fairly short reading assignments, with much help provided by "study questions" and "study guides"
    B. In college, students may be asked to read large chunks of material on their own, with few or no questions to serve as a guide

 III. Performance expected
    A. In high school, students often feel that there is one approved view or conclusion they are supposed to reach
    B. In college, students are often bombarded with opposing views on the same subject and left to make up their own minds

• The sample outline just given shows a **point-by-point comparison.** *One* feature of high school work is described (with examples) and then *immediately* compared with the corresponding situation in college. This way the reader can immediately see the similarity or the difference involved.

● In a **parallel-order comparison,** we would first describe *several* major features of high school work. We would then take up the corresponding features of college work *in the same order.* We would get an *overview* of each situation:

  I. High school work
    A. Noncontroversial materials
    B. Short assignments with many study helps
    C. Conformity to "approved" opinions

 II. College work
    A. Controversial subject matter
    B. Long assignments with few guides
    C. Opposed views

(3) Follow a process through its major stages. When we trace a process, the order we should follow is already built into our subject. Notice how faithfully the author of the following passage has stayed with the actual process by which we utilize the sun's energy:

> Last year, somewhere in Florida, on the leaves of a forgotten sugar-cane plant, a bit of sunlight ended its eight-minute dash to earth. Somehow, the plant turned that sunlight into sugar. Somehow, that sugar got into my sugar bowl and into my morning coffee. I sipped last year's sunshine at breakfast. Now it's in my blood, and it starts to feed these old architect-muscles. It's dark now, and I start for home on my bicycle. The muscled sunlight suddenly becomes pedal-power, then chainpull, wheel-spin, generator-whine, filament-heat, and finally—from the head-lamp—light again!—Malcolm Wells, *Environmental Action Bulletin*

When the process you trace is long or involved, make sure you do not lose your readers along the way. Make the major outlines stand out clearly. When you first study the history of jazz, for instance, you may find that it developed gradually, with many byways and dead alleys. But if you just present your findings step by little step, your readers will feel lost. The names and dates you mention will just become a blur in their minds. Help them find their way. *Mark off some major phrases:*

   I. Dixieland
  II. Big-band swing
 III. Bebop
 IV. Modern "concert" jazz

NOTE: Check your finished outlines for the following:

● *Avoid single subdivisions.* If there is a subdivision *A,* there should be a subdivision *B.* If there is a section numbered *1,* there should be a section numbered *2.* If a section covers only one major point, leave it undivided.

- *Avoid a long list of parallel elements, such as A–F or 1–8.* Try to split the sequence into two or three major groups.

- *Use similar wording or parallel structure for headings of the same rank.* For instance, *A.1* may read "To revive the student's interest." *A.2* and *A.3* should also be worded as infinitives: "To promote the student's participation"; "To develop the student's independent judgment."

- *In a* **topic outline,** *make each topic specific and informative.* In a **sentence outline,** make each subdivision a complete sentence. Make each sentence sum up an idea rather than merely indicate a topic.

- *Use conventional symbols and punctuation.* The following is part of a sentence outline. Study the way it uses Roman numerals for main headings, capitals for subheadings, and Arabic numerals for further subheadings:

```
Main Street Isn't Pennsylvania Avenue

Thesis:   A successful business career alone
          does not qualify an executive for
          government work.

   I.   Prominent business people have often
        held high positions in the federal
        government.

  II.   Business people often have qualifica-
        tions that government officials tend
        to lack.
        A.   They are in close contact with
             the general public.
        B.   They have thorough training in
             organizational problems.
             1.   They are trained in admin-
                  istrative efficiency.
             2.   They are cost-conscious.

 III.   But business executives often lack
        preparation for other aspects of
        government work. . . .
```

Composition

EXERCISE 1

Write an outline for a paper in which you *classify* one of the following:

1. homes in your community
2. cars owned by your neighbors
3. popular songs currently favored by young listeners
4. animals that have learned to coexist with civilization
5. buildings in a big city

(Your teacher may ask you to write a paper following the outline.)

EXERCISE 2

Suppose you have jotted down the following points for a paper on "The Hallmarks of Cheap Fiction." How would you sort out these points into major categories? Prepare a *topic outline*. Use Roman numerals for major headings and capital letters for subheadings.

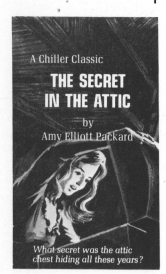

A Chiller Classic

THE SECRET IN THE ATTIC

by
Amy Elliott Packard

What secret was the attic chest hiding all these years?

1. The villians are all bad, with no shades of gray.
2. The hero and heroine ride off into the sunset to live happily ever after.
3. The hero succeeds in hairbreadth escapes and last-minute rescues that would never succeed in real life.
4. The heroine flowers from an ugly duckling into a ravishing beauty.
5. The red-blooded American boy triumphs over his enemies.
6. By a marvelous coincidence, the hero meets a long-lost friend on a South Sea island.
7. In the nick of time, the villain gets his amply deserved comeuppance.
8. The orphan is found to be the son (or daughter) of a rich banker.
9. The hero accidentally discovers documents that help him expose the villain.
10. In the chest in the attic, the poor heroine discovers documents that show her family to be the real owners of land worth a fortune.
11. In New York City, the heroine accidentally discovers her much-loved sister, believed dead but actually living under an assumed name.
12. The hero is mistaken for a famous outlaw, who looks and talks amazingly like him.

EXERCISE 3

Some things are very different in appearance and yet similar in basic design. A careful comparison and contrast can show both the similarity and the differences. Prepare an outline for such a detailed comparison. Use the *point-by-point* method. Choose one pair:

1. a Model-T Ford and a late-model car
2. a World War I fighter plane and a modern passenger jet
3. a human being and a chimpanzee
4. a beetle and a butterfly
5. a fiddle and a guitar

In studies of earliest history, we hear about the contrasting ways of life of different types of human beings: cave dwellers and cliff dwellers, or fruit gatherers and hunters. Write a *two-paragraph paper* about two contrasting modern types. Write one paragraph each about each member of the pair. Choose one:

EXERCISE 4

1. Cadillac owner and subcompact owner
2. house dweller and apartment dweller
3. armed forces people and civilian people
4. blue-collar people and white-collar people
5. adolescent and adult
6. athletic people and artistic people
7. opera goers and country music fans
8. outdoor people and indoor people
9. married parents and divorced parents
10. optimist and pessimist

Give three or four possible *major stages* for the following:

EXERCISE 5

1. the history of humanity
2. the development of a young person's attitude toward the other sex
3. the reputation of a president or other political leader
4. the development of a new fad
5. the development of a major new invention

(Be prepared to explain what each of the stages would be and why you would consider it a major or important phase.)

Divide a process into its major stages. Choose a hobby, manufacturing process, building project, or the like. Write an outline showing the major stages and intermediate steps. (Your teacher may ask you to write a paper following your outline.)

EXERCISE 6

Know how to attract and channel your reader's attention.

C2d

Titles, Introductions, Conclusions

Effective writers know how to attract attention. They leave us at the end with a strong, unified impression. Do the following to start a paper right and to finish it on a strong note:

(1) Make your title attractive and informative. An effective title beckons to the reader and says "READ." But at the same time, a good title gives your readers a clue to what they will find. Often, the title stakes out the *territory* to be covered:

How Words Are Born   The New St. Louis

WHAT'S IN A TITLE?

Look at the following titles of actual magazine articles. What kind of article does each title make you expect? Is there anything about the title that would be likely to catch a reader's attention? What kind of reader would be interested in each article? (Which of these would *you* want to read? Why?)

1. **How to Fight INFLATION**

2. **Is There Life Out There?**

3. **The folly of modern architecture**

4. **The Changing Status of Women in Developed Countries**

5. The never-before-seen Face of Mercury

6. A Pheasant Hunt to Remember

7. **Burning Waste to Make Electricity**

8. **Those Gas-Saving Gadgets--Do They or Don't They?**

9. **How Not To Get A Fair Trial**

10. **My Small War with the Coast Guard**

Often the title at the same time hints at the *key point*:

You Can't Live in the City
The Case for Early Marriage

Often the title shows the attitude of the writer, the *tone* he or she is going to adopt. What would be the tone in the articles?

Cheating: American Disgrace
Are IQ Tests Intelligent?
How to Turn Play into Work

Weak titles are too pretentious, too general, or too dull:

PRETENTIOUS: Facing the Challenge of Tomorrow
MORE HONEST: I Was Taught by a Computer
                 A Factory Without People

GENERAL: My Autobiography
MORE FOCUSED: Growing Up Confused
                 Confessions of a Mouse

DULL: Government and the People
MORE LIVELY: I Helped Elect the Mayor
                 Don't Write Your Senators

(2) *Use your introduction to draw your readers into the topic.*
The first few sentences of a short paper should give the answers
to questions like the following: "Why should I read this? What are
you trying to do? How are you going to do it?" The introduction
may show that the author will

• discuss a *topic that has often been neglected* or that has been
treated inadequately:

On Being the Right Size

The most obvious differences between different animals are differences of size, but for some reason the zoologists have paid singularly
little attention to them. In a large textbook of zoology before me I
find no indication that the eagle is larger than the sparrow, or the
hippopotamus bigger than the hare, though some grudging admissions are made in the case of the mouse and the whale.... (J. B. S.
Haldane)

• start from an *incident that has a special personal meaning:*

Shooting an Elephant

In Moulmein, in lower Burma, I was hated by large numbers of
people—the only time in my life that I have been important enough
for this to happen to me.... (George Orwell)

• present a *new solution* to a familiar problem:

How to Stop Littering

Antilitter signs litter the American landscape. Television, radio,
billboards, and even garbage cans ask us to "keep litter in its place"
and tell us "Don't be a litterbug." We get reminders that litter accu-
mulates on the nation's highways at the average of one cubic yard per
mile per month, and that it costs 28 million dollars per year to clean
it up. But these appeals to conscience have fallen on deaf ears....

● develop a striking *contrast:*

Aging and Everyone

Throughout human history until recent times, most human beings have died in infancy, and no more than a very small percentage survived to ripe old age, carrying with them the wisdom of their experience or the foolishness of their years. Now all is changing, thanks to antibodies, antibiotics, the surgeon's knife, and the welfare state.... (N. J. Berrill)

● approach a familiar problem in a challenging, provocative *new way:*

One Small Step

A riddle is making the rounds that goes like this: A man and his young son were in an automobile accident. The father was killed and the son, who was critically injured, was rushed to a hospital. As attendants wheeled the unconscious boy into the emergency room, the doctor on duty looked down at him and said, "My God, it's my son!" What was the relationship of the doctor to the injured boy? ... (Casey Miller and Kate Swift)

(3) Use your conclusion to reinforce your major point. A conclusion is not the same thing as a summary. Sometimes a summary is needed: When you have described a complicated process, you may want to look back over the major steps. When you have studied important objections, you may need a summary of your own point of view. But often a summary is merely lame *repetition.* Try alternatives like the following:

● Apply your major point to a *current situation:*

[an article on Washington's personality] ... There are times to smile and times to scowl. Washington lacked one of the basic qualities we have come to expect in the head of a chamber of commerce or the public relations director of a large company. He did not try to please everybody, all the time.

● Use a *striking example* to sum up or reinforce your main point:

[an article on the author's pride in her own country] ... in India, people turn out every election day in a larger percentage than anywhere else in the world to *choose* a government. They make a real holiday of it, decorating their oxcarts and dressing in their best clothes to go to the polls. Certainly one cannot pretend that there is nothing in India that needs to be changed, but somewhere in all this is a confidence and pleasure in being Indian, and in the country's ways.—Santha Rama Rau, *Return to India*

- Use a *quotation* to give added force to your own position:

[a paper on the shortcomings of "respectability"] . . . William Hazlitt said, "There is not any term that is oftener misapplied, or that is a stronger instance of the abuse of language, than this same word *respectable*." The trouble with respectable people is that they are too timid to do the things that would win our respect.

- Avoid the kind of conclusion that could be used *interchangeably* with other papers on similar subjects:

WEAK: . . . The teenagers who are concerned only with tomorrow night's date are going to become the adults who will run businesses, seek offices, educate the next generation of citizens, and decide world policies. If we are not able to respond to the challenge of tomorrow, we shall find ourselves ill-prepared and ill-equipped to deal with the jobs that must be done.

Was this a paper asking for support for the Scout movement? or advocating more homework? or suggesting a new kind of curriculum?

Remember: Avoid elaborate introductions that "beat around the bush." Avoid padded conclusions that repeat for the third time something you have already said.

How attractive and informative are the following *titles?* Which of them make you want to read what the author has to say? Which of them could serve as a model for the title of a student paper? Explain and defend your answers.

EXERCISE 1

1. Hope for the Blind
2. Detective Agencies
3. The Shame of Our Cities
4. Noah's Ark and Tomorrow's Zoo
5. Bemused in Buffalo
6. An Open Letter to the New Mayor
7. Death at an Early Age
8. How to Get Along with People
9. Beat the Drum Slowly
10. A Warning to a Wasteful World
11. Solving the Mysteries of College Applications
12. Portrait of a President
13. Cruising into Yesterday
14. How Hard Is College?
15. The Spirit of Democracy

EXERCISE 2

Look at the following *introductions*. How does each lead the reader into the topic? What kind of article do the title and the introduction make you expect? Would you want to go on reading? Why, or why not?

1.

AMERICA'S SPEEDING ANTELOPE

I lay down in the grass and began to wave my cap back and forth in the air. I was trying to take a picture of a wild pronghorn antelope buck that stood in the sagebrush a few hundred yards away looking at me. Antelope are wild, free spirits, bounding off across the plains to get away from people. But they also have a deep curiosity. . . . (George Laycock)

2.

An Eye for an Eye

"¡Estropeado!" was what Dr. X told me. "Beyond repair" would be a mild translation of the Castilian word, but the opinion did not surprise me. I had already been told by eleven other doctors in two other cities that the cornea of my left eye was beyond "conservative medical help." At the age of thirty-three, I was rapidly going blind in one eye because of a childhood injury, and I had had to stop work as a sculptor. . . .

3.

HOW TO CONTROL PESTS

Of the hundreds of thousands of species of insects and plants that are potentially damaging to our agricultural activities, only a few hundred are considered to be pests. The great majority are part of an ecological system of checks and balances which keeps their numbers below the level at which they become economically injurious. Inevitably, increased mobility of human populations and the mass application of agricultural technology have, in some cases, upset the natural balance . . . .

4.

Children, Divorce, and Welfare

In nineteenth-century America, children who had lost one parent were not uncommon. As health conditions improved, fewer children lost parents through death. Today, parents rarely die young. Most children who lose parents lose them through divorce. . . . (Mary Jo Bane)

5.

Lessons of the Street

John is a New York City plainclothes detective whose clothes are not all that plain. He wears webbed belts, bell-bottom slacks, and all-in-one suede and corduroy suits of a type purchasable at what the radio commercials refer to as "in" shops. This fondness for mod outfits makes him a bit unusual in his profession, most detectives favoring baggy slacks and white anklets or what John politely refers to as "period dress." But the clothing helps John blend into the background when he is at work. . . .

6.

Our Latin Americans

Over 2 million people make up New York's Latin-American community. For the most part they come from the Latin Caribbean: Puerto Rico, Cuba, and the Dominican Republic. The largest group from Spain's lost mainland empire is Colombian, followed by the Chileans. However, every country in Latin America has some representation, making the New York Latin community an especially rich and diverse one. . . .

7.

Things I Wish I'd Known

"Bewilderment" probably best describes the first feelings of every college freshman. Even those who look and act calm and self-assured have some little doubt or worry tucked away under that veneer of cool. It's a time of upheaval in your life-style, and you should expect change—and to change yourself. . . .

8.

Last Rites for Smallpox

On December 14, 1977, an international commission of public health experts from nine countries signed the death certificate for one of the most terrifying human afflictions ever known: *Variola major* smallpox. Meeting in Dacca, the capital of Bangladesh, two years after the last case of the disease had been detected, the experts certified that sufficient time had elapsed without traces of smallpox to safely say that the disease had been eradicated from the country. . . .

Composition

Which of the following passages sounds to you as if it would make a good *conclusion* to a paper or article? Describe in detail what would make it a strong or a weak conclusion.

1. ... This problem of anti-intellectualism is an important one. Perhaps it should be looked into a little further. In this fast-growing nation of ours, nothing is more important than the development of our minds.

2. ... The press was given its privileged status in order to question and, if necessary, counteract the exercise of government power. In that function it is defaulting. Writing in the *New York Review of Books,* Andrew Kopkind has described the real sources of news suppression: "In ways which journalists themselves perceive only dimly or not at all, they are bought, or compromised, or manipulated into confirming the official lies: not the little ones, which they delight in exposing, but the big ones, which they do not normally think of as lies at all, and which they cannot distinguish from the truth."

3. ... knowing the investment that this nation makes in the education of the young, we students of America will strive to be worthy of the trust put in us by our parents. With the knowledge and training we receive, we will become not only better students, but also better citizens.

4. ... When Christ was on the cross, the story goes, His persecutors were preparing a fourth spike made of silver to pierce his heart. Some Gypsies stole the spike, and Christ was spared the additional agony. God was so grateful that he gave the Gypsies permission to steal thereafter. I asked my hostess whether she believed the story. "How else can you explain it?" she replied. "Why can a Gypsy steal but he'll never get caught? The Gypsies don't have a church, and they don't have a country, but God made them free and He watches over us."

5. As I closed my suitcase, I thought of something my parents said months before, "Growing up is going away from home." How true that was. But it's also true that growing up is feeling free to go home again.

C2e
Carrying the Reader Along

Help your readers follow you from point to point.

How do writers carry their readers along?

Effective writers set their signals so that the reader knows from the beginning: "This is where we are headed." But they also make sure the reader does not get lost on the way. They employ devices that give their writing **coherence.** They make sure their ideas "hang together" as their readers move from one sentence and one paragraph to the next.

Try the following to help make your writing more coherent:

(1) Use transitional expressions to steer the reader in the right direction. These are like directional signals that say "now for the reason," or "here is an additional example," or "now let me draw the conclusion": The **transitional** signals easiest to spot list several examples or reasons in *numerical* order:

Guilt by Association

We are often quick to judge people by the company they keep. In days of aroused public opinion, people often judge others on the basis of guilt by association. This practice is wrong for several reasons. . . .

First, guilt by association goes counter to common experience. It assumes that a good cause becomes bad if it is supported by a few bad people. . . .

Second, guilt by association goes against basic principles of Anglo-American law. According to our laws, a person has the right to be judged as an individual, not as the member of a group. . . .

Third, guilt by association goes against some of our most cherished historical traditions. One thing that has always been part of our American way of life has been our faith in voluntary association as a way to get things done. . . .

Finally, guilt by association is wrong morally. It rests on the rotten-apple theory of society. It assumes that one wicked person can corrupt many basically good people. . . .

Many other transitional expressions trace the order of events *in time,* or take us from *cause to effect,* or from something desired to an *obstacle* in our way:

The Language of Chemistry

Like other scientists, chemists needed accurate technical terms for the substances they wanted to describe. They tried to get away from confusing and inaccurate familiar words and find more precise scientific names. . . .

Soon, however, chemists realized that the full names of chemical elements were often long and awkward. . . .

In addition, they realized the need for labels that chemists speaking different languages could easily recognize. . . .

Everyone, *therefore,* welcomed the invention of letter symbols for chemical elements. . . .

The *next* problem was to find a simple and clear way to show chemical compounds. . . .

Here are the most common transitional phrases and some of the purposes they serve:

ENUMERATION:	in the first place, in the second place; to begin with, first . . . second . . . third . . .; finally
CHRONOLOGY:	at first, now, then, later, at least, soon, in the meantime, gradually
ILLUSTRATION:	for example, for instance, to illustrate
LOGICAL CONCLUSION:	therefore, accordingly, as a result, consequently, hence
OBJECTION OR CONTRAST:	but, however, on the other hand, nevertheless, on the contrary
CONCESSION:	it is true that, granted that, no doubt
SUMMARY:	to conclude, to sum up, in short

(2) Make use of words and phrases that echo key ideas. Strengthen the network of **synonyms** and related terms that holds together a passage. When we find a network of terms like "justice," "fair distribution," "earned reward," and "equal shares," we know that the author is dealing with one point at a time.

In the following excerpt from an article, key words and phrases echo the idea of hunger and deprivation:

The Hungry World

It is difficult for the English-speaking peoples to understand the real meaning of *hunger.* Those who spent years in enemy prison camps are perhaps the only ones who have had to stare starvation in the face. . . .

Hunger is often associated with war. Farms are *deprived* of the necessary workers and equipment. Military campaigns *devastate* the countryside; retreating troops *destroy* food supplies. . . .

In a later excerpt from the same article, many words and expressions echo and develop the idea of erosion:

But the basic causes of starvation are independent of such relatively short-range developments. Perhaps the greatest single factor that has contributed to the present food problem is the inability to conquer the forces of soil *erosion.* Huge areas of the earth in the past have been devastated by bad farming; by plowing steep slopes and thus permitting rain to *wash soil away;* by permitting cattle to overgraze and thus *destroying the grass roots* which prevent wind erosion; by letting spring rains rush off land which has been *stripped of trees.* . . .

EXERCISE 1   In the following excerpt, point out all words or expressions that help us place events or follow the order of events *in time.*

A Day with a Lion Cub

By now we had established a routine for Elsa. The mornings were cool; it was then that we often watched the impala antelope leaping gracefully on the rifle range and listened to the chorus of the awakening birds. As soon as it got light Nuru released Elsa and both walked a short distance into the bush. The cub, full of unspent energy, chased everything she could find, including her own tail.

Then, when the sun got warm, she and Nuru settled under a shady tree and Elsa dozed while he read his Koran and sipped tea. Nuru always carried a rifle to protect them both against wild animals but was very good about following our instructions "to shout before shooting." He was genuinely fond of Elsa and handled her very well.

About teatime the two of them returned and we took over. First, Elsa had some milk. Then we wandered into the hills or walked in the plain. She climbed trees, appeared to sharpen her claws, followed exciting scents or stalked Grant's gazelle and gerenuk, which sometimes played hide-and-seek with her. Much to our surprise, she was fascinated by tortoises, which she rolled over and over. She loved playing, and never did she miss an opportunity of starting a game with us—we were her "pride" and she shared everything with us.

As darkness fell we returned home and took her to her enclosure, where her evening meal awaited her. It consisted of large quantities of raw meat, mostly sheep and goat. She got her roughage by breaking up the rib bones and the cartilages. As I held her bones for her, I would watch the muscles of her forehead moving powerfully. I always had to scratch the marrow out for her; she licked it greedily from my fingers, resting her heavy body upright against my arms. While this went on, Pati sat on the window sill watching us, content to know that soon her turn would come to spend the night cuddled around my neck and that then she would have me to herself.

Till then, I sat with Elsa, playing with her, sketching her, or reading. These evenings were our most intimate time, and I believe that her love for us was mostly fostered in these hours when, fed and happy, she could doze off with my thumb still in her mouth. It was only on moonlight nights that she became restless. Then she padded along the wire, listening intently, her nostrils quivering to catch the faintest scent which might bring a message from the mysterious night outside. When she was nervous, her paws became damp, and I could often judge her state of mind by holding them in my hands.—Joy Adamson, *Born Free*

EXERCISE 2

In the following excerpt, find all *synonyms and related terms* that have something to do with the presence or absence of water.

The Spreading Deserts

About fifteen percent of the human race live in dry lands, depending for survival on a marginally productive environment that is rapidly withering . . . .

The spreading of the deserts is not something new in human history. Some of the first civilizations grew in what are now the parched sands of the Middle East, in a region once known as the fertile crescent . . . .

Among the chief causes for the growth of the deserts are overgrazing of livestock, the cutting down of forests, and the wrong methods of working the soil. The need for firewood for warmth and cooking has caused the destruction of forests that meant shade and moisture. Often the spread of the encroaching desert is hastened by the concentration of human and livestock activities around the scarce waterholes and precious wells. . . .

Even irrigation, if it waterlogs poorly drained soils or deposits toxic salts, can help kill the land . . . .

In the past, people living in arid lands followed traditional practices that minimized damage to marginal areas. Nomads moved almost continually, allowing the vegetation of an area to recover before they visited it again. Some herders in the Middle East irrigated their pastures only every other year, moving their herds each year. People in some areas of India watered trees as acts of devotion, because they held them sacred . . . .

Today, large numbers of people and animals are crowded into overburdened areas. When drought comes, the capacity of the land is exceeded. Crowding around scarce water sources produces desiccation and erosion. . . .

EXERCISE 3

In a recent issue of a newsmagazine, find an article whose author has done an exceptionally good job of carrying the reader along. Find five paragraphs that start with a helpful transitional phrase or sentence. Copy these phrases and sentences. Be prepared to explain in class the role they played in the article.

C3

WRITING FROM EXPERIENCE

Draw on your own observation and experience.

Good writing draws on firsthand experience. It makes the reader feel: "This is real. This is related to what people do, think, and feel."

Remember:

(1) Draw on what people see. Learn to bring in the specific details that will enable your readers to visualize the actions that you describe. For example, it is harder to visualize a person who merely *walks* than a person who *shuffles, strides, limps, prances, wiggles, jumps, hops,* or *trots.*

(2) Draw on what people say. Reproduce what was *said* as well as what was done. In the following passage, can you see that the incident described becomes real to us as we listen to what is said? How does a detailed conversation make people more believable?

> "Hey girlie." I turned around. "You know where the park is?"
> "Sure. Straight up the block, then make a right and walk down a little. You'll see it right away."
> Alley Pond was a nice place to waste the day when you couldn't stay in school. . . . I was going to give them a few pointers, but the silence stopped me. It hit me in such an eerie way; I felt chilled to the bone, though I couldn't foresee why.
> "I sure do wish I had a dime. I have to call my mother."
> No one answered. Were they waiting for me? I knew why I had felt so uneasy, but I had fought the idea off as silly. Now I stood alone, the subject of ignorance.
> "Hey girlie, *you* got a dime?"

(3) Draw on what people feel. A good novel often seems real to us because the author knows how to make us share the emotions of ordinary people. Bernard Malamud, for instance, in *The Assistant,* tells the story of a neighborhood grocer struggling against poverty and crime.

What feelings is the reader made to share with the grocer and with the child in the following passage?

> The front door opened and a girl of ten entered, her face pinched and eyes excited. His heart held no welcome for her.
> "My mother says," she said quickly, "can you trust her till tomorrow for a pound of butter, loaf of rye bread and a small bottle of cider vinegar?"
> He knew the mother. "No more trust."
> The girl burst into tears.
> Morris gave her a quarter-pound of butter, the bread and vinegar. He found a penciled spot on the worn counter, near the cash register, and wrote a sum under "Drunk Woman." The total now came to $2.03, which he never hoped to see. But Ida would nag if she noticed a new figure, so he reduced the amount to $1.61. His peace—the little he lived with—was worth forty-two cents.

Composition

**PREVIEW
EXERCISE**

Describe a scene or an incident that you recently witnessed at a corner grocery, supermarket, gas station, bus stop, or similar everyday location. Include what the people actually saw, what they actually said, and what they actually felt.

C3a

Description

Do justice to the sights and sounds around you.

The descriptive writer is like someone who goes out with a camera and a tape recorder and then comes back to say: "Look at what I have seen. Listen to what I have heard." Remember the following guidelines for descriptive writing:

(1) Keep an eye out for detail. Do not just give your readers a general impression: "The room was cluttered" or "The shelves were neatly arranged." Bring in enough of what was there and how it looked for the reader to say, "I am beginning to get the picture."

Contrast the passages in the following pairs:

GENERAL: Each housing unit had prepared an elaborate float or display. Each float must have taken much time and energy to prepare. They were very ingenious.

DETAILED: Each housing unit had prepared an elaborate float or display. One prizewinner was an *enormous red bull* (the home team) *towing a corn cutter that mowed down cornstalks* (the opposing team) *and delivered them in bags*.

GENERAL: From my window, I could see a young man working in his apartment across the street. He was polishing a long table top. He was really working at it, giving it everything he had.

DETAILED: Framed in a lighted window level with mine in the apartment house across the street, I saw a young man *in a white T-shirt and white shorts* at work polishing a long, beautiful dark table top. It was obviously his own table in his own flat, and he was enjoying his occupation. He was *bent over* in perfect concentration, *rubbing, sandpapering, running the flat of his palm over the surface, standing back now and then to get the sheen of light on the fine wood.* (Katherine Anne Porter)

(2) Use vivid specific words. A routine writer relies too much on all-purpose words like *building, thing,* or *move.* The word *move* does not make us see a particular kind of motion. Look for words that would create a more vivid picture in the reader's mind: *lurch, jerk, stagger, slide, leap, hop, shift, totter, sway, glide, crawl, slip, shift, veer, careen,* and the like. In the excerpt on page 181, point out all words for specific objects, sights, sounds, and motions:

LET ME DESCRIBE THE SCENE

Pretend you have just arrived in this small, out-of-the-way town. Describe the scene you see. Make the description detailed enough so that your readers can see the scene in front of them. Try to make the readers feel what it is like to be here.

A LETTER FROM MY CELL

Pretend you are spending an indefinite amount of time in the place shown in this photograph. Write a letter in which you show your reader what the place looks like. Show your reader what it feels like to be here.

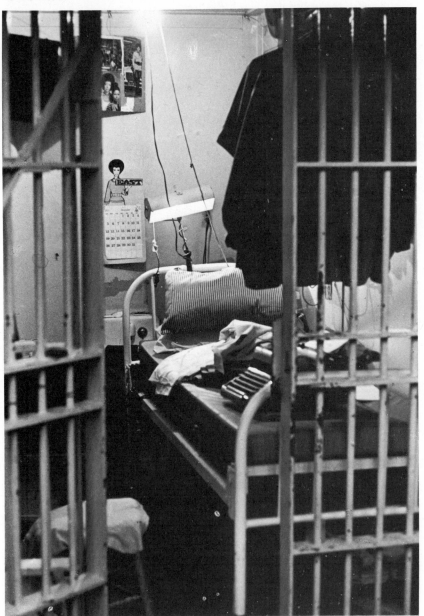

The car was going a wild forty-five miles an hour across the open and as Macomber watched, the buffalo got bigger and bigger until he could see the gray, hairless, scabby look of one huge bull and how his neck was a part of his shoulders and the shiny black of his horns as he galloped a little behind the others that were strung out in that steady plunging gait; and then, the car swaying as though it had just jumped a road, they drew up close and he could see the plunging hugeness of the bull, and the dust in his sparsely haired hide, the wide boss of horn and his outstretched, wide-nostrilled muzzle, and he was raising his rifle when Wilson shouted, "Not from the car, you fool!" and he had no fear, only hatred of Wilson, while the brakes clamped on and the car skidded, plowing sideways to an almost stop and Wilson was out on one side and he on the other, stumbling as his feet hit the still speeding-by of the earth, and then he was shooting at the bull as he moved away, hearing the bullets whunk into him, emptying his rifle at him as he moved steadily away, finally remembering to get his shots forward into the shoulder, and as he fumbled to re-load, he saw the bull was down.—Ernest Hemingway, "The Short Happy Life of Francis Macomber"

(3) Use comparisons and figurative words. We can begin to picture the body shell of a beetle when we are told whether it looks more like leather, or hard rubber, or a certain kind of metal. In the following passage, point out comparisons that help us imagine an animal that we may have never seen before:

From the deck of a vessel you may look down, hour after hour, on the shimmering discs of jellyfish, their gently pulsating bells dotting the surface as far as you can see. . . .

There are fierce little dragons half an inch long, the sharp-jawed arrowworms. There are gooseberry-like comb jellies, armed with grasping tentacles, and there are the shrimp-like euphausiids that strain food from the water with their bristly appendages.—Rachel Carson, *The Sea Around Us*

(4) Make your details add up. Include details that will help create a unifying overall impression for your readers. To help create a bustling street scene, the details you select should contribute movement and color. To help describe a nervous person, your details should stress movements and gestures that make the person seem fidgety, ill at ease.

Read the passage on the following page. How would you sum up in your own words the general picture that the reader carries along? Point out all words and phrases that help build up the same **dominant impression**:

We passed quite a number of tramps, singly or in couples—one squad, a family in a rickety one-horse wagon, with some baskets evidently their work and trade—the man seated on a low board, in front, driving —the gauntish woman by his side, with a baby well bundled in her arms, its little red feet and lower legs sticking out right towards us as we passed. In the wagon behind, we saw two (or three) crouching little children. It was a queer, taking, rather sad picture. If I had been alone and on foot, I should have stopped and held confab. But on our return nearly two hours afterward, we found them further along the same road, in a lonesome open spot, hauled aside, unhitched, and evidently going to camp for the night. The freed horse was not far off, quietly cropping the grass. The man was busy at the wagon, the boy had gathered some dry wood, and was making a fire—and as we went a little further we met the woman afoot. I could not see her face, in its great sunbonnet, but somehow her figure and gait told misery, terror, destitution. She had the rag-bundled, half-starved infant still in her arms, and in her hands held two or three baskets, which she had evidently taken to the next house for sale. A little barefoot five-year-old girl-child, with fine eyes, trotted behind her, clutching her gown.—Walt Whitman, *Specimen Days*

EXERCISE 1

Study the following samples of descriptive writing. How can the reader tell that the author of each was a good observer? For each passage do the following:

A. Point out all *specific concrete words* for sights and sounds in these passages.

B. Point out any examples of *comparisons* or of figurative language that the author uses.

C. Point out words or details that help us share in the writer's *feelings*.

D. Point out any details that help shape a *dominant impression*. In your own words, state the overall impression that stays in the reader's mind.

1. He watched their flight; bird after bird: a dark flash, a swerve, a flash again, a dart aside, a curve, a flutter of wings. He tried to count them before all their darting quivering bodies passed: six, ten, eleven: and wondered were they odd or even in number. Twelve, thirteen: for two came wheeling down from the upper sky. They were flying high and low but ever round and round in straight and curving lines and ever flying from left to right, circling about a temple of air. He listened to the cries: like the squeak of mice behind the wainscot: a shrill twofold note. But the notes were long and shrill and whirring, unlike the cry of vermin, falling a third or a fourth

and trilled as the flying beaks clove the air.—James Joyce, *A Portrait of the Artist as a Young Man*

2.   The Cross River picks its way down from the great mountains of the Cameroons until it runs sprawling and glittering into the great bowl of forest land around Mamfe. After being all froth, waterfalls, and eager chattering in the mountains, it settles down when it reaches this forest and runs sedately in its rocky bed. The gently moving waters create ribs of pure white sand across its width and wash the mud away from the tree roots, so that they look as though they stand at the edge of the water on a tangled writhing mass of octopus-like legs. It moves along majestically, its brown waters full of hippo and crocodile, and the warm air above it filled with swallows, blue and orange and white.—Gerald Durrell, *The Balfut Beagles*

3.   Keening harshly in his senility, the blind polar bear slowly and ceaselessly shakes his head in the stark heat of the July and mountain noon. His open eyes are blue. No one stops to look at him; an old farmer, in passing, sums up the old bear's situation by observing, with a ruthless chuckle, that he is a "back number." Patient and despairing, he sits on his yellowed haunches on the central rock of his pool, his huge toy paws wearing short boots of mud.—Jean Stafford, "In the Zoo"

4.   Mono Lake lies in a lifeless, treeless, hideous desert, eight thousand feet above the level of the sea, and is guarded by mountains two thousand feet higher, whose summits are always clothed in clouds. This solemn, silent, sailless sea—this lonely tenant of the loneliest spot on earth—is little graced with the picturesque. It is an unpretending expanse of grayish water, about a hundred miles in circumference, with two islands in its center, mere upheavals of rent and scorched and blistered lava, snowed over with gray banks and drifts of pumicestone and ashes, the winding sheet of the dead volcano, whose vast crater the lake has seized upon and occupied. —Mark Twain, *Roughing It*

5.   The eagles soared southward, high above the Valle Grande. They were almost too high to be seen. From their vantage point, the land below reached away on either side to the long, crooked tributaries of the range. Down the great open corridor to the south were the wooded slopes and the canyon, the desert and the far end of the earth bending on the sky. They caught sight of the rabbits and were deflected. They veered and banked, lowering themselves into the crater, gathering speed. By the time he knew of their presence, they were low and coming fast on either side of the pit, swooping with blinding speed. The male caught hold of the air and fell off, touching

upon the face of the cliff in order to flush the rabbits, while the female hurtled in to take her prey on the run. Nothing happened;
the rabbits did not move. She overshot the trap and screamed. She
was enraged and she hurled herself around in the air. She swung back
with a great clamor of her wings and fell with fury on the bait. He
saw her in the instant she struck. . . . In that split second when the
center of her weight touched down upon the trap he reached for her.
His hands closed upon her legs and he drew her down with all of his
strength. For one instant only did she recoil, splashing her great
wings down upon the beams and boughs—and she very nearly broke
from his grasp; but then she was down in the darkness of the well,
hooded, and she was still.—N. Scott Momaday, *House Made of Dawn*

EXERCISE 2

Look at the *specific details* included in each of the following
snapshot descriptions.

MODEL 1: The office of the student newspaper was a grubby, ill-lit room full
of pencil stubs, shreds of paper, paste, ink, broken chairs, typewriter ribbons, and candy wrappers.

MODEL 2: In the old-fashioned pantry, the shelves were laid out with rows
of jelly glasses and brown jugs and white stone-china jars with
blue whirligigs and words painted on them: coffee, tea, sugar,
ginger, cinnamon, allspice.

MODEL 3: On the far side of the room, sitting at a table alone, a small,
curiously beetle-like man was drinking a cup of coffee, his little
eyes darting suspicious glances from side to side. (George Orwell)

Write similar snapshot descriptions of *five* of the following:

- an attic, basement, or garage;
- a workshop or lab;
- a government office;
- a stranger you saw at a bus station or in a waiting room or similar
place;
- a student in a cafeteria or customer at a fast-food restaurant;
- a vintage car;
- an unusual building in your community;
- unusual fish in an aquarium.

EXERCISE 3

Study the way the following student-written paragraph leads
up to the unifying *overall impression*. Write a similar details-first
paragraph in which the unifying impression is one of the following:
frustration, effort, enthusiasm, indecision, resentment, triumph,
apathy.

I had forgotten my chemistry book and returned reluctantly to my locker on the third floor. In the dark hall I could barely see which book I had picked up so I stepped into the bright patch of light from the biology lab office. Then I saw Miss Browne, her white lab coat soiled and wrinkled, making notes on the creased pages of her notebook. Her slight figure was bent over the desk, and her light, shining hair was pulled into a bun on top of her head. I could see her shiny white name pin hanging crooked, as usual, from her rolled lapel. The ash tray to the right of the microscope was stuffed with the stubby remains of her cigarettes. <u>She was the perfect picture of concentration.</u>

PROSE MODEL 1

Study the following prose model. How does it illustrate the features of good descriptive writing? In this passage, an experienced writer describes the subdivision in which she lives. Note how she gives life and movement to what could be a static scene. Rather than describe the subdivision already built up, she shows it in the *process* of being built. Can you show how her following of this process gives a clear, overall pattern to this piece of writing? (Your teacher may ask you to prepare a rough outline.)

Study the following passage, and be prepared to answer the questions that follow it.

LOIS PHILLIPS HUDSON

Springtime in the Rockies

For anybody who grew up on the prairie, it was and is a remarkable experience to watch three or four hundred acres of fields and pasture becoming city. During the springs of my childhood I roamed alone over a half section—about the acreage of our Table Mesa subdivision, which is now populated by about ten times as many people as there were in the town where I went to school three miles from our farm. That town once seemed to me to be bursting with people; I suppose it would look quite different to me now. One street was paved, because it was also U.S. Highway 10, and there were a few blocks of cement sidewalk. But cement was never part of my idea of a prairie spring.

Nevertheless, when I looked out of my picture window my first spring in Table Mesa, what I saw was cement—cement on the move. We lived in the last completed house on our loop, and what seemed like the biggest fleet of cement trucks in the world rumbled by us, headed for the bulldozed lots between us and the prairie. Our house is called the Metropolitan, which seems a significant appellation, the two other "big-value" models are called the Trojan and the Apollo, and the largest and most expensive is called, also significantly, the Americana. Day after day, sidewalks, basements, patios, foundations, and driveways rolled by in their emulsive state, revolving in oblong tubs over howling engines and shuddering transmissions. Behind the cement trucks came the steel girder trucks and the lumber trucks loaded with prefabricated walls and gables. Then came the roofing trucks, the plumbers' trucks, the painters' trucks, and Melvin the Landscaper's trucks. Hot on their exhaust fumes came the trucks from the businesses in the new Table Mesa Shopping Center—the wall-to-wall rug trucks and the floor-to-ceiling drapery trucks, from shops that are now out of business, theirs being a relatively short-lived boom, not unlike the booms of the gold and silver ghost towns all around us, with collapsing roads called Bonanza, El Dorado, or Wall Street.

No sooner had the first parade of shiny trucks of prosperous subcontractors begun to dwindle than a second parade began —a parade of independent small businessmen, in ten-year-old pickups, scarred and dented Volkswagen buses, and fenderless, paintless panel trucks. Our neighbors, I thought, looking out of my picture window, are now free of the subcontractors and they are shopping around. This second parade brought, and still brings, the touches with which my neighbors "individualize" their homes. For example, a panel truck parked in front of the Trojan two doors down from us, and when it left two hours later, that Trojan had a brilliant red front door. Across the street a pickup arrived with a ten-foot blue spruce rooted in about three hundred pounds of burlap-wrapped dirt. I had been watching the man of the house for three weekends while he dug a vast hole in the lawn he had worked on every weekend before that, and I had been waiting for the dénouement. The sinewy, undernourished nursery worker and the sweating, overnourished accountant dragged the tree across the lawn and managed to set it upright in the hole. There will be blue lights on it come Christmas, I thought. That will be the dénouement. All blue lights.

To the Americana on our northern side, trucks brought great loads of fill, topsoil, and fertilizer, all dumped in conical piles in the driveway. Then came boulders, bulldozers to move the boulders, and men to build and plant terraces, borders, walks, and patios. I watched to see if spotlights would be installed under the boulders, as they were at the house on the corner, but instead our neighbor chose a white plaster rabbit with two white babies, an orange deer, three white ducks with orange bills, and a little black jockey in white shirt and orange pants. The yard ornaments repeated the color scheme of the Americana, which is built of black bricks and white siding trimmed with orange shutters.

During our first spring in Table Mesa we endured the worst windstorms in the recorded meteorological history of Colorado. The first storm came the night after we moved into our new house and registered gusts of over a hundred miles an hour. One of these gusts demolished a nearly completed building behind us, and all night long, sizable pieces of the wreckage blew into our house. All the windows in the children's bedroom were shattered, spraying glass over both sleeping girls. Our eight-foot picture window and the sliding glass doors of our patio bowed in and out as though they were made of cellophane, and the reflected light of our candle undulated with the glass as though it shone over waves of water. The next morning we found that parts of our new roof had been torn away and some of our siding was ripped, revealing to our apprehensive gaze the fact that it was not wood, but a kind of extra-heavy cardboard painted to look like wood, that stood between us and the hurricane.

I left my picture window that first spring and went out to see if I could still find my idea of prairie spring. . . . One block west of our new house, the bulldozers were still digging basements. I could see the world being newly made or unmade. The next block was roughly graded and set with stakes that seemed, with the expanse of the prairie behind them, oddly and frighteningly close together, even though the stakes marked out lots the size of our own. We were circumscribing ourselves in tiny bits of the earth, while the whole earth still called to us from beyond our imaginary lines.—from *The Reporter*

**READING
QUESTIONS**

1. Explain briefly each of the following words: *appellation, emulsive, dénouement, conical, undulate, expanse, circumscribe.* What uses of the word *Americana* do you know?

2. Suppose that for each of the seven phrases listed in the left-hand column on the following page the author had substituted the more general expression that appears in the right-hand column. Explain briefly what is *missing* from the second version.

I *roamed* over	I *moved* around in
our *loop*	our *street*
collapsing roads	roads *in poor condition*
howling engines	*noisy* engines
shuddering transmissions	*trembling* transmissions
parade of shiny trucks	*traffic* made up of shiny trucks
sinewy, undernourished	*lean,* undernourished nursery worker
nursery worker	

3. Point out several uses of specific detail that help *individualize* something —that set it apart from other similar things.
4. In the first two paragraphs, the author uses the word *cement* six times. Can you explain why this word is a key word in the essay? When you look at the essay as a whole, what does cement symbolize? How does the use of the word reflect the attitude of the author toward what she describes?
5. Show how and where the author makes use of comparison and contrast.

WRITING TOPICS

1. Write a paragraph in which you describe something by showing it in the *process* of being produced. You might describe, for instance, a special kind of cabinet, an ingenious toy, or a new and unusual article of clothing.

2. Write about some sight that represents a way of life about to pass out of existence. Here are some examples:

   - a once splendid building about to be torn down or up for sale;
   - a passenger train now discontinued (or about to be);
   - a once-busy railroad station now deserted;
   - a formerly elegant resort;
   - a famous park, for example, that has seen better days;
   - a neighborhood about to be redeveloped;
   - a small fishing village that is changing rapidly.

3. Assume that you are exploring your own familiar neighborhood as the scout for a landing party coming from an entirely different culture. Write a report about the familiar sights as if you were seeing them for the first time. How, for instance, would you make sure that people who have never seen a gas station will recognize one if they see it?

4. Much has been written about the "American Scene." Some observers claim that Americans like what is gaudy and extravagant, as shown in the design of our cars, for instance. Others find the skylines of our big cities and the sweeping arcs of our freeways beautiful and exhilarating. Concentrate on one major area— big-city architecture, outdoor advertising, freeway design, or the like. Use graphic description to show what it looks like to *you*.

Write about your own experience.

When you complain that you have nothing to write about, the obvious answer is: "Write about yourself." Write about what you know best: your own background, interests, problems, the people and events that helped shape your personality. Such writing is autobiographical; it deals with the author's own life. In writing autobiography, you look back over your own experience.

As you work on autobiographical papers, remember:

(1) Be selective. In 400 or 500 words, you cannot write the story of your life. You can take on tasks like the following:

- tell in detail the story of one major incident that marked a stage in your growing up;
- trace two or three key events that changed your mind about a person close to you;
- deal with a major stage in the development of one of your beliefs or attitudes: your attitude toward the church in which you grew up, your knowledge of people from different backgrounds.

(2) Make the setting real for your reader. The writer of autobiography in effect turns to the reader and says: "Imagine yourself in my place in a little town in Ohio ten years ago." The reader's natural reaction is "How *can* I?" The answer is "I will help you by recreating the scene and the events as concretely as I can."

Can you show what the authors of the following passages have done to "take you there"? Point out the kind of detail that only someone who lived through the incidents described would know.

> On the way to school in late spring and early fall, we would crack open watermelons in the growers' fields and eat just the hearts out of them, arriving at school all stuck together down the front with pink mud. Or we would detour around by Johansen's loquat tree, dump out the plain bread-and-butter sandwiches from our lunch bags, and fill up the sacks with dead-ripe, honey-sweet fruit. We kept the hard-boiled egg, though.—Dolly Connelly, "Game's End," *Atlantic*

> As I go back to the block now the back wall of the drugstore still rises up to test me. Every day we smashed a small black viciously hard regulation handball against it with fanatical cuts and drives and slams, beating and slashing at it almost in hatred for the blind strength of the wall itself. I was never good enough at handball, was always practicing some trick shot that might earn me esteem, and when I was weary of trying, would often bat a ball down Chester Street just to get myself to Blake Avenue. I have this memory of playing one-o'-cat by myself in the sleepy twilight, at a moment when everyone else had

left the block. . . . I would throw the ball in the air, hit it with my bat, then with perfect satisfaction drop the bat to the ground and run to the next sewer cover. Over and over I did this, from sewer cover to sewer cover, until I had worked my way to Blake Avenue and could see the park.—Alfred Kazin, *A Walker in the City*

(3) Help your reader see and hear the people involved in your account. Show the reader how they look, what they do, how they talk. In the following passage, we are given a portrait of a business executive concerned about burglaries at the company office. In your own words, what kind of person do we see and hear? How real does the person become to the reader?

We had interviewed the president of the company, Mac Gluttman—"Mr. Mac"—on Tuesday of the week. He was a short, stocky man with a square, blunt head lined on each side with cropped white hair. He had deep creases from his nose to his mouth, which turned heavily downward, and his elegant, custom-made suit fitted his Brooklyn-made body to perfection, emphasizing the thick shoulders and barrel chest. "No crummy two-bit thief is gonna take me," he said, jamming his powerful thumb into his chest. When he spoke, an old-time venom took possession of his voice, and he seemed like some intruder—some roughneck—behind his shining, expensive long desk. "I know this type, I know this kind of bum, ya know." He leaned forward, shaking his head to advise us he was going to level with us—we would understand that he was no dumbhead. We were speaking to a self-made man who didn't get things handed to him on a platter; he was not to the shoe-business born. The hard way, that's how he got where he was.—Dorothy Uhnak, *Policewoman*

(4) Make your reader share in your feelings. Do not just *talk* about what you felt. Make what you felt grow out of the situation, or out of the actual incident you describe. Stress what you did that *showed* your emotions. We know people are angry if we see them act out their anger—by a frown, by cutting remarks, by the way they slam the door on the way out.

In the following passage, what feelings does the author want you to share? How does the author help you share these feelings?

The mirror . . . is very large; it is inlaid inside of a brown wood wall in the room of a brownstone house. Next to it the window pours down so strong a light that the rest of the room is not reflected in the mirror. The image of the girl who approaches it is brought into relief. Against a foggy darkness, the girl of fifteen stands with frightened eyes. She is looking at her dress, a dress of shiny worn blue serge, which was fixed up for her out of an old one belonging to a cousin. It does not fit her. It is meager. It looks poor. The girl is looking at the worn shiny dark-blue serge dress with shame. It is the day she has been told in school that she is gifted for writing. They had come purposely into the class to tell her. In spite of being a foreigner, in spite of having to use the dictionary, she had written the best essay in the class. She who was always quiet and who did not wish to be noticed, was told to come up the aisle and speak to the English teacher before everyone, to hear the compliment. And the joy, the dazzling joy which had first struck her was instantly killed by the awareness of the dress. I did not want to get up, to be noticed. I was ashamed of this meager dress with a shine on it, its worn air, its orphan air, its hand-me-down air.—Anaïs Nin, *The Diary of Anaïs Nin*

(5) Try to put into words what an experience meant to you. In autobiographical writing, we do not merely try to remember. We try to understand.

In the following passage, an American biographer tells about her aged parents. Each of them has come to represent something to her—a way of looking at things, an attitude toward life. Explain in your own words what she is saying about her parents.

To my father old age spelled tranquillity; he who had been the most active and ambitious of men sat quietly by his window rereading the books he loved best—*Treasure Island,* *Vanity Fair, The White Company, Moby Dick*—and he read them not for their philosophy or "symbolism" but for the story pure and simple. "Have you read *Captain Fracasse* lately?" he would ask me gravely. "It is delicious. Let me just read you this page, where Agostino sets up the scarecrows in the field. . . . Can you sit down, have you time?"

His absorption and his pleasure in *Aztec Treasure Houses* and *Quentin Durward* irritated my mother, whose years only increased her native intensity, her relish for each small domestic detail of living. Her husband's withdrawal I believe she looked on as something slightly immoral. Once a year my mother's sister (herself in her early eighties) came from New York to spend a week with us. My mother contrived to make the day of arrival a turmoil such as only visiting queens can look for. Every car that passed our door was Aunt Cecilia's car. I remember one such day when my mother refused her much relished five o'clock cup of tea because the act of setting down the cup would slow her welcoming rush to the front door. My father who for days had been the victim of this mounting excitement of preparation, raised both arms to me across the room and waggled his fingers, smiling resignedly.

For me there was continual fascination in observing these two as they walked slowly toward their end, the one quieter, ever more remote, the other possessed of a kind of ferocious joy—or grief—in each passing moment as though she must savor it wholly, wholly, for it would not come again.—Catherine Drinker Bowen, "The Magnificence of Age," *Harper's*

Composition

Much autobiographical writing deals with the problems and obstacles someone encountered. But often the high point of an autobiographical narrative is some memorable achievement or experience of success. Study the following student-written example. How real does the author make the situation, the people involved, and his own feelings? Point out several things that make the author's account ring true.

Success Story

When I was in the seventh grade, I set a goal to become a varsity basketball player. For me, that was like wishing for peace in the world. In the seventh grade I was a terrible athlete. I was on the Junior High teams, but I played most of the games from the bench. I soon became discouraged; however, I was also angry. I wanted to prove that I could be as good a player as the others. Each summer I would practice hard. All this practice finally paid off my senior year, in the first game of the season.

I watched the ball as it arched through the air and dropped with a "swish" through the net. "Way to hit, man," yelled one of our guards. My uniform stuck to me like skin. It was the fourth quarter and my legs felt as if I was running through deep mud with heavy boots on. My arms throbbed from holding our opponents on defense. I had been in the game since the beginning.

The coach noticed me slowing down so he called a time out. There were three minutes left on the score board and we were up by two points. The coach's lips trembled as he stuttered, "Do you a-a think you can go a little longer?"

I looked at the coach's face. There was a bead of sweat dripping from his sideburns. His usually well-groomed black hair was tossed all around. The coach's brown eyes met with mine. Normally they seemed to look cold and angry. Now they appeared excited and wishful. I had always had the impression that he didn't like me. As I finally caught my breath, I replied, "Yea, I'll be okay."

My answer brought a little smile to the coach's face. "Good! Good!" he replied.

When the teams walked back on the court, the gym vibrated from the fans yelling and stomping. "Go, Trojans Go!" chanted the pep block. I had always dreamed of playing on the varsity. It was at this moment when I first realized I had reached my goal.

In the final three minutes of the game, we went on to win. But before it ended, something happened I'll never forget. The coach took me out with twenty seconds left. As I walked towards the bench, I stole a glance at the crowd; they were on their feet applauding. It was a standing ovation! I felt a lump gather in my throat as I continued walking. I then looked over to my coach, as he walked up to me with a smile from ear to ear. He gave me a bear hug that about made me faint. I hadn't even shaken hands with him before. This was the first time I had even been that close to him. But now I could see the trace of a tear in his eyes as he spoke: "You played a good game."

I will never forget those words and the way he threw his arms around me. It was his first year as a varsity coach and his first victory. We were not expecting to win.—Dean Cervenka

Your Turn: Write about a high point or memorable challenge in your own experience.

We do not always feel simple love or simple hate. A person we really like may at times make us very angry. A person we admire may do something that we condemn. Study the following student-written paper. Describe the writer's *mixed feelings* about his grandfather. (How do you think you would have felt?)

EXERCISE 2

My Grandfather

My grandfather was to me an example of a person who was both frightening and pitiful. He lived with us after my grandmother died. He lived with us for about nine years; then he died.

My grandfather was a frightening person to me, and he was a frightening person to my brother. Even my father sometimes seemed afraid of him. Mostly we became frightened on those times when Grandfather lost his temper. This happened quite often. Once he got mad at my father because my father forgot to bring him some chewing tobacco from the drugstore. He swore at him and cussed right in front of my mother. Another time he slapped my brother for nothing at all, for just spilling some vinegar on his shirt. Even if my grandfather wasn't losing his temper, he was always nasty and threatening to somebody. He threatened to shoot our neighbors'

dog if it didn't stay out of our yard. He wrote a
letter to my brother's math teacher and said he
would see that he got fired if my brother flunked.
He swore at the mailman one day when his social
security check did not come on time.

Even though my grandfather was a frightening
person, our family and relatives could not help but
pity him at times. He was very old, about 80, and
he had arthritis. He had nothing to do all day. He
had no place to go and no friends to visit or to visit
him. He must have been lonely most of the time. He
just seemed to live in the past. The only time I
can remember him enjoying himself was when he would
tell stories about when he had a farm back in
Wisconsin.

We felt both fear and pity for Grandfather, but
there was nothing we could do about it. Nobody cried
when he died.

Your Turn: Choose a person about whom you have mixed
feelings. Choose someone from real life, from history, or from your
reading. Write about the person.

EXERCISE 3

A German proverb says, "The unhoped-for often happens."
Write about an event (or a series of closely related events) where
things went contrary to expectation. For instance, you might write
about

- a childhood prank that turned serious;
- a project that turned out in an unexpected way;
- a holiday that departed from tradition;
- a competition that took an unexpected turn.

Write about something that happened to *you,* or something in
which you played a major part. Make a special effort to make the
scene and the events real for your reader.

PROSE MODEL 2

The author of the following excerpt is the American-born
daughter of immigrants from China. She says of herself, "From
infancy to my sixteenth year, I was reared according to nineteenth-
century ideals of Chinese womanhood." But like many other children

of immigrants, she eventually began to chart her own course between the traditional standards of her parents and the ways and ideals of her American environment. She began to ask: "Did a daughter have a right to expect more than a fate of obedience?" The following incident is a high point in her attempts to assert her independence.

Study the passage, and answer the questions that follow it.

JADE SNOW WONG

I Rebel Against Tradition

One afternoon on a Saturday, which was normally occupied with my housework job, I was unexpectedly released by my employer, who was departing for a country weekend. It was a rare joy to have free time, and I wanted to enjoy myself for a change. There had been a Chinese-American boy who shared some classes with me. Sometimes we had found each other walking to the same 8:00 A.M. class. He was not a special boy-friend, but I had enjoyed talking to him and had confided in him some of my problems. Impulsively, I telephoned him. I knew I must be breaking rules, and I felt shy and scared. At the same time, I was excited at this newly found forwardness, with nothing more purposeful than to suggest another walk together.

He understood my awkwardness and shared my anticipation. He asked me to "dress up" for my first movie date. My clothes were limited, but I changed to look more graceful in silk stockings and found a bright ribbon for my long black hair. Daddy watched, catching my mood, observing the dashing preparations. He asked me where I was going without his permission and with whom.

I refused to answer him. I thought of my rights! I thought he surely would not try to understand. Thereupon Daddy thundered his displeasure and forbade my departure.

I found a new courage as I heard my voice announce calmly that I was no longer a child, and if I could work my way through college, I would choose my own friends. It was my right as a person.

My mother heard the commotion and joined my father to face me; both appeared shocked and incredulous. Daddy at once demanded the source of this unfilial, non-Chinese theory. And when I quoted my college professor, reminding him that he had always felt teachers should be revered, my father denounced that professor as a foreigner who was disregarding the superiority of our Chinese culture, with its sound family strength. . . . My father did not spare me; I was condemned as an ingrate for echoing dishonorable opinions which should only be temporary whims, yet nonetheless inexcusable.

The scene was not yet over. I completed my proclamation to my father, who had never allowed me to learn how to dance, by adding that I was attending a movie with a boy I had met at college, unchaperoned.

My startled father was sure that my reputation would be subject to whispered innuendos. I must be bent on disgracing the family name. I was ruining my entire future. My mother underscored him by saying that I hadn't any notion of the problems endured by parents of a young girl.

I would not give in. I reminded them that they and I were not in China, that I wasn't going out with just anybody but someone I trusted! Daddy gave a roar that no man could be trusted, but I devastated them in declaring that I wished the freedom to find my own answers.

Both parents were thoroughly angered, scolded me for being shameless, and predicted that I would some day tell them I was wrong. But I dimly perceived that they were conceding defeat and were perplexed at this breakdown of their training. I was too old to beat and too bold to intimidate.—from "Puritans of the Orient," in Thomas C. Wheeler, ed., *The Immigrant Experience*

READING QUESTIONS

1. Define or explain briefly each of the following words: *confide, commotion, incredulous, unfilial, revered, ingrate, proclamation, innuendo.*
2. From what the author tells us about herself at the beginning, what picture do we form of her? Do a brief capsule portrait of the heroine of this account.
3. Do you understand or recognize the parents' point of view? How similar or how different is it compared with what you might expect in some other ethnic group? Explain the parents' side in the argument.
4. Often we express in words only part of what we feel. In this story, both the girl and her parents have some private thoughts and feelings that they do not verbalize during their encounter. What are they?
5. The idea we form of authority, and our attitude toward it, are an important part of our outlook. Coming to terms with authority is often a major challenge or problem in a person's growing up. Write a paragraph about "authority" as you have known it in your own experience.

WRITING TOPICS

1. The author of "I Rebel Against Tradition" wrote the following passage about her *early education* and its overall direction or purpose. Do you remember things that you were taught early in

your life? Was there a strong overall direction or purpose in what you were taught? Tell the story of your early training or education. Like the author of this excerpt, did you later rebel against the traditions of home?

> Very early in my life, the manners of a Chinese lady were taught to me: How to hold a pair of chopsticks (palm up, not down); how to hold a bowl of rice (one thumb on top, not resting in an open palm); how to pass something to elders (with both hands, never one); how to pour tea into the tiny, handleless porcelain cups (seven-eighths full so that the top edge would be cool enough to hold); how to eat from a center serving dish (only the piece in front of your place; never pick around); not to talk at table, not to show up outside of one's room without being fully dressed; not to be late, ever; not to be too playful. In a hundred and one ways, we were molded to be trouble-free, unobtrusive, quiescent, cooperative.

2. Margaret Mead said that there is "great contrast in the lives of the majority of Americans between the pattern of human relationships which they learn at home and the pattern they learn at school and out in the world. In many cases this contrast is a contrast between cultures, between homeways which are Polish or Italian or Irish, or at least stem from a completely different part of the United States, and school and outer-world ways which represent the more standard American culture." Does this contrast between homeways and outer-world ways still exist? Did you, or someone you know well or care about, experience any such contrast in upbringing? Or were the ways of home and those of school very similar? Tell your story.

3. What does it feel like to be different? Were you, or someone you know well or care about, ever an *outsider* in a group? Or, were you ever part of a group that kept someone out or treated others as outsiders? Tell your story. Discuss the possible reasons *why* a group treats others as outsiders.

Make your writing show that you have thought about your subject.

C4

WRITING AND THINKING

Sometimes people ask us simply for our ready-made opinion. They want to know where we stand on an issue. But when they read something we have written, they really expect *more*. They want to learn something from what we say. They want us to take a serious look at the evidence, and they want us to come up with some carefully considered conclusions.

C4a
Generalization

Formulate careful generalizations and support them effectively.

When we generalize, we go from the particular event or the individual person to the larger picture. We look at something that happens and say: "This is part of a *general pattern.*" The following are examples of the generalizations we encounter when we study a writer's work:

• An early traveler to the United States reports that many educational opportunities are open to American women and that they are free "to go out of the home to agitate for temperance, antislavery, and other reforms."

• An English writer, criticizing his country, writes that in England military leaders are more admired than scientists or poets.

• An American playwright says in a magazine article that the cowboy in American Westerns does not stand for the actual historical past but for what people *want* to believe the past was like.

Each of these statements represents a generalization that someone has produced by *totaling* up many individual observations.

The kind of thinking that produces generalizations from individual observations is standard procedure not only for the writer but also the scientist, the market research specialist, and many another expert. Here, for instance, are observations that a zoologist might have collected concerning the migrations of fish. When these observations are put together, they add up to a general pattern:

Ⓑ The shad go up the Chesapeake.

Ⓒ The alewives go up coastal streams in New England.

Ⓐ The Chinooks go up the Columbia.

Ⓓ The salmon go up the Penobscot and the Kennebec.

GENERALIZATION: In the spring, migrating fish leave the sea in order to ascend the great rivers.

In writing, we usually present the *result* first. We usually give the sum first—and then show what we have added up. We write as if the reader had said to us: "Tell me first how it *comes out.* You can tell me later how you *arrived* there." Here is a paragraph that follows the familiar pattern of "generalization first":

(Generalization)   *In the spring the sea is filled with migrating fishes, some of them bound for the mouths of great rivers, which they will ascend to deposit their spawn. Such are the*

(Observation A)	spring-run chinooks coming in from the deep Pacific feeding grounds to breast the rolling flood of the Colum-
(Observation B)	bia, the shad moving in to the Chesapeake and the Hudson and the Connecticut, the alewives seeking a hundred
(Observation C)	coastal streams of New England, the salmon feeling their
(Observation D)	way to the Penobscot and the Kennebec. For months or

years these fish have known only the vast spaces of the ocean. Now the spring sea and the maturing of their own bodies lead them back to the rivers of their birth.—Rachel Carson, *The Sea Around Us*

An honest generalization grows out of a whole set of such related observations. Do the following to help make your generalizations convincing to your readers:

(1) Limit your generalizations. Many generalizations go too far too fast. Few generalizations are really true of *all* Americans, *all* teenagers, or *everyone* in business. The less we know about Puerto Ricans, or Britishers, or Swedes, the more tempted we are to make sweeping generalizations about all of them. The more we find out about a group, the more aware we become of important differences that set its members apart.

Because each of the following statements includes one or more sweeping generalizations, each would make a skeptical reader say, "Not so fast!" Can you think of exceptions that would make you restate the generalization more cautiously?

SWEEPING: Teenagers today become aware of adult problems sooner than they used to. In the leisurely world of our grandparents, children were allowed to remain children for a few years longer than is the case today.

SWEEPING: The average American is unwilling to assume responsibility for the state of the rest of the world. While news commentators discuss famine or civil war abroad, the average American thinks about what type of fall suit to buy or speculates about the outcome of next Saturday's football game.

SWEEPING: The typical hero of the modern novel, story, or play is a drunk, a dope addict, or a sex fiend. He suffers from one or many neuroses and has a persecution complex and an overprotective mother. He is, in fact, a type of antihero.

(2) Support your generalizations. Good generalizations are the end result of many individual observations. Support your generalizations with those specific observations most likely to strike your reader as authentic, relevant, and important.

Here are typical kinds of supporting material for the generalizations that you might present to your reader:

GENERAL IDEA: Nobody is perfect.

SPECIFIC APPLICATION: That's why the pencil manufacturer equips pencils with erasers.

GENERAL IDEA: There is no point in inflicting harsh punishment on adolescents who have been subjected to irrational violence all their lives.

CASE HISTORY: The judge's voice boomed through the courtroom as he said, "I'm going to put you on probation in the custody of your parents. But I'll tell you this—if any boy of mine ever got caught smoking marijuana in the school washroom, I'd flog the hide off him with a horsewhip." The boy before the judge slowly rolled up the sleeve of his shirt. On his upper arm was a cluster of livid welts and blue-black bruises. "There's more of the same," the boy said, "on my back and shoulders, Judge. My old man's been doing just what you said twice a week for the last five years."

GENERAL IDEA: In America, pleasure and entertainment are big business.

STATISTICAL EVIDENCE: Leaders of our entertainment industry are the best paid men and women in the United States. Last year, the American people spent around thirty billion dollars for alcoholic beverages, theater and movie tickets, tobacco, cosmetics, and jewelry. We spend as much for moving pictures as for churches, more for beauty shops than for social service.

GENERAL IDEA: We are too afraid to rely on ourselves as our own authorities.

SUPPORTING ANECDOTE: There is a story about Thomas Hardy using the word "smalling" while writing something and then wondering whether there was any literary warrant for the word. So he went to the big Oxford dictionary and found that one well-known writer had used it previously: Thomas Hardy.

(3) Beware of repeating ready-made generalizations at second hand. The following statements are the kind that will make readers say: "I have heard this before. Have you really checked this general idea against your own experience and observation?" How would the following familiar-sounding statements stand up if you were to check them against your own experience?

- Money cannot buy happiness. The harried business executive who thinks only in financial terms is not a happy person.
- Americans would rather watch a game than play a game.
- Americans are passionately dedicated to the cause of freedom.
- People who want freedom must first shoulder responsibility.

The following statements are all generalizations in need of support. Which could you support? What would your evidence be? Which
would you find *hard* to support? Why?

1. Democracy is a mixture of majority rule and minority right.
2. Some American humane societies are currently accusing those con-
nected with rodeos of being cruel and inhuman to the animals. But these
critics have apparently not studied the sport very closely. Rodeoing is
a humane sport. The animals are well treated, with every effort made
to ensure their health and safety.
3. The term *progress* in the twentieth century has extremely mechanistic
connotations. We build new and better machines to further "progress."
4. The progress of society has never included progress toward tenderness
and compassion for the suffering and the distressed.
5. Hitchhiking is very popular with young people, but it is much more dangerous than most of them think.
6. Emigration has a bad effect on the society that is losing people this way.
It is usually the young, the ambitious, or the energetic who migrate.
7. For the great majority of workers, the work itself is disagreeable or
meaningless and the only meaning of the job is in the paycheck.
8. Women are increasingly found in jobs that used to be limited to men.
9. The American television audience seems to have an unlimited appetite
for brutal violence on the screen.
10. Many books most popular with the general reader are nonfiction.

Everybody is an individual. But when we watch people talk and
act, some general patterns do take shape. How good a judge are you
of the wishes and standards shared by many of the people around
you? Prepare an imaginary portrait of one of the following:

- the candidate the typical American voter would trust;
- the man (woman) the typical American girl (boy) wants to marry;
- the ideal minister for the typical American congregation;
- the woman most likely to succeed in American business or politics;
- the rising young actress or actor most likely to become the new favorite of the American television audience.

Read the following prose models as a forum on the ethnic identity of Americans. Look at the way the authors generalize about the
American past, "Americanism," and American values. Which of the
generalizations seem familiar or even obvious to you? Which seem
strange or doubtful? Which of these generalizations would you be
able to check against your own experience? (Answer the questions
that follow the three selections.)

PETER SCHRAG

The Decline of the Wasp

For most of of us who were born before World War II, America was a place to be discovered: it was imperfect, perhaps—needed some reform, some shaping up—but it did not need to be re-invented. It was all given, like a genetic code, waiting to unfold. We all wanted to learn the style, the proper accent, agreed on its validity, and while our interpretations and our heroes varied, they were all cut from the same stock. Cowboys, pioneers, athletes, entrepreneurs, men of letters: whatever we were of-fered we took pretty much as our own. Whether we were small-town boys or the children of urban immigrants, we shared an eagerness to become apprentices in the great open democracy, were ready to join up, wanting only to be accepted according to the terms that history and tradition had already established. It never occurred to us to think otherwise.

What held that world together was not just a belief in some standardized version of textbook Americanism, a catalogue of accepted values, but a particular class of people and institutions that we identified with our vision of the country. The people were white and Protestant: the institutions were English: Amer-ican culture was WASP. We paid lip service to the melting pot, but if, for instance, one's grandmother asked, "Is it good for the Jews?" there wasn't any question in her mind about who was running the country. The critics, the novelists, the poets, the social theorists, the men who articulated and analyzed American ideas, who governed our institutions, who embodied what we were or hoped to be—nearly all of them were WASPs: Hemingway, Fitzgerald, Eliot, MacLeish, Sandburg, Lewis, Steinbeck, Dewey, Santayana, the Jameses, Beard, Parrington, Edmund Wilson, Van Wyck Brooks, Lester Frank Ward, Oliver Wendell Holmes; *The Saturday Evening Post* under George Horace Lorimer (with covers by Norman Rockwell); *The Atlantic* under Edward Weeks; *Harper's* in the days of Frederick Lewis Allen—to name only a few, and only from the twentieth cen-tury. Of all the major figures discussed by Henry Steele Com-mager in *The American Mind,* not one is a Jew, a Catholic, or a Negro. The American mind was the WASP mind.

We grew up with them, they surrounded us: they were the heroes of the history we studied and the fantasy life we sought in those Monday-through-Friday radio serials. Even Hollywood, after all the creation of Jewish producers, never did much for pluralism. The stars were often ethnics—show business and sports constituting two major avenues for "outsiders" to make it into the mainstream—but their names and the roles they played rarely, if ever, acknowledged the existence of anything beyond that mainstream. The Hyman Kaplans were lovable jerks. Rochester said, "Yassuh, Mr. Benny" (did we realize that Benny was a Jew?) and anything beginning with Mike, Pat, or Abie was set up for a laugh. Hollywood's Jews sold the American dream strictly in WASP terms.

They—the WASPs—never thought of themselves as anything but Americans, nor did it occur to others to label them as anything special until, about twenty-five years ago their influence began to decline and they started to lose their cultural initiative and preeminence. There were, to be sure, regional distinctions, but whatever was "American" was WASP. Indeed, there was no "other"—was, that is, no domestic base of social commentary, no voice except their voice, for the discussion of "American" problems. The ethnics had their place and their strong loyalties, but insofar as that place was *American* it was defined by WASPs. We could distinguish Jews, Irishmen, Italians, Catholics, Poles, Negroes, Indians, Mexican-Americans, Japanese-Americans, but not WASPs. When WASPs were alienated it was because, as in the case of Henry Adams, the country had moved away from them, not because, as with the others, they regarded themselves as alien in heritage or tradition. (Southerners who had lost their war were—in that respect—alien, ethnically WASPs but also in some sense unwilling immigrants; they were among the first to be out of place in their own country.) For most WASPs, their complaints were proprietary. That is, the old place was going down because the tenants weren't keeping it up properly. They were the landlords of our culture, and their values, with rare exceptions, were those that defined it: hard work, perseverance, self-reliance, puritanism, the missionary spirit, and the rule of law.—*Harper's*

MICHAEL NOVAK

The Immigrant's America

All four of my grandparents, unknown to one another, arrived in America from the same county in Slovakia. My grandfather had a small farm in Pennsylvania; his wife died in a wagon accident. Meanwhile, a girl of fifteen arrived on Ellis Island, dizzy, a little ill from witnessing births and deaths and illnesses aboard the crowded ship, with a sign around her neck lettered "PASSAIC." There an aunt told her of the man who had lost his wife in Pennsylvania. She went. They were married. Inheriting his three children, each year for five years she had one of her own. She was among the lucky; only one died. When she was twenty-two, mother of seven, her husband died. And she resumed the work she had begun in Slovakia at the town home of a man known to us now only as "the Professor": she housecleaned and she laundered.

I heard this story only weeks ago. Strange that I had not asked insistently before. Odd that I should have such shallow knowledge of my roots. Amazing to me that I do not know what my family suffered, endured, learned, hoped these past six or seven generations. It is as if there were no project on which we all have been involved. As if history, in some way, began with my father and with me.

Let me hasten to add that the estrangement I have come to feel derives not only from a lack of family history. All my life, I have been made to feel a slight uneasiness when I must say my name. Under challenge in grammar school concerning my nationality, I had been instructed by my father to announce proudly: "American." When my family moved from the Slovak ghetto of Johnstown to the WASP suburb on the hill, my mother impressed upon us how well we must be dressed, and show good manners, and behave—people think of us as "different" and we mustn't give them any cause. "Whatever you do, marry a Slovak girl," was other advice to a similar end: "They cook. They clean. They take good care of you. For your own good."

When it was revealed to me that most movie stars and many other professionals had abandoned European names in order to feed American fantasies, I felt only a little sadness. One of my uncles, for business reasons and rather late in life, changed his name too, to a simple German variant. Not long, either, after World War II.

Nowhere in my schooling do I recall an attempt to put me in touch with my own history. The strategy was clearly to make an American of me. English literature, American literature; and even the history books, as I recall them, were peopled mainly by Anglo-Saxons from Boston (where most historians seemed to live). Not even my native Pennsylvania, let alone my Slovak forebears, counted for very many paragraphs. I don't remember feeling envy or regret: a feeling, perhaps, of unimportance, of remoteness, of not having heft enough to count.—*The Rise of the Unmeltable Ethnics*

JAMES BALDWIN

The Ancestral Homeland

At the time that I was growing up, Negroes in this country were taught to be ashamed of Africa. They were taught it bluntly, as I was, for example, by being told that Africa had never contributed "anything" to civilization. Or one was taught the same lesson more obliquely, and even more effectively, by watching nearly naked, dancing, comic-opera, cannibalistic savages in the movies. They were nearly always all bad, sometimes funny, sometimes both. If one of them was good, his goodness was proved by his loyalty to the white man. A baffling sort of goodness, particularly as one's father, who certainly wanted one to be "good," was more than likely to come home cursing—cursing the white man. . . .

But none of this is so for those who are young now. The power of the white world to control their identities was crumbling as they were born; and by the time they were able to react to the world, Africa was on the stage of history. This could not but have an extraordinary effect on their own morale, for it meant that they were not merely the descendants of slaves in a white, Protestant, and puritan country: they were also related to kings and princes in an ancestral homeland, far away. And this has proved to be a great antidote to the poison of self-hatred.—"East River, Downtown," *Nobody Knows My Name*

READING QUESTIONS

1. Explain or define briefly each of the following: (Schrag) *genetic code, entrepreneurs, social theorist, articulated, preeminence, proprietary;* (Novak) *insistently, estrangement, variant, forebears, remoteness, heft;* (Baldwin) *oblique, cannibalistic, baffling, morale, ancestral, antidote.*
2. What do each of the following terms mean to you? What ideas or association do they bring to mind? What are their connotations? Where or how do people encounter them? Who uses them?
   melting pot, Americanism, heritage, ethnic, mainstream, pluralism.
3. Which of the three authors stays closest to his own personal experience? For each author, point out one or more examples of writing close to firsthand personal experience. Then, for each author, point out one or more examples of large generalizations, stated or implied.
4. Select one or more generalizations that you are best equipped to test against *your* personal experience. Show how your own experience or observation would make you support or challenge the author's generalization.

5. Marya Mannes once said: "I remember the photograph albums so many families kept when I was a child. There, in our own, were these strange faces and strange clothes of the dead who preceded me: the tall, gaunt old baker in Poland, the opera singer in Germany, the immigrant furniture dealer in New York, the violinist in Breslau, the General near Kiel. . . ."

What kind of ancestor would have appeared in your own family album? Do a "portrait-in-words" of the person as you imagine him or her to have been.

WRITING TOPICS

1. Peter Schrag includes the following among the values that have helped shape American culture: hard work, perseverance, self-reliance, puritanism, the missionary spirit, and the rule of law. Choose *one* of these. Write about its role in American life as you know it today. What role does it play in people's lives? How strong is its influence?

2. An actor who had starred in many Hollywood Westerns once said: "I think Westerns have fed the public a false concept of the West. Kids around the world are growing up thinking one man will always ride into town to fight their battles while the rest of the community sits on its collective hands. In many of the television shows and Western movies, the hero is a kind of father-figure who fights alone for justice against the entire community." What general idea of "justice" would a viewer derive from current Western movies and television shows? Or, what general ideas about "crime" would a viewer derive from crime movies and shows? Use detailed examples.

3. Arthur Miller once said, "Any people have a conventional idea of what they are like. Americans fancy themselves, for instance, to be open-handed, on the side of justice, a little bit careless about what they buy, wasteful, but essentially good guys, optimistic." In your experience, what is the trait that Americans most often claim for themselves? Use evidence from speeches you have heard, editorials you have read, conversations you have participated in, and the like.

4. About the national symbols of England, E. M. Forster once said that "the national figure of England is Mr. Bull with his top hat, his comfortable clothes, his substantial stomach, and his substantial balance at the bank. Saint George may caper on banners and in the speeches of politicians, but it is John Bull who delivers the goods." Discuss two or three national symbols that reveal different aspects of *American* life.

Give exact meaning to key terms by careful definition.

It is hard for us to think clearly when our words are confused. Before we can think seriously about a subject, we may have to pin down what we mean by the words we use. We often have to make sure our key terms carry the right message. One way to make sure is to *define* our terms.

Definition sets limits. It maps out the territory a word covers. Here are some of the kinds of words that need definition:

NEW OR UNFAMILIAR TERMS: The most obvious examples of new or unfamiliar terms are words that the author has borrowed from another language:

> Some of the intensely close feeling a Mexican Indian child has for its mother is traceable to the omnipresent *rebozo, an oversized, hand-woven stole* that the mother is seldom without. The infant, carried about on her back in *that snug improvised hammock,* is always close to the warmth of the mother's body, and it remains close to her emotionally the rest of her life.

TECHNICAL TERMS: These serve as convenient labels but often need to be made clear to the nonexpert. For instance, an article on conservation of our natural resources may distinguish between "extractable resources"—coal, gas, oil—and "renewable resources"—soil, water, grass, timber, air.

RELATIVE TERMS: Words like *hot* and *cold* cover a whole range of meaning. To limit them to something specific, we need to fix a point on a scale. Watch out for words that raise questions of degree: When does "discipline" stop and "permissiveness" begin? When does a "careless" driver become "reckless"?

VAGUE TERMS: Some of the most important words in our lives mean different things to different people: *democratic, liberal, romantic, responsible.* What does the word *liberal* mean to the person speaking in the following excerpt from an interview? Does the word have other more familiar or more usual meanings?

> Our forefathers had the vision to set up a form of government—a constitution, a Bill of Rights—that gave us guidelines and an atmosphere that is extremely liberal. I don't mean "liberal" in the usual political sense; I mean the idealism that has given us room to grow. . . . Our forefathers deliberately got together and shaped the kind of government men dream of; they made it out of their own dreams.—"A Visit with Pearl Buck," *National Wildlife Magazine*

As you work up a definition of an important term, remember the advice given on the following page:

(1) Relate the word to the thing. An experienced writer shows us a word in action—shows us where, when, and to what it is applied. Do you agree that in each of the following passages the author quickly reaches the territory that the key term covers?

> Part of the educational program of the high school is carried on outside classrooms, in *"extracurricular"* activities—stamp, chess, art, French, math, Future Farmers, Future Teachers and similar clubs; student government activities and student publications; the school orchestra and band and glee club and Little Players, which give public performances; athletic teams and so forth.—Martin Mayer, *The Schools*

> To most Americans, *conservation* is the attempt to preserve parks and open spaces, so that people living in an industrial society can keep in contact with nature. The more crowded our cities, the more cluttered our roadsides, the more choking and eye smarting the air, the more we need grass and trees, birds, running streams, and quiet woods.

(2) Look for the common denominator. Once you have collected authentic examples of a word in action, you can ask: "What do these different instances have in common?" Suppose you and your classmates have collected the following list of things that help make a society "democratic":

- people choose their own rulers;
- people can associate without barriers of class or status;
- the government pays attention to public opinion;
- individuals choose their own jobs or careers;
- artists can be creative without fear of censorship;
- one person has the same rights or the same opportunities as another;
- newspapers do not take orders from higher authority;
- people can travel when and where they choose.

What do the different items on this list have in common? In all or most of these, the emphasis is on what individuals can and should do. The emphasis is on the potential of ordinary people. In many definitions of *democracy,* this common element plays the central role:

> The basis of the Athenian democracy was the conviction of all democracies—that average people can be depended upon to do their duty and to use good sense in doing it. *Trust the individual* was the avowed doctrine in Athens, and expressed or unexpressed, was common to Greece. (Edith Hamilton)

(3) Try to sum up clearly and exactly what you have found. A **formal definition** makes the writer sum up in one brief, exact statement the meaning of a key term. It thus makes the writer pull together what he or she has discovered.

A formal definition first places the term in a class, or *general category*. It thus tells us what kind of thing we are defining. It then narrows the choices by giving us the *distinctive features* of what we are defining. It thus sets it apart from other things of the same kind. A chipmunk is a type of squirrel (general category) that is smaller than most squirrels and has stripes down its back (distinctive features).

Here are some additional examples:

TERM	CLASS	FEATURES
History	is a recital in chronological order of events (so is a novel)	known to have occurred. (but now fiction is ruled out)
A paradox	is a statement that seems at first glance self-contradictory. (so is much mere nonsense)	but that is then found to express a truth. (now nonsense is excluded)
Democracy	is a form of government (so is a dictatorship)	in which major decisions are made by elected representatives of the people. (authoritarian governments are ruled out)

(4) Make your definition clear and convincing with supporting material. An **extended definition** brings in the examples that show what the definition means in practice. It supplies background. It clears up possible misunderstandings or confusions. Here are typical kinds of material that help us develop an extended definition of an important term:

HISTORICAL BACKGROUND:

In its primary historical significance, *democracy* refers to a form of government and only to government. A government is democratic to the extent that those who are affected by its decisions—leaving aside children—have a share, direct or more often indirect, through election of its agents or representatives, in determining the nature of the decisions. (Sidney Hook)

KEY EXAMPLE:

> Galileo hypothesized an experiment which proved that a marble rolling down one slope and then up another could never reach a point higher than its original elevation. Under ideal conditions, Galileo showed, however, that the marble would reach a height equal to its original elevation. This is what we now think of as *conservation of energy* in its simplest form. The energy of position which the marble possesses—because of its elevation—is transformed into energy of motion as it rolls down, and then back to energy of position as the marble rolls up the opposite slope. (Sir George Thompson)

CONTRAST WITH RELATED TERMS:

> *Sentimentality* is the evocation of a greater amount of feeling or emotion than is justified by the subject. It must not be confused with *sentiment*, which is merely another name for feeling or emotion, and which lacks the bad connotations of *sentimentality*. Some students confuse these two nouns because the adjective *sentimental* seems to be derived from both. *Sentimental* goes with *sentimentality*, not with *sentiment*. The poet who adopts a sentimental tone becomes more tearful or more ecstatic over the subject than it deserves. The sentimentalist is addicted to worn-out baby shoes, gray-haired mothers, and small animals—subjects certain to evoke an automatic response in a particular kind of reader. (College textbook)

EXERCISE 1

Write a brief informal definition for each italicized word in the following passages. Give a capsule definition to help the reader who asks: "What does this word stand for?"

1. The many clubs that form part of the extracurricular activities in high school are essentially *middle class;* they mirror typical features of the community's culture.
2. The truth is rarely pretty, though often *beautiful.*
3. Following directions of the board, the principal insisted on *conservative* dress for high school students.
4. Much literature of the Middle Ages shows people in the grip of *superstition.*
5. Modern life requires a certain amount of *regimentation.*
6. New Orleans is a very *romantic* city.
7. She always gave everyone very *sarcastic* answers.
8. Though my uncle was always friendly to people, he had become very *cynical* about human nature.
9. A person going into social work has to have a true *commitment* to helping people.
10. Censorship is a familiar feature of *totalitarian* societies.

List all the examples that come to mind when you think about the following terms. Do all the examples point in the same direction? Or are there two or three major directions? What would be a possible common denominator for each term?

EXERCISE 2

1. modern
2. bad taste
3. prejudice
4. narrow-mindedness
5. manners

Write a formal definition for *five* of the following terms.

EXERCISE 3

EXAMPLE: censor
(Answer) *A censor is an official who reads communications and deletes forbidden material.*

1. hymn   6. sauna
2. science   7. gerrymander
3. mystic   8. soap opera
4. decathlon   9. addiction
5. parole   10. optimism

Write a *two-paragraph* theme in which you define two contrasting terms. Write one paragraph about each member of the pair. Choose one of the following pairs:

EXERCISE 4

1. discipline and permissiveness
2. indifference and negligence
3. privacy and secrecy
4. respect and condescension
5. classical and popular

People often argue about what is news and what is editorializing, what is fact and what is propaganda. The following materials will give you a chance to define these and similar terms.

PROSE MODEL 4

HERBERT BRUCKER

The News Behind the News

The distinction between surface news and its background was first made long ago, in the heady social ferment let loose by that cataclysm on which the twentieth century is founded, World War I. There arose concern because the old man-bites-dog concept of news increasingly failed to give the public the essential meaning and significance of what was going on in an increasingly complicated world.

The answer was interpretive news. A convenient birthday might be the founding of *Time* in 1923. The Hadden-Luce plea was that the bare bones of the news, as reported in scattered snippets by even the best of the dailies, were often meaningless. It was necessary to organize the news into a coherent, colorful pattern. Because this diagnosis was sound, the newsmagazine has long since become part of the establishment—so much so that it too is now suspect. Nevertheless, it remains true that a weekly publication can pull together a more fully rounded and coherent view of current happenings than can a daily.

There is more to it, however, than the interval of publication. Indeed, the better dailies themselves are increasingly turning away from the bing-bang-biff, one-day-wonder stories of old. They still print the day's events. But they also detach reporters, or even teams of them, from the daily beat to produce carefully researched copy resembling a magazine article more than spot news.

This came about because of a long chain of experiences. In the mid-1920s, for example, thoughtful observers were struck by an act of journalistic genius that revealed the inadequacy of reporting merely the spectacular surface of events. At the time, the New York press found colorful fare in tales out of the Prohibition-and-gangster era. One such real-life whodunit ran on for days, as what the headlines called the Bobbed-Haired Bandit struck again and again in a series of Manhattan holdups. In due course, the young gun moll who had terrorized the town was caught, whereupon most papers dropped the story. But in time the late *World* published the full text of a social worker's carefully researched, factual report. It showed that this supposedly hard-bitten female, Celia Cooney, was nothing but a frightened child, a bit of human flotsam condemned never to have a chance in life from birth. The facts, as dug out by someone other than a reporter, were devastating in revealing the real causes of crime in modern society. They were equally devastating in revealing how much that was both fascinating and important the papers were missing.

READING QUESTIONS

1. Define or explain briefly the following: *social ferment, cataclysm, coherent, whodunit, flotsam, devastating.*
2. Explain the author's distinction between "surface" and "interpretive" news.

3. When you read a newspaper, do you look for the background and the explanations that help you understand the "surface news"? Give an example of a recent story about which you read background information that made you change your mind.

4. Look at the following brief comments about the function of the news media. What is each person saying? Give some example or illustration of what the person is talking about. Define briefly the key terms used.

   a. "The problem of what to report and how to report it will never be resolved, because the line between fact and the *subjective* view of that fact remains vague."

   b. "Eyewitness reports are obviously invaluable, both to *history* and to *journalism*. But they are not necessarily the whole truth."

   c. "There remains a simple test of the difference between interpretive news and *editorializing*—that can serve us still in this day of news conceived as *propaganda* to achieve a desired end, after the model of Dr. Goebbels and the Soviet hierarchy. It is this: Is the writer, by the internal evidence of what he or she writes, trying to explain the news or plug a cause?"

   d. "*Objectivity* is the *rationalization* for staying neutral, for not getting involved."

   e. "That people should live at peace with one another might be described as *truth,* but it is not a fact, nor is it news. That a certain number of children were born yesterday in Chicago is a *fact,* and the truth, but not *news.* Journalism involves an effort to discover, select, and assemble certain facts in a way that will be not only reasonably true but reasonably interesting—and therefore reasonably salable."

WRITING TOPICS

1. In each of the following pairs, the difference between the two key terms seems clear enough in theory. But it often proves hard to apply in practice. Choose one: "news vs. editorializing"; or "objectivity and subjectivity." Define the two opposing terms in the pair you choose. Use detailed examples from your observation of the news media to show what your definitions mean in practice.

2. People who are critical of American newspapers have in the past charged them with one or more of the following:

   • *sensationalism,* for instance, in the treatment of crime or sex;
   • *sentimentality,* for instance, in the treatment of children, weddings, and the like;
   • *bias,* for instance, in the treatment of minorities.

   Write a paper in which you define one of these key terms. Provide examples from your own observation of the news media. To judge from your own study, how fair or justified are the critics' charges?

3. In the words of a sociologist, "*crime* is an umbrella term held over the heads of some extraordinarily different kinds of things." Can you show that *crime* is indeed such an umbrella term? Can you nevertheless identify one or more important common elements? Or, write about another umbrella term that is applied to a great variety of different things. Choose one of the following: *controversial, modern, bad taste, decency*.

4. American historians like Frederick Jackson Turner have identified "individualism, working for good and for evil," as a dominant trait of the American national character, inherited at least in part from the days when the life of the frontier put a premium on self-reliance. How would you define *individualism* as it works in American life today? What role does it play in the life of the average person? Use detailed examples from your own observation and experience.

C4c

Argument

Learn how to present a convincing argument to the reader.

Argument shows relationships between ideas. It examines idea *A* and idea *B* and then shows how the two ideas, put together, help us reach idea *C*. The attitude of someone presenting an honest argument is: "Here are things we know—things we can agree on. Now here are the logical conclusions that we should draw from them."

Remember the following advice when you try to present a convincing argument to your reader:

(1) Identify a limited issue and do it justice. If you want your argument to convince your readers, you have to take clear aim. Each of the following paragraphs is focused on one clear-cut issue. In each case, the writer has asked: "What am I trying to prove?" In your own words, what is the issue in each case?

> U.S. black music is mainstream. This music, far from being simply Afro-American (whatever that is, the continent of Africa being as vast and varied as it is), is like the U.S. Negro himself, All-American. This is why so many other American musicians, like Paul Whiteman, George Gershwin, Benny Goodman, Woody Herman, Gerry Mulligan, and all the rest, identify with it so eagerly. The white American musician sounds most American when he sounds most like an American Negro. Otherwise he sounds like a European. . . . All Americans, even those committed to segregation, are, culturally speaking, closer to the blues than any song-and-dance group or tribe anywhere in Africa. The blues tradition is not indigenous to Africa. It is a U.S. tradition, indigenous to the United States.—Albert Murray, "Something Different, Something More," *Anger, and Beyond*

It would not be easy to find a responsible professional expert who sees any significant relation at all between the greater frankness of contemporary general literature and juvenile delinquency or misbehavior. As a matter of fact, most juvenile delinquents exhibit serious reading disabilities, averaging three years or more behind what is normal for their age-level. It is unusual to find in serious trouble with the authorities a youth whose capacity for sustained reading is adequate for an adult novel. Whatever creates juvenile delinquency, it is not the reading of works by John O'Hara or D. H. Lawrence or Vladimir Nabokov or, for that matter, Grace Metalious. In fact, it is the *inability* to do sustained reading, frustrating the youth at school and cutting off a major avenue of escape from the limits of what is usually a mean and sordid environment, that tends to breed rebellious delinquency.—Dan Lacy, "Obscenity and Censorship"

(2) *Weigh the evidence pro and con in order to reach a balanced conclusion.* When you evaluate a proposal or take a stand on an issue, look at the major arguments on both sides. A **"pro-and-con"** paper has more built-in suspense than a paper that makes a flat assertion at the beginning. The reader looks on as the evidence is weighed and the issue decided. When you discuss a proposal for a **new** kind of school or program, you can list the *advantages* first, and then point out *disadvantages*. You can then suggest a *modified* proposal that promises to achieve the benefits without the drawbacks. Here is a possible scheme for a paper:

I. People often ask for more vocational courses. These give both student and parents the feeling that the student is getting a "practical" education.

II. But some vocational courses prepare the student for jobs that automation and a changing technology are about to eliminate.

III. Vocational courses today should teach a student how to acquire *new* skills as jobs change.

(3) *Draw justified conclusions from what you know.* We interpret current events by relating them to previous experience. During a downpour, we see two badly damaged cars pulled over to the side of the highway. We are likely to think that one of the drivers lost control of the car on the rain-slick road. We relate the present incident to a general rule we have previously formed about accidents in the rain:

GENERAL RULE: In the rain, cars tend to skid on slick pavement and thus cause accidents.

SPECIFIC INCIDENT: This car has had an accident in the rain.

CONCLUSION: *Therefore,* this car must have skidded on the wet pavement.

When we carefully examine this conclusion, we will change the *must* to *may*. The conclusion is *probably* true. But, rain or no rain, *other* factors also cause accidents: defective steering wheels or inattentive drivers, and so on.

Much argument applies our general knowledge to individual cases. When we generalize, we look at many individual cases and reach a general conclusion. But then, when still another individual case comes along, we are ready to say: This is merely another example of the general rule we already know. The kind of reasoning that *applies* the general rule to the new example is called deductive reasoning, or **deduction.**

The more ironclad the general rule is, the more reliable the conclusions we can draw from it. When the general rule has the word *all* or *only* or *no* in it, it does not allow exceptions. We can confidently apply it to the individual case at issue:

GENERAL: Only persons over eighteen voted in the recent election.
SPECIFIC: Jim voted in the recent election.
CONCLUSION: Jim must be over eighteen.

GENERAL: No unaided human being can survive without air.
SPECIFIC: There is no air on the moon.
CONCLUSION: No unaided human being could survive on the moon.

When we draw such conclusions in the course of an argument, we should not try to get out of a general rule more than went into it. Learn to ask: How far exactly does the rule go—what ground does it cover? Look at the following argument:

GENERAL: All Communists read Karl Marx.
SPECIFIC: John Smith reads Karl Marx.
CONCLUSION: John Smith is a Communist.

Here, the conclusion goes *further* than the rule. There is nothing in the rule to exclude the possibility that, in addition to Communists, a great many *other* people also read Karl Marx. We could rewrite the rule as follows: "All Communists (and also many *non*-Communists) read Karl Marx."

(4) Consider important alternatives. Often an argument remains unconvincing because the readers are presented with a very narrow range of choice. They are pushed toward a "yes" or "no" answer when they really want to say "maybe" or "that depends." They are asked to choose *either* one solution *or* the other when they really want to ask: "Isn't there a *third* way out?" Often, when we are presented with a simple *either-or* choice, neither of the two alternatives fits the situation. We are presented with a **false dilemma.**

Before you present your readers with an *either-or* argument, see whether there is a third possibility that presents a way out. For instance, people often talk as if children are made to learn *either* by fear of punishment *or* by the hope of reward—a good grade, a pat on the back, or a place on the honor roll. But there is also a third possibility. The good student in math is often the one who *enjoys* solving problems. The best student in a Spanish class is often the one who likes to study a foreign language and to try it out. Many educators feel that children learn best when they enjoy what they are doing.

The following passages might each be part of a longer argument. Which passages make good sense to you? Explain what makes them seem logical or reasonable. In which passages does the author seem to jump to conclusions? How or why?

EXERCISE 1

1. Last year, Joe M. was arrested for taking things from a warehouse where he worked, though the case never came to trial. Two weeks after we hired him, the supervisor's wallet was stolen. Anyone looking at these facts can put two and two together.

2. When my uncle and aunt found they did not get along, they went to different marriage counselors, and they spent much money on psychologists. Finally, however, their marriage broke up anyway. Obviously, counseling alone is no cure-all for a troubled marriage.

3. Under primitive agricultural conditions, the farmer had few insect problems. These arose with the intensification of agriculture—the devotion of immense acreages to a single crop. Such a system set the stage for explosive increases in specific insect populations. . . . Nature has introduced great variety into the landscape, but man has displayed a passion for simplifying it. Thus he undoes the built-in checks and balances by which nature holds the species within bounds. One important natural check is a limit on the amount of suitable habitat for each species. Obviously then, an insect that lives on wheat can build up its population to much higher levels on a farm devoted to wheat than on one in which wheat is intermingled with other crops to which the insect is not adapted.—Rachel Carson, *Silent Spring*

4. On every IQ test, my brother has always scored way above the average. But he is a very slow reader and hardly ever reads unless he absolutely has to. It is high time that the school change its method of teaching reading.

5. Joan's parents did not allow her to take the flu shots that were offered everyone in the school last month. It must be against their religion.

6. Tax money spent on schools must benefit everyone equally. It cannot benefit a special group. Therefore, we cannot allow the government to use tax money in support of private schools.

7. It is often argued that guns do not kill—people do. If there is stricter gun control, criminals will find ways to get guns by illegal means. If guns are banned, violence will take other forms. But stricter gun control would make killing less easy. People inclined to violence would often be forced to think twice. An easy means of acting out their aggressive feelings would not be ready to hand. There is no doubt that stricter gun control would save lives.

EXERCISE 2 Have you ever listened carefully to a view *opposed* to your own? Write a paragraph in which you report as fully and impartially as you can a point of view with which you strongly disagree. Show that you can do justice to "the other side."

EXERCISE 3 Choose one of the following and line up several arguments pro and con:

- hunting
- banning handguns
- divorce
- professional wrestling
- banning smoking in public places
- legalized gambling
- more elective courses in high school

(Your teacher may ask you to present the arguments pro and con in a paper in which you draw your own balanced conclusion.)

EXERCISE 4 How do you react to the following discussion of a familiar issue? Identify several generalizations or conclusions that you agree with or that you would want to challenge. Point out examples of the author's bringing in *alternative* causes or solutions that others might have overlooked.

CHEATING

In my experience, the smartest kids in a class cheat as much as or more than the "dumb" ones. They realize that cheating is the easiest way out of the monotony of schoolwork, and they can rationalize their actions many ways. It is the best way to assure good grades, to relieve the pressure, and, besides, everybody does it—including adults and possibly the kids' own parents.

Faculty members and administrators are still distressed by the lack of honorable mores on the part of the students, even though they have been slightly infected by the students' casual attitudes. Their agony begins when the question of punishment for a cheater arises. As the severity of the punishment depends not only on the magnitude of the sin but on the motives and circumstances the teacher believes are present, the would-be punishers are beginning to ask why a student finds it necessary to cheat.

Of course, many teachers still dismiss the cheater as a lazy parasite who has nothing original to say or who just doesn't want to bother with the standard memorizing or thinking. But among the new breed of teachers appearing in the schools, conscience has weakened easy certainty. It is not the principle of the thing that bothers them, for most of our teachers and administrators are liberals and therefore awfully uncomfortable with strict applications of principle. Theirs is not to do or die, theirs is but to reason why.

He and she are usually young, interested, and popular with the students. The growing amount of cheating deeply concerns them, but they look upon the situation in a different light. More and more teachers are ready to suggest that maybe it's the schools' fault that students cheat; that schools have always taught students to fight for the best grade and to get it any way they can. They are beginning to question the traditional emphasis that society places on grades, and the pressure on students to *achieve*.

It could be said that this new attitude simply creates more excuses for lazy students, letting them off the hook too easily. Still, the questions remain to be raised and debated. With the importance of grades removed and a more flexible, individualized approach to teaching, would students feel less inclined to cheat, increasingly motivated to learn by themselves, and admit to being not as perfect as they would like?—Immy Humes, *Harper's*

The following prose model is an example of an editorial arguing an unpopular position. The author is known for his strong views, and his emotions are aroused by his topic. Nevertheless, he is aiming his argument at an intelligent reader. Can you show that he respects the reader's judgment? Study the selection carefully and answer the questions that follow it.

PROSE MODEL 5

NORMAN COUSINS

Who Killed Benny Paret?

I once had an interview with Mike Jacobs, the prize-fight promoter. I was a fledgling reporter at that time. My beat was education, but during the vacation season I found myself on varied assignments, all the way from ship news to sports reporting. In this way I found myself sitting opposite the most powerful figure in the boxing world.

There was nothing spectacular in Mr. Jacobs' manner or appearance; but when he spoke about prize fights, he was no longer a bland little man but a colossus who sounded the way Napoleon must have sounded when he reviewed a battle. You knew you were listening to Number One. His saying something made it true.

We discussed what to him was the only important element in successful promoting—how to please the crowd. So far as he was concerned, there was no mystery to it. You put killers in the ring and the people filled your arena. You hire boxing artists—men who are adroit at feinting, parrying, weaving, jabbing, and dancing, but who don't pack dynamite in their fists—and you wind up counting your empty seats. So you searched for the killers and sluggers and maulers—fellows who could hit with the force of a baseball bat.

I asked Mr. Jacobs if he was speaking literally when he said people came out to see the killer.

"They don't come out to see a tea party," he said evenly. "They come out to see the knockout. They come out to see a man hurt. If they think anything else, they're kidding themselves."

Some years ago, a young man by the name of Benny Paret was killed in the ring. The killing was seen by millions; it was on television. In the twelfth round, he was hit hard in the head several times, went down, was counted out, and never came out of the coma.

The Paret fight produced a flurry of investigations. Governor Rockefeller was shocked by what happened and appointed a committee to assess the responsibility. The New York State Boxing Commission decided to find out what was wrong. The District Attorney's office expressed its concern. One question that was solemnly studied in all three probes concerned the action of the referee. Did he act in time to stop the fight? Another question had to do with the role of the examining doctors who certified the physical fitness of the fighters before the bout. Still another question involved Mr. Paret's manager: did he rush his boy into the fight without adequate time to recuperate from the previous one?

In short, the investigators looked into every possible cause except the real one. Benny Paret was killed because the human fist delivers enough impact, when directed against the head, to produce a massive hemorrhage in the brain. The human brain is the most delicate and complex mechanism in all creation. It has a lacework of millions of highly fragile nerve connections. Nature attempts to protect this exquisitely intricate machinery by encasing it in a hard shell. Fortunately, the shell is thick enough to withstand a great deal of pounding. Nature, however, can protect man against everything except man himself. Not every blow to the head will kill a man—but there is always the risk of concussion and damage to the brain. A prize fighter may be able to survive even repeated brain concussions and go on fighting, but the damage to his brain may be permanent.

In any event, it is futile to investigate the referee's role and seek to determine whether he should have intervened to stop the fight earlier. That is not where the primary responsibility lies. The primary responsibility lies with the people who pay to see a man hurt. The referee who stops a fight too soon from the crowd's viewpoint can expect to be booed. The crowd wants the knockout; it wants to see a man stretched out on the canvas. This is the supreme moment in boxing. It is nonsense to talk about prize fighting as a test of boxing skills. No crowd was ever brought to its feet screaming and cheering at the sight of two men beautifully dodging and weaving out of each other's jabs. The time the crowd comes alive is when a man is hit hard over the heart or the head, when his mouthpiece flies out, when the blood squirts out of his nose or eyes, when he wobbles under the attack and his pursuer continues to smash at him with pole-axe impact.

Don't blame it on the referee. Don't even blame it on the fight managers. Put the blame where it belongs—on the prevailing mores that regard prize fighting as a perfectly proper enterprise and vehicle of entertainment. No one doubts that many people enjoy prize fighting and will miss it if it should be thrown out. And that is precisely the point.—from the *Saturday Review*

1. Explain briefly *bland, colossus, adroit, concussion, futile, mores*. Study the words the author uses to describe what the crowd sees during a fight. Would you say he is writing about boxing from hearsay or from close, first-hand observation? How can you tell?

READING QUESTIONS

2. Is this editorial clearly focused on a central issue? State it in your own words.
3. Can you point out one or more examples of a general principle being applied to a specific instance? How acceptable or convincing are the general assumptions from which the author argues?
4. Can you point out an important *distinction* that is crucial to the author's argument? How clearly or how fully is it worked out?
5. What is the author's attitude toward people who do *not* share his view?
6. How convincing is the author's argument as a whole? Does it convince *you*? Discuss his overall strategy, pointing out its strengths or weaknesses.

WRITING TOPICS

1. Find an issue which you have studied or with which you are personally concerned. Argue your position in such a way that a reasonable reader will respect your point of view. Where appropriate, weigh the arguments on the other side. Here are some possible choices:

   - police rights to question or search citizens;
   - public funds for private schools;
   - quotas for hiring or admission of minorities;
   - role of women in the armed services;
   - English as a requirement for U.S. citizenship;
   - reducing violence on television;
   - immigration policies;
   - treatment of juvenile offenders;
   - bilingual instruction.

2. Do you ever find yourself defending an *unpopular* view? Do you ever find yourself taking sides with a small minority? Can you think of an issue where you might want to play the "devil's advocate"? Argue your position on such an issue. Present arguments that might make people holding the majority view reconsider.

C4d

Persuasion

Learn how to help people change their minds.

Persuasion tries to change someone else's mind. Persuasive writing aims at *results*. The persuasive writer turns to us and says: "Buy my product! Hire my services! Support my program! Vote for my candidate!"

What can you do to make your writing persuasive? What does it take to influence the way people think or feel? Remember the following guidelines:

(1) Know your readers. Advertisers must know something about the needs and interests of their customers. Political candidates

EVERYBODY HAS A MESSAGE
Do you think these messages are effective?
Why, or why not?

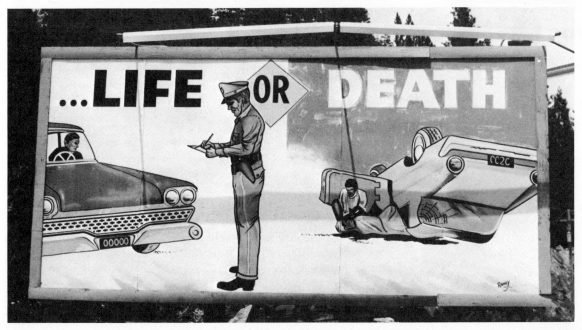

must know something about the feelings of the voters. When you want to persuade your readers, you must know something about what they believe, what they want, how they feel. You must be prepared to find some kind of common ground.

Each of the following passages appeals to basic interests or convictions that the author shares with the audience. What are these common interests or convictions?

Parks like Golden Gate Park in San Francisco or the beautiful parks of Denver are the result of the citizens' investment in their city's future. We are now enjoying the dividends of the money that earlier generations spent in making these cities beautiful. Therefore, we should in turn invest in the parks that will make our growing cities beautiful places to live for our children and children's children.

Clubs, fraternities, nations—these are the beloved barriers in the way of a workable world, these will have to surrender some of their rights and some of their ribs. . . . Anyone who remembers back to his fraternity days at college recalls the enthusiasts in his group, the rabid members, both old and young, who were obsessed with the mystical charm of membership in their particular order. They were usually men who were incapable of genuine brotherhood, or at least unaware of its implications. Fraternity begins when the exclusion formula is found to be distasteful. The effect of any organization of a social and brotherly nature is to strengthen rather than to diminish the lines which divide people into classes. The effect of states and nations is the same, and eventually these lines will have to be softened, these powers will have to be generalized.—E. B. White, *One Man's Meat*

(2) *Use language that strongly conveys the right attitudes and emotions.* It is hard to raise the reader's enthusiasm for the preservation of our forests and wildlife in the neutral, clinical language of the botanist, and geologist. In the following passage, point out the words that strongly convey the author's emotions.

The tragedy of the oceanic islands lies in the uniqueness, the irreplaceability of the species they have developed by the slow process of the ages. In a reasonable world men would have treated these islands as precious possessions, as natural museums filled with beautiful and curious works of creation, valuable beyond price because nowhere in the world are they duplicated. W. H. Hudson's lament for the birds of the Argentine pampas might even more truly have been spoken of the islands: "The beautiful has vanished and returns not." —Rachel Carson, *The Sea Around Us*

In much persuasive writing, *analogies* and *comparisons* help steer the reader's reactions. Can you show that the analogies in the following passages do not merely carry information but also suggest attitudes?

The parents who are trying to force their children *with an academic shoehorn* into colleges with academic standards way beyond the students' capacities are doing lasting harm.

We are living like the irresponsible *heirs of a millionaire uncle.* At an ever accelerating rate, we are now squandering the capital of metallic ores and fossil fuels accumulated in the earth's crust during hundreds of millions of years. How long can this spending spree go on? (Aldous Huxley)

(3) Go from the simple to the difficult, or from the obvious to the new. Reassure your readers by starting from what they already know or understand. Then take them step by step toward the new, the difficult, the controversial. Show how the following outline proceeds from what is easy to what is harder to accept.

A Police Officer's Right to Strike

I. The factory worker's right to strike is an established part of the American way of life.

II. White-collar workers are organizing and using the strike as a legitimate weapon.

III. In recent years, teacher strikes have improved the working conditions of teachers.

IV. It is hard to see how police officers can be denied a right granted to private and public employees alike.

(4) Bring out the weaknesses in an opponent's view. Point out telling contradictions or absurdities. The following passage is part of an article attacking hunting as a sport. Can you show in detail what the author does in order to demolish his opposition?

Let it be supposed that all hunters obey all regulations. Let it be supposed that no whiskey bottle is dropped to pollute any glen or dingle, no fence is broken, no fawn is shot, no forest is set afire, no robins are massacred in mistake for pheasants and no deer-hunters in mistake for porcupines (or possibly chipmunks). . . . The question persists: Is it a spectacle of manhood (which is to say of our distinctive humanness), when on a bracing morning we look out upon the autumn, draw an exhilarating breath, and cry "What a glorious day! How golden the light of the sun, how merry the caperings of creatures; *Gloria in excelsis Deo!* I will go out and kill something"?—Alan Devoe, "On Hunting," *The American Mercury*

(5) Do not try too hard to persuade. Try to keep your writing free of the following:

UNCONVINCING SUPERLATIVES: **Experienced readers are** tired of exaggeration. They have heard words like *tremendous, terrific, glamorous, thrilling,* and *unique* so many times that they are no longer impressed by them.

LOADED LANGUAGE: Do not rely on words that are *mere* words. What to one writer is the "steadily growing *burden* of school taxes" is to another writer "society's steadily growing *investment* in education." The experienced reader knows that in practice the words in each of the following pairs often mean much the same thing:

crony	trusted friend
bureaucrat	administrator
brutality	firmness
agitator	advocate
deal	settlement
regimentation	discipline

CHEAPENED IDEALS OR STANDARDS: Love of country is a powerful motive. But we cheapen it when we use it to help promote a pet scheme, or sell soap ("true American values . . . special money-saving coupons inside").

EXERCISE 1

Study the way the following passages influence the reader. What values or attitudes would the ideal reader of each passage have to share with the author? Point out all words that help make something sound good—and all words that help make something sound bad. What means does each author use to help turn the reader against things the author disapproves of? (How do *you* react to each passage?)

1. In the mythology which movies and books have created for the American West, the drifter has always been glorified at the direct expense of the settler. The drifter-figure has come to represent for us all that was romantic and free about the West. . . . There were, however, settlers who were not necessarily inferior to the drifters in their love of freedom. The cattlemen's not-so-latent contempt for the rodeo hand is based upon knowledge that rodeo hands have been content to fiddle while the West burned. The rancher's view is the precise opposite of that one gets from the movies. As they see it, rodeo hands are responsible only to the demands of their egos, take no care of the land itself, and have no respect for the labors or the traditions of the herdsman. They . . . have little patience, no love of work, and essentially crude skills. They are not very useful in intri-

cate cattlework and are seldom willing to stay around and do the dull but necessary chores once the fun of the roundup is over.—Larry McMurtry, "A Requiem for a Rodeo," *New York*

2. Writing an exciting biography about Warren Gamaliel Harding is like filming a chase sequence with a wooden Indian. Harding's instincts were all for posture. Like a suntanned Roman, he struck his Midwest Ciceronian pose and held it, occasionally delivering himself of the sort of speech that instantly self-destructs upon reaching the brain. Francis Russell, historian of Sacco and Vanzetti *(Tragedy in Dedham),* keeps his camera circling the 29th President of the United States and sometimes almost creates the illusion the body is twitching with life. . . . But he is up against one of the great political still lifes of modern times. The personal portrait that emerges reveals a man notable mainly for his mediocrity of mind and spirit—a rather lazy fellow for whom somebody else always had to open the door when opportunity knocked.—"Kiss Me, Harding," *Time*

3. My hope for the city's freedom from the curse of street disorders lies not so much in splendid constructions as in the humble, busy neighborhoods, in the type of people I see passing daily to and fro on nearby Upper Broadway or even enjoying the sunshine as they sit on the mid-traffic street benches. . . . I look for the solution of this question to the silent, unpretending efforts of public-school teachers and nuns and to cops and decent city officials and reasonable architects and friendly corner store keepers, and innumerable good persons, male and female, who tap typewriters in the ever mushrooming office buildings that madly crowd our limited space.—John LaFarge, "Brutality and the City," *Saturday Review*

4. According to the projections of demographers, the present world population of 3.6 billion will double by 2000 A.D. Then our planet will have to harbor two New Yorks instead of one, two Londons, two Tokyos, two Calcuttas, two Hong Kongs, one more of every existing human congregation. There will be double the highways and freeways to link them, double the consumption of oxygen by human and industrial and automotive combustion, double the air and water pollution, half the elbow room, a shrunken area of cropland that will have to be more and more intensively mined, a limited amount of parkland and open space trampled flat by the millions wanting to smell mown grass or show their children a squirrel.

Advertising is one of America's major industries. The methods and strategies of the advertiser have been much studied, criticized, and parodied. Study the sample paragraph on the following page. Then

EXERCISE 2

write a similar paragraph of your own. Identify one element that is strong in current advertising. Give several examples.

It is not difficult to recognize the widespread longing for the state of complete laziness and passivity. Our advertising appeals to it even more than to sex. There are, of course, many useful and labor-saving gadgets. But this usefulness often serves only as a rationalization for the appeal to complete passivity and receptivity. A package of breakfast cereal is being advertised as *"new—easier to eat."* An electric toaster is advertised with these words: ". . . the most distinctly different toaster in the world! Everything is done *for* you with this new toaster. You need not even bother to lower the bread. Power-action, through a unique electric motor, *gently takes the bread right out of your fingers!"* How many courses in languages or other subjects are announced with the slogan "effortless learning, no more of the old drudgery." Everybody knows the picture of the elderly couple in the advertisement of a life-insurance company, who have retired at the age of sixty, and spend their life in the complete bliss of having nothing to do except just travel.—Erich Fromm, *The Sane Society*

EXERCISE 3

Many modern readers have become wary of slick or insincere appeals to their generosity or their idealism. What would you say to enlist support for a cause that you sincerely believe in? Write a letter asking for support for a cause like the following:

- public television;
- the scout movement;
- help for a type of handicapped person you have been close to;
- an organization dedicated to fighting disease or poverty abroad.

PROSE MODEL 6

Magazines like *Harper's* or *Atlantic* publish many articles that try to arouse the public. The authors try to alert us to dangers or abuses. They try to enlist our support for a worthy cause. How does such an author try to arouse and influence public opinion? Study the following excerpt from an article. How do you react to this kind of writing? Does the author's persuasive strategy work? Why or why not?

HARRY M. CAUDILL

The Threatened Land

Most solid-state minerals lie much closer to the top than the Russian coal and the South African gold. War-spawned engines make it possible to dig them out from above by simply "stripping" away all the overlying rocks, dirt, trees, grass, and flowers. We have created surface-mining tools of unbelievable size, power, and effectiveness: gigantic bulldozers, power shovels and drills, huge but agile "highlifts," trucks that carry sixty tons per load, and cheap explosives compounded of petroleum and fertilizer. No mountain, however thickly capped with sandstone or granite, is proof against the men who come for its vitals.

Consider "Big Muskie," one of Ohio's tourist attractions and the pride of Central Ohio Coal Company. It stands twenty stories high, lifts a boom 310 feet long operated by a five-inch steel cable, and scrapes away 325 tons of overburden per scoop. Such machines are turned to the digging of phosphate, potash, clays, sand and gravel, copper, iron bauxite, and zinc. Iron and copper pits turn into awesome man-made canyons. Mountains are taken apart layer by layer. Plains are plowed to shreds and reduced to formless chaos. But men stay topside, casualties are fewer and less severe than in the underground mines, and fuels and ores reach mills and factories at lower costs. There is much to be said in support of strip-mining.

But there is another and sinister side of the coin. The lands we shred for minerals also feed, clothe, and shelter us, and when we dig we shrink our farms. . . .

Half of Iowa is underlain by strippable coal, as is 40 percent of Illinois. This is the nation's breadbasket, without which there would be little beef and pork for ourselves and no grain surpluses for sale to an underfed world. And the coal undergirds a fair-sized chunk of Texas, a third of Oklahoma, broad districts in New Mexico, Arizona, Colorado, Utah, Montana, Wyoming, Washington, and the Dakotas. . . . When the government opened the land for homesteading, it retained titles to the minerals in much of the land, and the Bureau of Land Management in the Interior Department has leased hundreds of thousands of acres for mining. The ranchers and farmers are seldom consulted until the machines are ready to rumble down onto their spreads. And if they resist, their "surface rights" can be condemned.

The best lands will go first. The coal is ubiquitous but strippers abhor overburden, so they will avoid the hills. Ranchers grow their hay on lowlands near the meandering streams and graze their cattle and sheep on the rugged, lightly watered backlands. On the hayfields the overburden is thin, the coal near the top. When the fields are stripped, ranches lose their viability because without hay livestock cannot be carried through the icy winters. When the hay is lost, the ranch is finished. In time, though, the rugged knobs and hills will be brought under "contour stripping," then "augering," and finally "top removal." Coal is life to a society hungering for heat and chemicals, and the ranches and farms will have no rest.—"There Is No Land to Spare," *Atlantic*

1. Define or explain briefly: *agile, compounded, vitals, sinister, undergird, ubiquitous, meander, viability, contour*. What are the connotations of the following words: *war-spawned, homestead, breadbasket?*

2. Point out all words that the author uses to arouse or alarm the reader. What words especially carry a sense of threat or of impending loss? What other words or passages are especially dramatic, making the reader pay attention?

3. A fair-minded reader wants a chance to look at the other side. Does the author provide the pro and con? How or where?

4. As fully as you can, describe the values or attitudes that the author expects readers to share. Give a "capsule portrait" of the author—tell us what he believes in, what his feelings are, how he talks to his readers.

5. Suppose you were given five minutes to speak up in defense of something that you consider precious or important but that is threatened by current developments. What would you choose to defend? What would you say?

1. Suppose voters in your state were considering a law designed to do one of the following:

   - make it easier for young people to get married;
   - make it easier for single people to adopt children;
   - make it easier for married people to get divorced;
   - make it easier for students to quit school;
   - make it easier for immigrants to come into the country;
   - make it easier for judges to put offenders on probation;
   - make it easier for the police to obtain evidence.

   Take a position pro or con on one of these proposed laws. Write a *letter to the editor* in which you try to persuade people committed to the opposite view.

2. Schools differ in how closely administrators supervise a school newspaper, literary magazine, yearbook, and the like. Could you persuade adults that they should adopt a "hands-off" policy toward student publications? (Would you be willing to take the position that "anything goes"?) Or, could you persuade your schoolmates that some basic restrictions are necessary? (Where would you draw the line?) Write a paper supporting your point of view as forcefully as you can.

3. Have you ever seen a promising reform or innovation rejected or inadequately carried out? Or, have you seen a worthwhile tradition or institution abolished or neglected? Write a paper in which you persuade your audience to give the project or institution in question a second chance.

Interpret and evaluate what you have read.

When you write about what you read, you try to answer questions like the following:

(1) "What do I make of this?"   When you answer this first and most basic question, you engage in **interpretation.** When you interpret your reading, you tell the reader: "This is what this author says. This is what I think the author is trying to do."

(2) "How do I react to this?"   A good book or an important article does not simply give us information. It gets us involved. It makes us think and feel. When we engage in **evaluation,** we show whether we considered the experience valuable or worthwhile. We explain why we agree or disagree.

(3) "How does this compare with other things I have read?" Comparison and contrast help us understand and judge. Weighing what others have said, we arrive at our own conclusions.

Help your reader understand and enjoy a poem, short story, novel, or play.

When you write about a story, poem, or play, you often sum up what happens in it. The following paragraph summarizes what happens in a famous story about a former college football player:

> Irwin Shaw's "The 80-Yard Run" is the story of an appallingly uninteresting fellow who was distinguished only by his talent as broken-field runner. In his sophomore year during a practice session, he gets the ball and goes beautifully, perfectly, for a 80-yard touchdown. It is a real moment of truth, in which things fit together and life, in a brilliant flash, has order and meaning. But before his junior year he injures himself, and his career is never the same. He carries the ball again but there is always someone in the way . . . things don't open up. He marries a woman who worshipped him as a halfback but gets bored with him in later life. . . . The halfback-husband takes a job as a traveling clothing salesman for colleges, returns to his own school and goes to the empty field to relive the moment of the 80-yard run.—Dan Wakefield, "In Defense of the Fullback," *Dissent*

If we have never read the story, this **plot summary** will give us a good idea of what the story is about. Even if we have read the story, this summary will remind us of the highlights. But at the same time, this summary leaves us with questions like the following:

- *Why* do things happen the way they do in this story?
- What kind of *person* is this former halfback—would the same kind of thing have happened to someone else?
- How does the story make us *feel?*
- What does it make us *think?*

When you try to answer such questions, you begin to talk about what the story means. You help your readers understand and enjoy the story. To give unity to a short critical paper, focus on one of the following:

(1) Examine a writer's use of language. Poets (and also novelists or playwrights) use language *imaginatively.* They make it do things we did not know it could do. Normally, for instance, words like *pompous, hate,* and *arrogant* would create a strongly negative picture. But the opposite is true when Helene Johnson uses the same words in her "Sonnet to a Negro in Harlem." She uses these words, but she uses them to express loyalty and admiration for the person to whom they apply. Can you explain *how* she does this in the following lines? How does she change the *connotations* of these words?

> You are disdainful and magnificent—
> Your perfect body and your *pompous* gait,
> Your dark eyes flashing solemnly with *hate.* . . .
>
> I love your laughter *arrogant* and bold.
> You are too splendid for this city street.

(2) Discuss a major character. When we first read a good story, we may be carried along by our interest in the action. John Steinbeck's story "Flight," for instance, keeps us in suspense as the boy Pepé is hunted down in the mountains after he has killed a man in a fight. But as we look back over the story, we realize that this is *Pepé's* story. It is the story of a boy who wanted to be an adult, proudly going on errands for his widowed mother:

> "Adiós, Mama," Pepé cried. "I will come back soon. You may send me often alone. I am a man."

It is the story of a boy who tried to act grown up when finding himself suddenly in an adult world:

> "I am a man now, Mama. The man said names to me I could not allow."

As you write about a character like Pepé, ask yourself questions like the following:

- What kind of general description does the author give of the person? (Steinbeck describes Pepé as a "gentle, affectionate boy.")
- What does the person *do* that reveals something about his character? (Pepé practices for hours throwing the long, heavy knife he has inherited from his father.)
- What do other people say about him? And what do they really *think* about him? (Pepé's mother "thought him fine and brave, but she never told him so.")

(3) Trace a unifying theme. When we read an announcement, we expect to find a message directly stated.

When we read a story or see a play, we may still look for the writer's message. But we expect to find it *acted out.* When we trace the **theme** of a story or a play, we try to sum up its overall meaning as it gradually unravels or falls into place.

Suppose we are reading a story like Stephen Crane's "The Open Boat." As we see the four shipwrecked men in their small lifeboat, we ask ourselves: Is there any question raised in our minds—and then *kept alive* by what happens in the rest of the story?

One idea that enters our minds again and again is that nature, far from being our real home, is really not made for us. We see the men in their boat, not much larger than a bathtub, surrounded by jagged and "barbarously abrupt and tall waves." The men have no eyes for the wild splendor of the shining, storm-tossed sea. They are absorbed in efforts that take all their limited strength. They are angered by the sea birds, unruffled and at home in a setting that threatens to destroy these exhausted human beings. When the men finally sight land, the surf keeps them from reaching shore. Again and again, the story makes us feel that we live in a world not made for us. We must look for warmth, friendship, and support to other human beings. The universe does not care whether we live or die. A critical paper could present this idea as the central theme. It could show the many ways this theme is echoed or acted out in different parts of the story.

(4) Examine the role of a key symbol. A **symbol** gives a visible shape to an idea. The cross is a familiar symbol of the Christian faith. Writers often choose their *own* symbols, gradually building up meanings and associations. They may build a whole poem or story around one or more symbols that focus our attention. By examining the role of such a symbol, we learn what the writer wants us to think and to feel.

WHAT'S IN A TITLE?

Look at the following book titles. What kind of book does each make you expect? What kind of person do you think wrote it? What kind of reader do you think would want to read it?

1. BRIAN PICCOLO: A SHORT SEASON

2. THE VOICE OF THE COYOTE

3. MARK TWAIN: GOD'S FOOL

4. THE NEW YORK TIMES BOOK OF MONEY

5. KGB: THE SECRET WORK OF SOVIET SECRET AGENTS

6. TINKER, TAILOR, SOLDIER, SPY

7. FREE TO BE...YOU AND ME

8. SLAUGHTER THE ANIMALS, POISON THE EARTH

9. DIVORCED IN AMERICA: AN ANATOMY OF LONELINESS

10. The Treasure of King Tut

In Ralph Ellison's novel *Invisible Man*, the narrator repeatedly encounters symbolic objects that vividly sum up for him major elements in the history of his own people. Here, for instance, is his first look at a "keepsake" kept by an older man who spent nineteen years on a chain gang before he finally broke the chain and escaped:

I took it in my hand, a thick, dark, oily piece of filed steel that had been twisted open and forced partly back into place, on which I saw marks that might have been made by the blade of a hatchet. It . . . bore the marks of haste and violence, looking as though it had been attacked and conquered before it stubbornly yielded.

In Ellison's novel, the leg-iron becomes one of the things that makes the young black feel united with the members of his own race. It becomes a symbol of the solidarity he feels with his black brothers.

NOTE: As you work on critical papers, remember a basic requirement: *Keep the reader in close contact with the actual work.* When you make general points, support them by referring directly to the work in front of you. Quote the actual words used by a poet. Point to specific events in a story. Refer in detail to the actions and words of a character in a play.

Study the following excerpt from a student paper about Antigone, the central character in the play of the same name by the Greek poet, Sophocles. Show how the student author has brought together short quotations from different parts of the play to support her estimate of Antigone's character. Show how she uses a longer quotation at a crucial point to show the key motive that makes Antigone act the way she does.

EXERCISE 1

```
            A Proud and Stubborn Spirit


     The chorus, in one instance, gives us a clue to
her personality by declaring, "the maid shows herself
passionate child of passionate sire, and knows not
how to bend before troubles."  Later, when Antigone
is on the way to her doom and is lamenting her fate,
the chorus replies, "thy self-willed temper hath
wrought thy ruin."  It also refers to Antigone as
mistress of her own fate, indicating that it feels it
is nobody's fault but her own that she finds herself
facing inevitable death.  When Antigone tells her
sister, Ismene, of her plans to bury Polyneices,
Ismene calls her "over-bold."  Creon is more vehement
in describing her.  He calls her a proud and "o'er-
stubborn" spirit.  He says, too, that she is "versed
in insolence."  However, Creon may perhaps be too
prejudiced against his niece to see her clearly.

     Let us then examine the conflict which makes this
passionate and self-willed girl choose the path that
leads to her destruction.  A famous scholar has said
that Antigone's tragic fate illustrates "the devotion
to a higher unseen law, resulting in revolt against,
```

and destruction by, the lower visible law." Antigone's religious motivation is very intense. This becomes evident when she tells her sister: "I owe a longer allegiance to the dead than to the living; in that world I shall abide forever. But if thou wilt, be guilty of dishonoring laws which the gods have established in honor." When she is arrested by the guards and brought to Creon, he asks her why she dared to transgress his edict and she replies:

> It was not Zeus that had published me that edict; not such are the laws set among men by the Justice who dwells with the gods below; nor deemed I that thy decrees were of such force that a mortal could override the unwritten and unfailing statutes of heaven. For their life is not of today or yesterday, but from all time, and no man knows when they were first put forth. Not through dread of any human pride could I answer to the gods for breaking these.

EXERCISE 2

In recent years, many women have been looking for books by and about women to help them better understand their own past and their future. Choose one of the following for a book report:

1. Alcott, Louisa May. *Little Women.* The classic American story of a family which involves the life experiences of four girls growing up.
2. Angelou, Maya. *I Know Why the Caged Bird Sings.* An autobiographical account of a black girl growing up in the thirties and forties.
3. Bolten, Carol. *Never Jam Today.* A fascinating account of the experiences of the American suffragettes from the point of view of a teenage girl.
4. Cather, Willa. *My Ántonia.* The American Dream as explicated by the life of an immigrant family and their daughter, Ántonia.
5. Duncan, Isadora. *My Life.* An autobiography of a liberated American woman who flamboyantly flashed across the American scene.
6. Ferber, Edna. *Giant.* A family saga of the American Southwest which features strong women.
7. Green, Hannah. *I Never Promised You a Rose Garden.* An account of a young woman's experience as she struggles to regain her mental health.
8. Jackson, Helen Hunt. *Ramona.* A tragedy of California Indians with a female protagonist.
9. Lindbergh, Anne Morrow. *Gift from the Sea.* A beautiful use of the language by a prominent and contemporary woman.

10. McCullers, Carson. *The Heart Is a Lonely Hunter*. A look at alienated people from the point of view of a lonely young woman.
11. Milford, Nancy. *Zelda*. The biographical account of a wife who was obscured by her more famous husband.
12. Mitchell, Margaret. *Gone with the Wind*. A Civil War account from the perspective of a Southern belle.
13. Oates, Joyce Carol. *Garden of Earthly Delights*. A migrant girl's life saga as she relates to her father, her husband, and her son.
14. O'Connor, Flannery, *Everything that Rises Must Converge*. A collection of short stories that feature violence from a woman's point of view.
15. Porter, Katherine Anne. *Pale Horse, Pale Rider*. Three short stories, one of which (the well-known "Noon Wine") depicts the difficulties of interpersonal relationships.
16. Wharton, Edith, *House of Mirth*. The restricted life-style of an aristocratic but impoverished woman protagonist.

WRITING TOPICS

1. Choose a character from a story, a novel, or a play whom you would call a rebel. What made this character a rebel? What kind of rebel was he or she? Can you identify with the rebel? Why or how? Write a character study that would help your reader know and understand the person.

2. What novel or play do you know that you would consider a great love story? Write about the *language* of love in the novel or play. What kinds of things do the lovers say to each other? Is what they say predictable or different? Why and how?

3. Do you ever read books that deal with illness, suicide, or death? Which of these books made the strongest impression on you? Write about the author's major theme and the way the theme was treated in the book.

4. What story or novel or play do you know in which one or more important symbols plays a central role? Write about what the symbols mean and how they work in the story or play.

C5b
The Research Paper

Interpret and evaluate evidence from several different sources.

Research means finding out for yourself. When you do research, you conduct your own independent investigation. You are no longer satisfied with what you have heard other people say. You no longer simply rely on an encyclopedia or a textbook, which summarizes the results of the investigations of others.

Remember the following general guidelines:

- *Try to find sources that take you close to firsthand observation or investigation.* When you are told that one of our early Presidents liked music, or that one of our great writers believed in telepathy, your attitude should be: "Let me see for myself." Whenever possible, find writers who rely on **primary sources**—eyewitness accounts, letters, contemporary newspaper reports, and the like.

- *Take in what you find.* The first question is not whether you agree or disagree with your source. Your first question is: "What does it say?" Look at what you find in *context.* Pay attention not only to a writer's conclusions but also to why and how those conclusions were reached.

- *Give credit where credit is due.* When you write down someone's exact words, make sure to put them in quotation marks. When you borrow someone's ideas, identify the person: "Acording to C. P. Snow . . ." Borrowing without acknowledgment is **plagiarism.** Someone accused of plagiarizing is accused of stealing from someone else's writing. You are welcome to repeat facts and theories that have become widely known. They are "common knowledge." But if someone else had to dig up these facts for you, or if the ideas are someone else's brain child, you should give credit to the other person.

When you write a research paper, you move through five major stages:

(1) Find a subject you can investigate by studying several different sources. Experts disagree. When you write a research paper, you will often have to weigh the conflicting testimony of different authorities. You will try to see where they agree and where they disagree. You will try to fill in the gaps in one source with evidence from another.

Here are some general subject areas. Find your own limited topic: Investigate in detail one key question or key problem that arises in your mind as you study some of the relevant materials.

OUR THREATENED WILDLIFE
Much has recently been written about the endangered species of our planet. You will find articles in sources like the following:

Audubon Magazine
Outdoor Life
Smithsonian Magazine
American Forests
Wildlife Magazine
books by writers like Rachel Carson and Loren Eiseley

NATIVE AMERICANS

Much has recently been written to correct the shortcomings or the bias in traditional accounts of the North American Indian. Look for some recent articles in magazines like *Harper's, Atlantic,* or *Smithsonian.* Look at stories or books by authors like N. Scott Momaday, Dorothy M. Thompson, Mari Sandoz, or Leslie Silko.

AMERICA THROUGH FOREIGN EYES

In the past, America was the land of opportunity and of liberty to millions of people abroad. In recent years, we have heard much about "anti-Americanism" abroad. How do foreign (or foreign-born) writers look at this country? What do they expect? What do they criticize?

Look at sources like the following:

- G. B. Shaw, *The Devil's Disciple*
- Graham Greene, *The Quiet American*
- Elia Kazan, *America, America*
- Evelyn Waugh, *The Loved One*
- D. H. Lawrence, *Studies in Classic American Literature*
- articles or books by authors like Alistair Cooke, Jacques Barzun, Simone de Beauvoir, J. B. Priestley
- interviews with foreign visitors

BLACK IDENTITY

Study the treatment of the theme of black identity or black pride in the work of several black Americans. Here are some black writers whose work you may want to read:

Frederick Douglass	Lorraine Hansberry
Paul Laurence Dunbar	Robert Hayden
Langston Hughes	Ralph Ellison
Gwendolyn Brooks	Arna Bontemps
Richard Wright	Nikki Giovanni

UTOPIA AND ANTI-UTOPIA

A utopia used to be an ideal society of the future as described in detail by a writer. But many modern accounts of the future are anti-utopias. They warn us against what the future holds in store for us. What accounts for this difference? Look at some of the following:

- Plato, *The Republic*
- Sir Thomas More, *Utopia*
- Jonathan Swift, Book IV of *Gulliver's Travels*
- Aldous Huxley, *Brave New World*
- E. M. Forster, "The Machine Stops"
- George Orwell, *1984*
- recent science fiction

(2) Keep a record of your sources for use during your project and in a final bibliography. The books you draw on in writing your paper may come from your school library, a nearby public library, or even a paperback bookstore.

See **R2** for a guide to library resources.

Write down a full description of every book, magazine article, or pamphlet on which you draw for material. For a book, note:

- full name of the author;
- complete title and any subtitle;
- where published, by whom, and what year;
- whether edited, revised, translated, and by whom.

For an article, note the author, title, issue of the magazine, and the page numbers.

For a short paper drawing only on two or three major sources, you may record all this information simply on a single sheet of notepaper. For a larger project, put the information for each source on a separate 3 x 5 **bibliography card.** These you can then easily alphabetize for use in your final bibliography at the end of your paper. On your bibliography cards (but not in your final bibliography) include the *library call number* for books you have obtained from a library:

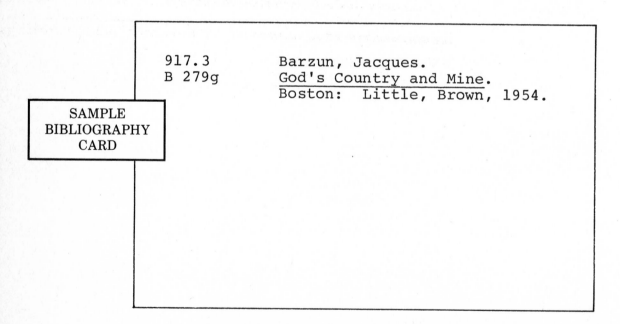

917.3
B 279g

Barzun, Jacques.
God's Country and Mine.
Boston: Little, Brown, 1954.

SAMPLE
BIBLIOGRAPHY
CARD

Use the following system to identify your sources both on your bibliography cards and in your final bibliography:

1. STANDARD ENTRY FOR A BOOK:

Ortiz, Victoria. <u>Sojourner Truth, a Self-Made
     Woman</u>. Philadelphia: Lippincott, 1974.

2. BOOK WITH A SUBTITLE:

Miller, Arthur. <u>Death of a Salesman: Certain
     Private Conversations in Two Acts and a
     Requiem</u>. New York: Viking Press, 1958.

3. BOOK WITH SEVERAL AUTHORS:

Main, C. F., and Peter J. Seng. <u>Poems</u>. Belmont,
     California: Wadsworth, 1961.

4. BOOK COMPILED FROM DIFFERENT SOURCES BY EDITOR:

Elwood, Roger, ed. <u>Future City</u>. New York: Simon
     & Schuster, 1973.

5. NEW EDITION OF OLDER BOOK:

Perrine, Laurence. <u>Sound and Sense: An Intro-
     duction to Poetry</u>. 5th ed. New York:
     Harcourt, 1978.

6. TRANSLATION:

Camus, Albert. <u>The Stranger</u>. Trans. Stuart
     Gilbert. New York: Vintage Books, 1958.

7. WORK WITH SEVERAL VOLUMES:

Trevelyan, G. M. <u>History of England</u>. 3 vols.
     Garden City, N. Y.: Doubleday, 1956.

8. BOOK NEWLY EDITED BY OTHER THAN AUTHOR:

Dickens, Charles. <u>Hard Times</u>. Ed. Robert
     Donald Spector. New York: Bantam Books,
     1964.

9. STANDARD ENTRY FOR ARTICLE:

Morrison, Theodore. "The Agitated Heart." <u>The
     Atlantic</u>, July 1967, pp. 72-79.

Revelle, Roger. "Food and Population." <u>Scientific
     American</u>, 231 (Sept. 1974), 161-170.

NOTE: For scholarly magazines, the Arabic numeral after the name
is the volume number (usually for all issues published during one
year). Note that the abbreviation "pp." for "pages" is omitted when
the volume number appears.

10. ANONYMOUS NEWSPAPER ARTICLE:

"A Shakespeare Festival." The Oakdale Register,
6 March 1979, p. 4, col. 3.

11. ARTICLE IN A COLLECTION:

Ornstein, Robert. "The Mystery of Hamlet." In
Hamlet: Enter Critic. Ed. Claire Sacks and
Edgar Whan. New York: Appleton, 1960.

12. ARTICLE IN ENCYCLOPEDIA:

"Drama." Encyclopaedia Britannica. 1958 ed.

13. TWO ENTRIES BY SAME AUTHOR:

Plimpton, George. Out of My League. New York:
Harper & Row, 1961.
----------. Paper Lion. New York: Harper & Row,
1965.

*(3) Take notes to record all information and quoted material
that you intend to use in your finished paper.* Take detailed notes
whenever you say to yourself:

- "This will help me prove a point."
- "This will provide essential background material for my
  readers."
- "This quotation will show the author's attitude on an important
  issue."
- "This excerpt from another writer's work will lend extra
  'weight' to my own point of view."

Many teachers recommend that you take notes on 4 x 6 cards.
With these cards, you can organize your paper easily by shuffling the
cards over and over until your thoughts and materials are in proper
order. Note at the top the tentative *subtopic* under which the material on the card would fit. Note at the bottom, in shortened form, the
author, the title, and the *exact page number* of the material. Limit
each card to one point, one step in an argument, one set of data—
material that you will not have to *split up* for use in different parts
of your paper.

Most of the notes you take will be of three major kinds:

SUMMARY OR PARAPHRASE—use summary or paraphrase when you summarize background information, sum up the events of a plot, or give
the gist of an argument. You are using your *own words:*

The following could be the final bibliography of a paper on "Sports and the Poet." Study the arrangement and punctuation of the different entries. Note that the entries are listed in alphabetical order, under the last name of the author or editor.

Francis, Robert. The Orb Weaver. Middletown, Conn.: Wesleyan Univ. Press, 1948.

Hadas, Moses, ed. The Greek Poets. New York: Random House, 1953.

Higgs, Robert J., and Neil D. Isaacs, eds. The Sporting Spirit: Athletes in Literature and Life. New York: Harcourt, 1977.

Kumine, Maxine W. Halfway. New York: Holt, Rinehart and Winston, 1961.

Mishima, Yukio. "Testament of a Samurai." Trans. Michael Gallagher. Sports Illustrated, 11 Jan. 1971, pp. 73-74.

Morrison, Lillian. Sprints and Distances: Sports in Poetry and the Poetry in Sport. New York: Crowell, 1965.

Pindar. The Odes of Pindar. Trans. Richard Lattimore. Chicago: Univ. of Chicago Press, 1947.

Robinson, E. A. Collected Poems of Edwin Arlington Robinson. New York: Macmillan, 1937.

Schulberg, Budd. "The Chinese Boxes of Muhammad Ali." Saturday Review, 55 (26 Feb. 1972), 28-30.

Stone, Gregory, ed. Games, Sport, and Power. New Brunswick, N. J.: E. P. Dutton, 1972.

SAMPLE NOTE CARD A

Humanity and Survival

The play shows Wilder's faith in the ability of humanity to survive the catastrophes it encounters. Although crushing setbacks are suffered, humanity is never beaten, but makes a fresh start. First, it survives the Ice Age. Next, it scrapes through decadence and the Flood. Finally it survives fascism and war.

Thornton Wilder, The Skin of Our Teeth

DIRECT QUOTATION—use direct quotation for important passages: They may show a key motive, state a major theme, or illustrate a characteristic attitude. Keep the exact *original wording:*

SAMPLE NOTE CARD B

Linda about Willy

"I don't say he's a great man. Willy Loman never made a lot of money. His name was never in the paper. He's not the finest character that ever lived. But he's a human being, and a terrible thing is happening to him. So attention must be paid. He's not to be allowed to fall into his grave like an old dog. Attention, attention must be finally paid to such a person."

Arthur Miller, Death of a Salesman, p. 56.

COMBINATION PARAPHRASE AND QUOTATION—use this combination to summarize and interpret important passages, while *keeping* directly quoted phrases and sentences from source materials that give your summary the authentic touch:

Majority rule

    Thoreau questions the democratic system of majority rule. In practice, the majority rules not "because it is most likely to be in the right" but because it is strongest. We should let our conscience decide what is right and wrong. "Must the citizen ever for a moment, or in the least degree, resign his conscience to the legislator? Why has every man a conscience, then?"

"Civil Disobedience," p. 37.

SAMPLE NOTE CARD C

As you write your note cards, ask yourself: "How *usable* will this be when I start writing the actual paper?" In a typical paragraph of your paper, you will *bring together* material from several closely related cards.

(4) Work out a strong overall pattern of organization. Early in your project, set up a working outline that will guide you in taking notes. Adjust and elaborate your outline as necessary in the light of your findings. As you go along, keep asking yourself: "What is my strategy for tackling this subject?" "What do I want each part of the paper to contribute to the whole?" "How and where does this material fit in with other findings?"

On the following page, study the outline for a paper comparing the treatment of a major theme in two American short stories. Can you see how the author's point-by-point comparison allows him to mesh material from his two major sources?

For more on outlines, see **C2c.**

Two Views of Guilt

THESIS: In both Stephen Crane's "The Blue Hotel" and Shirley Jackson's "The Lottery," innocent people die as the result of our inhumanity toward others. But Crane puts the blame on individuals, while Shirley Jackson blames society.

I. Our modern tendency to blame society for evil

II. Individual and society in the two stories

   A. The social setting in both stories
     1. Crane's characters each behave differently toward the victim.
       a. The hospitable landlord
       b. The belligerent son
       c. The disdainful gambler
     2. In "The Lottery," people act the same as members of a faceless mob.

   B. The victims in both stories
     1. The Swede turns people against him by his mixture of frantic suspicion and bullying bravado.
     2. In "The Lottery," all the townspeople take the "same chance" when the victim is selected by lot.

   C. The aftermath in both stories
     1. In Crane's story, the Easterner, a "bystander," recognizes his share of the guilt and points out the guilt of others.
     2. In "The Lottery," the killing is a customary ceremony in the community, and the people feel no guilt.

III. Crane's view of guilt is more convincing because his characters seem like real people.

(5) Make your evidence available for inspection. Identify your sources so that your readers can see for themselves. Detailed **documentation** directs your readers to the exact page in an article, book, or collection of documents where you found your evidence. By identi-

fying your sources, you are telling your readers: "You are welcome to check the original source to see whether I have quoted it accurately and represented it fairly."

Note how the footnote that goes with the following passage tells the reader exactly *where* the author found the quotation:

> Darwin's theory of evolution--that "species originated by means of natural selection, or through the preservation of the favored races in the struggle for life"--was hotly debated by his contemporaries.[1]

[1]These are Darwin's words, quoted by T. H. Huxley, "The Darwinian Hypothesis," Collected Essays, II: Darwiniana (New York, 1895), p. 1.

At the end of the sentence (or paragraph) that contains borrowed information or quoted material, insert a *raised* footnote number. Number all footnotes consecutively. At the bottom of the page, leave room for a footnote identifying the source of the borrowed or quoted material (Or you may put the footnotes on a separate sheet of paper at the end.)

Use the following system the *first time* you mention a source:

1. STANDARD FOOTNOTE FOR A BOOK:

[7]Hope Stoddard, Famous American Women (New York: Crowell, 1970), p. 34.

2. BOOK WITH SUBTITLE:

[3]Alice Griffin, Rebels and Lovers: Shakespeare's Young Heroes and Heroines (New York: New York Univ. Press, 1976), p. 79.

3. BOOK WITH SEVERAL AUTHORS:

[7]Jesse Burt and Robert B. Ferguson, Indians of the Southeast: Then and Now (Nashville: Abingdon Press, 1973), p. 18.

4. BOOK COMPILED BY EDITOR:

[13]Norman Rabkin, ed., Approaches to Shakespeare (New York: McGraw-Hill, 1964), pp. 9-10.

5. NEW EDITION OF OLDER BOOK:

[8]Albert C. Baugh, <u>A History of the English Language</u>, 2nd ed. (New York: Appleton, 1957), p. 115.

6. TRANSLATION:

[11]Eugene Ionesco, <u>Three Plays</u>, trans. Donald Watson (New York: Grove Press, 1958), p. 103.

7. ONE OF SEVERAL VOLUMES:

[2]Ethelou Yazzie, ed., <u>Navajo History</u> (Phoenix: Navajo Curriculum Center, 1972), I, 38.

8. BOOK EDITED BY OTHER THAN AUTHOR:

[19]Amelia Earhart, <u>The Last Flight</u>, ed. George Palmer Putnam (New York: Harcourt, 1939), p. 72.

9. STANDARD FOOTNOTE FOR ARTICLE:

[7]Ray B. West, Jr., "The Unity of Billy Budd," <u>Hudson Review</u>, 5 (Spring 1952), 124.

10. ANONYMOUS NEWSPAPER ARTICLE:

[8]"Albee's Powerful New Play," <u>The Allandale Times</u>, 17 June 1979, p. 3, col. 2.

11. ARTICLE IN COLLECTION:

[11]Honor M. V. Matthews, "Characters and Symbol in Macbeth," in <u>Approaches to Macbeth</u>, ed. Jay L. Halio (Belmont, California: Wadsworth, 1966), p. 89.

12. ARTICLE IN ENCYCLOPEDIA:

[3]"Symbol," <u>Encyclopaedia Britannica</u>, 1965, XXI, 701.

NOTE: The footnote differs from the bibliography entry in several ways. The footnote does *not* put the last name first. It does *not* use periods to separate the major parts. It *does* provide an exact page number. (In references to a Shakespeare play, you may substitute act and scene; in references to the Bible, chapter and verse as well as book: *Hamlet* III.ii or Judges 13:5.)

The *second time* and subsequent times you refer to a source, identify it by the author's last name. If you are using several sources by the same author, add a shortened version of the title:

1. ONE SOURCE BY AUTHOR:

   [7]Baugh, p. 78.

2. SEVERAL SOURCES BY SAME AUTHOR:

   [4]Baugh, *History*, p. 78.

ABBREVIATIONS FOUND IN FOOTNOTES

© *1965*	the copyright date, usually found on the *back* of the title page (unless the copyright on a book has been *renewed,* the copyright date is the official year of publication)
ca. or *c.*	Latin *circa,* "approximately"; used for approximate dates and figures (*ca.* 1952)
cf.	Latin *confer,* "compare"; often used loosely instead of *see* in the sense of "consult for further relevant material" (*Cf.* Ecclesiastes xii. 12)
et al.	Latin *et alii,* "and others"; used in references to books by several authors (G. B. Harrison *et al.*)
f., ff.	"and the following page," "and the following pages" (See pp. 16*f.*)
ibid.	Latin *ibidem,* "in the same place"; always points back to the last source cited
n.d.	"no date," date of publication unknown
op. cit.	Latin *opere citato,* "in the work already cited," usually preceded by the author's name: Baugh, *op. cit.,* p. 37
passim	Latin for "throughout"; "in various places in the work under discussion" (See pp. 54-56 *et passim*)
q.v.	Latin *quod vide;* "which you should consult"

Suppose you are investigating legislation regulating the design and use of automobiles. Below are sample passages by authors who might be experts. What kind of person is each writer? What side is he or she on? Would you trust the writer's judgment—why or why not?

1. The Detroit engine not only throws more garbage out of its exhaust into the air, but also demands the most lethal kind of gasoline which is loaded with anti-knock compounds, high and low speed additives, scavengers, deposit modifiers, anti-oxidants, metal deactivators, anti-rust agents, anti-icing agents, detergent additives and lubricants. And we have to breathe all of that bleep. Beyond failing to regulate the death-dealing capacity of automobiles, the fine gentlemen who run the country are still hard at work accommodating the monsters. Since 1947, the year we got serious about beginning to choke ourselves to death, all the governments of the United States—local, state and national—have spent $249 billion on highways. The largest single source of this money is the inviolate Highway Trust Fund, which is so holy that, in years when some of it is left unspent, the Treasury is actually obliged to pay interest on the unused portion of this vast amount of dough which flows from the federal tax on cars, tires, gas, etc.

2. Forced obsolescence has been much maligned. When production quantities exceed 350,000 units per year, the tooling is worn out anyway. Hence, the technical innovations evolved each year by engineers can just as well be incorporated when tools, dies, and machines are replaced. While Henry Ford may have saved a dollar or two per Model T (by making no important design changes), he spent over 100 million dollars in 1927 to make the change to the Model A. Yet only 4.5 million Model A's were produced before complete retooling was required for the 1932 V-8. From that time on, Ford retooled every year for a new and improved model. Even Ford capitulated to the inexorable march of technological advances.

3. As a driver, I object to the annoyance and expense of having my new car cluttered up with useless and even dangerous junk dreamed up by impractical sentimentalists in whom I have no faith. I mistrust these sentimental safety-thinkers because, as has been shown, they seldom bother to prove their assumptions or test their techniques scientifically. Therefore, I don't believe that all their cute safety gimmicks and clever safe-driving tricks actually work. I also mistrust them because they obviously consider that my time and that of millions of other Americans—at least that part of it spent on

rubber-tired wheels—is of no value whatever and can be wasted any way they see fit. I'm not denying that safety is important. Certainly there is a place for traffic "doctors"—people who specialize in accidents and how to prevent them—in our traffic systems, just as there's a place for school doctors in our school systems. But that place is not at the top of the pyramid. At the top, what are needed are some cold-blooded, hardnosed transportation specialists who'll consider their stopwatches and traffic counters as important as their accident statistics—people who'll understand that if you save a life but waste a lifetime doing it you're not really much ahead of the game.

In your school or public library, find *one* book or article in each of the following categories. Write a bibliography entry and a sample footnote for each.

EXERCISE 2

1. A book about the English language: its history, its structure, its uses or abuses.
2. A translation (some sample titles: Sophocles, *Antigone;* Henrik Ibsen, *A Doll's House;* Gunnel Beckman, *Admission to the Feast.*)
3. An article about a modern poet, such as Richard Brautigan, Sylvia Plath, or Anne Sexton; or about a modern playwright, such as Edward Albee, Eugene Ionesco, or Lorraine Hansberry.
4. One volume of a multivolume history.
5. A collection of science fiction stories.

Interpret all the information in the following footnotes. Point out anything that is unusual or difficult in these notes.

EXERCISE 3

[3]William Hazlitt, <u>Characters of Shakespeare's Plays</u>, Vol. IV of <u>The Complete Works of William Hazlitt</u> (London: J. M. Dent, 1930), p. 257.

[7]Walter Raleigh, ed., <u>Johnson on Shakespeare</u> (London: Oxford Univ. Press, 1952), p. 156.

[11]Edith Sitwell, "King Lear," <u>Atlantic,</u> 185 (May 1950), 58.

[2]Sholom J. Kahn, "'Enter Lear Mad,'" <u>Shakespeare Quarterly</u>, 8 (1957), 311-312.

[5]Samuel Taylor Coleridge, <u>Lectures and Notes on Shakespeare</u>, ed. T. Ashe (London: 1890), pp. 3-5.

EXERCISE 4
Study the way sources are quoted and identified in the following composite sample pages from student research papers. For each example, describe the procedure followed by the author.

SAMPLE A (Literary Topic)

BLOCK QUOTATION— PROSE

> And though after my skin worms destroy this body, yet in my flesh shall I see God: whom I shall see for myself, and mine eyes shall behold, and not another, though my veins be consumed with me.[4]

Job's inspirations are confirmed when the Voice in the Whirlwind shows him the greatness of God's power. He realizes that God is beyond our understanding:

KEY QUOTATION— SET OFF

> For he is not a man, that I should answer him, and we should come together in judgement.[5]

Robert Frost, in his "chapter forty-three of Job," shows that a God within the limits of human understanding would reduce life to a superficial charade.

---

[4] The Book of Job, 19:25-27.
[5] Job 9:32.

Frost's hypothetical God is easily recognized by us and easily portrayed by human media. "It's God./I'd know Him by Blake's picture anywhere." He lacks splendor and power: his court is constituted by Burning Bushes and Christmas Trees, by ornaments and gold-enameled nightingales. His throne, "a plywood flat, pre-fabricated," collapses on the fifth page of the poem.[6] Not only does God allow Job's wife to lodge a protest with Him, but, He allows Job to question the reason for his suffering in very human terms:

> The front of being answerable to no one
> I'm with You in maintaining to the public.
> But, Lord, we showed them what. The audience
> Has all gone home to bed. The play's played out.
> Come, after all these years--to satisfy me.
> I'm curious.[7]

LINES OF POETRY—
RUN IN
(SEPARATED BY
SLASH)

BLOCK
QUOTATION—
POETRY

---

[6]Robert Frost, _Complete Poems of Robert Frost_ (New York: Holt, 1949), p. 588.
   [7]Frost, p. 597.

SAMPLE B (Nonliterary Topic)

BLOCK
QUOTATION

> There in imposing majestic si-
> lence the vast silvery hulk of the
> Hindenburg hung motionless like a
> framed cloud. Everything within and
> without the ship was proceeding in
> an entirely normal manner. In only
> a few minutes more, the ship would
> reach the ground and her mooring
> mast safely and smoothly.[1]

This is how one observer described the German dirigible, Hindenburg, LZ-129, as it started its ill-fated attempted landing at Lakehurst, New Jersey, on May sixth, 1937. Within seconds, a ground engineer saw a small

QUOTED
PHRASES

spark "like static electricity" underneath the airship.[2] Moments later, the ship was gutted with fire. In thirty-two seconds the Hindenburg was gone, taking with it a final total of thir- ty-six lives. These were the first passenger fatalities in the history of commercial air- ship operation.[3]

"One of the most tragic and mysterious accidents in the pre-war [pre-World War II]

---

[1]A. A. Hoehling, Who Destroyed the Hindenburg? (Boston: Little, Brown, 1962), p. 103.
   [2]Hoehling, pp. 106-107.
   [3]"Airships," Encyclopaedia Britannica,
1968, I, 472.

history of air travel."[4] That was how German-
born missile expert Wernher van Braun described
the fiery death of the ship. There are many
possibilities as to the cause of the disaster
of May sixth, 1937, but the commissions that
investigated it could not reach a definite
conclusion. Until its destruction, the great
German airship was considered one of the great
accomplishments of modern technology. In this
paper I will discuss its structure and its
safety before and during the final voyage.

When one looked at the Hindenburg, it
seemed like a great monster. The gross weight
of equipment and fuel was 430,950 pounds.
With an additional 15,470 pounds for passengers
and 26,520 pounds for freight and mail, the
total lift under standard conditions was 472,
940 pounds or about 237 tons.[5] It measured
803 feet from nose to rudder tip, and was 146
feet high.

SUMMARY
OF
INFORMATION

PAGE NUMBER
OF PREFACE

---

[4]Hoehling, p. xiv.
[5]A. Klemin, "The Hindenburg," Scientific
American, 154 (June 1936), 330.

**FOR FURTHER
STUDY**

CREATIVE WRITING

There is no rigid line between ordinary prose and creative writing. Much everyday language has an imaginative touch. People using language for practical purposes often show that they love to play with words, or that they have an ear for a good story. They show that they can look at something old from an imaginative new point of view.

How much creative writing have you done? The following assignments will give you a chance to experiment. They will provide you with materials to discuss with your classmates.

ACTIVITY 1

An effective writer has an ear for words. A good writer knows how to sum up an idea in a vivid statement that rings true, in a sentence that we can repeat and remember. Choose one of the following two assignments:

A. Study the way the following sentences sum up an idea in a brief, memorable form. Write several similar statements of your own about the same topics: nature, life, greatness, beauty, voters, drivers.

- Nature made ferns for pure leaves, to show what she could do in that line. (Thoreau)
- Life is a banquet, and most of the people at it are starving.
- Greatness is a dream, which is what makes it enduring.
- Beauty is the strength of the salmon as she battles upstream to deliver her young.
- The President of this country is elected by the man who goes bowling on Thursday nights.
- The speed of an automobile is inversely proportional to the intelligence of the driver.
- The toad doesn't run for nothing. (African proverb)

B. Write half a dozen "modern proverbs," summing up a general observation in pointed, memorable form. Here are some possible models. (What was the original proverb in each case?)

It's a long street that has no parking meter.
He who laughs last will never be part of a studio audience.
Where there's muck there's headlines.
A watched bus never comes.
A penny earned is a penny spent.
A penny saved will probably be used for sales tax later.
Life is a bowl of pits—someone else got all the cherries.

Study the following five-line poems, or "cinquains." Can you see that each gives us a snapshot of something familiar? Read these poems out loud. Then write one or two five-line poems of your own.

ACTIVITY 2

Batman
flits across my rooftop,
sits on my TV antenna,
and pretends
he's a 200 lb. pigeon.   —Candy Fleming

> Honey
> Comb, the Queen Bee,
> Reigns with trifling, stoic
> Elegance, keeping her left eye
> Droneward.   —Paula Truesdell

When Emily Dickinson first published some of her poems, people found them very strange. Look at the following two examples. (Read them out loud.) How do you think they were different from what poetry lovers would have liked to see? Could you write a poem that readers would recognize as an imitation of Emily Dickinson's style?

ACTIVITY 3

The sky is low, the clouds are mean,
A traveling flake of snow
Across a barn or through a rut
Debates if it will go.

A narrow wind complains all day.
How someone treated him.
Nature, like us, is sometimes caught
Without her diadem.

Faith is a fine invention
When gentlemen can see,
But microscopes are prudent
In an emergency.

Read to yourself (and read aloud as well) examples of American *free verse:* one of the poems of Walt Whitman or Carl Sandburg, for instance. What are some of the features and effects such examples share? Try your hand at writing some free verse, keeping in mind its typical features and effects.

ACTIVITY 4

ACTIVITY 5

One of the oldest ways to communicate an idea and make the reader think about it is the *parable*. Study and describe the following example. Try your hand at writing a similar parable.

Damian was a poor man who lived in a modest house and did only small things. Every day after work he would stop and feed the birds which frequented his garden. He fed them bread crumbs which he had saved.

Duncan, on the other hand, had made it big in the world. He had a large home and servants, and he employed Damian as his gardener. Duncan had a large number of birdhouses and birdbaths located about his estate, and he supplied them with the finest seed. He also was an active member of an exclusive birdwatching club, and he owned quite an expensive pair of binoculars and a colorful Audubon portfolio.

Then there was Dunniger. He was a bird. He was free.

—from a student publication

ACTIVITY 6

In some modern fiction, the same story is told in turn by several different characters. Each one tells us what he or she has experienced and felt. Have you ever read a story or novel that employs this "multiple-reflector" technique? (William Faulkner's *The Sound and the Fury* is a famous example.) What special effects does this technique achieve? Write a story (or a poem) that presents several different versions of the same story as told by different participants or observers.

ACTIVITY 7

If you were a modern playwright, what kind of play would you want to write? On what kind of theme? With what kind of characters? Do one or both of the following:

1. Write a plot outline for a play you would like to write.
2. Write the dialogue for one key scene from the play.

(You may be able to arrange a trial staging in which some of your classmates read or act out the scene you have written.)

ACTIVITY 8

Satire uses humor as a weapon against things we want to criticize. Study the following paragraph from a description of an imaginary future society. What are the targets of the author's satire? What current trends has she projected into the future?

Write your own satire about some part of the current scene.

It had been a tiresome vacation. The other women in the dormitory were all right, but it was macaroni for breakfast, and there were so many organized sports. I had looked forward to the hike up to the National Forest Preserve, the largest forest left in the United States, but the trees didn't look at all the way they do in the postcards and brochures and Federal Beautification advertisements. They were spindly, and they all had little signs on saying which union they had been planted by. There were actually a lot more green picnic tables and cement Men's and Women's than there were trees. There was an electrified fence all around the forest to keep out unauthorized persons. The forest ranger talked about mountain jays, "bold little robbers," he said, "who will come and snatch the sandwich from your very hand," but I didn't see any. Perhaps because that was the weekly Watch Those Surplus Calories! Day for all the women, and so we didn't have any sandwiches. If I'd seen a mountain jay I might have snatched the sandwich from its very hand, who knows. Anyhow it was an exhausting week, and I wished I'd stayed home and practiced, even though I'd have lost a week's pay because staying home and practicing the viola doesn't count as planned implementation of recreational leisure as defined by the Federal Union of Unions.—Ursula K. Le Guin, "The New Atlantis"

How good are you at imitating a distinctive style? Try your hand at writing one of the following. Do your imitation as a brief story, as a script for an episode from a movie or television program, or whatever you consider appropriate:

ACTIVITY 9

- Columbus discovers the New World *Star Trek*-style;
- A day at the state (or federal) capitol reported in the style of *Julius Caesar, Macbeth,* or other Shakespeare play;
- A day at your house written in the style of a currently popular television program;
- A day at your school written in the style of a currently popular Western or detective series;
- A fairy tale retold in the style of a currently popular author.

(Or choose your own subject to be treated in a distinctive style of your own choice.)

Guide to Manuscript Revision

ab. . . . . . . Spell out abbreviation (M7b)

adv. . . . . . . Use adverb form (U2c)

agr . . . . . . Make verb agree with subject
            or pronoun with antecedent (U3a, U2d)

ap . . . . . . Use apostrophe (M2b)

cap . . . . . . Capitalize (M2a)

coll . . . . . . Use less colloquial word (U2a)

CS . . . . . . Revise comma splice (M4a)

d . . . . . . Improve diction (W3)

dev . . . . . . Develop your point (C1b, C2b)

div . . . . . . Revise word division (M7a)

DM . . . . . . Revise dangling modifier (U3c)

frag . . . . . . Revise sentence fragment (M3a)

FP . . . . . . Revise faulty parallelism (U3f)

awk . . . . . . Rewrite awkward sentence (U4)

lc . . . . . . Use lower case (M2a)

MM . . . . . . Shift misplaced modifier (U3c)

p . . . . . . Improve punctuation (M3-6)

¶ . . . . . . New paragraph (C1)

no¶ . . . . . . Take out paragraph break (C1)

ref . . . . . . Improve pronoun reference (U3b)

rep . . . . . . Avoid repetition (U3d)

shift . . . . . . Avoid shift in perspective (U3e)

sl . . . . . . Use less slangy word (U2a)

sp . . . . . . Revise misspelled word (M1)

st . . . . . . Improve sentence structure (U3, U4)

t . . . . . . Change tense of verb (U1a)

trans . . . . . . Provide better transition (C2e)

w . . . . . . Reduce wordiness (U4)

Chapter 4

Usage
Using Standard English

Chapter Preview 4

Use standard English effectively in speech and writing.

We are all aware of differences in the ways people use language. English sounds different in different parts of the country. We adapt our own use of language to suit different situations and different purposes. Differences in sound, in word choice, and in sentence structure are called differences in **usage.** When we study usage, we study the range and variety of our common language.

For practical purposes, the study of usage often concentrates on the most important distinction: the difference between **standard** English and other kinds of English. Schools teach standard English for the following reasons:

(1) Standard English has national currency. In the days before air travel and television, local varieties of a language could drift far apart. In countries like England and France, very different regional **dialects** developed over the centuries. A standard national language provides a common medium for education, information, and government. Today, standard English is the language of the schools, the media, and government in English-speaking countries around the world.

(2) For many people, standard English is job English. Today, almost any job requiring much paperwork or frequent contact with the public requires an effective command of standard English. Standard English is part of the price of admission to a wide range of occu-

pations, including those of office worker, teacher, journalist, insurance agent, lawyer, engineer, scientist, and physician.

(3) Standard English is needed for effective citizenship. It helps us hold our own any time we deal with officeholders and office workers. It helps us hold our own when we take care of our own official business and when we participate in community affairs.

COMMON USAGE PROBLEMS

A CHECKLIST

Adverb form required	U2c
Agreement—pronoun	U2d
Agreement—verb	U3a
Apostrophe missing or misused	M2b
Capitals missing or misused	M2a
Colloquial word	U2a
Comma splice	M4a
Comparison faulty or illogical	U3d
Dangling modifier	U3c
Deadwood	U4
Double negative	U1c
Lie/lay; sit/set	U2d
Like as connective	U2d
Misplaced modifier	U3c
Mixed construction	U3d
Parallelism	U3f
Passive overused	U4
Plural forms	U1c, 3a
Pronoun case	U2b
Pronoun form nonstandard	U1b
Pronoun reference	U3b
Sentence fragment	M3a
Shift in tense	U3e
Subjunctive	U2d
Verb form nonstandard	U1a
Who/whom	U2b
You overused	U3b, 3e

(M refers to Chapter 5, "Mechanics")

Usage

In serious speech and writing, people expect us to use formal standard English. Look at the blank space in each of the following sentences. Which of the three choices would be right in serious written English? Put the letter for the right choice after the number of the sentence. (Be prepared to discuss with your classmates the reasons for your choices.)

EXAMPLE: We had sent an invitation to his sister and _____ .
a. he   b. him   c. hisself

(Answer) *b*

1. Athletes have to take good care of _____ .
   a. theirselves   b. themself   c. themselves
2. John's fever has disappeared and _____ much better.
   a. feels   b. he feels   c. feeling
3. There are many regulations of which people are not _____ .
   a. aware   b. aware of   c. familiar
4. When a person loses, _____ may become discouraged.
   a. you   b. he or she   c. they
5. Someone could _____ her briefcase while she was gone.
   a. of stole   b. have stolen   c. have stole
6. Zeus, king of the gods, _____ his enemies with thunderbolts.
   a. struck   b. striking   c. zapped
7. All their hard work had never gotten my parents _____ .
   a. nowhere   b. nowheres   c. anywhere
8. The government had rewarded them _____ .
   a. real generously   b. very generously   c. real generous
9. The principal greeted us _____ nothing had happened.
   a. as   b. as if   c. like
10. Altering all the costumes _____ too much time.
    a. takes   b. take   c. taking
11. When the band did not appear, the audience _____ to boo.
    a. begins   b. began   c. begun
12. _____ enrollment goes up, the school will close.
    a. Without   b. On account of   c. Unless
13. His sister and _____ seldom if ever quarreled.
    a. him   b. hisself   c. he
14. Joe is one of those athletes who _____ always on the bench.
    a. is   b. are   c. being
15. Many people in our town _____ their own vegetables.
    a. grew   b. grown   c. growed
16. We never found the people for _____ the message was intended.
    a. whom   b. who   c. which
17. She enjoyed going out into the garden and _____ the leaves.
    a. rake   b. to rake   c. raking
18. Mary had traveled all over, but _____ had never appealed to me.
    a. travel   b. it   c. this

19. He had tried hard to get tickets for _____ .
    - a. he and I   b. himself and me   c. himself and I
20. _____ kind of mushroom might be poisonous.
    - a. Those   b. Them   c. That

Be able to speak and write standard English.

Standard English is business English: It is the language of memos, bills, reports, and catalogues. Standard English is office English: We use it whenever there are forms to be filled out, complaints to be filed, or benefits to be secured. Standard English is media English: We see it or hear it in newspapers and on TV.

Millions of Americans speak **nonstandard** English. Here are some things that make nonstandard *different* from standard English:

U1
STANDARD AND NONSTANDARD

VERB FORMS:	he *don't,* you *was,* I *says; knowed, growed, throwed;* have *wrote,* had *went;* I *seen* him
PRONOUN FORMS:	*hisself, theirself; this here* book, *that there* table; *them* coupons
CONNECTIVES:	*without* he pays the rent; *on account of* she was sick; *being as* he lived there
DOUBLE NEGATIVES:	we *don't* have *no* time; *never* hurt *nobody*
VOCABULARY:	*nowheres, nohow*

NONSTANDARD

Use the standard forms of English verbs.

Standard differs from nonstandard English in the forms of many common verbs. Here are some typical contrasts:

U1a
Standard Verb Forms

NONSTANDARD	STANDARD
we is, you is, they is	we are, you are, they are
we was, you was, they was	we were, you were, they were
ain't right, ain't got	isn't (is not) right, haven't got
he don't	he doesn't (does not)
I says	I say (present), I said (past)
knowed, growed, throwed	knew, grew, threw
have wrote, had went	have written, had gone
I done, I seen, I been	I've (I have) done, I've seen, I've been

Be sure of the following *standard forms:*

(1) Use the final –s *for third person, singular.* When we talk about the present, verbs change to show the change from "one single third party" to "several." This is the change from singular to plural:

SINGULAR: She *sings.*   He *talks.*   The bus *leaves.*
PLURAL: They *sing.*   They *talk.*   The buses *leave.*

We use the –s ending when talking not about the "first person" *(I, we)* or about the "second person" *(you)* but about the **third person** —someone or something else. *He, she,* and *it* are third-person pronouns. Use the –s ending for one single subject other than *I* or *you* for "action now":

NONSTANDARD: I says.
                  He like it.
                  She know.
STANDARD: He *likes* us.
                  She *knows* all about it.
                  It *snows* all the time.
                  The heater *makes* funny noises.
                  The clock *ticks.*
                  Joan *organizes* the meetings.
                  She always *says* the right things.

Be sure to use *doesn't* or *does not* for third person, singular:

NONSTANDARD: He don't like us.
                  She don't live here.
STANDARD: He *doesn't* like us.
                  She *doesn't* live here.
                  The door *doesn't* close.
                  It *doesn't* work.
                  The letter *doesn't* say.
                  The jacket *doesn't* fit.

(2) Use standard forms for the past tense. Almost all English verbs change from present to past. Such changes in time are called changes in tense. Most English verbs, the **regular** verbs, form their past by adding –d or –ed to their present forms: *work/worked, ask/ asked, hope/hoped.* Do not omit this –d or –ed ending from the past tense of regular verbs:

NONSTANDARD: Last summer, she *work* at the paper mill.
STANDARD: Last summer, she *worked* at the paper mill.

Other English verbs, the **irregular** verbs, make up their past forms in their own ways: *know/knew, grow/grew, throw/threw, bring/ brought. Knowed, growed, throwed,* and *brang* are nonstandard.

ENGLISH VERBS: A Checklist of Standard Forms

PRESENT	PAST	PERFECT
begin	began	have begun
bend	bent	have bent
blow	blew	have blown
break	broke	have broken
bring	brought	have brought
burst	burst	have burst
buy	bought	have bought
catch	caught	have caught
choose	chose	have chosen
come	came	have come
dig	dug	have dug
do	did	have done
drag	dragged	have dragged
draw	drew	have drawn
drink	drank	have drunk
drive	drove	have driven
drown	drowned	have drowned
eat	ate	have eaten
fall	fell	have fallen
fly	flew	have flown
freeze	froze	have frozen
get	got	have gotten (got)
go	went	have gone
grow	grew	have grown
know	knew	have known
prove	proved	have proved (proven)
ride	rode	have ridden
run	ran	have run
say	said	have said
see	saw	have seen
sing	sang	have sung
speak	spoke	have spoken
steal	stole	have stolen
swim	swam	have swum
swing	swung	have swung
take	took	have taken
tear	tore	have torn
throw	threw	have thrown
wear	wore	have worn
write	wrote	have written

GROUP 1

GROUP 2

GROUP 3

GROUP 4

(3) Use standard forms for the perfect tenses. Many verbs have one form for the simple past. They have another form for use after *have (has, had)*. We call the forms that use *have* the **perfect** tenses. They often show that something has happened recently, or that it still mattered when something else took place:

PRESENT: We *write* to each other regularly.

PAST: She usually *wrote* to us about Christmastime.

PERFECT: I *have* already *written* to the admissions office.

PAST PERFECT: She *had written* to them but received no reply.

The same form that follows *have* (the past participle) is also used in the passive form of the verb:

PASSIVE: Her letters *were written* in a hurry.

Study the verbs in the "Checklist of Standard Forms." Take up one group of ten verbs at a time. Remember: Forms like *have wrote* and *should have went* are nonstandard. Use *have written* and *should have gone* instead. *He done it* and *I seen him* are nonstandard. Include a form of *have:* He *has* done it. I *have* seen him.

NOTE: Sometimes dictionaries list *two possible standard forms:*

They *dived* (or *dove*) into the pool.
He *dreamed* (or *dreamt*) of a white Christmas.
They *lighted* (or *lit*) the fire.
The theory was *proved* (or *proven*) wrong.

(4) Use standard forms of be. *Be* is different from all other verbs. It has three present forms: *am, are, is.* It has two past forms: *was, were.* Study the following chart:

		SINGULAR	**PLURAL**
PRESENT	FIRST PERSON:	I *am* glad.	We *are* glad.
	SECOND PERSON:	You *are* right, Jim.	You *are* both right.
	THIRD PERSON:	Phil *is* absent. He *is* ill.	The parcels *are* here.
		Sue *is* here. She *is* well.	They *are* heavy.
		The food *is* ready. It *is* hot.	
PAST	FIRST PERSON:	I *was* glad.	We *were* glad.
	SECOND PERSON:	You *were* right, Jim.	You *were* both right.
	THIRD PERSON:	Phil *was* absent. He *was* ill.	The parcels *were* here.
		Sue *was* here. She *was* well.	They *were* heavy.
		The food *was* ready. It *was* hot.	

Remember: *We was, you was,* and *they was* are nonstandard. Use *we were, you were,* and *they were.*

STANDARD: We *are* ready.
They *are* our friends.
You *are* always welcome.

You *were* out of town.
We *were* disappointed.
They *were* working.

If your command of standard verb forms is unsure, use the following passages for *oral drill*. Read over each set of forms several times. Come back to this drill repeatedly over a number of weeks.

EXERCISE 1

1. I *say* yes, but my father *says* no. I *said* tomorrow, but my mother *said* today. Jim wants to leave, but his brother *doesn't.* Jean wants to go, but her sisters *don't.* She *doesn't* speak English, and her parents *don't* either. Fred *doesn't* dance, but his friends don't care. I *did* what I could. I *have done* nothing wrong.

2. Jim *threw* the ball. I *knew* it all the time. The wind *blew.* I have *known* him for years. I have *driven* her car. He's *done* it again. The dish was *broken.* The spy was *caught.* The story was *written.* The water had *frozen.* He had *dug* a ditch.

3. She had once *grown* flowers in the yard, but now nothing *grew* there. I *knew* his face but had never *known* his name. She *threw* back the ball I had *thrown* to her. We *drove* the same car we had *driven* east. He had always *eaten* what the others *ate* and had always *drunk* what they *drank.* We *swam* out to the float to which we had *swum* before.

4. He *is* tall. She *is* short. It *is* true. We *are* friends. You *are* right. They *are* wrong. He *was* here. She *was* there. It *was* new. We *were* tired. You *were* rude. They *were* gone. The dog *is* fed. The story *is* true. A page *is* missing. Roses *are* red. Violets *are* blue. Times *are* hard. The meeting *was* over. The night *was* warm. The people *were* happy. He *was* invited, but we *weren't* asked.

In each of the following sentences, fill in the *standard form of the verb* listed at the end. After the number of the sentence, write down the form that would fit into the blank space in the sentence. Do *not* add any auxiliaries not already supplied.

EXERCISE 2

1. He always listens when I _____ something. (say)
2. We _____ having dinner when we heard the news. (be)
3. We prayed as the sailors _____ a rope to the boat. (throw)

271

4. The crowd gasped when George _____ the ball. (catch)
5. If he _____ not call tomorrow, I am going to leave. (do)
6. Candidates today _____ more handsome than they used to be. (be)
7. He met a man he had _____ in the army. (know)
8. Last year's election _____ many surprises. (bring)
9. I had never _____ such a big crowd before. (see)
10. He had never _____ more than his share. (take)
11. Many students work while they _____ to college. (go)
12. Her aunt had _____ all the way from Indiana. (drive)
13. Pasternak had _____ poetry before he published *Dr. Zhivago*. (write)
14. When she arrived, the librarian had _____ home. (go)
15. I gave her your message the last time I _____ her. (see)
16. It was dark, and a cold wind _____ outside. (blow)
17. The family had _____ 600 miles in an attempt to reach Dayton by sunset. (ride)
18. The speaker _____ again after the audience had quieted down. (begin)
19. The singer never _____ the aria before. (sing)
20. Yesterday, Jean _____ the 200-meter race. (swim)
21. The boy had never _____ a tie. (wear)
22. The trees had _____ to tremendous height. (grow)
23. Your friends came looking for you while you _____ out. (be)
24. The lake had not _____ over in many years. (freeze)
25. In his family, close relatives kiss when they _____ goodbye. (say)

EXERCISE 3

Of the two choices given in each sentence, which is the right one? Write the standard form after the number of the sentence.

1. You should have *wrote/written* before your visit.
2. After my aunt moved, we *saw/seen* her only on holidays.
3. Mercury *doesn't/don't* appear on this photograph.
4. Hundreds of people *was/were* waiting in line.
5. The driver *threw/thrown* something from the passing car.
6. The typewriter had been *stole/stolen* from a downtown office.
7. Her assistant always *did/done* good work for her.
8. Most of the guests had already *went/gone* home.
9. By now, your check should have *came/come* in the mail.
10. My uncle Paul always *talk/talks* too much.
11. The members *meet/meets* every Monday in the recreation hall.
12. My friends *is/are* too shy to ask questions.
13. The building *been/has been* there since the town was founded.
14. The driver may have *took/taken* the wrong turn.
15. The neighbors had never *spoke/spoken* to us before.
16. Henry never *drove/driven* faster than the law allowed.

17. The ball bearings had been *wore/worn* out.
18. The games always *began/begun* punctually.
19. Someone had *tore/torn* a page from the magazine.
20. It started to rain while we *was/were* talking.

Use the standard forms of pronouns.

Nonstandard English often uses pronouns that are different from those of standard English. Here are some typical contrasts:

NONSTANDARD	STANDARD
my brother he left	my brother left
them books, them people	these books, those people
this here trip, that there box	this trip, that box
yourn, hisn, hern, ourn	yours, his, hers, ours
hisself, theirself	himself, themselves
ourself, yourself	ourselves, yourselves (plural)

Avoid the following nonstandard forms:

(1) Avoid nonstandard forms of **demonstrative** *pronouns.* These are the "pointing" pronouns: *this* and *these; that* and *those.* Avoid expressions like *this here book* or *that there shelf.* Do not use expressions like *them books* or *them people.*

STANDARD: Put *these books* back on *that shelf.*
 We ordered *those tires* from *this catalogue.*

(2) Avoid nonstandard forms of **reflexive** *pronouns.* These are the *–self* pronouns. The singular forms are *myself, yourself, himself, herself,* and *itself.* The plural forms are *ourselves, yourselves,* and *themselves.* They point back to someone or something in the same sentence. Avoid nonstandard forms *hisself, ourself, theirself* or *theirselves,* as well as *yourself* used as a plural.

STANDARD: The custodian had locked *himself* in.
 You and your sister should be proud of *yourselves.*
 My brothers felt sorry for *themselves.*

(3) Avoid nonstandard uses of **possessive** *pronouns.* At one time, many people used nonstandard forms like *yourn, hisn, hern,* or *ourn.* The standard forms for these are *yours, his, hers,* or *ours:*

STANDARD: He liked her drawing but criticized *yours* and *mine.*
 Instead of my car, you will have to borrow *his* or *hers.*

STANDARD FORMS OF PRONOUNS

A CHECKLIST			
DEMONSTRATIVE ("pointing" pronouns)	*this* book *these* words	*that* book *those* words	

POSSESSIVE (two sets)	*my* turn *your* friend *his* face *her* car *its* crib *our* house *their* luck	It's *mine.* It's *yours.* It's *his.* It's *hers.* It's *its.* It's *ours.* It's *theirs.*

REFLEXIVE ("*self*" pronouns)	I congratulated *myself.* You distinguished *yourself.* He questioned *himself.* She blamed *herself.* It speaks for *itself.* We think for *ourselves.* You distinguished *yourselves.* They fended for *themselves.*

INTENSIVE (same as reflexive)	He did it *himself.* They *themselves* told me.

NOTE: Standard English omits the added *he* or *she* in sentences like "My father, *he* asked them to leave" or "My aunt, *she* became a lawyer."

STANDARD: *My father asked* them to leave.
My aunt became a lawyer.

See **U2b** for subject and object forms of personal pronouns.

EXERCISE 1

Reinforce your command of standard pronoun forms by *oral drill.* Read over the following passage several times. If necessary, come back to this exercise repeatedly over a number of weeks.

1. Put *this* box on *that* shelf. Put *these* boxes on *those* shelves. Who brought *those* jars in? Where did you get *those* shoes?

2. You boys should make *yourselves* useful. We wrapped *ourselves* in our blankets. The stranger considered *himself* fortunate. They failed to protect *themselves* against mosquitoes.

NONSTANDARD: *Being as* she was our friend, we lent her the money.
STANDARD: *Because* she was our friend, we lent her the money.

NONSTANDARD: We were late *on account of* the car stalled.
STANDARD: We were late *because* the car stalled.

Without and *on account of* are standard as prepositions before a noun: *without* your help, *on account of* your friendship. They are nonstandard if they start a clause with its own subject and verb:

NONSTANDARD: We cannot pay the refund *without* you return the clock within a week.

STANDARD: We cannot pay the refund *unless* you return the clock within a week.

(5) Avoid using a *and* an *in nonstandard ways.* *An* is standard before words beginning with a vowel sound. *A* is standard only if the word does *not* start with a vowel sound:

AN: an ear, an ace, an offer, an easy task, an hour, an *F*
A: a car, a tree, a station, a horse, a *C*, a useful tool

(6) Avoid other familiar nonstandard expressions. Watch out for the following:

learned me   In standard English, a teacher *teaches* something to the student. The student *learns* something from the teacher.

STANDARD: *Teach* me what you have *learned.*
             I *learned* well in the classes she *taught.*

nowheres, some-
  wheres, nohow   The standard expressions are *nowhere, some-*
                       where, and *not at all:*

STANDARD: We had *nowhere* to turn.
             We hope to go *somewhere* special on vacation.
             We could *not* budge it *at all.*

off of   Use *off* or *from* instead of *off of:*

NONSTANDARD: She borrowed ten dollars *off of* her aunt.
STANDARD: She borrowed ten dollars *from* her aunt.

leave   In standard English, *leave* means "to go away from," and *let* means "to permit or allow":

NONSTANDARD: *Leave* me handle it.
STANDARD: *Let* me handle it.

EXERCISE 1	Use the following exercise for *oral drill*. All examples show the forms that are right in standard English. Read over each set of examples several times.

1. They *don't* live here *anymore*.
   Filbert *never* helped *anybody*.
   My uncle *never* gave *anybody anything*.
   She *didn't* leave *any* message.
   The candidate *isn't* indebted to *anybody*.

2. I *could hardly* lift the package.
   The driver *could barely* see the road.
   Jim *can hardly* write his own name.
   The money *will barely* pay the rent.

3. Our candidate will win *regardless* of these attacks.
   She will win the race *regardless*.
   We cannot fix the roof *without* help.
   We cannot fix the roof *unless* you help us.
   They canceled the hike *on account of* the rain.
   They canceled the hike *because* it rained.

4. She was *teaching* students who *learned* fast.
   The book *taught* me how to *learn* faster.
   When one applicant *leaves, let* the next person come in.
   Live and *let* live.
   We should *let* them solve their own problems.

5. *A* reader tore *a* page from *a* magazine.
   An angry group was trapped for *an* hour in *an* elevator.
   A con man sold *a* museum *a* fake painting.
   An artist sent *an* exact copy to *an* exhibition.
   The record showed *an A, a B,* and *an F*.

EXERCISE 2	Each of the following sentences has one word or expression in it that is nonstandard English. After the number of the sentence, write the standard form that should replace the nonstandard one.

EXAMPLE: We couldn't do nothing to talk him out of it.
(Answer) *anything*

1. The pilot couldn't barely see the landing lights.
2. The group had hiked about fifteen mile.
3. The vase had fallen off of the shelf.
4. We no longer try to build more faster cars.
5. In the living room we found a unexpected visitor.
6. The project continued irregardless of the bad publicity.
7. We looked for errors but didn't find none.

8. Being that he was a minor, the request was refused.
9. The situation will become desperate without help comes soon.
10. The papers never printed nothing about the meeting.
11. He never even bothered to make up a excuse.
12. We couldn't find nothing inaccurate in the report.
13. We should leave people make their own decisions.
14. Our prospects were poor on account of we had lost our best player.
15. I read somewheres that she signed a twenty-year lease.
16. These supplies won't hardly last until Christmas.
17. They had waited five year for the application to be approved.
18. The coach sent me to a eye specialist.
19. Newcomers usually can't find no work in this town.
20. Seeing as how it was late, we adjourned the meeting.

In each of the following sentences, which of the three italicized words or expressions is *nonstandard?* Put the letter for the nonstandard choice after the number of the sentence. If none of the three is nonstandard, write "None."

UNIT REVIEW EXERCISE

EXAMPLE: The company (a) *wouldn't* let (b) *a* employee admit (c) *an* error.
(Answer) *b*

1. The stranger introduced (a) *hisself* to (b) *us* (c) *without* embarrassment.
2. She (a) *didn't* telephone (b) *herself* (c) *on account of* she was sick.
3. (a) *We* don't have (b) *no* time for (c) *a* long argument.
4. We (a) *ourselves* should have (b) *went* to City Hall to (c) *complain*.
5. The accused (a) *insisted* that he (b) *done* (c) *no* wrong.
6. We (a) *learned* (b) *nothing* new from the (c) *long* report.
7. (a) *Our* hosts (b) *growed* these vegetables (c) *themselves*.
8. The committee (a) *had* received (b) *them* bills in (c) *an* unmarked envelope.
9. Last year, the senator (a) *himself* (b) *thank* people who (c) *made* large contributions.
10. (a) *A* simple denial (b) *don't* stop (c) *an* ugly rumor.
11. (a) *Regardless* of the hurry, I should have (b) *wrote* the note (c) *myself*.
12. I (a) *never* hear from your father (b) *unless* I call him (c) *myself*.
13. The crowd had (a) *waited* three or four (b) *hour* in (c) *a* driving rain.
14. I (a) *knew* the store had been (b) *torn* down (c) *without* a permit.
15. The quarrel (a) *begun* when he (b) *let* his dog sleep (c) *inside*.
16. My friends (a) *was* glad that I had (b) *brought* the map (c) *myself*.
17. Sometimes an owner (a) *can't* hardly recognize a (b) *car* that was (c) *stolen*.
18. We (a) *ourself* could not (b) *have* thawed out the (c) *frozen* pipes.
19. The manager (a) *herself* had (b) *taken* my name (c) *off* the list.
20. We (a) *were* glad that you two (b) *took* care of it (c) *yourself*.

U2
FORMAL AND INFORMAL

Shift from informal English to the more formal English appropriate in serious writing.

Within standard English, there are *functional varieties* fit for different occasions. **Formal** language goes with public occasions: official business, serious discussion, writing for a general audience. **Informal** language goes with a small circle of friends, casual talk, personal letters. Remember:

(1) Writing is generally more formal than speech. What we write down is generally more important than what we merely mention. It is usually intended for a larger audience. Formal written language indicates that we are taking our subject and our audience seriously.

(2) Effective writers avoid excessive formality as well as breezy informality. Effective formal English is vigorous and natural. If you always use the most formal word available, you will make your writing stilted and unnatural. Much effective English moves between the two extremes:

VERY FORMAL	IN-BETWEEN	VERY INFORMAL
retire	go to bed	hit the sack
fatigued	exhausted	bushed
vanquish	trounce	clobber

U2a
Informal Word Choice

Learn to recognize words with a limited range.

Many words are fit for all occasions. No matter how formal or informal the occasion, we can always call a hand a hand, or a house a house. But many other words are right only in the right context. They seem out of place when used elsewhere. *Kids, fake,* and *traipse* are informal words. We expect to hear them in casual conversation. Many dictionaries label such words **colloquial.** *Loaded, mutt,* and *latch onto* are **slang.** They are so informal that they may become disrespectful. Remember:

(1) Limit colloquial words to writing that is either very personal or meant to be humorous and entertaining. In writing meant to be taken seriously, avoid words like the following:

COLLOQUIAL:	act up	gripe	ornery
	enthused	hassle	pal
	fake	josh	skinny
	flunk	kid	sloppy
	folks	mean	stump
	gang up on	mess	swamp
	goof	mope	wangle

(2) Avoid trite, everyday figures of speech:

TRITE:	down to brass tacks	get on the ball
	elbow grease	get the show on the road
	pull all the stops	play ball
	hold your horses	polish the apple
	throw in the sponge	lie down on the job

(3) Use slang only for special effects. Many effective writers show that they have *learned from slang* about some of the things that make language colorful and vigorous. Much slang has a pointed, no-nonsense quality. Here are some typical slang words that are short and to the point: *blab, click, fizzle, jell, jibe, scram.* Much of our language is slang that has made the grade: *bogus, boom, carpetbagger, crook, graft, handout, hike, hobo, honky-tonk, racketeer.* But slang is limited in its usefulness because of its deliberate defiance of convention and respectability. "Head" becomes *bean,* "jail" becomes *jug* or *clink.* Slang metaphors are deliberately extravagant, exaggerated out of all proportion: "that kills me," "hit the ceiling," "fly off the handle," "go whole hog." In your own writing, use slang only when you can give it a witty, original twist and when your readers have a sense of humor.

(4) Use abbreviations and contractions sparingly. Many of the shortcuts of everyday speech are informal. Informal English uses many shortened words like *tux, lab, math, bike,* and *phone.* Informal English freely uses **contractions** like *shouldn't, don't, can't, won't, isn't,* and *aren't.*

NOTE: Some words are informal only in some of their uses. Watch out for the following:

INFORMAL	FORMAL
a *lot* of money	*much* money
a *bunch* of people	a *group* of people
fire someone	*dismiss* someone
looked *funny*	looked *strange*
got mad	*became angry*

Usage

EXERCISE 1

Which is the *more formal* choice in each of the following pairs? Write the letter for the more formal choice after the number of each pair—for instance, *7b*.

1. (a) party   (b) shindig
2. (a) nap   (b) snooze
3. (a) swell   (b) fine
4. (a) hoodwink   (b) bamboozle
5. (a) cockeyed   (b) absurd
6. (a) snoop   (b) pry
7. (a) gripe   (b) complain
8. (a) dazed   (b) groggy
9. (a) flatter   (b) butter up
10. (a) bunk   (b) nonsense
11. (a) yen   (b) yearning
12. (a) swipe   (b) steal
13. (a) dupe   (b) patsy
14. (a) lay for   (b) waylay
15. (a) horn in   (b) intrude
16. (a) failure   (b) flop
17. (a) weary   (b) fagged
18. (a) impudent   (b) sassy
19. (a) leery   (b) wary
20. (a) frisk   (b) search

EXERCISE 2

Put *F* for formal or *I* for informal after the number of each item. (Be prepared to discuss items that seem doubtful to you.)

1. snapshot
2. on the go
3. wise up
4. up to snuff
5. outlaw
6. snippy
7. hindsight
8. beside the point
9. pipe down
10. thug
11. on the double
12. nifty
13. back talk
14. penniless
15. kickback
16. pep
17. swindle
18. bawl out
19. checkup
20. big time

EXERCISE 3

The following passages range from formal to informal. Which seems to you most formal? Which most informal? From each passage, select five words or expressions that you can label formal or informal. (Compare your choices with those made by your classmates.)

1. In areas where television ownership has spread to the point of virtual universality, viewing reverts to a pattern which resembles that of radio listening in its prime. Viewing is now almost wholly within the family group, with outsiders not normally present. The television set remains the focal point of the family's typical evening activities. However, it probably no longer occupies the dominant position which it enjoyed in TV's earlier days, when other social activities slackened and even casual conversation was hushed in obedience to the set's demands.—Leo Bogart, *The Age of Television*

2. Another man made a valuable discovery because he forgot to wash his hands. He knocked off work in a laboratory to eat a roast beef sandwich, took one bite, and gagged. The sandwich was sickeningly sweet! In reaching for a glass of water, he noticed his hands were dirty. Could the dirt have anything to do with the unexpected sweetness of that sandwich? He examined the stuff he had been handling in the laboratory before lunch and thereby discovered saccharin.—W. Furness Thompson, "Why Don't Scientists Admit They Are Human?"

3. To hit the target, a person has to shoot off much ammunition. One of the marks of true genius is a quality of abundance. A rich, rollicking abundance, enough to give indigestion to ordinary people. Great artists turn it out in rolls, in swatches. They cover whole ceilings with paintings, they chip out a mountainside in stone, they write not one novel but a shelf full. It follows that some of their work is better than other. As much as a third of it may be pretty bad.—Catherine Drinker Bowen, "The Nature of the Artist"

4. There is an old and perhaps foolish query about the books which one would wish to take with him if he were to sojourn upon a desert island. But like some other foolish questions, the problem which it sets us is worth pondering. Upon the voyage of life there are a few books of which we may hope to make lifelong companions; and, as in the other relations of life, it behooves us, if we hope to avoid calamity on our voyage, to choose our mates with discretion.— Chauncey B. Tinker, *On Going to College*

5. If lost hunters would only stay put, they'd be fairly easy to find. But they rarely do. If they're inexperienced enough to lose themselves in the first place, they're inexperienced enough to get panicky. The thing to do, once you know you are lost, is to find a good, safe place to build a little fire, build it, fire three shots, and sit down and wait. If the shots aren't answered, wait a while till you are sure it's late enough for searchers to be out looking for you and shoot again. If you've plenty of shells with you, continue to do so every five minutes.—Louise Dickinson Rich, *We Took to the Woods*

EXERCISE 4

Informal language is around us every day. It offers us excellent opportunities for firsthand investigation of language in action. Prepare a short paper on *one* of the following topics:

1. What are the favorite *colloquial figures of speech* in your family or circle of friends? From what areas are they drawn? How familiar or how original are they?
2. Tell about the same episode, first in serious formal English for the benefit of teacher or parent, then in *current teenage slang.*

U2b

Pronoun Case

Use the formal forms of pronouns.

Most personal pronouns have two forms. We use *I* or *me, she* or *her, we* or *us,* depending on how the pronoun fits into the sentence. *I, he, she, we,* and *they* are the **subject** forms. We use these forms when the pronoun is the *subject* of the sentence. *Me, him, her, us,* and *them* are the **object** forms. We use these forms when the pronoun is the *object* of a verb. We also use them when the pronoun is the object of a preposition.

SUBJECT	OBJECT (OF VERB)	OBJECT (OF PREPOSITION)
I heard	he told *me*	with *me*
he arrived	I saw *him*	around *him*
she denied it	we believed *her*	against *her*
we had hoped	they betrayed *us*	without *us*
they deserve it	we noticed *them*	for *them*

We call the difference between subject form and object form a difference in pronoun **case.** In written English, and in formal speech, avoid familiar informal uses of pronoun forms:

(1) Choose the right pronoun when it is part of a **compound subject** *or* **compound object.** If there are several subjects for the same verb, use the form that would fit if there were only one subject. If there are several objects, use the form that would fit if there were only one object. Avoid expressions like *"Me* and Jim went" or "between you and *I."*

SUBJECT	OBJECT (OF VERB)	OBJECT (OF PREPOSITION)
Jim *and I* heard	he told Jim *and me*	between you *and me*
he and Fred did	we saw Fred *and him*	for Fred *and him*
she and Jill left	I asked Jill *and her*	about Jill *and her*

(2) Choose the right form when a pronoun combines with a noun. Use the subject form when a combination like "we Americans" or "we scouts" appears as a subject. Use the object form ("us Americans," "us scouts") when the combination appears as the object of a verb or preposition:

SUBJECT	OBJECT (OF VERB)	OBJECT (OF PREPOSITION)
we Texans cheered	they liked *us Texans*	among *us Texans*
we seniors did	he asked *us seniors*	against *us seniors*

(3) Use the subject form after a form of be. *Be (is, was, has been, will be)* is a linking verb and does not take an object. After the linking verb, formal English requires the subject form. In formal usage, avoid *it's him, that's her, it's us, it's them:*

FORMAL: It was *she* who had notified the police.
The police had known from the start it was *he.*

NOTE: Some informal uses of pronouns are so much a part of everyday speech that the formal choices have come to sound awkward. "It's me" is so generally accepted that "It is I" is almost never heard.

(4) Use the right form in shortened comparisons. Fill in the missing part of a comparison to decide whether the subject form or object form is right:

FORMAL: Ann writes better than *I* (do).
They know Ann better than (they know) *me.*

Few people are as considerate as *he* (is).
She had never liked anyone as much as (she liked) *him.*

(5) Use who *as a subject form and* whom *as an object form.* When used as a question word, *who* asks a question about the subject. Use it when *he, she,* or *they* are possible answers. *Whom* asks a question about the object of a verb or preposition. Use it when *him, her,* or *them* are possible answers:

FORMAL: *Who* sent the letter? (*He* did.)
Whom did you ask? (You asked *him.*)
With *whom* did you discuss it? (I discussed it with *her.*)

Who as a relative pronoun is the *subject* of its clause. *Whom* is the *object* of a verb or preposition in its clause:

The people/*who* knew her believed her. (*They* knew.)
Beth King,/*whom* he had met, introduced him. (He had met *her.*)
The girl/with *whom* I saw him was his sister. (I saw him with *her.*)

Usage

NOTE: Spoken English increasingly uses only *who* where written English requires a choice between *who* and *whom*. Remember to use *who* in reference to *persons, which* in reference to *things and ideas. That* may refer to both people and things:

The people *who* lived there had left abruptly.
The furniture, *which* they had left behind, was covered with dust.
We swept up the debris *that* littered the floor.

EXERCISE 1

Use the following exercise for *oral drill* of formal pronoun choices. Read over the examples in each set several times.

1. My brother *and I* had left. *He and* his brother arrived. He is inviting you *and me.* We saw *him and* his brother. This is strictly between you *and me.* He left a message for you *and her.*

2. *We Americans* welcome debate. They regarded *us Americans* with suspicion. This is hard for *us Americans* to understand. *We athletes* had few special privileges. The students supported *us athletes.* He always had time for *us athletes.*

3. It *was she* who made the suggestion. It *was they* who recommended it. The only ones left *were he* and his brother.

4. He plays better than *I.* The barber charged him more than *me.* He can do it as quickly as *I.* The accident injured him as badly as *her.*

5. The people *who* count support us. The people *whom* she named were well known. The people with *whom* she had talked all agreed. A friend *who* knew him volunteered. A woman *whom* she trusted was helping her. The woman for *whom* he had worked testified. *Who* is running for the position? *Whom* will the voters trust? Against *whom* will she be running?

EXERCISE 2

In each of the following sentences, choose the pronoun that would be right in formal written English. Write your choice after the number of the sentence.

1. Cheryl and *I/me* filled out the forms together.
2. The director had promised tickets to *she/her* and her sister.
3. *She/Her* and her trained chimpanzees were the hit of the show.
4. Few people on the team were as tall as *he/him.*
5. Everything I tell you is strictly between you and *I/me.*
6. The company promoted his fellow workers faster than *he/him.*
7. She hired handicapped people for *who/whom* a job meant not only a living but renewed self-respect.

8. To imagine the view of the world of a peasant in India is hard for *we/us* Americans.
9. Jim was disappointed that *he/him* and his friends were not selected.
10. For my sister and *I/me,* the theater was part of a distant world.
11. The Irish people *who/whom* had settled here had left Ireland during the Great Famine.
12. Rachel was chosen our first president, because it was *she/her* who first suggested our founding the club.
13. I never read an author *who/whom* I admired more.
14. A professional can do the work better than you or *I/me.*
15. Sometimes we meet someone *who/whom* we like instantly.
16. Against *who/whom* did King Arthur fight his battles?
17. In all these years, he has never had a friendly word for you and *I/me.*
18. There was no part of my aunt's farm that *we/us* boys had not explored.
19. No one knew that *he/him* and his friends had returned to the area.
20. *They/Them* and their parents had always farmed these acres.

Each of the following sentences includes an informal pronoun. After the number of the sentence, write the form that should replace the informal pronoun in written English.

1. He recognized the store where him and his brother used to work.
2. The person who called left a message for she and her sister.
3. We were sure it was them who had complained.
4. Us younger brothers were often treated badly.
5. We found out with who the arrangement had been made.
6. There is always trouble when him and his father start to argue.
7. Research is essential for a better future for you and I.
8. Her brother had always been less practical than her.
9. My sister and me are the only ones who go to Sunday school.
10. I recognized the person who the reporter had interviewed.

Know the adverb forms required in formal English.

Adjectives are words like *poor, obvious, happy,* and *careful.* Adverbs are words like *poorly, obviously, happily,* and *carefully.* Adjectives modify nouns. They tell us "which one?" or "what kind?" Adverbs modify verbs. They tell how, when, or where something is done:

ADJECTIVE: Only *poor* people lived there.
ADVERB: The whole team played *poorly.*

ADJECTIVE: The *quiet* girl finally spoke up.
ADVERB: The girl was talking *quietly.*

Informal English often uses adverb forms that are *the same* as the adjective. Formal English uses the *separate* adverb form whenever there is a choice. Remember:

(1) Avoid unmarked informal adverbs in formal English. Remember that adjectives may follow a linking verb that pins a label on the subject. Adverbs modify action verbs, telling us *where, when,* or *how* an action takes place:

ADJECTIVE	ADJECTIVE	ADVERB
easy work	seemed *easy*	won *easily*
loud hurrahs	sounded *loud*	speak *loudly*
careful words	has been *careful*	did it *carefully*
considerable pain	was *considerable*	changed *considerably*
a *good* deed	tasted *good*	worked *well*

Be sure to use the form with *–ly* to replace the unmarked informal adverbs in expressions like "She worked *steady*" and "It had changed *considerable*":

FORMAL: The crew was working *steadily.*   They suffered *terribly.*
Our town changed *considerably.*   I left *quickly.*

NOTE: A few adverb forms are unmarked even in formal English: *long, fast, right, much, thus, wrong.*

ADJECTIVE	ADJECTIVE	ADVERB
a *long* march	was *long*	waited *long*
a *fast* move	seemed *fast*	acted *fast*
the *right* tone	looked *right*	acted *right*

(2) Use well *and* badly *as formal adverbs to replace* good *and* bad. Avoid expressions like "clean it *good*" or "it was working *good.*" Use *well* to show approval of how something is done:

FORMAL: She is a *good* athlete. She plays *well.*
We bought a *good* heater. It works *well.*
A *good* teacher taught her. She paints *well.*

It was a *bad* mistake. They were hurt *badly.*
It was a *bad* start. It ended *badly.*

Remember that the adjective forms follow linking verbs: It sounds *good.* I feel *bad.* Everything tasted *bad.*

NOTE: The most common use of *well* is as the formal adverb to go with *good*: a *good* talk; he talked *well*. However, *well* is also used as an adjective in expressions like "He is not *well*" and "The sick child got *well* again."

(3) Avoid informal expressions like real smart *or* awful fast. In formal English, we use the form with *–ly* to modify other adjectives and other adverbs: *really smart, awfully fast, truly sorry, exceptionally well*. When *real* and *awful* are used as informal intensifiers in this way, the best replacement is often *very* or *extremely*. Use *fairly* to replace the *pretty* in *pretty good*.

INFORMAL	FORMAL
pretty cold	*fairly* cold
real fast	*very* fast
awful slow	*extremely* slow
mighty proud	*very* proud

(4) Avoid the informal sure *used as a sentence modifier.* Use *surely* or *certainly* as an adverb that applies to a whole statement.

FORMAL: They *certainly* know their job.
Surely there is some other way.

For more on adjective and adverb forms, see **S1e.**

The following sentences show the right uses of adjectives and adverbs in formal English. Read over the sentences in each pair several times.

EXERCISE 1

1. It was a *marvelous* concert. The orchestra played *marvelously*.
2. He was a *careless* driver. He drove *carelessly*.
3. *Considerable* damage was done. The dam weakened *considerably*.
4. She has been a *steady* customer. They worked *steadily*.
5. The mourners looked *solemn*. The minister spoke *solemnly*.
6. My uncle was *generous*. He helped us *generously*.
7. The task seemed *easy*. We accomplished it *easily*.
8. We had a *good* team. It did *well*.
9. The road looked *good*. She handled the car *well*.
10. We had some *good* and some *bad* players. Some played *well*, and others *badly*.
11. We had a *good* start and a *bad* finish. The race started *well* but ended *badly*.
12. The shirt was *real* silk. The exam was *really* difficult.

13. The hills made a *pretty* picture. The picture came out *fairly* well.
14. The quarterback made an *awful* mistake. It was *extremely* costly.
15. She needed a *sure* footing. She can *surely* do better.
16. We have to set a *certain* date. We *certainly* appreciate your health.
17. We have had *extreme* temperatures. It was *extremely* cold.
18. He took a *wrong* turn. We handled things *wrong*.
19. We took the *fast* bus. Things were changing *fast*.
20. Vote for the *right* candidate. You guessed *right*.

EXERCISE 2

Check all adverb forms in the following sentences. Put *S* (for satisfactory) after the number of the sentence if the adverbs in the sentence are right for formal English. If there is an unmarked informal adverb, write down the formal adverb that should replace it.

EXAMPLE: We met the deadline easy.
(Answer) *easily*

1. The car looked good and ran well.
2. It sure meant considerable expense.
3. Their public relations had improved considerable.
4. My grandfather pretended that he did not hear good.
5. We were never sure whether he would act right.
6. Unfortunately the instructions are not really clear.
7. Everyone was awful sorry to see the coach leave.
8. He never again worked steady after the accident.
9. The soup smelled strange and tasted really terrible.
10. Our relay team had been surprisingly fast in the tryouts.
11. She submitted designs that were real imaginative.
12. The caller sounded pretty desperate.
13. The new principal handled the situation extremely well.
14. The spark plugs had crusted over really bad.
15. She wrote down the address careful.
16. He described the whole incident breathlessly.
17. Walter always tried to fool people much too obvious.
18. The governor's image suffered badly during the campaign.
19. The latest offer sounds real good.
20. Because of their truly heroic efforts, no one was hurt bad.

EXERCISE 3

After the number of each of the following sentences, write the choice appropriate in written English.

1. His mother never learned to speak Spanish very *good/well*.
2. Opposition to the regime weakened *considerable/considerably*.
3. For the first time, the news from home sounded *good/well*.
4. She had never heard the piece played so *good/well*.

5. His withdrawal *sure/surely* surprised everyone.
6. We were never *sure/surely* what he would do next.
7. She never succeeded in making the point *real/really* clear.
8. Tim had never had to earn a living in the *real/really* world.
9. The musicians played the piece rather *bad/badly*.
10. Whenever I asked for my allowance, my parents pretended they did not hear very *good/well*.

Recognize expressions that are too informal for serious written English.

Everyday talk is more informal than serious speech and writing. Avoid the following forms and expressions in formal English:

(1) Avoid these kind *and* those kind. The *these kind* in "These kind of cars" mixes singular and plural. Use *this kind* and *that kind* for one kind. Use *these kinds* and *those kinds* for several kinds:

ONE KIND: *This kind* of sweetener has been banned.
We studied *this kind* of mushroom.
We had read about *that kind* of battery.

SEVERAL: We studied all *these kinds* of mushrooms.
Those kinds of tools are in a different department.

(2) Avoid the informal like *in "like I said" and "like we told you."* Formal English uses *like* as a preposition: *like* my mother, *like* a river. Do not use *like* as a connective to start a clause that has its own subject and verb. Use *as* or *as if* instead:

PREPOSITION: He acted *like* a real friend.
They look *like* their parents.
The building looked *like* a barn.

CONNECTIVE: He acted *as if* we had insulted him.
It looks *as if* it will snow again.
She had acted *as* a friend should act.

(3) Avoid the informal was *in "If I was you."* After *if* and *as if*, use *were* instead to show that something is contrary to fact— impossible or not now true. This special form to show the opposite of something real or factual is the **subjunctive**. We use it also in expressions like "I wish it *were* true."

SUBJUNCTIVE: If I *were* you, I would resign.
He would have a better chance if he *were* taller.
They talked about their dog as if it *were* a person.
I wish it *were* vacation time.

NOTE: Other special subjunctive forms appear after verbs like *request, command, order, suggest:*

She requested that the case *be* reopened.
I suggested that the group *disband* (or should *disband*).
She ordered that he *leave.*

(4) Avoid the informal uses of lay *and* set. In formal English, the verb for "being seated" is *sit* or *sit down.* Its past form is *sat* or *sat down.* The verb for "stretching out" is *lie* or *lie down.* Its past form is *lay* or *lay down.*

Remember: We just sit or lie. But we set or lay *something:*

LIE/LAY	INTRANSITIVE: (S–V)	I *lie* in the sun. (present) He will *lie* in the sun. (future) We *lay* in the sun all day. (past) We have *lain* in the sun. (perfect) She was *lying* in the sun. (progressive)
	TRANSITIVE: (S–V–O)	I *lay* my burden down. (present) She will *lay* the cornerstone. (future) We *laid* our cards on the table. (past) We have *laid* tile. (perfect) I am *laying* bricks. (progressive)
SIT/SET	INTRANSITIVE: (S–V)	I always *sit* here. (present) He will not *sit* still. (future) We *sat* there quietly. (past) We have often *sat* there. (perfect) Why are you *sitting* here? (progressive)
	TRANSITIVE: (S–V–O)	I *set* the table. (present) He will *set* it down over here. (future) She *set* up her headquarters. (past) He has *set* his burden down. (perfect) She was *setting* a precedent. (progressive)

(5) Avoid using plural pronouns to point back to words like everybody *and* nobody. *Everybody (everyone), anybody (anyone), somebody (someone),* and *nobody (no one)* are **indefinite** pronouns. Though they refer to people in general, these words are treated as singulars in formal English. Avoid informal expressions like "Everybody took *theirs*" or "Nobody got *their* money back." Formal English requires singular pronouns like *he (him, his)* or *she (her)* to follow one of the indefinite pronouns. The same rule applies to *one* and *a person:*

FORMAL: *Everyone* knew *her* assignment.

Nobody told *his* family about the plan.

If *anybody* needs extra help, *she* should say so.

If *a person* is always criticized, *she* becomes unsure of *herself.*

I was always told that *one* should solve *his* (or *one's*) own problems.

NOTE: To many readers, *he* or *him* seems misleading when *everybody* or *somebody* stands for both men and women. *He or she* (or *him or her*) is more accurate, but some readers consider it awkward. Often the best solution is to make the whole sentence plural:

INFORMAL: *Everybody* parked *their* car behind the house.

FORMAL: *Everybody* parked *his or her* car behind the house.

FORMAL: *All the guests* parked *their* cars behind the house.

(6) Become aware of other informal expressions. Avoid the informal *most* in "*most* everybody." Use *almost* or *nearly* instead. Avoid the following as informal: *had ought to, used to could, didn't use to:*

FORMAL: *Almost* everyone had heard the announcement.

You *ought to have* warned us.

We *used to be able* to walk through the fields.

Wealthy people *did not usually* live here.

NOTE: Many expressions that used to be considered informal are today avoided only by very conservative writers. See the "Glossary of Usage" (U5) for expressions like the following:

- different than
- due to
- reason is because
- split infinitive

Use the following exercise for *oral drill* of expressions that are right for written English. Read over the examples in each set several times.

EXERCISE 1

1. The builder recommended *this kind* of reinforcement. *This kind* of deer is almost extinct. Her father knew all *these kinds* of wines. *That kind* of roll is not made anymore. It was hard to choose among all *those kinds* of bread.

2. He talks Spanish *like* a native. She talks Spanish *as if* she were a native. We acted *like* cowards. We did *as* we were told. The scaffolding looked *like* a giant steel web. The scaffold looked *as if* it would topple.

3. He acted as if he *were* my long-lost brother. The bird looked as if it *were* a plane. If I *were* you, I would refuse. If she *were* my friend, she would act differently.

4. If he *were* in town, he would call us. If he *was* in town, we will hear about it. She would not work if she *were* ill. She should not have worked if she *was* ill.

5. I suggest that she *return* the money. We recommend that the contract *be* renewed. I wish the work *were* finished. The workers demanded that the law *be* changed. I insist that she *tell* me herself. They moved that the meeting *be* adjourned.

6. I know better than to *lie* in the sun. Last summer we *lay* on the beach all day. The letter had *lain* on his desk for weeks. I want to *lie* down. When I stayed with my uncle, he always *lay* down after lunch for a nap. He should have *lain* down for a rest. The boards were just *lying* there.

7. Hens *lay* eggs. We are now *laying* the foundation. The foundations have been *laid*. The boards have to be *laid* end to end. Last year we *laid* new tile.

8. The person was just *sitting* there. When we left, he still *sat* there. He had *sat* there all day. Come in and *sit* down. We should *sit* in the back of the room. He told us to *sit* still.

9. We have to *set* a deadline. We are *setting* a precedent. He had *set* the load down in the wrong place.

10. Somebody has left *her* lights on. A person should not be required to tell *his* innermost thoughts. Everybody has the right to state *his or her* opinion. *No one* on our team has really reached *her* full potential.

EXERCISE 2

Which of the two choices in each of the following sentences is more formal? After the number of the sentence, write the choice that is appropriate in serious written English.

EXAMPLE: Everything was done *like/as* it should be.
(Answer) *as*

1. Everyone on our gymnastics team did *her/their* best.
2. *That/Those* kinds of cakes have always sold well here.
3. Our proposals had simply been *lying/laying* on the shelf.
4. The owners behaved as if the country *was/were* still in the Middle Ages.
5. The plane dropped to the ground as if it *was/were* a stone.
6. Thousands were *sitting/setting* in the rain waiting.
7. We used to *could/be able to* buy fresh fruit in the marketplace.
8. People were *lying/laying* odds three to one against his election.
9. We demanded that the matter *was/be* reopened.
10. People were *lying/laying* on benches and along the walls.

11. We refused to *sit/set* there doing nothing.
12. We had *set/sat* up all night waiting for the eclipse.
13. I had never seen *this/these* kind of application.
14. The lawn looked *like/as if* it had never been mowed.
15. A person should choose *his or her/their* own career.
16. His aunt talked to him as if he *was/were* not very bright.
17. If the check *was/were* forged, it will be hard to prove the forger's identity.
18. My grandfather hugged me *like/as* a bear.
19. Wrappers and paper cups were *lying/laying* everywhere.
20. *That/Those* kind of statistics will not impress the voters.

In each of the following sentences, which of the two choices would be right in formal written English? Write the formal choice after the number of the sentence.

1. The trip came as a complete surprise for my sister and *I/me*.
2. For a moment, Greg looked *like/as if* he were going to cry.
3. Sometimes we wish the farm *was/were* still run the old way.
4. The governor always avoided *that/those* kinds of questions.
5. She tried to make the bear lose interest by *lying/laying* still.
6. The new machine never worked as *good/well* as it should have.
7. She told everyone to *who/whom* she had mentioned the incident.
8. According to Ed, *they/them* and the neighbors had never quarreled.
9. We were told to put all our *gripes/complaints* in writing.
10. She always had a friendly word for *we/us* musicians.
11. The nation had treated its minorities *bad/badly*.
12. The year had been *real/really* successful for all of us.
13. The store was *sitting/setting* up a new checkout system.
14. They denied that they had driven *reckless/recklessly*.
15. She thanked all those *who/whom* had supported her.
16. As we expected, the game developed into a *real/really* contest.
17. Few of my friends know as much about cars as *I/me*.
18. No one in the sorority talked much about *her/their* grades.
19. The referee's decision had made our coach very *mad/angry*.
20. Business had been *pretty/rather* slow all year.

Revise your written sentences to make them clear and effective.

In conversation, we often leave something half said and then return to it later. We start a sentence one way and finish it another way. A good written sentence is more finished and more carefully put together. It follows a clear pattern that the reader can follow. Learn how to revise sentences that seem hastily written or confused.

U3a

Revising for Agreement

Check agreement between the subject and its verb.

Most English nouns and pronouns have one form for singular and another for plural: one *plane*/several *planes;* one *accident*/several *accidents.* When a noun or pronoun is the subject of a sentence, the sentence often shows this difference twice. The verb as well as the noun may change from singular to plural. We say that the verb **agrees** with the subject:

SINGULAR	PLURAL
Her friend *was* happy.	Her friends *were* happy.
The race *has* started.	The races *have* started.
He *plays* the flute.	They *play* in the band.

Agreement shows in many verb forms using a form of *be* (*is*/*are, was*/*were*) or of *have* (*has*/*have*). With other forms, agreement survives only in the present tense, in speaking about a third party ("third person"): *speaks*/*speak; admits*/*admit.*

Check for agreement in the following situations:

(1) Check for agreement when something comes between the subject and its verb. The subject may be one thing among several. It may be a quality or an activity that applies to several things. Make the verb agree with its true subject. Material that comes between subject and verb does not affect agreement:

Enrollment in these courses *has* gone down.
The *attitude* of the teachers *is* changing.

Saving endangered animals *requires* much patient effort.
Filling in the questionnaires *takes* hours.

A similar kind of wedge may come between a plural subject and its verb:

The *spectators* in the top section *see* very little.
The *neighbors* who filed the charge *have* changed their minds.

(2) Check for agreement in sentences with more than one subject. We call two subjects joined by *and* or *or* a **compound subject.** *And* adds two singular subjects and turns them into a plural. *Or* may merely make us choose between them and leave them singular. *As well as* and *together with* are used as prepositions and leave a singular subject singular:

PLURAL: Hiking and swimming *were* her only recreation.
SINGULAR: His brother or a friend *has* always helped him out.
SINGULAR: The colonel together with a few diehards *was* still holding out.

NOTE: A compound subject may be singular when the whole combination is the name of a single thing:

SINGULAR: His friend and lifelong companion *has* left him.
SINGULAR: Ham and eggs *was* her favorite breakfast.
SINGULAR: The Stars and Stripes *was* fluttering in the wind.

(3) Check for agreement when the subject follows the verb. In informal English, we often start a sentence with *there is* or *there was* regardless of whether a singular or a plural subject follows. Make sure that the verb that follows *there* agrees in number with the postponed subject:

SINGULAR: There *is* little *hope* for a new beginning.
PLURAL: There *were dozens* of boxes to be put on the shelves.
PLURAL: There *were a church and a cemetery* at the top of the hill.

Make the verb agree with a postponed subject in sentences like the following:

In the box *were thousands* of dollars in old coins.

(4) Check for agreement when form and meaning do not clearly point in the same direction. **Each** and *either* point to more than one person or thing. But we are thinking of each individually:

SINGULAR: *Each* of the applicants *is* interviewed.
SINGULAR: *Either* answer *was* acceptable.

• **Collective nouns,** such as *class, team, police, jury,* and *committee* are singular when we think of the whole group together. They are plural when we think of the members of the group:

SINGULAR: The team *is* changing its strategy.
PLURAL: The team *were* changing their clothes.

• Expressions like *two-thirds* or *thirty dollars* are singular when they stand for the whole amount. *A number of* is plural when it means "several":

SINGULAR: *Three dollars is* too little.
Five hours was more than enough time.
Three-fourths of the oil *was* already gone.

PLURAL: *A number of* people *were* still waiting.

• *Fields of study* may be plural in form and yet be treated as singulars. *None,* once only a singular, is now used as both singular and plural:

Physics *has* always fascinated me.
None *has* (or *have*) ever complained.

(5) Check for agreement in relative clauses. After *who, which* and *that,* the verb agrees with whatever noun the relative clause as a whole modifies:

SINGULAR: He is *the only one* of her relatives who really *cares.*
(Only *one* cares.)

PLURAL: He always was one of *those people* who really *care.*
(*Several* care.)

(6) Check for agreement with unusual Latin or Greek plurals:

SINGULAR	PLURAL
This *phenomenon* is new.	These *phenomena* are new.
The *medium* is the message.	The *media* are powerful.
This *criterion* is irrelevant.	These *criteria* are irrelevant.

The word *data,* originally a plural ("pieces of information"), is now also used as a singular:

This *data* means little.
These *data* mean little.

(7) Check for agreement of other sentence elements. Sometimes sentence elements other than the verb need to be changed to bring them into **logical agreement** with the subject:

ILLOGICAL: *His parents* had spent most of their *life* abroad.
LOGICAL: *His parents* had spent most of their *lives* abroad.

EXERCISE 1

All of the following examples show how agreement is handled in formal written English. Read over the examples in each set several times.

1. The usefulness of these inventions *is* limited.
   The implication of her findings *remains* unclear.
   Understanding their motives *is* difficult.
   Finding replacements *takes* time.

2. The sheriff and a deputy *are* conducting the search.
   The sheriff together with two deputies *is* conducting the search.
   A number of local citizens *have* joined the search.
   The mayor as well as several council members *has* opposed the plan.

3. All *arrive* together, but each *leaves* separately.
   Either *is* eligible, but neither *has* applied.
   Everyone *comes* to the meeting, but a number of people *leave* early.

4. There *is* a newcomer living there.
   There *are* newcomers living there.
   There *are* a newcomer and his family living there.
   There *is* a cabin by the lake.
   There *are* a cabin and small store by the lake.
   There *are* cabins by the lake.

5. Thoreau is one of the writers who *have* preached civil disobedience.
   He is not the only one who *has* written about it.
   I am not one of those who *recommend* the use of force.
   Jean was one of those girls who *enter* every contest.
   He was one of those politicians who *respond* to every change in the wind.

6. The first criterion *is* clarity, but other criteria *are* equally important.
   The first medium of mass communication *was* the press, but soon other media *were* equally important.
   The phenomenon *has* attracted much attention, though similar phenomena *have* gone unnoticed.

How would you handle agreement in the following sentences? After the number of each sentence, write the choice appropriate to *written English*.

EXERCISE 2

1. The time spent traveling and the wear and tear on one's nerves *makes/make* commuting a poor bargain.
2. There *was/were* no trees or any form of shade.
3. More active participation in sports by young people *has/have* been encouraged by public officials.
4. At Christmastime, the children wait impatiently to open the presents that *has/have* been put under the tree.
5. Other arguments against early marriage *is/are* low earning power and the responsibility of unexpected children.
6. In the lobby of the museum, a rich display of flowers *fills/fill* the air with fragrance.
7. A doctor and a nurse *has/have* a responsibility to live up to the code of ethics of their profession.
8. I found that friendliness and a few casual words *was/were* effective in selling.
9. There *is/are* always several college-entrance tests coming up at this time of the year.
10. How can anyone remember all the rules that *is/are* listed in the manual?
11. South Africa is one of those countries that *does/do* not have a single national language.

12. The language of many white settlers *was/were* Dutch.
13. Almost everyone among their descendants *has/have* learned English as a second language.
14. Either *is/are* understood by many South Africans today.
15. A number of Dutch words *has/have* become part of South African English.
16. Having two official languages *complicates/complicate* politics in Canada.
17. My friend Robert is one of those Canadians from Quebec who *speaks/speak* French.
18. French Canadians have often felt that they were at a disadvantage in furthering their *career/careers*.
19. The media in Canada *is/are* now using French more widely than before.
20. There *has/have* been many arguments about the language of instruction in Canada's schools.

EXERCISE 3

In each of the following sentences, a verb (or auxiliary) does not follow the rules for agreement in written English. Change the word so that it will agree with its subject. Write the changed form of the word after the number of the sentence.

1. The design of bridges along the highway add to the scenic view.
2. A politician must say what a voter want to hear.
3. The beauty of our modern highways are being destroyed by litter.
4. My father and I was working as usual.
5. Every student actually need a double education, physical and mental.
6. On the ground floor, there is a workshop and some storage rooms.
7. The general attitude of the people I talked to were very poor.
8. For the average apprentice, the years devoted to learning a trade has been well spent.
9. The responsibilities of a team leader includes cheering up team members who have a defeatist attitude.
10. A sharp increase in violent crimes are reported in our local newspapers.
11. My uncle and his family still practices the old orthodox faith.
12. There was often only fifty or sixty people interested enough to come to the polls and vote.
13. Inflammatory speeches by local politicians often aggravates the already tense situation.
14. Reading the long explanations of ballot propositions have become a chore for the voter.
15. The precision of these exercises always amaze the spectators.
16. The criteria for admission to the program includes initiative and poise.
17. My mother is one of those people who believes in high standards.
18. The dropout rate for students at the school have gone up every year.
19. Hidden at the very bottom of the drawer was some old coins.
20. His lifestyle as well as his sharp tongue have alienated the workers.

Make the reference of your pronouns clear.

Pronouns are pointing words. *He* may point to *James* or to *Paul.* *She* may point to *Sue* or to *Jean.* We call the word that a pronoun points to its **antecedent**—"what has gone before." A pronoun becomes confusing when it does not point clearly to its antecedent. A pronoun becomes ambiguous when we cannot tell which of two people or things is meant.

To make things clear, you may have to *drop* a confusing pronoun and spell out what it stands for:

CONFUSING: He reached for the dog's leash, but *it* ran away.
                 (the leash?)
CLEAR: When he reached for its leash, *the dog* ran away.

You may be able to make a pronoun clearer by *shifting* things in a sentence:

CONFUSING: *The mayor* and *Bob Greene* discussed *his* resignation.

CLEAR: *Bob Greene* discussed *his* resignation with the mayor.

(1) Make the pronoun point to something clearly stated. Do not let it refer to something hinted or implied. Revise sentences if *it* or *they* points to an **implied antecedent:**

CONFUSING: Her mother had been a *musician,* and the daughter too chose *it* as a career. (A musician is not "it.")
CLEAR: Her mother had been a musician, and the daughter too chose *music* as a career.

CONFUSING: We used to be invited to many different places, but *they* gradually stopped coming.
CLEAR: We used to receive many different *invitations,* but *they* gradually stopped coming.

Avoid the informal *they* that points to "the people concerned":

INFORMAL: We had just gotten our tickets when *they* announced our flight to Istanbul.
FORMAL: We had just gotten our tickets when *a voice* announced our flight to Istanbul.

INFORMAL: At Oakdale College, *they* require two years of French.
FORMAL: *Oakdale College* requires two years of French.

(2) Avoid vague this *and* which. These pronouns are often ambiguous when they point back to the whole idea expressed in what has gone before. Revise ambiguous **idea reference** as shown in the examples on the next page:

CONFUSING: As a teacher, I would try hard not to play favorites. *This* is the best way to gain the students' confidence. (*What* is the best way—playing favorites or *not* playing favorites?)

CLEAR: As a teacher, I would try hard not to play favorites. Complete *impartiality* is the best way to gain the students' confidence.

CONFUSING: He refused to practice the tuba, *which* annoyed his parents.

CLEAR: He refused to practice the tuba. *This stubbornness* annoyed his parents.

(3) Avoid the informal you. *You* is informal when it points to people in general. Use it to mean "you, the reader."

INFORMAL: *You* have to work full time at being a parent. (Many of your readers are not parents.)

FORMAL: A parent's job is full-time work.

For shifts in pronoun reference, see **U3e.**

EXERCISE 1

Check the italicized pronouns for *clear reference*. Put *S* (satisfactory) after the number of the sentence if the pronoun points clearly to its antecedent. Put *U* (unsatisfactory) if the reference is confusing or informal. (Your teacher may ask you to revise the unsatisfactory sentences.)

1. It is hard to believe that we are lacking nurses, for *this* should be a field too highly regarded to suffer a shortage.
2. His neighbor had neglected to return the rake *that* he had loaned to her.
3. Many of us have been depressed, but not all of us know how to get rid of *it*.
4. We stopped at a Navajo trading post and bought several items that *they* had made.
5. Herman hated editors because *they* kept rejecting his manuscripts.
6. City children are cheated when *they* build modern schools only in the suburbs.
7. What makes marine corps training different is that its purpose is to turn *you* into a different person.
8. Skydiving fascinated me because *it* introduced me to a new world.
9. The voters turned against the party leaders because *they* believed in private property.
10. We decided on a brick wall because *it* is easier to carry and to handle than concrete blocks.
11. My father and my uncle quarrel constantly because *he* is very self-righteous.
12. When there was a disagreement, we referred *it* to the supervisor.
13. The lake had frozen over, but *it* was not thick enough for skating.
14. They changed the safety regulations, *which* made people very angry.

15. The mother resumed *her* career when the daughter started school.
16. We usually went around the corner to the Baptist chapel and used *their* parking lot.
17. People used to hunt wolves from airplanes. *This* practice has been banned.
18. The fire, *which* spread very rapidly, was set by an arsonist.
19. He called his father about the keys to *his* car.
20. In several states, *they* have legalized gambling.

In the following paragraph, check the italicized pronouns for *clear reference*. Put *S* (satisfactory) after the number of the sentence if the pronoun points clearly to what it stands for. Put *U* (unsatisfactory) if the reference is confusing or informal. (Your teacher may ask you to revise the unsatisfactory sentences.)

(1) Have *you* ever heard "paper" pronounced like "piper," or "my shirt" like "me shirt"? (2) In World War II, many American GIs heard this kind of pronunciation when *they* were stationed in Australia. (3) In Australia, *they* speak a kind of English similar in many ways to that of Great Britain. (4) The British originally sent convicts there because *they* had no use for the continent. (5) Later, when free immigrants followed, *they* found a climate, plants, and animals different from those of their native England. (6) They learned words like "wombat," "kangaroo," and "boomerang," *which* were taken from the language of the Australian aborigines. (7) Australia is a long trip around the world from England, *which* has made close contacts difficult. (8) But in education and politics, *you* follow British models, and everyday language owes much to British slang. (9) In Australia, *you* call a man a "cove" rather than a "guy" or a "fellow." (10) Australians feel close to the British because they consider *it* their mother country.

Place modifiers carefully in a sentence.

A modifier changes or narrows the meaning of another part of the sentence. A **dangling modifier** appears in a sentence *without* the word or phrase that it is supposed to modify:

DANGLING: *Working silently,* the attempts at rescue continued.
REVISED: Working silently, *the crew* continued the attempts at rescue.

A **misplaced modifier** seems to go *with the wrong part* of a sentence:

MISPLACED: *Stubbornly refusing to move,* George whipped the mules.
REVISED: *Stubbornly refusing to move,* the mules were whipped by George.

A "squinting modifier" may seem to look in the wrong direction:

MISPLACED: The people you see *at night* work at other jobs.
REVISED: The people you see work at other jobs *at night.*

Check placement of five kinds of modifiers:

(1) Place adverbs where they point clearly to what they modify.
Adverbs like *only, just,* and *almost* are confusing when they appear in the wrong place:

CONFUSING: You have to notify the supervisor *only* in an emergency.
CLEAR: You have to notify *only* the supervisor in an emergency.
CLEAR: You have to notify the supervisor in emergencies *only.*

CONFUSING: We had *almost* enough to eat for everyone.
CLEAR: We had enough to eat for *almost* everyone.

(2) Move prepositional phrases if necessary. They start with a preposition like *at, with, on, by, for, through,* or *without.* These prepositions bring a noun and other possible material into the sentence:

MISPLACED: She sent me a bill for the teeth she had filled *by mail.*
REVISED: She sent me a bill *by mail* for the teeth she had filled.

(3) Revise dangling and misplaced verbal phrases. Many dangling or misplaced modifiers start with a verbal like *cleaning, driving, opening;* or like *driven, written, opened.* To revise them, shift or add things in the sentence as needed:

DANGLING: *Coming around a bend,* the mountain suddenly loomed large.
REVISED: *As we came* around a bend, the mountain suddenly loomed large.
REVISED: Coming around a bend, *we suddenly saw* the large mountain.

MISPLACED: *Written in a strange script,* we studied the mysterious message.
REVISED: We studied the mysterious message, *written in a strange script.*

(4) Make appositives point clearly to what they modify. An appositive is a second noun that tells us more about another noun (or sometimes, a pronoun): "Margaret Smith, *the senator.*" Make sure the appositive relates clearly to the other noun:

MISPLACED: There was only one case before the judge, *a confirmed alcoholic.*
REVISED: Only one case, involving *a confirmed alcoholic,* was before the judge.

(5) Make relative clauses point clearly to what they modify. Make sure the *who, which,* or *that* at the beginning of the clause points in the right direction:

CONFUSING: We heard about the boat of a friend *that had capsized.*
REVISED: We heard about a friend's boat *that had capsized.*

NOTE: Some verbals are technically danglers but are acceptable in formal English. They show the intention or attitude of the speaker or writer. They point to an implied "I" or "we":

ACCEPTABLE: *Generally speaking,* there has been little change.
ACCEPTABLE: *Considering his background,* he is doing well.

Check the following sentences for *dangling, misplaced,* or *confusing modifiers.* Write *S* after the number of the sentence if all modifiers are satisfactory. Write *U* if one or more modifiers are unsatisfactory. (Your teacher may ask you to revise the unsatisfactory sentences.)

EXERCISE 1

1. She declined the invitation to speak at the meeting with regret.
2. Though announced three times, Jean was late for the examination.
3. Having taken history the year before, I saw no need to take it again.
4. Having finished my dinner, the waiter removed the dishes.
5. Bleeding from a cut above the left eye, the champion was severely handicapped.
6. I kept calling the old number after it was changed by mistake.
7. Considering his qualifications, his salary is already too high.
8. High school graduates handicap themselves by not entering college in many different ways.
9. Labeled immoral by the city officials, large crowds came to see the movie.
10. Frantically manipulating the controls, she finally succeeded in stabilizing the plane.
11. Painted in three bright colors, we could not make up our minds to buy the car.
12. He steadily applied his file to the steel grille barring the window.
13. At the age of twelve, Grandfather invited me to Canada.
14. He had strong feelings about the issues that he could not disguise.
15. Special meals were prepared for tourists only in Spain.
16. Having eaten earlier, we were no longer hungry.
17. Half asleep in our jeep, a herd of elephants suddenly blocked the road.
18. The students were unaware of the prowl cars that had appeared on the scene.
19. Always saying hello to me, I wondered who the handsome stranger was.
20. An incurable optimist, Carl was looking for a job offering travel and an expense account.

Revise each of the following sentences to bring out the intended meaning more clearly.

EXERCISE 2

1. We sent supplies for the victims that were badly needed.
2. Sitting down for dinner, the telephone suddenly rang.

3. Shipped by mistake, I had to return the bracelet.
4. We both had read the advertisement, a furniture sale.
5. Doing all our shopping at the discount store, the prices are usually more reasonable.
6. Blocking two lanes of traffic, a police officer was checking the car.
7. Being a sickly child, my grandmother had always spoiled me.
8. Turning a suspicious color, we threw out the mushrooms.
9. By the end of the day, the crews had only contained one of the fires.
10. I found a book about prisoners who escaped by accident.

U3d
Mixed Construction

Avoid unnecessary repetition and other kinds of mixed construction.

Revise sentences that confuse two different ways of saying the same thing. When we speak, we often start a sentence one way. Then we change to what may seem a better way. Look for the following kinds of duplication and mixed construction:

(1) Remove unnecessary repetition of sentence parts. In hasty writing, parts of the sentence machinery may appear twice. Look for unnecessary duplication of connectives like *that,* or of prepositions like *on, to,* and *with:*

CONFUSED: I know *that* when the chips are down *that* he will be on our side.
REVISED: I know that he will be on our side when the chips are down.
REVISED: I know *that* when the chips are down he will be on our side.

NOTE: Sometimes, we go too far in leaving out elements that seem to duplicate some other part of a sentence. When a similar idea is expressed by two *different* prepositions, or by two *different* verb forms, both are needed:

INFORMAL: He never *has* and never *will admit* his mistake.
FORMAL: He never has *admitted* and never will *admit* his mistake.

INFORMAL: She was enthusiastic and loyal to the project.
FORMAL: She was enthusiastic *about* and loyal *to* the project.

INFORMAL: My work is *as good,* if not *better, than* yours.
FORMAL: My work is as good *as,* if not better *than,* yours.

(2) Revise sentences that unintentionally repeat the same idea in different ways. We call such sentences **redundant.** (Something is redundant when it "overflows.") "At three A.M. in the morning" is redundant because "three A.M." has to be in the morning. Take out the second italicized part in sentences like the following:

In the long run, it will *eventually* pay off.
He *returned* the car *back* to the shop.

In hasty writing, the verb of a sentence may repeat all or part of the subject:

CONFUSED: *The choice* of the site *was selected* by a committee.
REVISED: *The choice* of the site *was made* by a committee.
REVISED: *The site was selected* by a committee.

(3) Revise sentences if two ways of putting the sentence together have become mixed. Make the sentence follow either one possible pattern or the other:

MIXED: *In case of* an accident *should be reported* to the office.
CLEAR: *In case of an accident,* notify the office.
CLEAR: Accidents *should be reported* to the office.

MIXED: *He worked* as little as possible and *still pass the course.*
CLEAR: *He tried to work* little and still *pass* the course.
CLEAR: *He worked* as little as possible while still *passing* the course.

MIXED: *The participation* in club activities was overcrowded.
CLEAR: *The club meetings were* always *overcrowded.*
CLEAR: *Participation* in club activities *was* very *lively.*

MIXED: Her job is *an inspector* in quality control.
CLEAR: *She* is *an inspector* in quality control.
CLEAR: *Her job* is *that* of an inspector in quality control.

Avoid confusion of *because* and *because of:*

MIXED: We made a detour *because of* the bridge *was closed.*
CLEAR: We made a detour *because* the bridge *was closed.*
CLEAR: We made a detour *because of* a closed bridge.

(4) Avoid informal adverbial clauses that replace a noun in a sentence. When and *because* usually introduce *adverbial* clauses. They show the time or the reason for what happens in the main clause. Avoid a *when* clause after *is* in definitions. The *when* clause would then take the place of a noun:

INFORMAL: Nepotism *is when* relatives receive special favors.
FORMAL: Nepotism *is the practice* of giving special favors to relatives.

Avoid using a *because* clause that replaces the subject of the main clause:

INFORMAL: *Because he is your friend* does not mean he is mine.
FORMAL: *That he is your friend* does not mean he is mine.
FORMAL: *Just because he is your friend,* he is not necessarily mine.

(5) Revise illogical or incomplete comparisons. Comparisons easily move off the track as they go from the one thing being compared to the other, as shown on the following page:

Usage

ILLOGICAL: His own *reputation* was equal to his *father*.

REVISED: His own *reputation* was equal to *that* of his father.

REVISED: *His* own reputation was equal to his *father's*.

ILLOGICAL: The math teacher knew more than *anyone* on the staff.

LOGICAL: The math teacher knew more than *anyone else* on the staff.

AMBIGUOUS: I understood the parents better than the boys.

CLEAR: I understood the parents better than the boys *did*.

CLEAR: I understood the parents better than *I did* the boys.

EXERCISE 1

Check the following sentences for *confused construction* or *illogical comparisons*. Write *S* after the number of the sentence if it is satisfactory. Write *U* if it is unsatisfactory. (Your teacher may ask you to revise unsatisfactory sentences.)

1. Her kindness was unlike anyone I have ever met.
2. The students demonstrated in favor of higher standards and against overemphasis on athletics.
3. Accidents can and do happen to people like you and me.
4. Because the cabin was damaged does not mean that we should cancel the fishing trip.
5. A student should be graded in English on the same basis as any other class.
6. His mother's attitude was much more liberal than his father's.
7. I finally saw the play of which he had told me about.
8. It is preferable but not absolutely necessary that marriage partners share common interests.
9. The purpose of the device was designed to serve as a warning system.
10. Parole is when a prisoner is released before serving a full sentence.
11. Watching the crowd was as entertaining as watching the fight.
12. I believe that with the right attitude that early marriage can be made to work.
13. She has dozens of toy animals that she buys with her own money and places them around the room.
14. Few poets ever have or ever will equal Emily Dickinson.
15. Young people really conform more readily than adults.
16. The judge blamed the boys more than their parents.
17. We had to study because of an exam was being given the next day.
18. The use of the football helmet today is used not only for protection but also as a weapon.
19. Young people just cannot or will not understand the way the older generation felt about a home and children.
20. Discipline, to me, is a school with teachers who keep the students under control.

Revise the following sentences for unnecessary repetition and other kinds of mixed construction.

1. I forgot the name of the officer to whom I reported the incident to.
2. Her ability does not equal the player whose place she took.
3. A landslide is when a candidate buries the opposition.
4. Because he has a pleasing personality does not mean he will be an effective mayor.
5. My friends always have and will help me in an emergency.
6. At the beginning of her career, Marian started as a society reporter for the *Daily Mirror*.
7. The purpose of the review was intended to keep us from repeating the error.
8. Their intentions are good but seem unable to live up to them.
9. We received the first installment from the customer but has not paid us since.
10. He hated to be prevented or hampered in doing what he had decided to do.

Avoid confusing shifts in point of view.

U3e

Shifts in Perspective

As you write, be aware of how you look at people and events. For instance, you may describe events as though they were happening now. Or you may describe them as having happened in the past. If you shift back and forth between present and past, you will confuse the reader. A sentence is **consistent** if it keeps the same perspective toward people and events.

Look for three kinds of shift:

(1) Avoid shifts in time. The **tense** forms of verbs show the relationship of events in time. Do not shift from the past *to the present* when some event becomes especially vivid in your mind:

SHIFT: As we *drove* along, the horse suddenly *panics* and almost *overthrows* the cart.
CONSISTENT: As we *drove* along, the horse suddenly *panicked* and almost *overthrew* the cart.

Use the **perfect** tense, formed with *have* or *has,* for something that has happened in the past but still matters. Use the **past perfect,** formed with *had,* for a time *before* other events in the past took place:

PERFECT: I remember (now) what I *have learned.*
During this decade, many new techniques *have developed* (and are now being used).
PAST PERFECT: I remembered what I *had learned.*
By 1970, many new techniques *had been developed.*

Do not show events as happening at the same time if one actually came before the other:

SHIFT: My father *showed us* where he *served* as an apprentice.
CONSISTENT: My father *showed us* where he *had served* as an apprentice.

(2) Avoid shifts in reference. Stay with one way of referring to yourself, to your reader, or to people in general. Do not start with an expression like *one* or *a person* and then shift to *you:*

SHIFT: There are some things *a person* ought to know before *you* travel abroad.
CONSISTENT: There are some things *people* ought to know before *they* travel abroad.
CONSISTENT: There are some things *a person* ought to know before *he or she* travels abroad.

EVENTS IN TIME

PRESENT (present or habitual action, or past events treated *as if* they were happening now):

When I *see* him, I *laugh.*

PAST (events past and done with):

When I *saw* him, I *laughed.*

PERFECT (past events with a bearing on the *present*):

I profit now from what I *have learned.*

PAST PERFECT (past events *prior to* other events in the past):

I profited from what I *had already learned.*

Do not shift from a reference to yourself to a reference to people in general:

SHIFT: *I* do not want to live in a tract where all *your* neighbors know everything *you* do.
CONSISTENT: *I* do not want to live in a tract where all *my* neighbors know everything *I* do.

(3) Avoid shifts to the passive. The **passive** makes the target or the result of an action the subject of the sentence. It turns the usual "actor-action" pattern of the active sentence around, as shown in the following example:

ACTIVE: The guide *explained* the exhibits.
PASSIVE: The exhibits *had been loaned* by their owners.

Do not shift from the active to the passive when *the same person (or thing)* is still doing things in the sentence:

SHIFT: The partners *obtained* a loan, and a restaurant *was started*.

CONSISTENT: The partners *obtained* a loan and *started* a restaurant.

SHIFT: Totalitarians *urge* us to give all to the cause, and close personal ties *are considered* a luxury.

CONSISTENT: Totalitarians *urge* us to give all to the cause; they *consider* close personal ties a luxury.

NOTE: Often an account actually moves from the present to the past, or from one person to the other. Confusing *shifts* result when there is a switch in tense but not in time, or when pronouns change but the person stays the same.

EXERCISE 1

Which of the following sentences are *consistent* in perspective? Put *S* (for satisfactory) after the number of each such sentence. Which sentences show a confusing *shift* in point of view? Put *U* (for unsatisfactory) after the number of each of these. (Your teacher may ask you to revise the unsatisfactory sentences.)

1. When I walk past the small neighborhood grocery stores and corner restaurants, I feel at home, among my own people.
2. When one is writing a paper, you must first collect your thoughts.
3. The Welsh have built themselves some of the ugliest villages in the world, but they love literature and music.
4. My uncle had been trained as an architect but made a living selling real estate in New York City.
5. Scientists have already conquered polio, and the cause of cancer is being searched for in a big way today.
6. In a little shack with a Coca-Cola sign, an old woman sells souvenirs and sweetens the air with popular recordings.
7. Chiropractors believe that most of a person's illnesses are due to dislocated vertebra in your spine.
8. As they cautiously advanced into the cave, the earth begins to tremble and rocks start tumbling down the side of the mountain.
9. When one compares today's language with that of Shakespeare's time, many differences are observed.
10. In my childhood, cattle were still rounded up for sale in the fields behind our house, and pigs were herded down our street.
11. At halftime our team had a comfortable lead, but early in the second half the visitors suddenly draw to within three points.
12. On Saturday mornings, we always mowed the lawn, swept the sidewalk, and the car was washed later.
13. If you want to pass the course, all work should be turned in on time.

14. A young person should think seriously about college, because there you are exposed to new people and ideas.
15. The city finally opened its new convention center, which the voters had approved eight years earlier.
16. When you study photography, lab work has to be done on time and work schedules have to be met.
17. When workers work in the same factory for many years, occupational diseases may be contracted.
18. A good camp counselor knows what to do when an emergency arises.
19. My grandmother told me about her brother who was a child prodigy.
20. Much treasure had been buried in the tomb, and the entrance had been carefully sealed.

EXERCISE 2

How would you revise each of the following sentences to shift the point of view? Rewrite the italicized part of each sentence.

EXAMPLE: As we reached the top of the hill, *a shot suddenly rings out.*
(Answer)   *a shot suddenly rang out*

1. I could not marry a person *who always criticizes your habits.*
2. The dentist seemed very competent, *and my tooth was extracted without a problem.*
3. I was dreaming about a sunny day in the woods *when the alarm clock goes off.*
4. Students naturally wonder *what will happen to you when you leave school.*
5. The excavations for the new office building took place in an area *where the Aztec priests prepared human sacrifices.*
6. We washed the good china by hand, *and it was carefully stored until the next holiday.*
7. A person with a college degree can no longer be sure *that an employer will hire you right away.*
8. Few people in the stadium seemed to pay any attention *when the band plays the national anthem.*
9. The teacher drew a diagram on the chalkboard, *and all details were carefully explained.*
10. We watch out for unusual birds, *and many interesting specimens have already been seen.*

U3f

Parallel Structure

Line up similar sentence parts in parallel form.

Sentence parts joined by *and, or,* or *but* should be the same kind of word. A noun should be linked to a noun. An adjective should be linked to an adjective. When a vehicle has four wheels, we align the wheels so that they will run parallel. When a sentence has several similar parts, we make them **parallel** to help keep the sentence on its track. In each of the following, the linked parts are the same kind of word:

The crowd *whistled* and *cheered*.
She was *a* good *manager* but *a* poor *politician*.
My friends were always wildly *optimistic* or completely *depressed*.

Do the following to revise sentences so that linked sentence parts will be parallel:

(1) Change parts that are not parallel from one category to another. Two sentence elements joined by *and, or,* or *but* should be in the same category. For instance, these coordinators should not link an adjective to a noun, or a phrase to a clause, or an infinitive to a verbal noun:

OFF-BALANCE: The production was *lavish* but *a disappointment*.
PARALLEL: The production was *lavish* but *disappointing*.

OFF-BALANCE: He left *without a penny* and *after he had lost all his friends*.
PARALLEL: He left after he had lost *all his money* and *all his friends*.

OFF-BALANCE: She liked *to eat* well and frequent *traveling*.
PARALLEL: She liked to *eat* well and *travel* frequently.

(2) If necessary, add something to the sentence to make it parallel. Or take out the *and* altogether:

OFF-BALANCE: She *had finished* algebra and now *taking* geometry.
PARALLEL: She *had finished* algebra and *was* now *taking* geometry.

OFF-BALANCE: She was *a native* of Maine and *who loved the sea*.
PARALLEL: She was a native of Maine who loved the sea.

(3) Make three or more parts parallel when they appear in a **series.** When three or more things are linked, the first two may be parallel. Then the third upsets the pattern. (Sometimes all three parts of a series are different kinds of words.)

OFF-BALANCE: The receiver is *small, compact,* and *uses* flashlight batteries.
PARALLEL: The receiver is *small, compact,* and *inexpensive*.
PARALLEL: The receiver *costs* little, *runs* on flashlight batteries, and *fits* into a purse.

OFF-BALANCE: She liked to *swim, play tennis,* and many other *sports*.
PARALLEL: She liked *swimming, tennis,* and many other *sports*.

(4) Use parallel elements with **paired connectives.** Check for parallel structure when similar elements are joined by combinations like *not only . . . but also* or *either . . . or.* Make sure the *not*

only or the *either* appears in the most logical position:

OFF-BALANCE: He not only called him a liar but also *a thief*.

PARALLEL: He called him not only *a liar* but also *a thief*.

OFF-BALANCE: We should either *turn back* now or *going ahead* without constant second thoughts.

PARALLEL: We should either *turn back* now or *go ahead* without constant second thoughts.

EXERCISE 1

Which of the following sentences are parallel in structure? Put *S* (for satisfactory) after the number of each such sentence. Which sentences are off-balance? Put *FP* (for faulty parallelism) after the number of each such sentence. (Your teacher may ask you to revise the unsatisfactory sentences.)

1. The first dictionaries explained words that English had borrowed from Latin, French, and Greek.
2. She wanted to know how one enters the contest, what the rules are, and about the judges.
3. He pulled up a chair to the shelf, took down the family Bible, and began to read.
4. She returned to pay the rent and because she had left some belongings.
5. The new coach was relaxed, cordial, and we felt immediately at ease.
6. Word books at first gave only the spelling and meaning of hard words.
7. Most of the other passengers were teenagers and who considered the outing fun.
8. Every morning, my father read not only the local newspaper but also two or three out-of-town dailies.
9. He was falsely accused, imprisoned for life, but then made his escape.
10. The use of atomic weapons would destroy our cities and ruining what is left of our ancient cultures.
11. The dresses she sold were stylish, different, and at a good price.
12. One of the first dictionaries had "choice" words in the first part and not so choice words in the second.
13. The hero of the old-fashioned Western loves his horse and stands for right and justice.
14. We studied the proposal carefully and weighing the pros and cons.
15. The new manager was a hard worker and very intelligent.
16. His ambition was to retire from politics and living a life of leisure.
17. She asked us either to approve the report or to find a new treasurer.
18. The Greeks wrote their dictionaries by hand and called them "lexicons."
19. He is a member of the VFW, the YMCA, and an active supporter of many community projects.
20. A knowledge of Latin is useful not only to physicians and pharmacists but also to students of law.

How would you revise the faulty parallelism in each of the following sentences? Rewrite the italicized part of each sentence on a separate piece of paper.

EXERCISE 2

EXAMPLE: They liked riding their dirt bikes *and stir up clouds of dust.*
(Answer) *and stirring up clouds of dust*

1. She wanted her daughter to finish school *and having a good start in life.*
2. In some parts of the desert, ancient markings *are still visible and a great tourist attraction.*
3. Gina promised to be careful *and that she would write soon.*
4. My cousins like to wrestle, jump, *or any other kind of exercise.*
5. My aunt and her family were always *either planning a trip or a big reunion.*
6. He was always worried *about his grades or what he would do in later life.*
7. The coach told us that our record was disappointing *and to work harder.*
8. The boss showed us how the apples were boxed *and the arrangements for storage.*
9. Emily was a great organizer of picnics, hayrides, *and how to raise funds.*
10. Attendance at the game *was not only hurt by the poor weather but also by high ticket prices.*

Choose between the two ways of completing each of the following sentences. The right choice will make the sentence acceptable in serious written English. The wrong choice will bring about a familiar sentence problem, such as lack of agreement, confusing or mixed construction, or a shift in point of view. Put the letter for the right choice after the number of the sentence.

UNIT REVIEW EXERCISE

1. Every student had to give two short reports _____
   (a) and a research paper had to be completed.
   (b) and complete a research paper.

2. When a person travels in a foreign country, _____
   (a) he or she should respect the local laws.
   (b) you should respect the local laws.

3. Plea bargaining is _____
   (a) when a defendant is allowed to plead guilty to a lesser charge.
   (b) the practice of letting a defendant plead guilty to a lesser charge.

4. Driving through the animal park, _____
   (a) lions may trot by close to the visitor's car.
   (b) visitors may see lions trot by close to their cars.

5. Choosing intelligently between two candidates _____
   (a) is becoming harder for the voter.
   (b) are becoming harder for the voter.

6. Vandals have cost our schools millions _____
   (a) and strained already tight budgets.
   (b) and straining already tight budgets.

7. The actors of our own theater group were _____
   (a) almost as good as the tour company.
   (b) almost as good as those of the tour company.

8. The barber shop had _____
   (a) old-fashioned chairs for its customers with reclining backs.
   (b) old-fashioned chairs with reclining backs for its customers.

9. We had promised her _____
   (a) that when she reapplied we would hire her.
   (b) that when she reapplied that we would hire her.

10. She was a good teacher _____
    (a) and patient when students complained.
    (b) and a patient listener when students complained.

11. He was a great expert on _____
    (a) how to write invitations and what to wear to parties.
    (b) writing invitations and what to wear to parties.

12. My aunt is one of those people _____
    (a) who always have an encouraging word for everyone.
    (b) who always has an encouraging word for everyone.

13. Because he is from my part of the country _____
    (a) does not mean I have to vote for him.
    (b) I do not necessarily have to vote for him.

14. The guide told us how to stay warm in the rain _____
    (a) and other good advice.
    (b) and gave us other good advice.

15. We were enjoying the quiet afternoon _____
    (a) when a motorcycle starts roaring up and down the street.
    (b) when a motorcycle started to roar up and down the street.

16. The choice of the building site _____
    (a) was made by the school board.
    (b) was selected by the school board.

17. My aunt was very unhappy _____
    (a) when they raised her taxes.
    (b) when the government raised her taxes.

18. Interest in do-it-yourself courses _____
    (a) have increased steadily over the years.
    (b) has increased steadily over the years.

19. My parents were farmers, _____
    (a) but my poor health made it impossible for me.
    (b) but my poor health made farming impossible for me.

20. Vaudeville troupers went _____
    (a) wherever there were a hall and an audience waiting for them.
    (b) wherever there was a hall and an audience waiting for them.

Make your sentences clear and effective instead of awkward or roundabout.

Awkward and roundabout language is like a fogged-up windshield. It gets in the way. It prevents the reader from seeing your point clearly and directly. Remember the following advice when trying to make your sentences clear and effective:

U4

EFFECTIVE SENTENCE STYLE

(1) Use active verbs where overuse of nouns would make a sentence static. The right verb can help make a sentence go. It can give us actions or events to *visualize.* Try translating what things *are* into what people *do:*

STATIC: Violent *argument* over the smallest issues resulted every time there was a *reunion* of the family.

BETTER: Every time the members of my family *met,* they *argued* violently over the smallest issues.

(2) Use active constructions where the passive would be awkward or too impersonal. The passive is most appropriate when we want to emphasize the result or the target, not the "doer":

EFFECTIVE: *Repairs,* except what you could do for yourself, *had* to *be sanctioned* by remote committees. (George Orwell)

The passive gets in the way when who or what *makes things happen* is really the more important part of the sentence. The passive becomes bureaucratic and impersonal when people responsible for actions disappear from the sentence altogether, as shown in the following examples:

AWKWARD: *Preparations are being made* by opponents of the bill for an extended advertising campaign.

BETTER: *Opponents of* the bill *are planning* an extensive advertising campaign.

BUREAUCRATIC: *All* personnel *records will be* periodically *evaluated* in the light of established company policy.

BETTER: *Management will* periodically *evaluate* the records of all employees.

(3) Remove the deadwood *from sentences using impersonal or roundabout constructions.* Often a sentence moves more briskly after you remove fillers like *one, a person,* or *there is:*

AWKWARD: When *one* is a teacher in a big-city school, *he or she* obtains a firsthand look at our urban problems.

BETTER: A *teacher* in a big-city school can take a firsthand look at our urban problems.

AWKWARD: When a *person* who is still a teenager joins the army, *there is* a tremendous adjustment to be faced.

BETTER: A *teenager* who joins the army faces a tremendous adjustment.

Often, a phrase can carry the same meaning as a longer dependent clause:

LENGTHY: The mansion, *which had been built* to last hundreds of years, belonged to Mike Fawley, *who was a wealthy rancher.*

COMPACT: The mansion, *built* to last hundreds of years, belonged to Mike Fawley, *a wealthy rancher.*

(4) Revise or break up sentences in which several dependent clauses work against each other. Sometimes several similar clauses follow one another in "house-that-Jack-built" fashion. Sometimes a clause at the end seems to cancel out a clause at the beginning, producing a teeter-totter effect:

OVERLOAD: We sat watching the waves *that* were driven along by the storm *that* was building up.

BETTER: We sat watching the waves *driven along* by the storm that was building up.

OVERLOAD: *If we finish in time,* we might go walking *if we feel like it.*

BETTER: *If* we finish in time, *and if* we feel like it, we might go walking.

(5) Vary sentence length and sentence rhythm. Use long, elaborate sentences for careful explanation or detailed examples. Use a short sentence to drive home a key point:

We live in an age of rising seas. Along all the coasts of the United States a continuing rise of sea level has been perceptible on the tide gauges of the Coast and Geodetic Survey since 1930. . . . (Rachel Carson)

I now saw Death as near as I believe I have ever seen Him. He was swimming in the water at our side, whispering from time to time in the rising wind which continued to carry the boat away from us at about the same speed we could swim. *No help was near. Unaided we could never reach the shore.* I was not only an easy, but a fast swimmer, having represented my House at Harrow, when our team defeated all comers. *I now swam for life.* (Sir Winston Churchill)

• Vary your sentence openings. For instance, move a modifier or a dependent clause to the beginning of the sentence:

For six years now he had been a hunter. *For six years now* he had heard the best of all talking. (William Faulkner)

At a thousand feet, and on down to the very end of the sun's rays, silvery fishes are common. . . . *At depths greater than 1500 feet,* all the fishes are black, deep violet, or brown. (Rachel Carson)

Experiment with interrupting elements that break up the familiar Subject—Verb or Subject—Verb—Object pattern:

Life, *at all times full of pain,* is more painful in our time than in the two centuries that preceded it. (Bertrand Russell)

Rewrite the following sentences to make them more direct, more compact, or more effective.

EXERCISE 1

1. In being a teacher, it is important not to show any favoritism.
2. After all these requirements are met by the candidate, there is still a personal interview to be faced.
3. My selection of a career has been due in part to my parents' influence.
4. We loved to hear the ancient bells that hang in the church towers, which have survived centuries of war and poverty.
5. As a newcomer in politics, one must avoid making charges that are founded on hearsay.
6. My views of marriage have been acquired gradually and have not been shaped by any one instance.
7. The availability of sufficient funds is a prerequisite for the person who desires to go to college.
8. Careful attention should be paid by those who hire a football coach to his emotional stability.
9. A substantial part of my earnings was expended for room and board.
10. The qualifications required of a person who wants to enter a school of nursing vary in different locations.
11. I little realized why my ancestors came to America before I wrote this theme.
12. Brian drives a truck which he informs me that his mother doesn't allow him to haul anything in it.
13. Every time in a tearjerker someone in connection with it or being the main character dies or suffers a serious loss.
14. Learning the great historical events and the great deeds of important people was all we were taught to learn.
15. An examination of the typical business executive will reveal that the excessive pressures of modern life are a primary cause of poor mental and physical health.

EXERCISE 2

Each of the following sentences is a model of varied and effective sentence style. Write a close imitation of each sentence. Use material of your own choice, but follow the overall pattern of the original as much as you can.

1. The first European ever to sail across the wide Pacific was curious about the hidden worlds beneath his ship. (Rachel Carson)
2. Rather than love, than money, than fame, give me truth. (Thoreau)
3. Jesus, in a world of arrogant Pharisees and egoistic Romans, thought that purity and poverty were one. (D. H. Lawrence)
4. To describe with precision even the simplest object is extremely difficult. (Aldous Huxley)
5. People will not look forward to posterity who never look backward to their ancestors. (Edmund Burke)
6. On a huge hill, cragged and steep, truth stands. (John Donne)

EXERCISE 3

Look at the following example of a sentence put through its paces. Then write two different additional versions of the sample sentences listed below. Make changes that produce sentence variety.

EXAMPLE: The shivering survivor told the grim story, sobbing uncontrollably.

(Answers) *Shivering, sobbing uncontrollably, the survivor told the grim story.*

The survivor who told the grim story was shivering and sobbing uncontrollably.

The survivor—shivering, sobbing uncontrollably—told the grim story.

1. The old man recited the verses with many a splendid gesture.
2. The injured and dazed pilot hung on in the cockpit of the damaged plane.
3. The children in the empty lot went on with their games, dancing and singing.

U5

GLOSSARY OF USAGE

Check the current status of expressions frequently criticized.

An effective speaker and writer is aware of the standards and preferences of the audience. The following glossary reviews the current status of expressions that have been frequently criticized.

Abbreviations in the entries of the glossary refer to the following authoritative guides to modern usage:

W III: *Webster's Third New International Dictionary,* the unabridged volume on which books like *Webster's New Collegiate Dictionary* are based.

BRYANT: Margaret M. Bryant, editor, *Current American Usage.*

PERRIN: Porter G. Perrin, *Writer's Guide and Index to English.*

a, an.   In standard English, use *a* when the next sound you *pro-nounce* is a consonant. Use *an* when the next sound you *pronounce* is a vowel:

A: a trip, a board, a house, a cold winter, a useful tool, a *C*
AN: an error, an honor, an invitation, an unpaid bill, an *A*

ain't.   The best-known single feature of nonstandard speech. Some-times used facetiously in informal writing. In first-person questions, many Americans find "ain't I" more natural than "am I not" ("I'm your friend, ain't I?"). *Advice:* Avoid all uses of *ain't* in speech and writing.

amount, number.   *Number* is more exact than *amount* with things that can be individually counted:

EXACT: A large *number* (not *amount*) of people were waiting.

And, But.   The use of *and* or *but* at the beginning of a sentence is found "in the best writing" (Bryant). Many modern writers prefer the initial *and* or *but* to heavier connectives like *moreover, further-more,* or *however.*

and/or.   This combination is sometimes necessary in commercial or official documents. In ordinary prose the combination is awkward and annoying.

as.   *As* is nonstandard as a substitute for *that* or *who.* As a substitute for *because* it is standard but sometimes criticized as ambiguous:

NONSTANDARD: I don't know *as* I can come.
NONSTANDARD: Those *as* knew her avoided her.

AMBIGUOUS: *As* we talked about war, I remembered Bill.
UNAMBIGUOUS: *Because* we talked about war, I remembered Bill.
UNAMBIGUOUS: *While* we talked about war, I remembered Bill.

being as, being that.   Nonstandard when they stand for *because* or *since:*

NONSTANDARD: *Being as* he was the mayor's son, we invited him.
STANDARD: *Because* he was the mayor's son, we invited him.

between, among. *Between* is related to *two* and *twain*. Traditional handbooks limit *between* to two of a kind ("choose *between* right and wrong"). They require *among* for more than two ("choose *among* many candidates"). But *between* is also appropriate when more than two things can be considered in pairs of two:

ACCEPTABLE: He had sand *between* his toes.

ACCEPTABLE: Bilateral agreements exist *between* many countries.

blame for, blame on. Both *blame for* and *blame on* are standard English, appearing with about equal frequency in publications like *Time* and *The New York Times* (Bryant). But some writers consider *blame on* informal:

INFORMAL: He blamed the disaster *on* his subordinates.

FORMAL: He blamed his subordinates *for* the disaster.

can, may. *Can* in the sense of "have permission" was once labeled careless or incorrect. It is now "used interchangeably with *may*" in standard spoken English (W III). But in more formal written English, *can* is still used to show ability, while *may* is used instead to show permission:

INFORMAL: *Can* I go now?

FORMAL: Each player *may* (permission) take as much as she *can* (ability) carry.

cannot help but. Some teachers and editors object to *cannot help but* as illogical or confused.

SAFE: I cannot help *admiring* his courage.

could of, might of. To transcribe informal speech, use *could've, might've*. In formal writing, use the more formal *could have, might have, should have.*

couple of. *A couple of minutes,* in the sense of "several," is informal. *A couple dollars,* without the connecting *of,* is nonstandard.

different than. *Different than* is standard American English, but *different from* is preferred in formal writing.

STANDARD: Things didn't seem any different *than* usual. (Walter Van Tilburg Clark)

FORMAL: He looked different *from* what I had expected.

disinterested, uninterested. In formal writing, *disinterested* usually means "not swayed by personal, selfish interest": "We were sure he would be a *disinterested* judge." Many readers object to *disinterested* when it is used to mean "uninterested" or "indifferent."

double comparative, double superlative. To show degree, adjectives use endings (bigg*er*, bigg*est*) or intensifiers (*more* convenient, *most* convenient). At one time, the ending and the intensifier could reinforce each other, as in Shakespeare's "the *most* unkind*est* cut of all." Today, such double comparatives or double superlatives are nonstandard.

double negative. In Chaucer's and Shakespeare's English, several negative words like *not, no,* or *never* reinforced each other in the same sentence. In modern English, such duplication is nonstandard. Less obvious double negatives, in which a word like *hardly* or *scarcely* repeats the negative idea, "are colloquial in nature and at times are used by well-known writers" (Bryant).

NONSTANDARD: A little rain *never* hurt *no* one.
NONSTANDARD: It's them that haven*'t no* common sense that make trouble on this island. (William Golding)

INFORMAL: We couldn*'t hardly* get into the house.
INFORMAL: He couldn*'t scarcely* walk straight.
FORMAL: He could *scarcely* walk straight.

due to (as a preposition). *Due to* is generally accepted when *due* serves as an adjective: "His absence was *due to* ill health." As a preposition meaning "because of," *due to* used to be condemned, but it occurs "in writing produced and edited by unquestionably educated persons" (Bryant).

DEBATABLE: He canceled his trip *due to* ill health.
SAFE: He canceled his trip *because of* ill health.

etc. *Et cetera* is Latin for "and so on." Therefore, *and etc.* is redundant. *Ect.* is a common misspelling.

get, be. The word *get* is often used in informal English as an emphatic and unambiguous passive auxiliary instead of the more formal *be* (Perrin):

INFORMAL: Several of his colleagues *had gotten* promoted.
FORMAL: Several of his colleagues *had been* promoted.

hadn't ought to. Use *ought not to have* instead.

DEBATABLE: He *hadn't ought to* mention the incident.
SAFE: He *ought not to have* mentioned the incident.

if, whether. People were formerly taught to avoid *if* to express doubt or uncertainty after verbs like *ask, don't know, wonder,* and *doubt.*

FORMAL: I wonder *whether* his information is reliable.

in, into. Formal writing often requires *into* rather than *in* to indicate direction: "He came *into* (not *in*) the room."

infer, imply. In formal usage, *imply* means "*point* to a conclusion." *Infer* means "*draw* a conclusion." But in much informal usage, *infer* is used as a synonym of *imply* ("a horse . . . *infers* only weight and speed while Lion *inferred* not only courage . . . but endurance"— William Faulkner).

FORMAL: From what he *implied* throughout his talk, we *inferred* that our chances were nil.

irregardless. Though often heard in informal speech, *irregardless* instead of *regardless* is widely considered nonstandard. Avoid.

learn, teach. *Learn* used to mean both "learn" and "teach." In the sense of "teach," *learn* has become nonstandard.

STANDARD: Students *learn* what teachers *teach.*

leave, let. *Leave* in the sense of "permit, allow, let" is considered nonstandard.

NONSTANDARD: You wouldn't *leave* nobody else hug and kiss you.
STANDARD: You wouldn't *let* anybody else kiss you.

less, fewer. People used to be taught to use *fewer* for "count nouns" ("fewer accidents") and *less* for "mass nouns," measured by quantity or bulk ("less water"). But many modern writers use *less* with countable items ("They felt that they would sooner have had *less* figures and more food"—George Orwell). By using *fewer* with countable items, however, you avoid criticism:

FORMAL: There were *fewer* complaints than we had expected.

like (as a connective). *Like* is acceptable in all varieties of English as a preposition: "The girl looked *like* her mother." It is also commonly heard as a connective taking the place of *as, as if,* or *as though* at the beginning of a clause: "Do *like* I tell you." According to Perrin, this use of *like* "is certainly now within the range of Standard English." But since many people are prejudiced against it, "writers should avoid it except in distinctly informal papers."

INFORMAL: "What's up?" I asked Canby . . . "Lynching, I'd judge," he said, *like* it didn't interest him. (Walter Van Tilburg Clark)

FORMAL: "Lynching, I'd judge," he said, *as if* it did not interest him.

most, almost. *Most* in the sense of "almost" or "nearly" is considered informal.

INFORMAL: *Most* everybody was there.

FORMAL: *Almost* everybody was there.

myself. *Myself* has long been a more emphatic substitute for *I* or *me* when the pronoun is one of several subjects or objects: "Front to front / Bring thou this fiend of Scotland, and *myself*" (*Macbeth,* Act IV, Sc. 3). But this use of *myself* has often been condemned in formal English.

SAFE: Mrs. Graham and *I* (not *myself*) will expect you in the afternoon after three o'clock.

off of. *Off of* instead of *off* or *from* is common in informal educated speech but considered nonstandard by many teachers and editors. Avoid.

FORMAL: The storm tore the roof *off* (not *off of*) the building.

FORMAL: He borrowed the money *from* (not *off of*) his mother.

possessive of inanimate nouns. A traditional rule limited the use of the possessive with *–'s* to nouns referring to living things (the *girl's* purse), and to nouns involving measurement (a *day's* work, a *dollar's* worth). For inanimate nouns, the rule required *of* (not "the *car's* roof" but "the roof *of* the car"). This rule goes counter to standard usage and is no longer observed:

STANDARD: Duncan is in his grave; After *life's* fitful fever he sleeps well. (*Macbeth,* Act III, Sc. 2)

STANDARD: He leadeth me in the path of righteousness for his *name's* sake. (Psalms)

possessives with verbal nouns. A traditional rule, still sometimes observed in formal writing, required the *possessive* form of noun or pronoun before a verbal noun in sentences like the following:

INFORMAL: No one objected to *John* taking the job.
FORMAL: No one objected to *John's* taking the job.

INFORMAL: I cannot imagine *him* driving there alone.
FORMAL: I cannot imagine *his* driving there alone.

preposition at the end of a sentence. The rule against ending a sentence with a preposition has been abandoned by most teachers and editors. The final preposition has long been idiomatic English and occurs in the work of the best writers:

> Thy blood is cold;
> Thou hast no speculation in those eyes,
> Which thou dost glare *with*. (*Macbeth,* Act III, Sc. 4)

A writer may, however, move the preposition ahead in order to place another word in an emphatic position at the end:

EMPHATIC: Do not ask *for* whom the bell tolls. (John Donne)

reason is because. This expression is "in reputable use though disapproved by some" (W III). But "because of widespread prejudice against the construction" (Perrin), students do well to use *reason is that* instead:

SAFE: The *reason* we do not have enlightened legislation in this area *is that* no one has the courage to speak out.

seeing as how. Nonstandard for *because:*

NONSTANDARD: *Seeing as how* she was an old friend, I lent her the money.
STANDARD: *Because* she was an old friend, I lent her the money.

shall, will. At one time, handbooks required *shall* for future action after first person pronouns (I *shall* try; we *shall* leave at eight). But *will* is now acceptable in written English to almost all teachers and editors. The more emphatic *shall* often indicates strong determination, definite obligation, or authoritative command. It is also common in polite first-person questions:

FORMAL: I *shall* return.
FORMAL: In no case *shall* payments exceed 5 percent.
FORMAL: *Shall* we dance?

split infinitive. The modifier that comes between *to* and the rest of the infinitive (to *really* understand) was once widely criticized but today this split infinitive is accepted by most teachers and editors. Awkwardness may result when *more than one word* splits the infinitive:

AWKWARD: The captain ordered us *to* with all possible speed *return* to our battle stations.

BETTER: The captain ordered us *to return* to our battle stations with all possible speed.

superlative in reference to two. "The *tallest* one of the twins" used to be criticized as illogical. "The *taller* one of the twins" is preferred in formal English. Save *tallest* and other superlatives for comparisons of three or more.

INFORMAL: Which of the two is the *best* speaker?

FORMAL: Which of the two is the *better* speaker?

unique, perfect, equal. It used to be argued that one thing cannot be *more* unique, *more* perfect, or *more* equal than another. If something is unique, it is "one of a kind" and cannot be *more* so; if something is perfect, it cannot be *improved; equal,* by definition, does not allow for comparative statements using *more.*

SAFE: Our aim must be to make educational opportunities *more nearly* equal.

SAFE: This antique vase is *unique,* therefore priceless.

used to, didn't use to, used to could. Formal English does not employ *used to* in questions or negative statements with *did.* This usage is considered nonstandard.

INFORMAL: She *didn't use to* live here.

FORMAL: She *used not* to live here.

Used to could is nonstandard for *used to be able.*

wait on, wait for. *Wait on,* used instead of *wait for,* occurs in informal speech and writing, but most teachers and editors expect *wait for* in formal English.

INFORMAL: "We might as well sit down," Davies said. "They're *waiting on* Bartlett anyway." (Walter Van Tilburg Clark)

FORMAL: Recording artists have long *waited for* copyright legislation to protect their rights.

where at, where to. In formal English, *where* takes the place of both *where to* and *where at*.

INFORMAL: Where are you *at?*
              Where do you want it sent *to?*
FORMAL: Where are you?
              Where do you want it sent?

Where used instead of *that* ("I read in the paper *where* taxes are going up") is informal.

without, on account of. *Without* and *on account of* are prepositions in standard use. They are nonstandard as connectives, introducing a clause:

NONSTANDARD: The manager can't let you into the theater *without* you have your ticket.
STANDARD: The manager can't let you into the theater *unless* you have your ticket.

NONSTANDARD: We missed the show *on account of* the bus was late.
STANDARD: We missed the show *because* the bus was late.

GLOSSARY REVIEW

In each of the following sentences, *one* of the three italicized expressions is widely considered nonstandard or excessively informal. Put the letter preceding it after the number of the sentence.

1. A person (a) *like* our governor finds it (b) *hard* to act (c) *like* he had no desire to run for President.
2. (a) *Regardless* of what her story was, the guards (b) *hadn't ought to* let in a (c) *total* stranger.
3. (a) *Without* another word, he (b) *took* his broom and started to sweep the leaves (c) *off of* the sidewalk.
4. When I (a) *left* him, he had only (b) *a couple* dollars left and was (c) *waiting for* a check from home.
5. Jim was (a) *unable* to (b) *leave* town (c) *on account of* he was scheduled to act in an insecticide commercial.
6. She strongly (a) *implied* that she wanted us to (b) *leave,* but we stayed on (c) *irregardless.*
7. (a) *Being as* he was new, we had to (b) *teach* him (c) *where* to store the different kinds of merchandise.
8. I (a) *inferred* from his remarks that at one time he (b) *could of* been the (c) *most* influential man in town.
9. (a) *Most* everybody I knew (b) *used to* come to the station to (c) *wait for* the afternoon train.
10. She had (a) *always* received a fair (b) *number* of complaints, but they (c) *didn't use to* bother her.

THE VARIETY OF ENGLISH

English has been spoken by many different people at different times and in different places. Today, English is the national language not only of Great Britain and the United States, but also of Australia, New Zealand, and Canada. Millions of people throughout the world learn English as a second language because it serves as an international language of trade, science, and technology. The following assignments will give you an opportunity to explore some of the range and variety of English.

Look at the following sampling of English as it might have been spoken on the Mississippi a hundred years ago. Point out any features of nonstandard English that are still current today.

> Pretty soon I see a black something floating on the water away off to stabboard and quartering behind us. I see he was looking at it, too. I says:
> "What's that?" he says, sort of pettish:
> "'Tain't nothing but an old empty bar'l."
> "An empty bar'l!" says I, "why," says I, "a spy-glass is a fool to *your* eyes. How can you tell it's an empty bar'l?" He says:
> "I don't know; I reckon it ain't a bar'l, but I thought it might be," says he.
> "Yes," I says, "so it might be, and it might be anything else too; a body can't tell nothing about it, such a distance as that," I says.
> We hadn't nothing else to do, so we kept on watching it. By and by I says:
> "Why, looky-here, Dick Allbright, that thing's a-gaining on us, I believe."
> He never said nothing. The thing gained and gained, and I judged it must be a dog that was about tired out. Well, we swung down into the crossing, and the thing floated across the bright streak of the moonshine, and by George, it *was* a bar'l. Says I:
> "Dick Allbright, what made you think that thing was a bar'l, when it was a half a mile off?" says I. Says he:
> "I don't know." Says I:
> "You tell me, Dick Allbright." Says he:
> "Well, I knowed it was a bar'l; I've seen it before; lots has seen it; they says it's a ha'nted bar'l."—Mark Twain, *Life on the Mississippi*

FOR FURTHER STUDY

ACTIVITY 1

What are some of the differences between American and *British* English? Be prepared to report to your classmates on any firsthand experience with British English that you might have had.

1. To judge from your own experience or from information in your dictionary, what is the typical British pronunciation of the following words?

blackguard	Warwick
boatswain	waistcoat
halfpenny	schedule
twopence	Gloucester
Southwark	tomato

2. For each of the following words, what is an everyday meaning that might be unfamiliar to the American visitor to Great Britain?

lift	master
tube	knacker
spanner	corn
torch	lorry
minerals	dust bin
bonnet	hoarding
boot	bowler
chemist	maize
wireless	bobby
fender	guinea

Scotland was until the Act of Union in 1707 a separate kingdom, with its own traditions in government, religion, language, and literature. Here are some words and meanings that dictionaries list as part of Scottish English: *dub* ("puddle"), *ikla* ("each, every"), *winnock* ("window"), *unco* ("very, extremely"), *canny* ("quiet"), *drouthy* ("thirsty").

These are some of the features that set Scottish English apart from that spoken farther south in the British Isles:

1. Old English words that survived in Scotland but not in standard English:

   kale (cabbage), *bairn* (child), *snell* (quick), *lift* (air), *mickle* (much)

2. Scandinavian borrowings, as in the following lines from Robert Burns:

I *kent* her heart was a' my ain   (knew)
Poor beastie, thou *maun* live   (must)
An folk begin to tak the *gate*   (road)

3. Words testifying to centuries of French influence:

For you sae *dounce,* ye sneer at this   (sober, from *doux*)

Have you encountered Scottish English in the dialect poems of Robert Burns? Select fifteen or twenty lines from a poem like "Tam O'Shanter" and report on the dialect features you encounter there.

In the following short excerpts from a play, the characters speak an **Irish** version of English. To judge from the written text, what features of pronunciation would make Irish English *sound* different from American English? What *words and expressions* are there that would be strange or unfamiliar to an American? What features of *sentence structure* set these passages apart from ordinary American English?

Have you encountered any of the features of Irish English in the speech of Americans of Irish descent?

1. No answer, eh? An' me afther seein' a light in th' window. Maybe they are out. For their own sakes, I hope they are; for it's hardly an honourable thing to gainsay a neighbour's knock.

2. At long last, afther hard sthrainin', me an' Sammy have got the tune down in tested clefs, crotchets, an' quavers, fair set down to be sung be anyone in thrue time. An' Sammy's below, in his gay suit for the Show, waitin' to be called up to let yous hear th' song sung as only Sammy can sing it.

3. All bark, but no bite! We know him of old: a decent oul' blatherer. Sure, doesn't he often buy violets and snowdhrops, even, for little Ursula, below, tellin' her she mustn't put them before a graven image, knowin' full well that that was th' first thing she'd hurry home to do.

4. Is it dhreamin' I am? Is somethin' happenin' to me, or is it happenin' to you? O, man, it's mixin' mirth with madness you are at thinkin' St. Pathrick ever looped his neck in an orange sash, or tapped out a tune on a Protestant dhrum!—Sean O'Casey, *Red Roses for Me*

ACTIVITY 4

Chapter 5

Mechanics
Words on the Page

Chapter Preview 5

Know the English writing system and make it serve your purpose.

Our writing system is the result of thousands of years of trial and error. Here are some historical facts that help explain what made our writing system what it is:

(1) Our alphabet was originally developed to write down languages different from our own. The earliest writing systems had used picture symbols for whole words. Alphabetic writing developed when people started to use symbols for the sounds *making up* a word.

(2) Our writing system has changed more slowly than the spoken language. Since books were first printed in English, speech has changed considerably, but spelling has tended to stay the same. We use many spellings that once stood for sounds but are now silent:

throu*gh*, ni*gh*t, li*gh*t, ou*gh*t
*h*ave, li*v*e

(3) Over the centuries, our writing system has developed features that are merely conventional. They are not absolutely necessary to carry meaning. We know that e. e. cummings was a person even though he refused to use capital letters in his name.

THE STORY OF THE ALPHABET

EGYPTIAN ca. 2000 BC		SEMITIC ca. 1700 BC	WEST SEMITIC ca. 1200 BC	GREEK ca. 500 BC	EARLY ROMAN
	head of ox			A	A
	corner of wall			Γ	C
	man with both arms raised			E	E II
	ripples			M	M
	cobra				N M
	eye			○	○
	sandal strap			T	T

Mechanics

How well do you know basic requirements for satisfactory spelling and punctuation? Study the three possible choices for the blank space in each of the following passages. Put the letter of the best choice after the number of the passage.

EXAMPLE: That year the team had an excell_____ record.
       a. ant   b. ent   c. int

(Answer) *b*

1. They chose the right person for the _____ position.
   a. assistants   b. assistant's   c. assistants'

2. The locksmith _____ the nick of time.
   a. arrived. In   b. arrived; in   c. arrived in

3. The front office _____ been notified immediately.
   a. should of   b. should have   c. shouldve

4. The company had moved to _____.
   a. Dallas, Texas   b. Dallas Texas   c. Dallas, texas

5. There had been a very defi_____ improvement.
   a. nite   b. nate   c. nnit

6. The same thing had _____ several times before.
   a. ocurred   b. occurred   c. occured

7. The children loved stories about _____ and goblins.
   a. ghosts witches   b. ghosts; witches   c. ghosts, witches,

8. I looked for the _____ had parked the car.
   a. person. Who   b. person; who   c. person who

9. The whole family always was together on _____.
   a. Christmas Day   b. Christmas day   c. christmas day

10. Some plants need _____ others need much sun.
   a. shade whereas   b. shade, whereas   c. shade. Whereas

11. She would not tell us _____ painting she preferred.
   a. whos   b. whose   c. who's

12. The sheriff bel_____ved little of what we told him.
   a. ie   b. ei   c. ea

13. We hurried to the _____ the bus had left.
   a. corner, however   b. corner however,   c. corner; however,

14. Everyone was enjoying the three _____ holiday.
   a. day's   b. days'   c. days

15. Your mother must have been a very coura_____ person.
   a. geous   b. gous   c. dgeous

16. Several _____ lived together in the small house.
    a. family's   b. families   c. familys

17. We were going to have a _____ talk.
    a. heart to heart   b. heart, to heart   c. heart-to-heart

18. He always talked to _____ to Jim or me.
    a. Rae, never   b. Rae never   c. Rae; never

19. The book was called _____.
    a. *Black elk speaks*   b. *Black Elk speaks*   c. *Black Elk Speaks*

20. The _____ message was recorded in the White House.
    a. presidents   b. President's   c. Presidents

Master your spelling problems by regular spelling work.

Poor spelling puts a barrier between your message and the reader. Whenever there is competition for the reader's attention, poor spellers put themselves at the end of the line. If you have a spelling problem, remember the following advice:

(1) Identify words that cause trouble for you. Some common words are misspelled over and over again: *believe, definite, athlete.* Keep a spelling log. Include among the common spelling demons all those words that you have misspelled on quizzes, exams themes

(2) Solve your spelling problems by building the right habit. A word ceases to be a spelling problem when the correct spelling has become *automatic.* Over and over again, run your eyes over the individual letters and the shape of the word as a whole. Give the word a chance to become firmly imprinted in your mind. Spell the letters out loud, so that your ears as well as your eyes will remember the word. Trace the word repeatedly in exceptionally large letters.

(3) Learn how to find a difficult word in the dictionary. In English, as the result of many changes in the spoken language, there is only a very imperfect fit between sign and sound. Many sounds are spelled several different ways. Take inventory of the different ways the same sound may be spelled. Study the accompanying chart.

Use spelling rules to help you with words that follow a common pattern.

English spelling does not follow simple rules. However, some groups of words do follow a common pattern. The rule that applies to them will usually have its exceptions. But it will help you memorize many words that you would otherwise have to learn one by one.

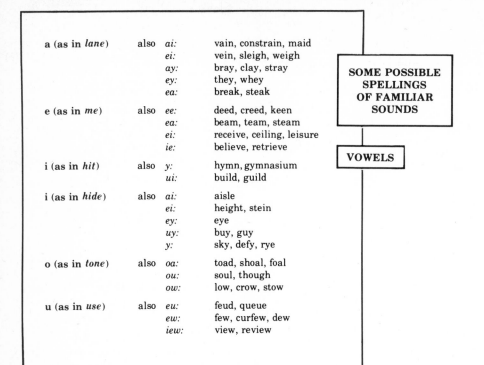

SOME POSSIBLE SPELLINGS OF FAMILIAR SOUNDS

VOWELS

a (as in *lane*)	also	*ai:*	vain, constrain, maid
		ei:	vein, sleigh, weigh
		ay:	bray, clay, stray
		ey:	they, whey
		ea:	break, steak
e (as in *me*)	also	*ee:*	deed, creed, keen
		ea:	beam, team, steam
		ei:	receive, ceiling, leisure
		ie:	believe, retrieve
i (as in *hit*)	also	*y:*	hymn, gymnasium
		ui:	build, guild
i (as in *hide*)	also	*ai:*	aisle
		ei:	height, stein
		ey:	eye
		uy:	buy, guy
		y:	sky, defy, rye
o (as in *tone*)	also	*oa:*	toad, shoal, foal
		ou:	soul, though
		ow:	low, crow, stow
u (as in *use*)	also	*eu:*	feud, queue
		ew:	few, curfew, dew
		iew:	view, review

CONSONANTS

f (as in *father*)	also	*ph:*	phone, phrase, emphatic
		gh:	laugh, cough, enough
g (as in *go*)	also	*gh:*	ghost, ghastly
		gu:	guess, guest, brogue
h (as in *hot*)	also	*wh:*	whole, who
j (as in *jam*)	also	*g:*	gypsy, oxygen, logic
		dg:	budget, knowledge, grudge
k (as in *kin*)	also	*c:*	castle, account, coat
		ch:	chemist, chlorinate, chrome
		qu:	clique
n (as in *noon*)	also	*gn:*	gnat, gnarled, gnash
		kn:	knife, knave, knight
		pn:	pneumonia
r (as in *run*)	also	*rh:*	rhythm, rhapsody, rhubarb
		wr:	wrong, wrangle, wry
s (as in *sit*)	also	*c:*	cent, decide, decimate
		sc:	scent, descent, science
		ps:	psychology, psalm, pseudonym
sh (as in *shine*)	also	*ch:*	machine, chef
		ci:	special, vicious, delicious
		si:	impression, possession, tension
		ti:	notion, imagination
		sci:	conscious, conscience
z (as in *zero*)	also	*x:*	xylophone

(1) Spell i *before* e *except after* c. In some words the *ee* sound is spelled *ie,* in others *ei*. When you sort out these words, you get the following pattern:

ie:	believe, achieve, grief, niece, piece (of pie)
cei:	receive, ceiling, conceited, receipt, deceive

I BEFORE *E*

In the second group, the *ei* always follows *c*. Exceptions:

ei:	either, neither, leisure, seize, weird
cie:	financier, species

(2) Double a single final consonant before endings that start with a vowel. In many words, we double a final consonant before the verb endings *–ed* and *–ing,* or the adjective endings *–er* and *–est*. Remember the following instructions:

• Make sure the final letter is a single consonant, coming after a single vowel:

big	bigger, biggest
fat	fatter, fattest, fattening
hop	hopper, hopped, hopping
hot	hotter, hottest
plan	planner, planned, planning
red	redder, reddening, reddest
run	runner, running
scrap	scrapped, scrapping
slip	slipper, slipped, slipping
win	winner, winning

DOUBLED CONSONANT

• Do *not* double the consonant if the final syllable has a double vowel (*oo, oa, ea,* etc.) or a silent *e:*

DOUBLE VOWEL	SILENT E
heat—heated, heating	*hate*—hated, hating
read—reading, reader	*plane*—planed, planing
neat—neater, neatest	*love*—lover, loving
sleep—sleeper, sleeping	*hope*—hoped, hoping
doom—dooming, doomed	*dome*—domed, doming

NO DOUBLING

● Contrast pairs like the following:

plan—pla*nn*ed   plane—pla*n*ed
hop—ho*pp*ing   hope—ho*p*ing
scrap—scra*pp*ed   scrape—scra*p*ed
slip—sli*pp*ed   sleep—slee*p*ing
red—re*dd*er   read—rea*d*ing

● Double the consonant only if it is part of the syllable that is *stressed* as you pronounce the word. Do not double the letter if the stress shifts away from the syllable:

DOUBLING	NO DOUBLING
ad**mit**, ad**mit**ted	**ben**efit, **ben**efited
over**lap**, over**lap**ping	de**vel**op, de**vel**oping
re**gret**, re**gret**ted	ex**hib**it, ex**hib**ited
be**gin**, be**gin**ning	**weak**en, **weak**ening
for**get**, for**get**ting	**orb**it, **orb**iting
re**fer**, re**ferr**ed	**ref**erence
pre**fer**, pre**ferr**ing	**pref**erable

(3) Drop a silent e *before an ending that starts with a vowel.* Keep the silent *e* if the ending starts with a consonant:

SILENT *E*		VOWEL	CONSONANT
	love	loving	lovely
	bore	boring	boredom
	fate	fatal	fateful
	like	likable	likely
	state	stating	statement

Exceptions: *argue—argument, true—truly, due—duly, mile —mileage, whole—wholly.* Also, do not apply this rule to the *e* that accounts for the *dge* sound in chang*e*able, courag*e*ous, and out- rag*e*ous; or the *ss* sound in notic*e*able.

(4) Change a final single y *to* i *or* ie *before endings other than* -ing. Change the *y* to *ie* when you add *–s.* Change it to *i* before most other endings. Keep the *y* before *–ing:*

ie:	try—tries, dry—dries, family—families, quantity—quantities, carry—carries, hurry—hurries		FINAL *Y*
i:	easy—easily, beauty—beautiful, happy—happiness, dry—drier, copy—copied		
y:	carrying, studying, copying, hurrying		

When it follows another vowel, the *y* usually remains unchanged: *played, joys, delays, valleys, grayness.*

Exceptions: *day—daily, pay—paid, say—said, gay—gaily, lay—laid.*

(5) Know the spellings of unusual plurals. A number of common words change their spelling when we go from one to several, from singular to plural:

SINGULAR *o:*	hero	potato	tomato	veto	motto
PLURAL *oes:*	heroes	potatoes	tomatoes	vetoes	mottoes

SINGULAR *man:*	man	woman	freshman	postman	fireman
PLURAL *men:*	men	women	freshmen	postmen	firemen

SINGULAR *f (fe):*	life	knife	calf	wife	half
PLURAL *ves:*	lives	knives	calves	wives	halves

NOTE: Some of the less common words ending in *o* or *f* do not change their spelling in the plural: *solo—solos, soprano—sopranos, cello—cellos; hoof—hoofs* (or *hooves*), *scarf—scarfs* (or *scarves*). Check your dictionary when you are in doubt.

On a separate sheet, write down the words called for in the following instructions.

EXERCISE 1

1. Fill in *ei* or *ie:* dec_____ve, conc_____t, n_____ce, bel_____f, rec_____ve, c_____ling, bel_____ve, s_____ze, ach_____vement, conc_____vable.
2. Write the *plural* of the following words: quantity, postman, parody, fly, hero, family, freshman, woman, knife, potato, quality, valley, property, veto.
3. Write the *past tense* of the following verbs: shun, hope, permit, edit, plan, cheat, play, tip, float, say, stop, regret, pay, blot, entrap.
4. Add *–ing* to the following words, making the necessary changes in spelling: like, prefer, orbit, commit, wipe, overlap, carry, dry, run, hurry, benefit, study, hate, drop, plan.
5. Add *–er* to the following words, making the necessary changes in spelling: red, sad, swim, lonely, busy, hot, carry, dim, write, white.

6. Add *–able* to the following words, making the necessary changes in spelling: change, notice, envy, regret, enjoy, break, admire, love, pay, debate, use.
7. Look up the *plural* forms of the following words in your dictionary: buffalo, cargo, Eskimo, mosquito, motto, piano, wharf.

EXERCISE 2

Of the two possible words in each sentence, write down the one that fits the context best.

1. We had *planed/planned* the attack carefully.
2. Unjust immigration laws once *barred/bared* minority groups.
3. The choir boys were *robed/robbed* in white.
4. We *scraped/scrapped* our plans for a big reception.
5. We were *hoping/hopping* against hope for an end to the rain.
6. Travelers looked forward to *dining/dinning* on the train.
7. He had *planed/planned* and sanded the wood himself.
8. The noise of the engine was *dining/dinning* in her ears.
9. The late show was a *griping/gripping* suspense drama.
10. After the loss, she had *pined/pinned* away.

EXERCISE 3

In each of the following numbered sets, one lettered item is misspelled. Write the correct spelling of that word after the number of the set.

1. (a) deplaned (b) unplanned (c) planed ahead
2. (a) studied (b) studing (c) studies
3. (a) true (b) dues (c) arguement
4. (a) dayly (b) delayed (c) paid
5. (a) referred (b) referring (c) referrence
6. (a) heros (b) solos (c) potatoes
7. (a) deceit (b) recieve (c) species
8. (a) forgetful (b) regretful (c) forgeting
9. (a) occured (b) occurrence (c) occur
10. (a) families (b) beauties (c) beautyful
11. (a) noticable (b) courageous (c) likable
12. (a) wholly (b) truely (c) duly
13. (a) knifes (b) hoofs (c) halves
14. (a) winning (b) thinner (c) begining
15. (a) happiness (b) copys (c) copying
16. (a) loveing (b) lovely (c) lovable
17. (a) niether (b) seize (c) niece
18. (a) regrets (b) regreted (c) regretting
19. (a) believe (b) achieve (c) liesure
20. (a) runner-up (b) runing (c) reruns

Make a special effort to master confusing pairs.

Learn to distinguish the words in three major types of confusing pairs:

(1) Know how to spell the same root word in different uses:

courte*ous*	but	court*e*sy
curi*ous*	but	curi*o*sity
descri*be*	but	descri*p*tion
four, fo*ur*teen	but	f*or*ty
gener*ous*	but	gener*o*sity
ni*ne,* ni*ne*ty	but	ni*n*th
prono*u*nce	but	pron*u*nciation
spe*ak*ing	but	spe*ech*
till	but	un*til*
wri*t*ing	but	wri*tt*en

Remember the following:

We advi*se* you to try. (verb)
He gave us advi*ce*.   (noun)

We pa*ss*ed the turnoff. (verb)
Let us forget the pa*st*.   (noun)

We found little prejudi*ce*.   (noun)
He was extremely prejudi*ced*.   (adjective)

We us*e* cardboard and tape. (present)
We us*ed* to meet in the hall. (past)

(2) Know how to spell words that sound similar or alike:

accept: He *acc*epted my apology; his terms are not *acc*eptable; I cannot *acc*ept the money

except: everyone *exc*ept Judy; she made an *exc*eption for us; to *exc*ept (exempt, exclude) present company

adopt: to ad*o*pt a proposal (in its present form); put a child up for ad*o*ption

adapt: to ad*a*pt a plan to one's needs (to make it fit better); an ad*a*pt-able worker (who fits in); an ad*a*ptation of the story

capital: Paris is the capit*al* of France; a bank needs capit*al*; print in capit*al* letters

capitol: the capit*ol* is the building where the legislature meets

censor:	in wartime letters are cen*sor*ed; object to cen*sor*ship
censure:	he was cen*sure*d (blamed, condemned) for his behavior; a vote of cen*sure*
cite:	he was *c*ited for bravery; she *c*ited several books by experts
site:	the *s*ite of the new school (it's situated there)
counsel:	the coun*sel*ing staff coun*sel*s, or gives advice (its members are coun*sel*ors)
council:	a city coun*cil* is a governing board or committee (its members are coun*cil*ors)
desert:	we drove through the de*s*ert; she de*s*erted her friends; he got his just de*s*erts
dessert:	we had pie for de*ss*ert
effect:	she *eff*ected many changes (she brought them about, produced them); far-reaching *eff*ects; an *eff*ective speech
affect:	it *aff*ected my grade (had an influence on it); the bill won't *aff*ect (change) your status; he spoke with an *aff*ected (artificial) accent
its:	*its* hood, *its* end (belonging to it)
it's:	*it's* (it is) too late
personal:	these are my own perso*nal* affairs; he got too perso*nal*
personnel:	the manager hired additional perso*nnel;* the organization had a perso*nnel* problem
presents:	he bought us presen*ts* (gifts)
presence:	your presen*ce* is essential (opposite of absen*ce*)
principal:	her princi*pal* (main) argument; a school princi*pal* (chief administrator); the princi*pal* (original sum) of a loan
principle:	princi*ples* (rules, standards) of conduct; he acted on princi*ple*
quiet:	be qui*et;* a qui*et* neighborhood
quite:	the house was qu*ite* old; not qu*ite* ready
than:	(*a* in comparisons) brighter *than* before
then:	(*e* for time) now and *then;* let's go *then*

there:	here and *there; there's* no room
their:	*their* car, *their* behavior (belonging to them)
they're:	*they're* (they are) gone

to:	*to* church, *to* school (direction); started *to* run (infinitive)
too:	*too* soon, *too* hot (degree); he, *too* (also)

weather:	stormy *weather*; to *weather* the storm
whether:	*whe*ther or not; ask *whe*ther it's true

whose:	wh*ose* house is it? (belonging to whom?); the driver *whose* car stalled
who's:	*who's* (who is) to blame?; the driver *who's* (who is) responsible

(3) Know how to spell words with parts that sound similar or alike.

–able:	accept*a*ble, avail*a*ble, indispens*a*ble (as in dispens*a*ry)
–ible:	poss*i*ble (also poss*i*bility), plaus*i*ble, irresist*i*ble

–ance:	attend*a*nce, perform*a*nce, acquaint*a*nce, guid*a*nce
–ence:	occurr*e*nce, experi*e*nce, exist*e*nce, excell*e*nce

–ant:	attend*a*nt, brilli*a*nt, abund*a*nt, predomin*a*nt
–ent:	excell*e*nt, promin*e*nt, independ*e*nt, differ*e*nt

–cede:	prec*ede*, sec*ede*, conc*ede*
–ceed:	succ*eed*, proc*eed* (but procedure)

NOTE: Make sure to spell out the *have* that sounds like a shortened *of* in the following combinations:

could *have* come	(never *could of*)
should *have* stayed	(never *should of*)
would *have* written	(never *would of*)
might *have* worked	(never *might of*)

After the number of each sentence, write down the word that fits the context.

EXERCISE 1

1. We cannot *accept/except* the invitation.
2. The move did not *affect/effect* his seniority.
3. He should listen to my *advise/advice*.

4. You might ask him *whether/weather* he knows.
5. She taught the *principles/principals* of mathematics.
6. No one *except/accept* my brother had applied for the job.
7. Her aunt was never *prejudice/prejudiced* against Catholics.
8. The house where he *use/used* to live has burned down.
9. The blow had *affected/effected* his hearing.
10. He spoke in the *presents/presence* of witnesses.
11. We had not seen them for *quite/quiet* a long time.
12. Electricians often make more money *than/then* teachers.
13. Guests had to show *there/their* identity cards.
14. She mentioned a doctor *whose/who's* name I have forgotten.
15. She was *cited/sited* for careless driving.
16. The new president *effected/affected* many changes in procedure.
17. It was *to/too* soon to concede defeat.
18. The loan sheet listed *principal/principle* and interest.
19. I was afraid he would *desert/dessert* us at the last minute.
20. The symphony orchestra had *its/it's* tenth anniversary.

EXERCISE 2

Write down the following words, inserting the missing letter (or letters).

1. ·indispens_____ble
2. emin_____nt
3. abund_____nce
4. irresist_____ble
5. proc_____d
6. permiss_____ble
7. perform_____nce
8. exist_____nce
9. curi_____sity
10. experi_____nce
11. attend_____nt
12. occurr_____nce
13. succ_____d
14. plaus_____ble
15. pron_____nciation
16. excell_____nt
17. prec_____ding
18. acquaint_____nce
19. gener_____sity
20. proc_____dure

EXERCISE 3

For each of the following pairs, write two short sentences using the words in context: *cast/caste, cue/queue, click/clique, aid/aide, aisle/isle, key/quay, dying/dyeing, peek/peak, moral/morale, a lot/allot.*

M1c
Spelling Lists

Study words frequently misspelled in order to avoid predictable errors.

The following boxes contain several hundred words frequently misspelled by student writers. Study the words in one box, and then have someone dictate them to you. Give special attention to the words that give you trouble.

GROUP 1

absence	accuses	adequate
abundance	accustom	admit
accept	achievement	adolescent
accessible	acknowledgment	advantageous
accidentally	acquaintance	advertisement
accommodate	acquire	afraid
accompanied	acquitted	against
accomplish	across	aggravate
accumulate	actuality	aggressive
accurately	address	a lot

GROUP 2

allotted	analysis	appreciate
allowed	analyze	approach
all right	annual	appropriate
already	anticipate	approximately
altar	anxiety	area
altogether	apologize	argue
always	apparent	arguing
amateur	appearance	argument
among	applies	arising
amount	applying	arrangement

GROUP 3

article	basically	breath
ascend	basis	brilliant
assent	beauty	Britain
athlete	becoming	burial
attack	before	busy
attendance	beginning	business
audience	belief	
authority	believe	calendar
	beneficial	candidate
bargain	benefited	career

Mechanics

careless	clothes	competition
carrying	coarse	competitor
ceiling	column	completely
cemetery	comfortable	conceivable
challenge	comfortably	conceive
changeable	coming	concentrate
character	commercial	condemn
chief	committed	confident
choose	committee	confidential
chose	companies	conscience

conscientious	courageous	decision
conscious	course	definite
considerably	courteous	definitely
consistent	criticism	definition
continually	criticize	dependent
control	curiosity	describe
controlled		description
convenience	dealt	desirable
convenient	deceit	despair
coolly	deceive	desperate

destruction	disappearance	during
develop	disappoint	
development	disastrous	ecstasy
device	discipline	efficiency
difference	disease	efficient
different	disgusted	eighth
difficult	dissatisfaction	eliminate
dilemma	dissatisfied	embarrass
dining	doesn't	embarrassment
disagree	due	eminent

GROUP 7

emphasize	exceptionally	families
endeavor	exercise	fashion
enough	exhaust	favorite
entertain	existence	foreign
environment	experience	forward
equipped	explanation	friend
especially	extraordinary	fulfill
etc.	extremely	fundamentally
exaggerate		further
excellent	familiar	

GROUP 8

gaiety	happily	hungry
generally	happiness	hurriedly
genius	height	hypocrisy
government	heroes	hypocrite
governor	heroine	
grammar	hindrance	ignorant
group	hopeful	imaginary
guaranteed	huge	imagination
guidance	humorous	immediately
	hundred	immensely

GROUP 9

incidentally	interpret	laboratory
indefinite	interrupt	laid
independent	involve	leisure
indispensable	irrelevant	library
inevitable	irresistible	likely
influence	itself	literature
ingenious		livelihood
intellectual	jealous	loneliness
intelligence		losing
interest	knowledge	

Mechanics

magnificent	method	necessarily
maintain	mileage	necessary
maintenance	miniature	ninety
maneuver	minute	noticeable
manufacturer	mischievous	
marriage	morale	obstacle
mathematics	muscle	occasion
meant	mysterious	occasionally
medicine		occurred
medieval	naïve	occurrence

omit	paralysis	permanent
operate	paralyze	persistent
opinion	particularly	persuade
opponent	passed	pertain
opportunity	past	phase
optimism	peace	philosophy
original	peculiar	physical
	perceive	piece
paid	perform	playwright
parallel	performance	political

possess	principal	pursue
possession	principle	
possible	privilege	quantity
practical	probably	
practice	procedure	really
precede	proceed	receive
prejudice	professional	recognize
prepare	prominent	recommend
prevalent	propaganda	regard
primitive	psychology	relief

GROUP 13

relieve	sacrifice	similar
religion	safety	simple
repetition	satisfactorily	sincerely
representative	schedule	sophomore
resource	seize	speech
response	sense	sponsor
reveal	separate	strength
rhythm	several	stretch
ridiculous	shining	strictly
	significance	studying

GROUP 14

subtle	thorough	various
succeed	together	villain
successful	tragedy	
sufficient	transferred	weird
superintendent	tremendous	writing
surprise		women
	undoubtedly	
temperament	unnecessary	
tendency	useful	
therefore	using	

A WRITER MUST KNOW HOW TO SPELL

difference

VALIDITY   POLLUTION   compassion

HISTORY   *politician*   PREVENTION

Mechanics

Use memory aids like the following to help fix the right spelling of familiar spelling problems in your mind. Read the aids in each set over several times.

A. 1. He *accepted* the blame for the *accident*.
2. We can care a little, *a lot,* or a whole *lot.*
3. *All right* means *all* is *right*.
4. The *inning* is *beginning*.
5. *Eve* and St*eve believe.*
6. The *bus* company was back *in business*.
7. Her *conscience* made her *conscious* of her guilt.
8. The *finicky* player was *definitely fini*shed.
9. He was a *friend* to the *end*.
10. People who *govern* are a *government*.

B. 11. *Margaret* likes *grammar*.
12. *Hoping* is better than m*oping*.
13. They *brought bricks* for the *library*.
14. The re*cess* was *necessary*.
15. She had been *occ*upied on that *occasion*.
16. Double *r* occu*rr*ed in *occurred*.
17. She made a *pers*onal appearance at every *perf*ormance.
18. The *principal* was everybody's *pal*.
19. He paid us tr*iple* on *principle*.
20. She will *probably* represent us cap*ably*.

C. 21. We w*ant* the same *quantity*.
22. We *received* the money for a new *ceiling*.
23. Double *m* is recom*m*ended in *recommend*.
24. We *ate* at *separate* tables.
25. The *larger* bird was *similar* to a *lark*.
26. *Studying* is done in a *study*.
27. Accelerate if you want to *succeed*.
28. When the *surfer surf*aced we were *surprised*.
29. The *villain* went to Sp*ain*.
30. The factory hired *men* and *women*.

Test your mastery of common spelling problems by having someone dictate the following sentences to you. They contain *100 frequently misspelled words* included in the preceding section.

1. *Successful propaganda* requires a *thorough knowledge* of *psychology*.
2. The *performance* of *amateur athletes* is *occasionally disappointing*.
3. The *sponsor interrupted* the *tragedy* with *ridiculous commercials*.
4. *Optimism* makes us *seize* on *hopeful* signs in *disastrous occurrences*.
5. His *irrestible strength* made him *approach* the *obstacle confidently*.

352

6. The *courageous heroine coolly eliminated* the *villain.*
7. He *always accuses* his *opponents* of *prejudice* or *hypocrisy.*
8. *Intellectual discipline* is as *necessary* as *genius* or *imagination.*
9. The *candidate addressed* her *arguments* to a *courteous audience.*
10. Our *writing course* dealt with *description* and *definition.*
11. We did not *anticipate* the *extraordinary anxiety* of our *adolescent friend.*
12. The *authorities consistently emphasize* the *influence* of the *environment.*
13. The *efficient manufacturer accurately analyzed* the new *procedure.*
14. Her *peculiar character* made her *choose beauty* over *convenience.*
15. Our *business* was *eliminated* by the *aggressive advertisements* of the *competition.*
16. His *changeable* and *jealous temperament* drove his *acquaintances* to *despair.*
17. *Disgusted* with *medicine,* he was *beginning* a new *career* in *mathematics.*
18. The *dissatisfied committee condemned* his *careless methods.*
19. The *governor continually criticized* those with *different opinions.*
20. He *accidentally* met *destruction during* a *speech* on *safety.*

UNIT REVIEW EXERCISE

In each of the following sentences, one word has been misspelled. Write the correctly spelled word after the number of the sentence.

1. They had reccommended a long list of books for summer reading.
2. He was not the only one who's rights were denied.
3. We all have to except and respect responsibility.
4. The judge studied them carefully, periodically peaking over the top of his glasses.
5. I couldn't tell if it was a business matter or mearly a friendly call.
6. For the owner of a small store, a robbery can be a catastrophy.
7. Voters today are more intellegent and sophisticated than ever before.
8. Sarcasm to me is a very evil thing, unless it effects no one.
9. Campus life is often dominated by snobbish little clicks.
10. Bringing a child into the world creates alot of responsibilities.
11. From the top of the hill, we could see the river with it's many barges and boats.
12. He claimed that the reports of injuries had been exagerated.
13. The new principle received many angry calls from parents.
14. We have started a new proceedure for accepting applications.
15. The pronounciation of the word used to be different.
16. My teachers took attendence at the beginning of the hour.
17. All of my friends were studing in the library.
18. He had had similiar warnings on several preceding occasions.
19. Many former amatures are now professional players.
20. She was asked to play at a benefit preformance.

CAPITALIZED NAMES
An Overview

PERSONAL NAMES	PEOPLE:	Eleanor Roosevelt, Langston Hughes, William Faulkner, Edna St. Vincent Millay
	TITLES:	Dr. Brothers, Senator Kennedy, Queen Elizabeth, Pope John, the President
	IMAGINARY PEOPLE:	Apollo, Captain Nemo, Jane Eyre, the Wizard of Oz, Maid Marian
GEOGRAPHIC NAMES	CONTINENTS:	Asia, America, Europe, Australia, the Antarctic
	COUNTRIES:	United States of America, Canada, Great Britain, Mexico, Denmark, Japan
	REGIONS:	the Southwest, the East, the Near East, the Midwest
	STATES:	Iowa, South Dakota, Louisiana, New Hampshire
	CITIES:	Oklahoma City, Houston, Baltimore, Los Angeles; Washington, D.C.
	SIGHTS:	Lake Erie, Mount Hood, Death Valley, Walden Pond
	ADDRESSES:	Park Lane, Fleet Avenue, Oak Street, Independence Square
CALENDAR NAMES	MONTHS:	January, March, July, October
	WEEKDAYS:	Monday, Wednesday, Saturday, Sunday
	HOLIDAYS:	Labor Day, Thanksgiving, Easter, the Sabbath, Mother's Day, the Fourth of July
INSTITUTIONAL NAMES	INSTITUTIONS:	the Supreme Court, the Department of Agriculture, the U.S. Senate
	BUSINESSES:	Ford Motor Company, General Electric, Sears
	SCHOOLS:	Oakdale High School, Las Vistas Junior College, University of Maine
	GROUPS:	the Democratic Party, the American Legion, the Garment Workers' Union
RELIGIOUS NAMES	PROPER NAMES:	the Virgin Mary, St. Thomas, Luther
	FAITHS:	Christian, Muslim, Jewish, Buddhist
	DENOMINATIONS:	Methodist, Mormon, Unitarian, Roman Catholic

Know how to use capital letters, apostrophes, and hyphens.

When we put words on a page, we use not only the ordinary alphabet but also capital letters and special marks. These marks often do not have an exact equivalent in speech. They are not pronounced in a way that would clearly signal when to put them in. We therefore have to study and practice the proper use of these marks in formal writing.

Use capital letters for proper names, for most of the words in a title, and for the first word of a sentence.

The most basic function of a capital letter is to start a **proper name.** A proper name sets an individual or a group off from other examples of the same kind. Look at the difference between general words and proper names in the following examples:

GENERAL WORD: student, senior, athlete, swimmer
PROPER NAME: Dennis, Marcia, Susan, Pablo

GENERAL WORD: tribe, nation, people, visitor
PROPER NAME: Cherokees, Danes, Mexicans, Canadians

GENERAL WORD: car, vehicle, motorcycle, truck
PROPER NAME: Ford, Toyota, Chevrolet, Volkswagen

In addition, capital letters serve some special purposes: We capitalize the pronoun *I.* We capitalize the first word of a new sentence.

Remember:

(1) Capitalize the first word of a sentence. Also capitalize the first word in a quotation that is a complete sentence:

The leader of the group said: "We did our best."

(2) Capitalize all major words in titles. Capitalize the first word in titles of books, newspapers, articles, poems, movies, songs, television shows, and the like. Also capitalize all other words in such titles except articles *(a, an, the);* prepositions *(at, of, for, with,* and the like); and connectives *(and, but, when, if,* and the like). Capitalize even the prepositions and connectives when they have five or more letters *(through, without, across, about).*

NOTE: Capitalize words this way when you write the title of your *own* theme and when you mention a book or article *in* your theme. The titles you mention, but not the title of your own theme, should also be italicized.

Study the use of capital letters in the following titles of books and articles:

The Future of Doctoring

A Serious Preacher Takes a Stand

The Shifting Focus of Faith

All About Pigeons

Truth-Telling for Couples

A Man at the Top of His Trade

Across the Sahara by Camel

How to Know Where You Are

See **M6b** for italicizing of titles.

(3) Capitalize the names and initials of persons. Also capitalize any titles or ranks used with the name. Study the contrast between a general and a specific use of a title or rank:

GENERAL WORD: The mayors of several nearby cities attended.

PROPER NAME: Both Mayor Gurnek and Mayor Carlson signed the document.

GENERAL WORD: The other judge had disqualified himself.

PROPER NAME: The defense had asked Judge Byrnes to disqualify himself.

We capitalize *Father* and *Mother* and similar family names when we use them as the name of the person. We do not capitalize them when they follow a pronoun like *my, his,* or *her:*

GENERAL WORD: My mother and her father got along well.

PROPER NAME: I know Father was right.

NOTE: We sometimes use a title alone. "A *president*," "a *queen*," or "a *pope*" means "one of several." "The *President*," "the *Queen*," or "the *Pope*" means "the only one."

(4) Capitalize the names of major groups. Study the capitals used with religions, denominations, nationalities, races, and political parties:

Protestant, Episcopalian, Canadian, Eskimo, Democratic

Remember that words like *democratic* and *republican* are also used to describe a type of institution or idea:

GENERAL WORD: Ancient Greece developed *democratic institutions.* (examples of a type)

PROPER NAME: She voted for the *Democratic party.* (name of one party)

(5) Capitalize the names of places and geographical features. Use a capital letter for the names of countries, states, cities, towns, streets, rivers, mountains, lakes, and the like:

Sweden, Florida, Los Angeles, Outer Drive, Mount Hood
the Ohio River, Lake Tahoe, Purvis Tunnel

(6) Capitalize the names of buildings and institutions. Use a capital letter for the names of churches, schools, clubs, and other organizations. Study the difference between general and proper names in the following pair:

GENERAL WORD: A girl from my high school was taken to the hospital.

PROPER NAME: A girl from Independence High School was admitted to Greenfield Community Hospital.

(7) Capitalize the names of historical events, periods, and documents. Study the following pairs:

GENERAL WORD: They fought in two world wars.

PROPER NAME: They fought in World War I and World War II.

GENERAL WORD: The constitutions of several states have been changed.

PROPER NAME: The Constitution of the United States has been amended several times.

(8) Capitalize calendar names: days of the week, months, and holidays. Do *not* capitalize the names of the seasons:

Wednesday, October, Easter, the Fourth of July, Christmas
spring, summer, autumn, winter

(9) Capitalize compass points only when they name a region.
For example, capitalize the South, the Northwest, the East. Do not
capitalize compass points when they show a general direction:

GENERAL WORD: She had to turn east to reach the lake.
PROPER NAME: She had spent all her life in the East.

GENERAL WORD: The wind was coming from the southwest.
PROPER NAME: They worked on irrigation projects in the Southwest.

GENERAL WORD: He moved from south of Chicago to south of Detroit.
PROPER NAME: He had been born in the South.

(10) Capitalize the names of all languages. Do not capitalize
the names of other school subjects, unless they are in a course title:

Students were studying French, German, or Spanish.
Few Americans know Russian or Chinese.

My sister had taken Algebra I and Geometry IIB.
I have always preferred art and music to physics and math.

(11) Capitalize the name of the Deity. Also capitalize all pronouns referring to Him. The names of sacred figures, the Bible,
and parts of the Bible are also generally capitalized:

The Lord gives and He may take away; blessed be His name.
Virgin Mary, Holy Ghost, Genesis

(12) Capitalize adjectives made from proper nouns. But do
not capitalize the nouns following such adjectives unless they themselves are proper nouns:

Brazilian coffee (shipped from Brazil)
Danish pastry (first made in Denmark)
French bread (first made in France)
an African country (located in Africa)
a Roman emperor (who reigned in Rome)

*(13) When something has been named after a person, capitalize
the person's name:*

Geiger counter, Ferris wheel, Morse code

Sometimes the person who gave something its name has been
forgotten, and a lowercase letter is used:

diesel engine, a maverick senator, pasteurized milk

(14) Capitalize trade names of all kinds. Do not capitalize
the word following the trade name unless it is part of it:

Handicraft tools, Alka-Seltzer, Bayer Aspirin, a Xerox copier

NOTE: Do not capitalize the following when they are part of a proper name: the articles *(the, a, an);* short prepositions and connectives —less than five letters *(of, by, with; and):*

Institute for Foreign Studies
Museum of the Visual Arts
Fourth of July
National Telegraph and Telegram

Use the following section for *habit building*. Read the examples in each set over several times. Pay special attention to pairs where the same word is used once with and once without a capital letter.

EXERCISE 1

1. An assessor, Assessor Smith; the president of the company, President Kennedy; police officers, Officer O'Malley.
2. A village street, Greenwich Village; a city in Kansas, Kansas City; a county courthouse, Santa Clara County; an island in the Pacific, Staten Island; a side street, a shop on Main Street.
3. A Ford sedan, the Ford Motor Company; Westinghouse appliances, a Walt Disney movie, a Dodge truck.
4. *Much Ado About Nothing, The Mayor of Casterbridge, The Power and the Glory, The War of the Worlds, The Man Without a Country.*
5. Greek gods, the Christian God, the Old Testament, the Bible, a Buddhist temple, a Methodist minister, Catholic beliefs.
6. In the South, drive south from Los Angeles; a city in the East, east of the city.
7. This last spring, this fall, in June and September, every Wednesday; closed on Sundays, open on weekdays; Easter vacation.
8. The Middle Ages, the Victorian period, the Elizabethan stage, the Great Depression.
9. Many civil wars, the Civil War; republican institutions, the Republican candidate; a democratic country, Democratic voters.
10. The Bill of Rights, the Fourth of July, the Declaration of Independence, the U.S. Senate, the U.S. Army, the *Congressional Record.*

In each of the following sentences, which words should have been capitalized? Write down and capitalize all such words after the number of each sentence. (Do not include the first word of the sentence.)

EXERCISE 2

1. The twenties was a colorful period in american history.
2. A great jazz musician, louis armstrong, played in king oliver's band in chicago.

3. Everybody's favorite was will rogers, an oklahoma cowboy who was part indian.
4. The president, a republican, often appeared in public as a cowboy or indian chief.
5. A swedish actress named greta garbo helped make hollywood a household word on both sides of the atlantic.
6. For a time, marcus garvey was the leader of a black movement promoting a return to africa.
7. In the east, new york became a mecca for journalists, with publications ranging from *the new yorker* to hearst's *daily mirror.*
8. At notre dame in south bend, indiana, knute rockne's teams helped make football a favorite american spectator sport.
9. In the south, baptists and methodists, quoting the bible, accused teachers of teaching darwinian evolution and marxist economics.
10. A generation of brilliant writers was publishing american classics like *the great gatsby, this side of paradise, a farewell to arms,* and *main street.*

EXERCISE 3
After the number of each sentence, write down and capitalize each word that should start with a capital letter. (Do not include the first word of the sentence.)

1. The history of europe has often been dominated by powerful individuals, from frederick the great and napoleon through hitler and stalin.
2. In america, history has often been made by groups of anonymous men and women.
3. The first spanish explorers were followed by jesuit priests aiming to convert the natives to christianity.
4. Later, the fur traders—french, british, and russian—pushed in for beaver and other pelts.
5. Members of protestant minorities—the puritans, the quakers—colonized new england and pennsylvania.
6. In books like *the scarlet letter* and *the house of the seven gables,* nathaniel hawthorne described the puritans, who had tamed the wilderness with bible and gun.
7. In the war of independence, a citizen army put democracy and republican institutions in the place of the government of king george.
8. After the louisiana purchase, the mississippi became the center of a way of life described by mark twain in *life on the mississippi.*
9. In the great plains of the west, the wild horses and cattle were rounded up and driven to kansas or texas by cowboys and cattle ranchers who had often been citizens of the confederacy during the civil war.
10. The gold fields of california and the comstock lode brought new yorkers, southerners, and midwesterners across the rocky mountains or into san francisco harbor.

Use the apostrophe to show contractions and the possessive of nouns.

Like a capital letter, the apostrophe is strictly a *written* symbol. We cannot hear it when we read a sentence aloud. Know the
three major uses of the apostrophe:

(1) Use the apostrophe to show the omission of sounds or letters.
Spoken English (and informal written English) makes frequent use
of **contractions.** These are shortened forms of *be, have,* and auxiliaries like *will (would), can (could),* and the like.

As long as *there's* light, *we're* brave enough.
So we *can't* have a signal fire.
We're beaten.

Many contractions include a shortened form of *not: can't,
haven't, don't, isn't, wouldn't, won't.* Take care not to misspell these,
especially *doesn't (does not).* Some contractions sound like other
forms that have different uses. Make sure to spell them differently:

it's *(it is)*	*It's* too early.
its *(of it)*	The ship kept *its* course.
who's *(who is)*	*Who's* next?
whose *(of whom)*	*Whose* coat is that?
they're *(they are)*	*They're* right.
their *(of them)*	*Their* cabin was deserted.

USES OF THE APOSTROPHE

That's why

A FAN'S NOTES

They're worth
waiting for.

A report on Women's Studies

CHILDREN'S FUND   **I didn't realize**

Webster's American Biographies

NOTE: Limit your use of contractions to personal letters and informal or humorous themes. Feel free to use an occasional *don't* or *it's* even in more serious papers. But avoid contractions in formal reports, research papers, or letters of application.

(2) Use the apostrophe for the possessive of nouns and some pronouns.   The **possessive** shows where something belongs or what it is part of. Usually, the same relationship could also be shown by the preposition *of.* The most usual form of the possessive shows the singular noun followed by the apostrophe plus *s:*

SINGULAR: *Greg's* father (the father *of* Greg)
his *sister's* graduation (the graduation *of* his sister)
Jean Brown's store (the store *of* Jean Brown)
the *family's* outing (the outing *of* the family)
the *prophet's* beard (the beard *of* the prophet)

Remember:

• When the plain form of the noun already has an *s* at the end, do not *add* a second *s* to make the possessive. This rule applies to all −*s* plurals:

PLURAL: the *girls'* pool (the pool of the *girls*)
the *slaves'* revolt (the revolt of the *slaves*)
the *teachers'* records (the records of the *teachers*)
the *families'* homes (the homes of several *families*)

• Not *all* plural nouns have the plural −*s.* They then form the regular possessive with apostrophe plus *s:*

women's wages, the *children's* hour

• The possessive is used in many expressions dealing with *time, price,* or *measurement:*

SINGULAR: a *day's* work, an *hour's* wait, *today's* paper, last *year's* meeting, a *moment's* notice, a good *night's* sleep, a *dollar's* worth
PLURAL: two *weeks'* pay, three *dollars'* worth, six *weeks'* notice

• Only *indefinite pronouns* use the apostrophe. Never use the apostrophe with possessive pronouns like *its, hers, ours, theirs, yours:*

INDEFINITE: *one's* relatives, *someone's* uncle, *anybody's* guess, no *one's* fault
POSSESSIVE: it is *hers,* it was either *ours* or *theirs,* has run *its* course

NOTE: For *proper names* ending with *s,* the use of a second −*s* for the possessive is *optional:*

Charles' birthday (or *Charles's* birthday)
Charles *Dickens'* novels (or Charles *Dickens's* novels)

(3) Use the apostrophe to separate the plural –s from the name of a letter or of a number, or from a word discussed as a word:

Her record showed all *A's* and *B's.*
His number consisted of seven *3's* in a row.
It was a speech with many *if's* and *but's.*

EXERCISE 1

Each of the following shows the right spelling of possessive forms and contractions. Explain why or how the apostrophe was used or omitted in each of the examples.

1. *They're* drawings that *don't* appeal to *everyone's* taste.
2. *It's* illegal to identify these positions as *women's* jobs.
3. She got into the *driver's* seat of my *cousin's* car.
4. The boy was wearing *someone's* old woolen overcoat, with *its* belt dragging behind him.
5. In the *man's* arms is the *couple's* youngest child.
6. *Dolores'* silence might have been brought on by a jealous reaction, but *mine* was occasioned by pure surprise. (Maya Angelou)
7. When the announcer read the *winners'* names, *hers* was missing from the list.
8. The *burglars'* muddy footprints were all over my *aunt's* new carpet.
9. Slowly the red drained from *Jack's* cheeks. His gaze avoided the embarrassment of linking with *another's* eye. (William Golding)
10. They separate the grain from the chaff by tossing the straw in the air. This was their *fathers'* method. And it is likely it will be their *sons'.* (William O. Douglas)

EXERCISE 2

Rewrite each of the following. Substitute the possessive form or the contraction using the apostrophe.

1. could not agree
2. the fence of the neighbor
3. the taxes of my neighbors
4. through the fault of nobody
5. against the orders of his doctor
6. does not matter
7. do not worry
8. a workshop of teachers
9. a vacation of two months
10. the objections of her family
11. the feud of our families
12. the rights of women
13. for the sake of the child
14. in the best interest of the children
15. the friends of Agnes
16. the pay of half a day
17. they are late again
18. to the surprise of everyone
19. have not harmed anyone
20. the deliberations of the jury
21. the instructions of the judge
22. the lawyer of the accused
23. the reactions of the spectators
24. cannot hurt
25. the bedrooms of her sisters

EXERCISE 3

Write down the right choice after the number of the sentence.

1. Through her illness she lost several *week's/weeks'* pay.
2. He felt that his private life was *nobodys/nobody's* business.
3. Over the years he had collected about ten *dollar's/dollars'* worth of nails.
4. It must be nerve-racking to be a test *pilot's/pilots* insurance agent.
5. We watched the *spectator's/spectators* and their reactions.
6. He was worried about his *children's/childrens'* future.
7. Several new *family's/families* had moved in.
8. We have the man *who's/whose* fingerprints match those on the gun.
9. We can never be absolutely sure *who's/whose* to blame for an accident.
10. Carl loved to send people on a *fools/fool's* errand.
11. Nobody can be *everybodys/everybody's* friend.
12. You always give me good advice when *it's/its* too late.
13. People look for a scapegoat when *they're/their* angry or hurt.
14. Peter had always been his *family's/families'* black sheep.
15. The husbands commiserated over their *family's/families'* misfortunes.
16. The board refused to rescind *it's/its* earlier decision.
17. It was all in a *day's/days* work.
18. The mayor accepted the *commissioners/commissioner's* resignation.
19. The minister always called all of us *Gods/God's* children.
20. It seems as if *everyones/everyone's* grandfather had to walk ten miles barefoot to school.

M2c

Using Hyphens

Use the hyphen in compound words that have not yet become a single word.

Use the hyphen in the following situations:

(1) Use the hyphen in compound numbers from twenty-one *to* ninety-nine:

The minimum age had been changed from *twenty-five* to *twenty-one*.

(2) Use the hyphen for combinations that are at the halfway stage between one word and several. We call combined words **compound words.** Some have already merged into a single word. Others are still separate. Still others are hyphenated:

ONE WORD: headache, darkroom, highway, newspaper, stepmother, grandfather, birthplace, bittersweet, freestyle, greenbelt, heavyweight, typewriter

SEVERAL WORDS: high school, labor union, commander in chief, second cousin, bird dog, ground plan, pony express, side effect

HYPHEN: bull's-eye, cave-in, court-martial, great-grandfather, in-laws, brother-in-law, Mexican-American, left-handed, merry-go-round, hand-picked, able-bodied

Make sure to get the following right:

ONE WORD: today, tomorrow, nevertheless, nowadays
TWO WORDS: all right, a lot, be able, no one

NOTE: Many words that used to be hyphenated are now written solidly. Others are used either way. When you are in doubt, use the word the way it is listed in your dictionary.

(3) Use the hyphen to separate some prefixes from the word that follows.   A **prefix** is an exchangeable part that can appear in front of many different words. Most prefixes combine with the word that follows into a single unit. Put a hyphen after the prefix in the following situations:

- After *all–, ex–* (when it means "former"), and *self–;*

all-knowing, all-powerful
ex-champion, ex-president
self-conscious, self-respect

- Before a *capital* letter:

all-American, pro-British
anti-German, non-Catholic

- Between two *identical vowels:*

anti-intellectual
semi-independent

(4) Use the hyphen with group modifiers.   Several words that are normally separate may combine as a **group modifier** that is put in front of a noun. Use hyphens whenever such a group of words takes the place of a single adjective: *first-class* mail, *four-wheel* drive, *high-grade* ore.

SEPARATE: He described the process *step by step.*
HYPHENS: We wanted a *step-by-step* account.

SEPARATE: The meal was *well balanced.*
HYPHENS: They served a *well-balanced* meal.

SEPARATE: We decided to *wait and see.*
HYPHENS: She adopted a *wait-and-see* attitude.

Do not use hyphens when one part of the group modifier is an adverb ending in *–ly: a rapidly growing* city, a *carefully prepared* demonstration.

For hyphen dividing words at end of line, see **M7a.**

Mechanics

Use the following as a habit-building exercise. All examples show the *right* spelling of hyphenated words and of combinations spelled as one word or as several words. Read the examples in each set over several times.

1. thirty-six, eighteen, ninety-four, eighty-three, twenty-one.
2. grandmother, stepfather, mother-in-law, in-laws, great-grandmother.
3. drive-in, old-fashioned, cave-in, turnout, one-sided, a one-time associate.
4. a full-size car, a three-stage rocket, wall-to-wall carpets, a heart-to-heart talk, a left-of-center government, middle-of-the-road policies, a once-in-a-lifetime opportunity.
5. English-speaking nations, freedom-loving citizens, world-shaking events, a smoke-filled room.
6. high-class ore, a well-earned rest, a hard-hitting account, a smoothly running engine, happily smiling listeners.
7. ex-husband, ex-senator, self-styled, self-confident; un-American, pro-British, anti-German, neo-Nazi; all-powerful.
8. travel first class, send it by first-class mail; he brought us up to date, an up-to-the-minute summary.
9. the Italian-American community, an Anglo-Irish family, a Mexican-American tradition.
10. pseudo-scientific, quasi-religious; postwar.

After the number of each group of words, write it the way it should appear. Use hyphens where they are required. Make changes only if they are necessary. (Your teacher may ask you to check examples in your dictionary.)

EXAMPLE: an ex champion
(Answer) *an ex-champion*

1. by parcel post
2. the local post master
3. a matter of fact announcement
4. a pre fabricated house
5. a deep seated suspicion
6. a slow motion study
7. infra red rays
8. a key note speech
9. Marion's kin folk
10. her brown eyed cousin
11. rear wheel drive
12. a clear cut explanation
13. strong anti British feeling
14. a new fangled invention
15. for newly weds
16. an ex colony
17. her self righteous attitude
18. a double edged sword
19. much double talk
20. had double parked the car
21. the give and take of conversation
22. a give away program
23. a hit and run driver
24. in the locker room
25. a grass roots campaign

In each sentence, find the combination that needs one or more hyphens. *Write the hyphenated combination* after the number of the sentence.

1. He was surprised at the anti Americanism of his Japanese friends.
2. She explained step by step how to make a person to person call.
3. What had been a strictly spontaneous movement turned into a well organized campaign.
4. The ex governor had had strong support from the labor unions.
5. Up to the minute news coverage seldom examines any event in depth.
6. The candidate promised to conduct a down to the grassroots campaign.
7. The quickly formed committee promised an in depth study of the problem.
8. Pat was changing from a happy go lucky student to a serious junior executive.
9. His self confidence was badly shaken by her curt reply.
10. A government with almost equally powerful branches is preferable to a single all powerful executive.

Look at the three possible choices for the blank in each of the following sentences. After the number of the sentence, put the letter for the right choice.

1. We always watched the parade on _____ .
   a. Columbus day   b. columbus day   c. Columbus Day
2. She and her friends had visited the Museum _____ Art.
   a. of Modern   b. of modern   c. Of Modern
3. The form asked questions about my _____ source of income.
   a. families   b. families'   c. family's
4. She had asked the _____ to appear on her talk show.
   a. ex governor   b. ex-governor   c. exgovernor
5. That year, winter came early in the _____ .
   a. midwest   b. Midwest   c. mid-west
6. The title of the book was *I Know Why* _____ *Sings*.
   a. *the Caged Bird*   b. *The Caged Bird*   c. *the caged Bird*
7. The jury wanted to reread several _____ testimony.
   a. witnesses   b. witness'   c. witnesses'
8. She had tried out for the _____ relay team.
   a. women's   b. womans   c. womens
9. The law required tenants to give _____ notice.
   a. two weeks   b. two weeks'   c. two week's
10. Pat wanted to study at one of our _____ .
    a. state colleges   b. state college's   c. State Colleges
11. Bill had grown up in a largely _____ .
    a. Polish Suburb   b. Polish suburb   c. polish suburb

12. The picture showed the _____ office in the White House.
    a. presidents   b. president's   c. President's
13. Several _____ had applied for the new government grants.
    a. city's   b. cities'   c. cities
14. The ship sailed _____ for several days.
    a. southeast   b. Southeast   c. South-East
15. He had been an _____ basketball player.
    a. all-American   b. allAmerican   c. all-american
16. She was reading a book called *Hands* _____ *Sea.*
    a. *across the*   b. *Across the*   c. *across The*
17. It was a case of one _____ judgment against another's.
    a. person's   b. persons   c. persons'
18. That was the first time she had gone against _____ wishes.
    a. Mothers'   b. mother's   c. Mother's
19. The announcer gave us a _____ account.
    a. play by play   b. playbyplay   c. play-by-play
20. England has long had _____ institutions.
    a. true democratic   b. true Democratic   c. true-democratic

M3

END PUNCTUATION

Mark the end of a sentence by a period, a question mark, or an exclamation mark.

There are several ways of saying "This is John." When we let our voice drop off at the end, we show that we have completed a statement: "This is John." When we make the pitch rise at the end we are asking a question: "This is John?" If pitch stays level at the end, we show that we are going to continue the sentence: "This is John, who lives next door." These and similar differences are signaled in writing by punctuation. End punctuation shows we have completed a unit that can stand by itself.

M3a

Sentences and Fragments

Use the period at the end of a complete sentence.

The **period** separates one complete sentence from another. A complete sentence has its own subject and its own verb. (In request sentences, the subject has often been left out, but *you* is understood as the subject.) To be able to stand by itself, a complete sentence must *not* be subordinated to another sentence by the following:

SUBORDINATING CONNECTIVES	RELATIVE PRONOUNS
if	who
when	which
because	that
whereas	

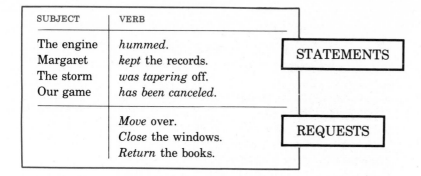

SUBJECT	VERB	
The engine	*hummed.*	
Margaret	*kept* the records.	**STATEMENTS**
The storm	*was tapering* off.	
Our game	*has been canceled.*	
	Move over.	
	Close the windows.	**REQUESTS**
	Return the books.	

When the period sets off a group of words that is not a complete sentence, the result is a **sentence fragment.** Avoid the sentence fragment in serious writing. Often, what causes a fragment is the lack of all or part of the verb. Often, both part of the verb and a possible subject are missing.

FRAGMENT: We had a big surprise. *My brother from Chicago.*
COMPLETE: We had a big surprise. My brother *arrived* from Chicago.

FRAGMENT: We listened to Jim. *Singing the blues.*
COMPLETE: We listened to Jim. *He was* singing the blues.

Avoid especially four kinds of sentence fragments:

(1) Do not separate prepositional phrases from the rest of the sentence.   Prepositional phrases start with a preposition like *in, at, with, for, on,* or *without.* Do not separate them from the sentence to which they belong:

FRAGMENT: He tried to eat his rice. *With chopsticks.*
COMPLETE: He tried to eat his rice *with chopsticks.*

FRAGMENT: She found the missing gloves. *On the back seat.*
COMPLETE: She found the missing gloves *on the back seat.*

(2) Do not separate appositives from the rest of the sentence.   An appositive is a second noun that is put after the first noun and gives us further information about it. Often the second noun carries with it other material to make up an appositive phrase. There is no verb to make a second complete sentence:

FRAGMENT: She had bought a secondhand car. *A station wagon.*
COMPLETE: She had bought a secondhand car, *a station wagon.*

FRAGMENT: They were looking for Jim. *The runner-up.*
COMPLETE: They were looking for Jim, *the runner-up.*

PUNCTUATION MARKS
A Reference Chart

COMMA
before coordinating connectives	M4a
with adverbial clauses	M4b
with relative clauses	M4c
with nonrestrictive modifiers	M5a
after introductory modifiers	M5a
with adverbial connectives	M4a
with *especially, namely, for example*	M3a
with *of course* and other sentence modifiers	M5a
between items in a series	M5b
in a series of parallel clauses	M4a
between coordinate adjectives	M5b
with dates, addresses, and the like	M5b
with direct address and other light interrupters	M5c
between contrasted elements	M5c
with quotations	M6a

SEMICOLON
between independent clauses	M4a
before adverbial connectives	M4a
before coordinating connectives	M4a
between items in a series	M5b

COLON
to introduce a list or explanation	M3a
to introduce a quotation	M6a

PERIOD
at end of sentence	M3a
ellipsis	M6a
with abbreviations	M7b

DASH
break in thought	M3a
with heavy interrupters	M5c

QUOTATION MARKS
with direct quotation	M6a
quotation within quotation	M6a
with slang or technical terms	M6b
to set off titles	M6b

EXCLAMATION MARK	M3b
QUESTION MARK	M3b
PARENTHESES	M5c

(3) Do not separate verbals from the rest of the sentence. Many verbal phrases start with an *–ing* form (participle) or a *to* form (infinitive). To become part of a complete verb, such forms have to follow an auxiliary like *am, was, has, had, will, can, may,* or *should.* Do not separate verbals from the sentence if there is no auxiliary:

FRAGMENT: They were busy in the kitchen. *Baking their own bread.*
COMPLETE: They were busy in the kitchen, *baking their own bread.*

FRAGMENT: We turned the boat around. *To head for shore.*
COMPLETE: We turned the boat around *to head for shore.*

(4) Do not separate dependent clauses from their main clauses. A clause that starts with a subordinator—*if, because, although, whereas*—cannot stand by itself. It turns into a fragment when separated from the main clause by a period. A clause that starts with a relative pronoun—*who, which, that*—also turns into a fragment when set off:

FRAGMENT: Heat makes metal expand. *Whereas cold makes it shrink.*
COMPLETE: Heat makes metal expand, *whereas cold makes it shrink.*

FRAGMENT: We went to Buffalo. *Which is his hometown.*
COMPLETE: We went to Buffalo, *which is his hometown.*

Remember the major ways a sentence fragment may be revised:

• Tie most adverbs and prepositional phrases, and many verbals, into the preceding sentence without any punctuation. Use *no* comma or other mark:

We are changing the policy *gradually.*
We will meet you later *at the corner of Main Street.*
They went to the office *to register.*

• Use a **comma** rather than a period to set off most appositives and many verbals and dependent clauses:

She had bought a secondhand car, *a convertible.*
They were busy in the kitchen, *preparing a big meal.*

• Use the **comma** when you add examples to a more general statement after *such as, especially, for example, for instance,* and *namely.* In formal writing, use a *second* comma after the last three:

He kept exotic fish, *such as Japanese carp.*
Her friends loved Europe, *especially France.*

Look out for the unexpected, *for instance, a stalled car.*

See **M4** and **M5** for detailed instructions on using the comma.

● Use the **colon** to tie a *list, description,* or *explanation* to the more general statement that came before:

Only two of us were given a scholarship: *Martha Livingston and Boyd Wilmette.*

The bison was life to the tribes of the plains: *the Sioux, the Cheyenne, the wild-riding Comanche.*

● Use a **dash** when you want to keep something separate as an *afterthought:*

We are changing the policy—*gradually.*

He left Newton Jail—*a free man.*

● Sometimes it is difficult to tie a sentence fragment to the preceding sentence. Turn such a fragment into a *complete separate sentence:*

FRAGMENT: We tried to change his mind. *Being a futile effort.*

REVISED: We tried to change his mind. *It was a futile effort.*

NOTE: **Permissible fragments** appear in writing when the writer deliberately imitates the natural flow of speech or thought. You will find such fragments in the following:

● Written records of *conversation,* or prose that records the give-and-take of dialogue:

"I'd rather be myself," he said. *"Myself and nasty. Not somebody else, however jolly."* (Aldous Huxley)

● *Narrative* or informal essays that record naturally rambling thought:

I don't think it's fortunate to write. *Or clever.* It's cleverer to converse. (Sylvia Ashton-Warner)

● *Description* that records impressions the way they move through the mind of the observer:

The plains vary here even more than usual—sometimes a long sterile stretch of scores of miles—then green, fertile and grassy, an equal length. *Some very large herds of sheep.* (Walt Whitman)

You may use such permissible fragments when reporting a conversation or writing a story. Avoid these fragments when writing an expository paper devoted to serious discussion, argument, or research.

In which of the following does the period separate two complete sentences? Put *S* for satisfactory after the number of the passage. In which of the following does the period cause a sentence fragment? Put *Frag* for fragment after the number of the passage.

1. She had only one goal. To graduate.
2. An elderly man was standing up. Nobody on the bus noticed.
3. Wilma Rudolph became famous during the 1960 Olympics. She won three gold medals.
4. The teacher walked around the classroom several times. Looking for cheaters.
5. The movers left the piano with five keys damaged. Strictly Laurel and Hardy.
6. Rudyard Kipling named his wolf man Mowgli. Shere Khan was Mowgli's rival.
7. Not all of Shakespeare's female characters are Lady Macbeths. Or Ophelias either.
8. He said he wanted only neat papers. Neat writing and "neat" ideas.
9. Most driving tests are the same. Stopping at signals and parking.
10. My grandparents had a dozen cats. Caring for their pets kept them happy.
11. One part of Hawaii is covered with black sand and volcanic rock. The other part is covered with trees and flowers.
12. Sarah had gone back to Toronto. To live with a wealthy aunt.
13. Dolores was painting the ceiling. Splattering white paint over the blue walls.
14. One comic-book hero appeared on the covers of six million copies that year. The Amazing Spider-Man.
15. Wilma Rudolph starred in the 100-meter and 200-meter dashes. She also served as anchor of the 400-meter relay team.
16. The sprinter had survived severe childhood diseases. Pneumonia and scarlet fever.
17. At first Mowgli climbed trees like a sloth. Later he jumped from branch to branch.
18. Minnesota is famous for its lakes. It is called the "Land of 10,000 Lakes."
19. The comedian was eating his own sandwich out of a brown bag. At a fancy restaurant.
20. More insulation is being used. Thermal windows are put in.

What would be the right punctuation at the break in each of the following passages? On a separate sheet of paper, put the appropriate abbreviation after the number of each passage: *P* for period; *Cm* for comma; *Cl* for colon; *No* for no punctuation. Limit yourself to these four choices. Use no other marks.

(Your teacher may ask you to write these sentences out with their correct punctuation. When you do, remember to capitalize the first word after a period.)

1. Opinions differ on many things _____ for instance, human nature.
2. Some writers admire humanity _____ they consider people good.
3. People naturally treat others _____ with kindness.
4. Wrongdoing is caused by other factors _____ poverty or oppression.
5. People are innocent and good _____ in their natural state.
6. Other writers believe in the opposite _____ a natural tendency toward evil.
7. They stress two basic qualities _____ selfishness and cruelty.
8. People learn to be good _____ through fear of punishment.
9. They soon forget the rules of civilization _____ in an emergency.
10. This view prevails in a book that is read _____ by many high school students.
11. The book is a British novel _____ namely, Golding's *Lord of the Flies*.
12. Golding describes a group of boys _____ going back to savagery.
13. The setting of the book is a solitary island _____ the time is after a nuclear war.
14. There are no adults left _____ to maintain discipline.
15. At first the boys hold on to civilized procedures _____ for example, the election of a leader.
16. The boys carry on their British traditions _____ such as respecting differences of opinion.
17. Gradually tensions appear _____ under the civilized surface.
18. Soon they are ruled by two primitive influences _____ force and primitive superstition.
19. The book may be a parable _____ the story has a larger meaning.
20. Perhaps the same thing could happen _____ on a larger scale.

M3b
Questions and Exclamations

Use question marks and exclamation marks where necessary.

Use marks to show that something is not a simple ordinary statement:

(1) Use the question mark to end sentences that ask for a reply. Many questions are signaled by question words like *who, whom, whose, which, when, where, what, why,* and *how:*

Who is your friend?
What is the point?
Which is the shortest way?
Why should we have to pay?
How could they solve their problem?

Many questions are signaled by a reversal of the subject and its verb (or auxiliary):

Was the plane on time?
Did he tell the truth?
Could they have used a different road?
Have her parents been told?

Remember to put the question mark at the end of a *long* question:

Where does factual truth end and editorializing begin?

NOTE: Feel free to use either the question mark or the period after requests worded as questions for the sake of *politeness:*

Will you please return to the office at three o'clock?
Will you please return to the office at three o'clock.

(2) Use the exclamation mark for special emphasis.   It shows that something is urgent, or that it is unusual, or that it is a surprise. It marks orders, shouts, or urgent requests. Use it as needed with single words, groups of words, or complete sentences:

Stop!   We lost the game!
Come back!   The supplies are gone!
What a break!   What stories they used to tell!

Most of the following sentences show acceptable end punctuation. Put *S* for satisfactory after the number of each such sentence. Find the sentences that are unsatisfactory. Put *U* after the number of each of these.

EXERCISE

1. What could have brought them to this out-of-the-way place?
2. Wasn't it Charles Dickens who wrote *A Tale of Two Cities.*
3. Will you please fill in the attached form and return it to our office.
4. These are the people who represent us in Congress!
5. How well he knew every nook and cranny of the old house!
6. What can a man do if his family turns against him.
7. Why does she always have to quote Ayn Rand?
8. Don't ever show your face in this house again!
9. Would you kindly pass this information on to your friends.
10. How are we going to make up for the wrong already done.
11. How many highways do we need?
12. Do soldiers have to follow orders without thinking.
13. At one time, the place sold hamburgers for 19 cents!
14. How can she expect us to store things for her for six months.
15. Does a single vote make any difference.

16. Did anyone remember to lock the doors?
17. Our Constitution registers the desires of our ancestors.
18. Imagine flying without being surrounded by tons upon tons of metal!
19. Our human desire to fly is as old as the myth of Daedalus and Icarus.
20. Be calm!

UNIT REVIEW EXERCISE

Put *S* for satisfactory after the number of each passage with the right punctuation. Put *U* if a passage is unsatisfactory because of a sentence fragment or other punctuation problem.

1. Some famous American writers wrote about the Old South. They described a vanishing way of life.
2. Several well-known writers were from Mississippi. Including William Faulkner.
3. Katherine Anne Porter wrote many short stories. She was from Texas.
4. Some well-known stories about young America are by Joyce Carol Oates. A writer from the state of New York.
5. She writes about familiar modern topics, for instance, loneliness and violence.
6. What do young Americans look for in their favorite books and stories?
7. Are you surprised by their interest in stories about handicapped people or about serious illness.
8. Young readers often like two quite different things: sad stories and mad-cap humor.
9. A very old theme is again very popular. A love of nature and a respect for all living things.
10. Much adolescent fiction deals with the same basic topic—growing up.
11. Some of the books have a serious purpose. For example, to warn against drugs.
12. How many young readers look for books helping them to choose a career.
13. The plot of an adolescent novel often sounds familiar. Sometimes the main character runs away from home.
14. Often the hero or heroine leaves home only for a time. Returning after a series of adventures.
15. Familiar kinds of adults appear in these books. Both good and bad.
16. One familiar kind is the very strict teacher. Another familiar kind is the kindly stranger.
17. Often the kindly or good people are eccentrics. They may act very strange at first.
18. Often the main character learns from someone in the family. Like an older sister or brother.
19. What kind of hero do young readers admire?
20. They like books about familiar models of achievement, such as athletes and mountain climbers.

Know when to put the comma or the semicolon between two clauses.

A complete sentence has its own subject and verb. (In requests, the subject may be omitted, or "understood.") Two such Subject–Verb units may become subsentences in a larger combined sentence. We then call them **clauses.**

To punctuate such combinations, we have to learn to recognize the different types of clauses and the different ways we have of tying them together.

See **S4** for a review of clauses.

Know when to use the comma or the semicolon between independent clauses.

We call two clauses independent when they are joined only loosely. We could separate them again and keep them apart by a period. There are three major ways we can link two independent clauses in a larger combined sentence:

(1) Use a comma when two clauses are joined by a coordinator. The seven coordinating connectives are found everywhere in ordinary prose: *and, but, so, for, yet, or,* and *nor.* The **comma** is the most typical punctuation when one of these words joins two clauses:

Paul had slept very little, *and* he felt grimy and uncomfortable. (Willa Cather)
She applied for the job, *but* the position had been filled.
He was no bigger than I was, *so* I thought him fair game. (Winston Churchill)
Something strange was happening to Piggy, *for* he was gasping for breath. (William Golding)
Clouds had appeared in the sky, *yet* no rain fell.
We should call them now, *or* it will be too late.

Notice the *reversal* of subject and verb caused by *nor:*

Sue never volunteered a comment, *nor* did she ever ask a question.

More than two independent clauses may be linked by coordinators in the same sentence. Note the *three* independent clauses in the following excerpt:

America comes out of Europe, *but* these people have never seen America, *nor* have most of them seen more of Europe than the hamlet at the foot of their mountain. (James Baldwin)

NOTE: All the connectives in this group also have *other* uses. These often require no punctuation. Often, a coordinator joins two words or phrases:

> The city needed more parks *and* playgrounds.

(2) Use a semicolon when two independent clauses are joined by an adverbial connective. Adverbial connectives are words like *however, therefore, consequently, nevertheless, besides, moreover, furthermore, accordingly, indeed, instead,* and *in fact.* Put a **semicolon** between the two clauses joined by one of these words:

> We all had doubts; *therefore,* we tabled the motion.
> He likes to read; *in fact,* he does little else.
> The tenants had complained; *nevertheless,* no repairs were made.

This kind of connective may *shift its place* in the second clause. The semicolon stays at the point where the two clauses join:

> My uncle had moved out; *however,* his son still lived there.
> My uncle had moved out; his son, *however,* still lived there.
> My uncle had moved out; his son still lived there, *however.*

NOTE: In formal writing, as in all of these examples, a **comma** usually keeps the adverbial connective apart from the rest of the second clause. If the connective appears in the middle of the second clause, *two* commas are needed. The commas used to set off adverbial connectives are *optional* in informal writing:

INFORMAL: Jim never came to the meeting; he went home *instead.*

(3) Use a semicolon when there is no connective between independent clauses that are closely related. Often two statements go together even though there is no connective to join them. A **semicolon** may then replace the period. In this case, the first word of the second statement is *not* capitalized:

> The room was empty; papers littered the floor.
> Some stood in stony silence; others wept.

> Nothing is wasted in the sea; every particle of material is used over and over again. (Rachel Carson)

(4) Do not use a comma or omit punctuation altogether where a semicolon is required. When you leave out the semicolon, the result is a **fused sentence:**

FUSED: Billie Jean King had enjoyed track and baseball she became a tennis champion.
REVISED: Billie Jean King had enjoyed track and baseball; she became a tennis champion.

FUSED: She had written *Women Who Win* it told the stories of several well-known sports figures.

REVISED: She had written *Women Who Win;* it told the stories of several well-known sports figures.

When you use a comma where a semicolon is required, the result is a **comma splice:**

COMMA SPLICE: We exceeded our goal, the drive was a success.

REVISED: We exceeded our goal; the drive was a success.

COMMA SPLICE: She had been promised a raise, however it never came.

REVISED: She had been promised a raise; however, it never came.

Some writers use the comma between independent clauses that are very similar in structure or in meaning. In your own writing, use the semicolon to be safe. Avoid the comma unless *three or more* similar clauses combine in the same sentence:

SAFE: The drums rumbled, the bugles called, the fifes shrilled.

NOTE: Here are possible *variations* from the most common practice:

• A **period** is possible with adverbial connectives, and also at times with coordinators, for a stronger break. Both kinds of connectives leave the clauses they join independent. The period does not cause a sentence fragment:

The auditorium had been declared unsafe. *Therefore,* all programs scheduled for the fall had to be canceled.

All that year the animals worked like slaves. *But* they were happy in their work. (George Orwell)

• A **semicolon** is possible with coordinating connectives, especially if the two clauses are *long or complicated:*

There was the exciting world of hunting, tactics, and skill; and there was the dull world of work and common sense.

• A **colon** may join two clauses when the second is the *explanation or result* of the first:

There was complete silence over the town: everybody was asleep. (Graham Greene)

• *And, but,* and *or* appear *without* punctuation between clauses that are very short or very closely related:

He had been walking all day *and* he was very tired. (Graham Greene)

See **S4a** for fuller treatment of independent clauses.

EXERCISE 1

Read the following adapted version of a student paper. What punctuation marks would you put in the blank spaces? After the number of the sentence, put *C* for comma, *SC* for semicolon, or *No* for no punctuation. (Do not use any additional periods. Use punctuation only if there are two complete clauses.)

1. My father took us to the ball game _____ the Giants were playing the Dodgers.
2. They played in San Francisco _____ and the Giants won by six to four.
3. There was a special attraction for us _____ it was bat day.
4. I got a bat _____ but my brother didn't get one.
5. The first six innings went by _____ without any special events.
6. In the seventh inning, my father went for refreshments _____ so my brother and I were alone for a few minutes.
7. A man two seats away from us died _____ he just fell down.
8. I remember his face _____ it was like a plastic mask.
9. People wiped his face with wet cloths _____ however, he just lay there.
10. Then some attendants came with a stretcher _____ and he was taken away.
11. The newspaper the next day listed the man _____ as dead from a heart attack.
12. My father came back a few minutes later _____ therefore, he didn't see the incident.
13. The people around us talked about the dead man for a while _____ they soon went back to their popcorn, however.
14. The game went on _____ the teams did not even stop playing ball.
15. My brother and I sat in the car _____ in silence during the long drive home.

EXERCISE 2

Many of the sentences in this exercise show the right punctuation between independent clauses. Put *S* for satisfactory after the number of each such sentence. Other sentences illustrate the comma splice. Put *CS* after the number of each of these. A few of the sentences illustrate the fused sentence. Put *FS* after the number of each of these. (Your teacher may ask you to revise the unsatisfactory sentences.)

1. Children need a feeling of security; otherwise, no amount of discipline will help.
2. Our dog never spends a whole day in peace, it engages in at least one fight with the neighborhood mongrels.
3. All at once classes begin, and the realities of college life become all too evident.
4. The first history test is taken; the first physics experiment is done.
5. Their faces were different, but they dressed like twins.

6. Some student groups do almost nothing some are concerned with activities outside of school.
7. Friendship is like marriage, you have to work together for success.
8. The campus is a study in contrasts, for the new architecture makes the old more noticeable.
9. The teacher never explained anything he just told us to write and hand in our papers at the end of the period.
10. We five girls live together, not one of us knew any of the others before.
11. A home is no longer just a home; it is expected to be a showplace.
12. There was no sign of recent occupancy in the cabin, nor was there any message.
13. There was something wrong with the airport, it was under water.
14. Black coral grows up to heights of ten feet; the branches of the coral tree are thin and delicate.
15. Our society is founded on compromise, therefore force should be used only as a last resort.
16. The new principal announced strict new rules; however, she soon learned when to allow exceptions.
17. The doctor washed her hands, she was dead tired.
18. A few buzzards looked down from the roof with indifference; dogs lay quietly in the sun.
19. He built another magnificent tomb, this one was of black marble.
20. We had been warned to stay inside; we went out, nevertheless.

What would be the right punctuation at the numbered breaks in each of the following sentences? Put *C* for comma after the number of the break if a *coordinator* joins two clauses. Put *S* for semicolon if an *adverbial* connective joins two clauses. Put *No* if the break occurs *within* a clause rather than between two clauses.

EXERCISE 3

A. Canada has powerful minorities _____(1) and can be governed _____(2) only in a spirit of compromise.
B. Canadians differ in language _____(3) and culture _____(4) therefore, they lack a strong single identity.
C. They long avoided all national symbols _____(5) in recent years, however, they have developed a new passion _____(6) for asserting themselves as Canadians.
D. Much of Canada has been settled by the English _____(7) and the Scots _____(8) the Maritime Provinces, in fact, have long been inhabited mostly by dyed-in-the-wool Britishers.
E. These provinces were always the British stronghold _____(9) for many Loyalists had left the United States _____(10) for this part of Canada.
F. Toronto is the most American of the cities _____(11) yet the natives still think of it _____(12) as a British town.

G. France lost its Canadian territories long ago _____(13) but French culture still flourishes in the province of Québec.

H. Many French Canadians have become bilingual _____(14) most, however, have never given up French _____(15) nor are they likely to do so.

I. Not only their common language _____(16) but also their European pattern of life gives French Canadians a strong sense of unity _____(17) their political influence is strong, consequently.

J. The province of Québec is old France and new France _____(18) it is still North America, nevertheless.

K. American influence is felt everywhere _____(19) and many families have relatives _____(20) across the border.

M4b
Adverbial Clauses

Use the comma to set off nonrestrictive adverbial clauses.

Subordinating connectives do not merely join a second clause loosely to the first. They subordinate it, turning it into a dependent clause. The clauses they help us work into the larger sentence are typically **adverbial clauses.** Like adverbs, they tell us when, where, why, or how. They may come *before* as well as after the main clause:

NORMAL: We were miles from the camp *when the storm broke.*
REVERSED: *When the storm broke,* we were miles from the camp.

NORMAL: The game will be canceled *if the rain continues.*
REVERSED: *If the rain continues,* the game will be canceled.

Some adverbial clauses require no punctuation; others are set off by a comma. Remember three major possibilities:

(1) Use no punctuation when you add a restrictive clause.   Most subordinators deal with time, place, or conditions: *when, while, before, after, since, until, where, if, unless, as, as long as.* The clause they introduce often makes all the difference to the meaning of the whole statement. Such a clause narrows down the meaning of the main clause in an important way. It is called a **restrictive** clause.

The added dependent clause in each of the following examples *restricts* the meaning of the original statement:

You can have the day off.
You can have the day off *if you find a substitute.* (only then)

The town was safe.
The town was safe *until the dam broke.* (only until then)

(2) Use a comma *when you add a nonrestrictive clause.*   Some subordinators set up a contrast: *though, although, whereas, no matter what, no matter how.* The clause they introduce does *not* change the

meaning of the main clause. It merely points out that something else is *also* true. Such clauses are **nonrestrictive.** They are set off by a break in the spoken sentence, and by a comma in writing:

> We enjoyed the trip, *though* (also true) the weather was bad.
> He was a British subject, *although* (also true) he lived in Spain.

In each of the following examples, each of the two statements is true separately:

> Arabs are Muslims, *whereas* Ethiopians are Christians.
> He always failed, *no matter how* he tried.

(3) Use a comma *when the dependent clause comes first.* Use this comma to show where the main clause starts, regardless of whether the adverbial clause is restrictive or nonrestrictive:

> *Where the stream came out of the canyon,* the trail left it.
> *As they struggled to and fro,* the table was overturned. (Hawthorne)

NOTE: A few subordinating connectives work two different ways. With *because* and *so that*, use no punctuation if the main point of the sentence *follows* the connective. Use the **comma** if the main point is in the main clause. The adverbial clause then merely gives further information:

> Why are you leaving?
> I am leaving *because I have to study.*
> What are you doing?
> *I am leaving,* because I have to study.

> A house can be designed *so that it utilizes all available sunshine.*
> (Dependent clause states the *purpose*.)
> *The house had been built close to the river,* so that water kept seeping
>   into the basement. (Dependent clause *adds* an unintended result.)

What should be the punctuation at the break shown in each of the following sentences? Put *C* after the number of the sentence if there should be a comma. Put *No* if no punctuation is required.

1. Skiers head for the slopes _____ after the first heavy snows fall.
2. We could not pry the door open _____ no matter how hard we tried.
3. People in Argentina speak Spanish _____ whereas people in Brazil speak Portuguese.
4. You should never leave your keys behind _____ when you leave your car.
5. The branch office will be closed _____ unless business improves.
6. When the workers started excavating _____ they found the remnants of an Aztec temple.

7. We remained confident _____ although our team was the underdog.
8. Since the program was announced _____ many applicants have signed up.
9. The engine started overheating _____ as we reached the hilltop.
10. The guards disconnected the alarm _____ before they opened the safe.
11. After she left home _____ she went to business school.
12. The salmon reach their spawning grounds _____ though many obstacles block their way.
13. He made new friends easily _____ so that he was seldom alone.
14. The instructor showed us what to do _____ while help was on the way.
15. You will find the camp _____ where the road starts to angle away from the lake.
16. The Maoris are Polynesian _____ whereas most other New Zealanders are of British descent.
17. Everything in the cabin shook and trembled _____ as the big plane rumbled down the runway.
18. As long as you pay your dues _____ you will remain a member.
19. Although there had been many protests _____ the slaughter of the seals continued.
20. We will have to wait _____ until the weather improves.

EXERCISE 2

What would be the most typical punctuation at the break in each of the following sentences? Put *C* after the number of the sentence if the dependent clause should be set off by a comma. Put *No* if no comma is required.

1. Although Australia is a large country _____ Australian speech is everywhere much alike.
2. People sound the same in Queensland and New South Wales _____ whereas in England speech varies from one region to another.
3. We can see the reason for this difference _____ if we look at the country's history.
4. Australian speech is relatively uniform _____ because local dialects take centuries to grow.
5. They develop _____ where groups of people live by themselves.
6. But few people settled down in isolated communities _____ after they came to Australia.
7. Ever since the continent was opened up _____ there has been a large, shifting population.
8. Most of them move _____ because their jobs require them to.
9. People cannot work in sheep-shearing and harvesting _____ unless they move with the seasons.
10. Teachers and ministers go _____ where they are needed.
11. There has been little chance for the development of regional dialects _____ since radio and television made their appearance.

12. People listen to the same programs _____ no matter where they live.
13. But language differences do exist in Australia _____ though they do not follow geographic boundaries.
14. Many people consider British English the best kind _____ so that the language of the schools is close to standard British English.
15. At home most Australians speak "broad" Australian _____ no matter how much teachers frown on popular speech.
16. Speakers of broad Australian say *piper* _____ when they mean paper.
17. When they mean piper _____ they say *poiper.*
18. As you would expect _____ educated Australians differ in their attitude toward popular speech.
19. Some believe good English to be the same everywhere _____ so that any departure from British English is automatically bad.
20. Others do not object to differences in pronunciation _____ as long as they do not interfere with communication.

Use the comma to set off nonrestrictive clauses.

M4c

Relative and Noun Clauses

Learn how to punctuate two special kinds of dependent clauses. The relative pronouns *(who, whom, whose, which, that)* start a **relative clause.** Relative clauses fill in information about one of the nouns in the main clause:

> They had a small child *who kept them awake at night.*
> The mayor, *who had skirted the issues,* was reelected.

That and question words like *why, how, where,* and *when* serve as special connectives starting a **noun clause.** A noun clause takes the place of one of the nouns in the main part of the sentence:

NOUN: Jim told us *the truth.*
NOUN CLAUSE: Jim told us *that the house was empty.*

See **S4c** for a review of relative clauses and noun clauses.

Remember:

(1) Use no commas for relative clauses that are essential to the meaning of a sentence. Use no comma with *who (whom, whose)* and *which* when the relative clause is **restrictive.** A restrictive clause is needed to identify something. It tells us who, or which one, or what kind. It becomes an essential part of the sentence:

RESTRICTIVE: We looked for the driver *who had parked the truck.*
RESTRICTIVE: The actor *who played Hamlet* was outstanding.

Often, something or somebody has already been identified. For instance, we know the name. The relative clause then merely adds information. It is **nonrestrictive**—not an essential part of the main statement. The nonrestrictive clause is set off by a **comma:**

NONRESTRICTIVE: We looked for Jean, *who had parked the truck.*

Use *two* commas when a nonrestrictive clause *interrupts* the main clause:

NONRESTRICTIVE: Laurence Olivier, *who played Hamlet,* was outstanding.

NOTE: When *that* is used as a relative pronoun, the clause that follows is usually restrictive. Use no comma:

RESTRICTIVE: The car *that followed them* belonged to a private investigator.

The *that* is often left out in such sentences. Punctuation remains the same—no comma:

RESTRICTIVE: The poems *he wrote* were about flowers and sunsets.
We were worried about the car *my sister drove.*

(2) Use no comma to separate a noun clause from the rest of the sentence.   Use no punctuation when *that* or question words like *why, how, where,* and *when* start a noun clause. Noun clauses become part of the sentence without a break in speech and without punctuation in writing:

No one knew *where the equipment had been stored.*
I suddenly remembered *that the library was closed.*
The article explained *how it is done.*

(3) Punctuate all clauses that modify a noun the way you do relative clauses.   Not all clauses starting with *where, when, after,* and similar words are adverbial clauses. Instead, they may modify a noun in the main clause. Set them off if they are nonrestrictive:

RESTRICTIVE: He took us to the spot *where he had buried the treasure.*
NONRESTRICTIVE: She returned to Canada, *where they had lived several years.*

RESTRICTIVE: There was a time *when they were close friends.*
NONRESTRICTIVE: We went there in the fall, *when the leaves were just turning color.*

EXERCISE 1

After the number of each sentence, put *S* if punctuation is satisfactory. Put *U* if punctuation is unsatisfactory.

1. Billie Jean King, who talked to herself on the tennis court charmed the British spectators.
2. Dick Gregory, who became famous as a comedian, had trained himself as a runner in high school.

3. The instructions did not explain how the panels fitted together.
4. Tennis which used to be a sport for the few now has a large following.
5. George Eliot, whose real name was Mary Ann Cross, wrote several great Victorian novels.
6. The guards kept out any visitors, who did not have identification.
7. Some athletes find it hard to remember, that football is only a game.
8. The lecturer talked about new sources of energy that scientists were exploring.
9. He sometimes talked about prejudice, which he had encountered in many different places.
10. They had gone to a part of Mexico where the great Zapotec ruins can be seen to this day.
11. An applicant who does not get a job right away, should try again.
12. The great trains that used to cross the country are no more.
13. She described the prejudices that hurt the handicapped.
14. I asked my oldest brother who knows everything about birds.
15. His parents never really understood what had gone wrong.
16. The firm hired an applicant, whom several companies had rejected.
17. I usually saw her at Christmas, when the whole family came together.
18. She discovered that, people rarely change lifelong habits.
19. Soccer, which is a fairly recent import, has swept the country.
20. We reported the incident to the principal, who promised to investigate.

What would be the right punctuation at the breaks in each of the following sentences? Put *C* after the number of the sentence if a *nonrestrictive clause* requires one or more commas. Put *No* after the number of the sentence if no comma is required.

EXERCISE 2

1. Americans _____ who seldom know foreign languages _____ usually read the masterpieces of world literature in English.
2. People _____ who study translations _____ sometimes complain of their poor quality.
3. Robert Frost said _____ that poetry is lost in translation.
4. We should remember _____ that great poets have practiced the translator's art.
5. The writers _____ who produced the masterpieces of our literature _____ often knew other languages.
6. The author of *The Canterbury Tales* was Chaucer _____ who translated poems from the French.
7. John Milton _____ who wrote *Paradise Lost* _____ had written sonnets in Italian.
8. Coleridge _____ whose "Ancient Mariner" is known to every student _____ had studied German poetry.
9. Anyone _____ who wants to use language well _____ learns much from other languages.

10. Ezra Pound is one of the greatest poets _____ America has produced.
11. Some of the poems _____ that made him famous _____ were translated from Latin.
12. He knew Chinese _____ which is rarely studied in this country.
13. American writers are read in translation by the millions abroad _____ who love American literature.
14. Edgar Allan Poe _____ who wrote "The Tell-Tale Heart" and similar stories _____ was translated by a French poet.
15. French students _____ who know American authors _____ usually read them in French translations.
16. Writers _____ who write about foreign cultures _____ often know the language of the country well.
17. Margaret Mead _____ whose book about New Guinea became a classic _____ started her research by learning the native language.
18. Pearl Buck wrote about China _____ where she lived for many years.
19. Some writers wrote their best-known books in a language _____ that they had learned in later life.
20. Joseph Conrad _____ who wrote *Lord Jim* _____ spoke Polish as a child.

The Good Earth

PEARL S. BUCK

UNIT REVIEW EXERCISE

Most of the following sentences show the right punctuation for a sentence combining two clauses. Put *S* for satisfactory after the number of each such sentence. The remaining sentences illustrate unsatisfactory punctuation. Look for the following especially: (1) fused sentences, with no punctuation where there should be a comma or a semicolon; (2) comma splices, where there should be a semicolon *instead* of a comma; (3) unnecessary commas—a comma used with a restrictive clause or a noun clause. Put *U* after the number of each unsatisfactory sentence.

1. We threw more twigs on the fire, which started to hiss and sputter.
2. The auction had been widely advertised, yet very few buyers came.
3. Many pesticides were banned they were harmful to wildlife.
4. The bond issue was approved; the stadium was never built, however.
5. Retired people liked the place, for the mild climate kept fuel bills low.
6. Game was becoming scarce, therefore the tribe moved on.
7. My grandfather loved stories that had a happy ending.
8. The judges had decided, that they would not award a first prize.
9. Sullivan, who built some of America's first skyscrapers, designed a famous building in St. Louis.
10. The buffalo, which was once the king of the plains almost became extinct.
11. Turning salt water into drinking water is expensive; moreover, it consumes precious energy.
12. We must learn to use less energy, or the lights will go out in our cities.
13. Speed limits are unpopular, they nevertheless save many lives.
14. The Dutch at one time ruled Indonesia; the French ruled Indochina.

15. Some sports require expensive equipment, whereas others require only our arms or legs.
16. Few people can learn, unless they have a real desire to improve.
17. My uncle lived alone he never married.
18. When the tidal wave struck, most of the people had already evacuated their homes.
19. I passed the news on to my brother Greg who immediately telephoned our parents.
20. We had to cross the frozen river, although the ice was thin and very treacherous.

Know when to to use commas or other inside punctuation.

Within a single clause, there is no punctuation between the most basic elements. We do not normally put punctuation between the subject and the verb, or the verb and its completers. Even when modifiers are added, they may become an essential part of what the sentence says. They then blend into it without a break. None of the following sentences needs any inside punctuation:

His sister Eileen studied law in the evenings.
The people in the front row were applauding.
The road to the village had been blocked by an avalanche.

Know which sentence parts blend into a sentence without a break and which are set off by commas or other inside punctuation.

Use commas to set off nonrestrictive modifiers.

The basic elements in a sentence often carry along modifiers that clarify or in some way limit their meaning. Know the situations where a modifier requires a comma:

(1) Use no commas with essential modifiers. A modifier that follows a noun may help us single out one thing among several, or one kind of thing among several kinds. It narrows down the possibilities. It helps us *identify* something. Such a modifier is **restrictive** and requires *no punctuation*.

The girl *in the blue dress* asked me your name.
(Which girl? The one *in the blue dress*)

Newspapers *critical of the régime* were shut down.
(Which newspapers? Those *critical of the régime*)

The student *sitting next to me* explained the assignment.
(Which one? The one *sitting next to me*)

M5

**INSIDE
PUNCTUATION**

M5a

**Punctuating
Modifiers**

COMMAS FOR INSIDE PUNCTUATION
A Summary

The *comma* used for inside punctuation appears with the following sentence elements:

(1) *nonrestrictive modifiers*—modifiers *not used* to single out one or one of a kind:

> The Lincoln Memorial, *a magnificent structure,* was next.

(2) *sentence modifiers*—modifiers that seem to apply to the sentence as a whole rather than to any one part:

> *To keep out the deer,* they built a wooden fence.

(3) *series* of three or more elements of the same kind:

> We talked about *art, music, and poetry.*

(4) *dates, addresses, and measurements* with two or more parts:

> The family had moved to *Houston, Texas.*

(5) *interchangeable adjectives* modifying the same noun:

> The settlers discovered a *cool, moist* valley.

(6) *names, questions, and comments* added to a sentence:

> Your application, *Jean,* has been received.

(7) *alternatives* inserted for contrast after *not* or *never:*

> I wanted the wrench, *not the pliers.*

---

(2) Use the comma with nonessential modifiers. When something has already been identified, the modifier merely adds further information. It does not single something out. It is **nonrestrictive.** Such a modifier is set off by a **comma.** Use *two* commas if the sentence continues after the modifier:

> He introduced me to Laverne Brown, *the new librarian.*
> Europeans, *living on a crowded continent,* envy our wide-open spaces.
> Helen Keller, *born blind and deaf,* became famous.

(3) Set off sentence modifiers. Some modifiers apply to the sentence as a whole. Set them off by one or more **commas** when they are stressed enough to be set apart in speech by slight breaks. Set off *any verbal or verbal phrase* at the beginning of a sentence. Set

off any verbal or verbal phrase that appears later in the sentence but applies to the sentence as a whole:

> *To make rabbit stew,* first catch the rabbit.
> *Considering the risk,* the price seems reasonable.

> Hunting, *to be frank,* has never appealed to me.
> He did quite well, *considering his lack of experience.*

(4) Set off long introductory modifiers. As a rule of thumb, use the comma with any introductory modifier of more than three words:

> *For a person of her talents,* it was an easy task.
> *More than twenty years ago,* he had asked her to marry him.

(5) Set off transitional expressions and the like in formal writing. Here are some of the expressions set off by one or more commas in formal writing: *after all, of course, unfortunately, on the whole, as a rule, certainly, on the other hand, for example.*

> The performance, *on the whole,* was not a success.
> The money will have to be returned, *of course.*
> *As a rule,* we consider only written applications.

Most of the following sentences show the right punctuation with modifiers. Put *S* after the number of each such sentence. Put *U* if punctuation is unsatisfactory.

EXERCISE 1

1. Edinburgh, the capital of Scotland, is a beautiful old city.
2. Pyramids built before the arrival of the Spaniards, still exist in Mexico.
3. They had one child, a girl.
4. Leaving the simple life of the farm, they joined the hurrying crowds of the city.
5. Aided by a scholarship student athletes can finish school without constant financial worries.
6. She sat in silence almost all the way, wrapped in her own meditations. (Jane Austen)
7. Richard Wright told the story of his growing up in *Black Boy,* his autobiography.
8. People singing in the choir are often highly trained musicians.
9. In opera and drama, women's roles were first played by men.
10. In addition to her autobiography and many other books Simone de Beauvoir wrote *The Second Sex.*
11. Our language has many expressions, showing contempt for other nationalities.
12. After graduating, she took a job as a day-care instructor.
13. His wife had died some years before, leaving him a young widower with two little girls and a baby boy. (Dorothy Canfield Fisher)

14. To save time we prepared all our materials the day before.
15. Grandfather, dozing in his armchair by the fire, came to with a start.
16. Margaret Chase Smith, the senator from Maine was widely known and admired.
17. The face of the presiding judge, clean-shaven and pale, looked at him without expression.
18. He stood stiffly in the shade, a small man dressed in a shabby dark city suit, carrying a small attaché case. (Graham Greene)
19. She sat there like a black question mark, ready to go, ready to stay.
20. Business was not too bad considering the location.

EXERCISE 2

Put *C* after the number of the sentence if you would use a comma to set off the modifier at the beginning or at the end of the sentence. Put *C* also if you would use *two* commas to set off a modifier appearing in the middle of the sentence. Put *No* after the number of the sentence for no punctuation.

1. To please their audience _____ popular writers often use stock characters.
2. The men and women _____ populating the pages of a novel _____ sometimes seem strangely familiar.
3. Characters _____ proving popular with audiences _____ may appear in play after play.
4. Imitated over and over _____ such stock characters become stereotypes.
5. Audiences _____ flocking to the theaters of ancient Rome _____ watched the miser and the braggart soldier.
6. Charles Dickens _____ writing in nineteenth-century England _____ made use of the kindly old capitalist.
7. Hollywood _____ dream capital of the world _____ has acquainted millions with the stock characters of the Western novel.
8. The bully _____ whiskey-eyed and unshaven _____ terrorizes the citizens of a small Western town.
9. To save the hero _____ the owner of the saloon throws herself in the path of the deadly bullet.
10. Everyone remembers Robin Hood _____ the merry outlaw.
11. Robbing the rich and helping the poor _____ Robin is one of many scofflaw heroes.
12. James Fenimore Cooper _____ the author of the Leatherstocking tales _____ shows us noble Indians.
13. Another stock character of American fiction is Uncle Tom _____ the faithful slave.
14. A stereotype _____ found in recent American fiction _____ is the Jewish mother.
15. What stereotypes have you encountered in books _____ read by young people?

Use commas where several elements of the same kind appear in a sentence.

Several items of the same kind often take the place of a single sentence part. When we have several parts of the same kind, there is often a connective like *and* or *or* to **coordinate** them—to tie them together. Often there are punctuation marks in addition to or in place of a connective:

(1) Use commas between elements in a series. Three or more elements of the same kind are called a **series.** In the most common kind of series, **commas** appear between the elements of a series, with the last comma followed by a connective that ties the whole group together. Study this *"A, B,* and *C"* pattern in each of the following examples:

> *Jim, Chad,* and *Jeremy* came to say good-bye.
> His face appears on *monuments, coins,* and *stamps.*
> We could order a *salami, bologna,* or *liverwurst* sandwich.

> *Cabot, Frobisher,* and *Davis sought* the passage to the northwest, *failed,* and *turned back.* (Rachel Carson)

A series can be expanded to *more than three* items:

> Ford showed that one could *raise* wages, *cut* prices, *produce* in tremendous volume, and still *make* millions.

The slots in the series may be filled not just by single words, but by groups of words or whole clauses:

> The *trumpets blared,* the *banners fluttered,* and the *band marched* out onto the field.

NOTE: The last comma in a series is *optional.* Use it in your own writing, because it is never wrong.

(2) Use semicolons in a series where commas would be confusing. Sometimes the separate parts of a series already contain commas. Use **semicolons** instead of additional commas to show the major breaks:

> Three witnesses testified for the defense: *Claire,* the accused's wife; *Jim,* his best friend; and *Pat Brown,* his immediate supervisor at the meat-packing plant.

(3) Use commas with information that comes in several parts. Dates, addresses, page references, and similar information often come in two or more parts. Use **commas** between the different ele-

ADDRESSES COME IN SEVERAL PARTS

The Metropolitan Museum of Art
255 Gracie Station, New York 10028

Aluminum Company
of America, 349-J Alcoa
Building, Pittsburgh,
PA 15219

Box 403, Warwick, Rhode Island

ments. Use another comma *after the whole group,* unless the last word is also the last word of the sentence:

The date was *Monday, December 18, 1978.*
The gold rush at *Cripple Creek, Colorado,* was the last really big one south of Canada.
He lived at *39 Pine Street, Oakland, California.*
Chapter 5, Volume II, deals with regional history.
Look at *Chapter 3, page 45.*

Commas also separate the different parts of *measurements* that use more than one unit of measurement. Here no additional comma is used after the last item:

The frame was *3 feet, 3 inches* wide.
He entered *6 pounds, 2 ounces* as the net weight.
The track event took *2 minutes, 4 seconds.*

(4) Use commas between interchangeable adjectives. Two or more adjectives may modify the same noun. Sometimes these come in different layers. For instance, we first call someone a *public servant* and then say what kind: a *loyal public servant. Loyal* and *public* are not interchangeable (a *public loyal servant* would not make sense). When two adjectives *are* interchangeable, they may be coordinated by *and,* or instead by a **comma:**

a tall *and* handsome stranger $\longrightarrow$ a *tall, handsome* stranger
(a handsome and tall stranger)

a friendly *and* happy crowd $\longrightarrow$ a *friendly, happy* crowd
(a happy and friendly crowd)

(5) Use a comma to show some kinds of repetition. A second word or phrase may repeat, reinforce, or explain the first. A **comma** appears between the two:

> She told him *to improvise, to be flexible.*
> We need players who are *alert, quick in body and mind.*

Most of the following sentences show the right punctuation of equal sentence parts. Put *S* for satisfactory after the number of each such sentence. Put *U* if punctuation is unsatisfactory.

EXERCISE 1

1. The author had devoted her career to teaching, lecturing, and writing about the arts of the world.
2. It was a warm, cloudless night.
3. The university is located in Ann Arbor, Washtenaw County Michigan.
4. My aunts were knowledgeable, gossipy, and pious.
5. One old woman was pulling the door open in short, gradual jerks. (Eudora Welty)
6. I like to spend my spare time swimming hiking or raising horses.
7. They had moved from Memphis, Tennessee, to Chicago, Illinois.
8. They had known Einstein, the scientist; Dorothy Parker, the writer; and James Thurber, the humorist.
9. One little bit of yeast grows multiplies, rises, and expands until it raises up an entire loaf.
10. Wyomia Tyus was a young sprinter from Los Angeles, California.
11. She had run the 100 meters in a record 11.4 seconds.
12. She ran the exact same distance in 11 seconds flat in Mexico City, Mexico.
13. Tyus was an exceptionally lean, agile, and graceful runner.
14. She was five foot seven and one-half inches tall.
15. She grew up in Griffin, Georgia, on a dairy farm.
16. She was offered a four-year scholarship at Tennessee State, Nashville Tennessee.
17. In later years, Wyomia Tyus ran as a hard-working, ambitious pro.
18. Typical prize money was $500 for winning $250 for second, and $100 for third.
19. Sponsors sometimes pay additional amounts, bonuses for special achievement.
20. Track stars, swimmers, and gymnasts are usually among the popular heroes of the Olympic Games.

What punctuation would you use at each of the numbered breaks in the following sentences? After the number of each break, put *C* for comma, *S* for semicolon, or *No* if no punctuation is required.

EXERCISE 2

Include all optional commas.

A. The typical _____(1) Yankee was a tall _____(2) loose-jointed figure with sallow cheeks _____(3) a sharp nose _____(4) and an eye _____(5) to the main chance.

B. The lean-jawed _____(6) soft-spoken _____(7) gambler carried two six-guns _____(8) beneath the frock coat made in Omaha _____(9) Nebraska.

C. Quantrill _____(10) Jesse James _____(11) and Sam Bass _____(12) are among the leaders of famous _____(13) outlaw _____(14) bands.

D. The best-known figures of American folklore are Daniel Boone _____ (15) the woods ranger in his coonskin cap _____(16) Davy Crockett _____ (17) the backwoods boaster _____(18) and Paul Bunyan _____(19) the prodigious lumberjack.

E. Davy Crockett could outboast any man alive _____(20) grin the bark off a tree _____(21) and hug a bear _____(22) too close for comfort.

F. The stereotyped _____(23) Southern colonel wears a black _____(24) slouch hat _____(25) and shoestring tie while sitting in the familiar _____ (26) rocking chair drinking mint juleps.

G. A good Western novel has gunfighters _____(27) law officers _____(28) cattle kings _____(29) chiefs _____(30) gamblers _____(31) sheep-herders _____(32) miners _____(33) and scouts.

H. The Pilgrims _____(34) the Quakers _____(35) and the Mor-mons _____(36) undertook difficult _____(37) dangerous migrations to escape _____(38) religious persecution.

I. Carson City _____(39) Nevada _____(40) is the center of a famous mining district in the American West.

M5c

Punctuating Interrupters

Use commas or other marks to set off interrupters.

Especially in conversation, we often *interrupt* a sentence. We interrupt what we are saying in order to call the listener by name. We stop to add some information that we forgot to mention. There are three major ways of setting off such interrupters from the rest of the sentence:

(1) Use commas to set off light interrupters. Light inter-rupters blend into the sentence with only a slight break. They need two **commas** when they appear in the middle of a sentence. They need only one comma when they are at the beginning or end. Use the commas that go with light interrupters when you

● address the listener or reader:

Your record, *Ralph,* is disappointing.
Here are the books, *Mrs. Cardoza.*
Friends, Romans, countrymen, lend me your ears. *(Julius Caesar)*

- show how true something is, or who thought so:

Her appeal, *it seems,* was not successful.
They will refund the money, *I am sure.*

- start a sentence with *yes, no, well, why,* or a similar expression:

Yes, we heard all about it.
Why, she never even mentioned it.
"*Well,* Julio," said his brother with desperate charm.

- follow a statement with a tag question:

He is your friend, *isn't he?*
So she locked the door, *did she?*

- add something for contrast after *not* or *never:*

He always mentioned his children, *never his wife.*
I come to bury Caesar, *not to praise him. (Julius Caesar)*

- shift something to an unusual position in a sentence:

Bureaucracy, *in a technical age like ours,* is inevitable. (E. M. Forster)

(2) Use dashes to set off heavy interrupters. Heavy interrupters cause a definite break in speech and are set off in writing by dashes. Overuse of the dash makes for jerky, disconnected writing. Use the dashes that go with heavy interrupters when you

- stop in order to insert a complete sentence:

Aunt Mary had known her—*Aunt Mary was two years older*—but she lived a thousand miles away now and was not well. (Dorothy M. Johnson)

- add a modifier that is exceptionally long or contains commas:

Noise—*hums, hisses, rumbles, pops, clicks, and the like*—has ruined many a recording.

- make something stand out for an especially strong effect:

This is what he left behind—*a country in ruins.*
On the floor of the Capitol is a pattern made from six flags—*the flags of Spain, Mexico, France, the United States, the Confederacy, and Texas.*

(3) Use parentheses to enclose less important information. Less important information is often given in a lower tone of voice and

appears in writing in **parentheses.** Use parentheses instead of dashes when you

- insert a complete sentence as an aside:

Jamaica *(I went there last June)* is a fascinating place.
During the rains the village *(it was really no more)* slipped into the mud.

- provide page references, dates, or other supplementary information:

The anecdote about the two tramps *(p. 67)* seemed familiar.
The anniversary *(October 15)* will be a gala event.
Samuel Clemens *(better known as Mark Twain)* was a great satirist.

NOTE: When a whole sentence appears *separately* in parentheses, it carries its own end punctuation with it:

Exactly how many volumes Alger wrote is not known. *(One biographer ran the total up to 119.)*

EXERCISE 1

Most of the following sentences show the right punctuation with *interrupters.* Put *S* for satisfactory after the number of each such sentence. Put *U* for unsatisfactory after the number of each sentence that needs to be revised. (Be prepared to explain in class what went wrong.)

1. English spelling, we all know, is haunted by ghosts.
2. The *h* in *ghost* (as well as in *ghastly* and *aghast*) stands for nothing.
3. Three of the letters in *through*—a perfectly ordinary word—do not stand for any sounds.
4. Many less common words—*knight, thoroughfare, knickknack*—have three or more silent letters.
5. British spelling, believe it or not is even more conservative than American.
6. The British still spell *gaol* (pronounced *jail*).
7. Some progress, it is true, has been made toward modernized spelling.
8. Noah Webster (the American lexicographer) helped us get rid of the *k* in *musick* and *logick*.
9. The word *programme* (still often seen in England) is now spelled *program*.
10. Other modernized spellings *catalog, plow, thru* have met with varying degrees of success.
11. Has no one tried, you might ask, to develop a streamlined spelling system for our language?
12. Yes, there have been many schemes for spelling reform.

13. But the arguments against thorough reform are obvious aren't they?
14. We cannot simply reprint all books, can we?
15. Why every typewriter in the English-speaking countries would have to be equipped with the new letters.

What would be the right punctuation at each of the numbered breaks in the following sentences? After the number of each break, put one of the following:

EXERCISE 2

    C for comma;
    D for dash;
    P for parenthesis;
    No for no punctuation.

(Use no other marks. Write on a separate sheet.)

A. Yes _____(1) our main office has moved to Omaha _____(2) Nebraska.
B. Her little brother _____(3) her parents both worked _____(4) answered the phone.
C. The drawbacks of modern technology _____(5) pollution _____(6) health hazards _____(7) wasted resources _____(8) receive much publicity.
D. The project _____(9) everyone agrees _____(10) was a success.
E. Well _____(11) you did your best _____(12) Ellen.
F. Her book (first published in 1932 _____(13) is now out of print _____(14) it seems.
G. Your transcript _____(15) we really must have it soon _____(16) has still not arrived.
H. The club meets on Wednesdays _____(17) not Mondays _____(18) doesn't it?
I. Your grandfather _____(19) Susan _____(20) left his children only one thing _____(21) a mountain of debts.
J. Why _____(22) does Ellen _____(23) always do the work _____(24) never her brother?
K. The informant's name appears in chapter 7 _____(25) p. 76.

What should be the punctuation at the blank spaces in each of the following sentences? After the number of each space, write one of the following:

UNIT REVIEW EXERCISE

    C for comma;
    SC for semicolon;
    D for dash;
    No for no punctuation.

(Use no other marks. Write on a separate sheet.)

A. Eleanor Roosevelt was a tireless _____(1) dedicated _____(2) idealist.
B. She was admired for her energy _____(3) loved for her interest in people _____(4) and attacked for her independent views.
C. Theodore Roosevelt _____(5) her uncle _____(6) had been President of the United States _____(7) before World War I.
D. Franklin Delano Roosevelt _____(8) he was President for three historic terms _____(9) was her husband.
E. After her husband's death _____(10) Eleanor Roosevelt served as delegate to the United Nations.
F. She wrote _____(11) a newspaper column _____(12) spoke on radio _____(13) and appeared on TV.
G. Her personal kindness was remembered by people like Emma Bugbee _____(14) reporter for the *Herald Tribune* _____(15) Ruby Black _____(16) correspondent for the United Press _____(17) and Henrietta Nesbitt _____(18) housekeeper at the White House.
H. In the days after Eleanor Roosevelt's death _____(19) a woman _____(20) living in Tacoma _____(21) Washington _____(22) received a check for ten dollars.
I. A hitchhiker _____(23) it seems _____(24) had once been picked up by the First Lady.
J. To show his gratitude _____(25) he had named his daughter after Mrs. Roosevelt.
K. Mrs. Roosevelt _____(26) hearing the news _____(27) asked to be the girl's godmother.
L. The girl grew up _____(28) married _____(29) and moved to Tacoma.
M. A check for ten dollars made out to her _____(30) arrived from her godmother on every birthday.

M6
QUOTATION

Know how to work quoted material into your text.

We often repeat words and ideas not our own. We then make it clear by punctuation and other means that we are recording what someone else said, or copying what someone else wrote.

M6a
Direct Quotation

Use quotation marks to set off someone's exact words.

When you repeat someone's exact words, you are using **direct** quotation. Material quoted word for word is enclosed in **quotation marks**.

Punctuate direct quotations as follows:

(1) Use a comma to separate a short quotation from its credit tag. Usually, a **comma** separates the quotation from the introductory statement—the credit tag that shows its source. The comma

is used regardless of whether the credit tag appears at the beginning
or at the end:

> He said, "There is nothing we can do."
> "We have no record of your payment," she replied.
> "The warranty had expired," the letter said.

If the credit tag *splits* a sentence, you need two commas. If the
credit tag *separates* two complete sentences, you need a comma before
it and a **period** after it:

> "In Tucson," she said, "you can go across the border to shop."
> "We like color and music," she said. "It's part of our heritage."

(2) Use the colon to introduce long or formal quotations: Long
quotations are often introduced by a **colon** rather than by a comma:

> Dr. Harriet Dustan explained a common attitude of doctors: "Most phy-
> sicians believe sickness is for other people, not for them. It is an insult
> for a doctor to be sick."

When a single quoted word or phrase appears in a sentence, you
do *not* need a comma or a colon to set it off:

> He said "Buenos días" to a man with a gun who sat in a small patch of
> shade against a wall. (Graham Greene)

(3) Know how to place the final quotation mark. When a quotation ends or is interrupted, commas and periods stay inside the
quotation. They come *before* the final quotation mark. Semicolons
go outside the quotation. They *follow* the final quotation mark:

> He said, "It's perfectly safe"; besides, we had no choice.

Question marks go inside the quotation if the quoted part asks
a question. They go outside if you are asking a question *about the
quotation.* Exclamation marks go inside if the quoted part was
shouted or had strong stress on it. They go outside if you are making
a strong point *about the quotation:*

> He said slowly, "How long will it stay afloat?"
> Did you actually hear her say, "You'll be sorry"?
> Rita kept shouting: "We are much too late!"
> Don't you ever tell me, "You people are all alike"!

NOTE: When the credit tag follows a question or exclamation, do
not use a comma in addition to the other marks:

> "What's the use of it?" she asked.

(4) Show quotations within a quotation. Use **single quotation marks** to show that the person you are quoting is in turn quoting somebody else:

> Voltaire said, "I never made but one prayer to God, a very short one: 'O Lord, make my enemies ridiculous.' "

(5) Show where something has been left out. Omissions from a quotation are shown by three spaced periods, called an **ellipsis.** Use four periods if the omission includes the period at the end of a complete sentence:

> As John Gardner has said, "Favoritism . . . judges the individual on the basis of his relationships rather than on ability and character."

(6) Show where something has been added. Comments or corrections added to a quotation are put between **square brackets:**

> The report said: "On Monday, October [actually October 4], we set out across the ice."
> He said, "The mayor of one Western city [Portland?] was attacked for having placed fourteen relatives in city jobs."

(7) Know how to set off unusual or exceptionally long quotations. When quotations run to more than half a dozen lines, they are often treated as **block quotations.** These are *not* set off by quotation marks. They are indented and, in a typed paper, single-spaced.

See sample pages in **C5b** for examples of block quotations.

Lines of poetry and of dialogue are also set off in special ways. A full line or more of poetry is usually set off as a block quotation:

> He read the opening lines of a poem by Gwendolyn Brooks:
> To be in love
> Is to touch things with a lighter hand.

In quoting dialogue, we start a *new paragraph* for each change of speaker:

> "Mr. Lorry, look upon the prisoner. Was he one of those two passengers?"
> "I cannot undertake to say that he was."
> "Does he resemble either of these two passengers?"
> "Both were so wrapped up, and the night was so dark, and we were all so reserved, that I cannot undertake to say even that."
> (Charles Dickens)

NOTE: The first word of a quotation is *capitalized* if it was the first word of a sentence in the original text.

The following examples all show the right way of punctuating quotations. Explain why each was punctuated the way it was. Point out what is different or unusual about some of the examples.

1. He said, "We have found your father."
2. "You are very kind," the girl replied.
3. The current issue quotes a saying that contains a great deal of truth: "There is always a Jones ahead of the Jones you keep up with."
4. "Right you are, Crofton!" said Mr. Henchy fiercely.
5. "Sir," said the honest young newsboy, "you have given me a dime by mistake. The newspaper costs only a penny."
6. Edgar Allan Poe wrote, "I love fame. . . . I would have incense arise in my honor from every hamlet."
7. The phrase "I'm just a country boy" has become the favored gambit of sophisticated and wily men. (John W. Gardner)
8. Mencken said, "Conscience is the inner voice which warns us that somebody may be looking"!
9. Was it Hamilton who said, "Your people, sir, is a great beast"?
10. Mr. Henchy continued: "He was the only man that could keep that bag of cats in order. 'Down, ye dogs! Lie down, ye curs!' That's the way he treated them."
11. "The thing is this," said Merrylegs. "Ginger has a bad habit of biting and snapping." (Anna Sewell)
12. She kept asking, "Where are you taking me?"
13. The yearly report stated: "The company's operations in the Congo [now Zaire] have been greatly expanded."
14. "We do not trust you," their leader said; "nevertheless, we will try to help you one more time."
15. Without the cry of "Hot dogs!" a football game is not really complete.

After the number of each sentence, write down the mark or marks missing at the blank space in the sentence.

EXAMPLE: "We are leaving soon _____ she quickly said to her mother.

(Answer) ,"

1. "Nogales _____ she said, "is a border town."
2. She said, "Have you ever tried the mangos or the tortillas _____
3. "Fruits are insect carriers," he said _____ Eat the fresh fruit while still across the line."
4. "Do we need a visa to keep going down the road _____ he wanted to know.
5. The visitor asked, "Is there any true unspoiled desert left _____
6. The chamber of commerce brochure was full of purple prose _____ Lizards slither, rattlesnakes rattle, cactus and wild flowers wait for a few inches of rain to burst into bloom."

7. "Genuine Indian jewelry!" our angry friend kept shouting. "Made in Hong Kong _____

8. What did he mean when he said, "The town is a free port _____

9. "She was always criticizing," he drily said, "what she called the 'spirit of mañana _____

10. "The old adobe buildings," he said _____ are reserved as museum pieces surrounded by glass and concrete."

11. The diary entry said: "Every day the director tells the staff, 'Things will be better soon _____

12. "Stop _____ the guard said. "Everyone off the truck!"

13. What a comeback for a player who had said "I'm through _____

14. The stranger said, "Dr. Garrett lives here, doesn't he _____

15. Does she have to keep saying, "It's all the same to me _____

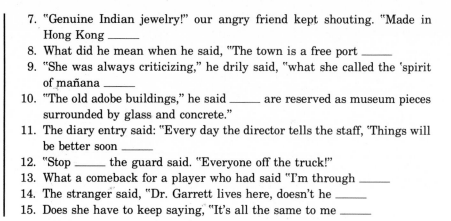

M6b
Indirect Quotation and Words Set Off

Use no punctuation with indirect quotations, but set off phrases quoted word for word.

We do not always reproduce the exact wording of what someone said. Instead we repeat it in our own words. This way of quoting someone is called **indirect** quotation. Indirect quotations often start with the special connective *that* or question words like *how, why, what,* and *where.* Such indirect quotations fit into the sentence *without punctuation*—no comma, no quotation marks:

INDIRECT: She wrote *that winter had come early.*
INDIRECT: He explained *why interest rates were going up.*
INDIRECT: The mechanic asked me *what the problem was.*

A direct quotation looks at things from the point of view of the *speaker,* at the time the speaker was talking. An indirect quotation looks at things from the point of view of the person who *quotes,* at the time of quoting. Notice how references to persons and to time change in the following pairs:

DIRECT: He asked, "Why *do you follow me?*"
INDIRECT: He asked why *she followed him.*

DIRECT: The inspector said, "But no one *saw you* leave."
INDIRECT: The inspector said that no one *had seen me* leave.

Even when you are not using direct quotation, set the following off from your own text:

(1) Set off quoted words and phrases. Even in indirect quotations, show when you have kept some of the original words—because they are striking, or typical of the speaker, or especially

important. Enclose such words and phrases (but not the rest of the quotation) in **quotation marks:**

> She said she did not want her son to marry "below his station."

(2) Set off difficult or new technical and other unusual terms. **Quotation marks** show that they are new or deserve special attention:

> The engine had an "afterburner" especially designed for this plane.
> The new pioneers would be the "backtrailers," moving from the Plains States to Chicago, Boston, or New York.

(3) Set off words discussed as words, as in a discussion of word meanings. Use **italics** (or underlining in typed and handwritten papers) for this purpose:

> To describe the wedge-shaped fender in front of a locomotive, the Americans used the word *cowcatcher,* the British used the word *plow.*

(4) Set off words borrowed from foreign languages and still considered foreign. For instance, many scientific and legal terms are borrowed from Latin. Use **italics:**

> The killer whale *(Orcinus orca)* is a fierce animal 20 to 30 feet long.
> The lawyer entered a plea of *nolo contendere.*

(5) Set off titles of publications. For *complete publications* —such as books and magazines—use **italics.** For *separate parts* of a publication—such as a chapter of a book, an article in a magazine, a poem in a collection—use **quotation marks:**

> "The Emperor of Ice-Cream" is included in *Poems* by Wallace Stevens.

NOTE: Students often use quotation marks to set off words—often slang terms—for humorous effect (I was happy to see all my "chums" again). This practice is much overdone.

Which of the following sentences include a direct quotation? Which include an indirect quotation? Copy each sentence, punctuating it correctly.

EXERCISE 1

1. The speaker said let me give you an example of conspicuous waste
2. The director explained how the program would help families
3. The speaker said that the blame for higher prices often must be placed on the consumer
4. True peace in the region the author wrote will not come in our time
5. The official told me that I needed three copies of the form
6. We asked the guard why the museum was closed

7. She asked us why do you always make the same mistake
8. These projections do not tell us what the future of the country will really be
9. We saw the train leave my uncle said we stood by helplessly
10. The viewer feels like asking why am I asked to consider this

The following passages show the right way of setting off words and phrases. Explain why each was set off the way it was.

1. The name *Alaska* comes from the Aleut word *Alayeska,* meaning "the great land."
2. Books like *Risen from the Ranks* and *Bound to Rise* showed generations of young Americans the road to fame and fortune.
3. The text of "Lucy in the Sky" appears in *The Book of Beatle Lyrics.*
4. She explained the difference between a *de facto* government and a government *de jure.*
5. The brown rat *(rattus norvegicus)* and the black rat *(rattus rattus)* are both common in the United States.
6. A California newspaper called Easterners "the unhappy inhabitants of the frozen East."
7. She had written an article called "The Language of Gestures" for *Redbook* magazine.
8. His book had been the first to distinguish between "self-directed" and "other-directed" people.
9. The speaker claimed that business firms are wasting much energy by "lighting up buildings like Christmas trees."
10. The term *karma* is explained in the chapter on "Hindu Beliefs" in *The Book of World Religions.*

Look at the following passages. What punctuation is needed in each of the blank spaces? After the number of the passage, put one or more marks as required. Put *No* for no punctuation. (Be prepared to explain the punctuation of quotations and the use of italics in these passages.)

1. The *Atlantic* printed an article called "Is There a Computer in Your Future _____
2. It explained what "input" or a _____ print-out" is.
3. The article said _____ that computers already do much of our thinking for us.
4. It said: "Words like *program* have acquired new meanings _____
5. Some people predict a future when people as well as computers will be "programmed _____
6. The first computerized dating service was called "Operation Match _____

7. The sign on the door said _____ Welcome!"

8. The interviewer asked _____ how old and how tall I was.

9. "Would you be happy _____ he asked, "with a person who wasn't very affectionate?"

10. "This number is not in service anymore _____ said the operator.

11. The questionnaire included questions like "Do you try to avoid cracks in sidewalks _____

12. "The computer does not work magic," the man said _____ The human touch is still required."

13. The instructions read: "React to the following statement: 'Everyone should look for a spouse _____

14. He asked _____ what I thought of dirty dishes left in the sink.

15. What would you require in a "compatible date _____

16. The letter said _____ I have two cats, and I am interested in horses and nature walks."

17. "Dear Pat _____ I wrote back, "I hate cats and especially horses."

18. The questionnaire asked _____ how important religion was in my life.

19. "Why did you lie to the computer _____ he asked indignantly.

20. "The computer replaces Cupid _____ the ad began.

M7
MANUSCRIPT FORM

Hand in clean and legible copy observing standard form.

The outward appearance of your paper shows what you think of your reader. Show that you care about your reader's convenience, eyesight, and standards of neatness.

M7a
Preparing Copy

Write or type your papers neatly, legibly, and in standard form.

Observe the following guidelines:

(1) Keep your handwriting clear and legible. Keep the loops open in letters like *e*. Keep the dots right over each *i*, and cross your *t*'s. Do not run together combinations like *mm, mn, ing, tion*. Avoid excessive slanting and excessive crowding. If your teacher does not require any special type of theme paper, use paper of *standard size*, ruled in *wide* lines.

(2) Type your papers whenever you can. Type the original copy on *nontransparent* paper—unlined, of standard size. Semi-transparent sheets (onionskin) are for carbon copies. *Double-space* all material except block quotations and footnotes. Leave two spaces after a period or other end punctuation. Use two hyphens—with no space on either side—to make a dash.

(3) Leave adequate margins. Leave about an inch and a half on the left and at the top. Leave about an inch on the right and at the bottom. *Indent* the first line of a paragraph—about an inch in longhand, or five spaces in typed copy.

(4) Capitalize words in the title of your paper as you would in a title you mention. Observe the three *don'ts* for the title you give to your own theme. Do *not* underline or italicize it. Do *not* enclose it in quotation marks unless it is a quotation. Do *not* put a period at the end, but use a question mark or exclamation point where needed.

```
A Forgotten Neighborhood
Who Am I?
Up, Up, and Away!
```

See also **M2a.**

(5) Proofread a first draft carefully for misspellings or typing errors. The following last-minute corrections are permissible on the final copy if they are neat and few in number:

• Draw a line through words or phrases you want to omit. Do *not* use parentheses or square brackets for this purpose:

```
We knew that if we were late that our .....
```

• To correct a word, draw a line through it and write the corrected word in the space immediately above. Do *not* cross out or insert individual letters:

```
            implied
He inferred we were cheating.
```

• To add a missing word, insert a caret (∧) and write the word immediately above:

```
                    is
A new census being planned.
              ∧
```

• To change the paragraphing of a paper, insert the symbol ¶ to indicate an additional paragraph break. Insert *no*¶ in the margin to indicate that an existing paragraph break should be ignored.

```
. . . was finished. ¶ The second part of the
program. . . .
```

(6) Divide words as recommended by your dictionary. Most dictionaries use centered dots to show the possible breaks (com·pli·ment). Divide words only if otherwise you would have an uneven right margin. Use the hyphen to divide words.

Remember:

• Do not set off *single letters,* as for instance in *about, alone, many, via.* Do not set off the *–ed* ending in words like *asked* and *complained.*

• When a word is clearly a *combination* of other meaningful parts, divide at the point where the original parts are joined: *blue·bird, harm·ful.*

• Divide *hyphenated words* only at the point where the hyphen occurs, for instance in *un-American* or *sister-in-law.*

• Do not divide the *last word* on a page.

(7) Underline, or italicize, for emphasis. Use this device only rarely, when clearly appropriate:

```
The teacher was expected to present the
evaluation to the parent in person.
```

Use abbreviations and figures only where they are appropriate.

Abbreviations and figures save time and space. In ordinary writing, however, avoid excessive shortcuts:

(1) Use abbreviations only if they are acceptable in ordinary writing:

• Before or after *names,* the titles *Mr., Mrs., Ms., Dr., St.* (Saint); the abbreviations *Jr.* and *Sr.;* degrees like *M.D.* and *Ph.D.:*

We were introduced to Mr. and Mrs. Jones.
The sign identified her as Jean E. Gielgud, M.D.

• Before or after *numerals,* the abbreviations *No.,* A.D. and B.C., A.M. and P.M. (or *a.m.* and *p.m.*); and the symbol *$:*

The battle of Marathon was fought in 490 B.C.
The plane leaves at 9:25 A.M.

• *Initials* standing for the name of agencies, business firms,

M7b
Abbreviations and Numbers

technical processes, and the like, providing these initials are in common use:

> The union was affiliated with the AFL-CIO.
> Her article was critical of the CIA and the FBI.
> He had worked for agencies like UNICEF and UNESCO.

• *Latin abbreviations* such as *e.g.* (for example), *etc.* (and so on), *i.e.* (that is). (The modern tendency is to use the corresponding English expressions instead.)

> The water problems may be solved by new technology, e.g., desalinization.

(2) Know abbreviations that we use only for special purposes. Some abbreviations are acceptable in addresses, business records, and the like, but are *spelled out* in ordinary writing:

• Names of *countries, states, streets,* and the like (with a few exceptions: *U.S.S.R.;* Washington, *D.C.*):

> Their offices in the United States were in Pittsburgh, Pennsylvania.
> The company had moved from Brown Street to Constitution Avenue.

• *Units of measurement* like *lb.* (pound), *oz.* (ounce), *ft.* (foot), with the exception of *mph* and *rpm:*

> The fish she caught weighed 3 pounds, 2 ounces.

(3) Use exact figures where needed. Figures are generally acceptable in references to dates and years, street numbers, and page numbers. Use them also for exact sums and technical measurements, especially those referring to percentages or including decimal points:

> The meeting was held on November 29, 1978.
> He lived at 2965 Sycamore Street, Apartment 9.
> The population had grown to 37,650 inhabitants.
> At a rate of 7.8 percent, the interest was $23.45.

(4) Know which figures to spell out. The following are usually spelled out: numbers from one to ten; round numbers requiring no more than two words; a number at the beginning of a sentence. (When they are spelled out, compound numbers from 21 to 99 are hyphenated.)

> He had sold twenty-five prints at a hundred dollars each.
> Twenty-two years ago conditions were different.
> The horses were from three to six years old.

Put *S* after the number of each sentence in which any use of abbreviations and numbers is satisfactory. Rewrite a sentence if abbreviations or numbers would be unsatisfactory in ordinary writing.

EXERCISE

1. Each member was asked to contribute $10.00 or more.
2. She could not decide whether to attend a local J.C. or go to the state univ.
3. The PTA held a national convention in Washington, D.C.
4. The shareholders received a dividend of $2.23 per share.
5. 17 voted for, 3 against, and two abstained.
6. They had moved from Vermilion, South Dakota, to Lafayette, Indiana.
7. The dr. told him to lose at least twenty lbs.
8. He was looking for players who measured close to six feet and weighed close to two hundred pounds.
9. Doctor Sprack first came to Oakland, Calif., in 1978.
10. The exact time elapsed had been 34.7 seconds.

Chapter 6

Oral Language
Public Speech

Chapter Preview 6

Know how to reach your audience.

During an effective public speech, the people in the audience do not just sit there. They are drawn in; they participate. They frown as the speaker poses a problem. They listen in silence to a solemn admonition or a serious charge. They break into laughter at a flash of wit.

Remember the following hints for speakers:

TAKE IN YOUR SURROUNDINGS: Look around before you start talking. Arrange your notes, the lectern, and the mike the way you want them *before* you start.

SPEAK FREELY FROM NOTES: Few people can read a prepared speech, or recite it from memory, and still sound *natural*. Effective speakers often have their material in front of them. They put it into words freshly as they go along.

MOVE NATURALLY: Feel free to use your arms and hands for gestures that reinforce what you say. Step back half a step, raise your head, look at your audience as you ask an important question or make an important statement.

KEEP IT CURRENT: Make your talk sound live by working in last-minute examples: "On my way to class I noticed. . . ." "We all saw yesterday's headline. . . ."

CUT WHERE NECESSARY: Don't race the clock. If you run overtime, omit examples or detailed explanations. Make sure you don't have to stop before you reach your main point.

Choose one or more of the following for limbering-up activities:

1. Get an older person to tell you about his or her experience and outlook on life. Try to tape or write down the person's own or approximate words. Then tell the person's story in those words, assuming the role of the person.
2. Choose a topic on which you have strong feelings but that at the same time has a lighter side. Give a short talk that makes your listeners think while appealing to their sense of humor.
3. Find several short poems or prose passages on a favorite topic: love, friendship, the passing of time, or the like. Prepare to read them with a brief informal introduction and connecting words.

Know how to prepare a short talk and present it effectively to an audience.

Have you ever studied a tape recording or a transcript of a successful talk? How did the speaker approach and hold the audience? What are some of the elements you find when you study a successful speaker's approach?

Remember and practice the following:

(1) Know your subject.   To talk about any topic with conviction, you have to have "lived with it" for a while. Immerse yourself in your subject. Read about it; talk about it; think about it. Be able to respond to questions by saying: "I'm glad you asked me—I know all about this!"

(2) Bring things clearly into focus.   Take clear aim; do not scatter your shots. If you have an important proposal to present, make sure it does not get lost among various other points. Make it stand out clearly. Summarize it; repeat it; reinforce it.

(3) Organize your material.   A speaker must know how to lay things out in his or her own mind. Work out a simple basic strategy. Give your listeners an overall plan they can follow: four major steps in a process, or three possible ways of solving a problem, or three major objections to a project. If you have sorted your material out under three major headings, or if your argument moves through three major steps, make sure your audience gets a clear signal as you move from one point to the next.

(4) Make yourself understood.   Hunt for examples that will make your audience understand a difficult point. Look for analogies that will bring a technical point close to the nonexpert. Suppose a lecturer wanted to make the point that language is shaped by the culture of a people—it reflects where and how they live. Examples like the following would help make this point clear to the listeners:

Arabic has many words relating to the sicknesses of camels, because Arabs have many camels, and camels have many sicknesses. English is almost destitute of words relating to the sickness of camels, because if they are sick, we leave it to the zoo. When the Lord's Prayer was first translated into Eskimo, it read, "Give us this day our daily fish," because Eskimos didn't have bread in those days and wouldn't have understood. (Bergen Evans)

(5) Identify with your audience. Ask yourself: "What do I and my audience have in common?" "How can I relate my topic to the background and interests of my listeners?" Suppose a lecturer is making the point that differences in language develop naturally. They are a normal, everyday thing. If lecturing in Missouri, the speaker might look for an example *from* Missouri: Old-timers pronounce the name of the city "Saint Louie"; others "Saint Louis." If lecturing in Illinois, the speaker might point out that people from Vienna, Illinois, call it "Vienna," with the *i* pronounced "eye." (A man trying to cash a bogus check was caught because he claimed to be from Vienna but did not pronounce it right.)

Remember: In effective public speaking, there is *two-way* communication. The speaker senses the reactions of the audience. To do a "live" presentation, learn to think on your feet. Shift gears as needed to go back over an important point, or to build up enthusiasm, or to explain a possible misunderstanding.

(6) Keep your material up to date. Link your subject to what is current or topical. By using current examples, you can show that you are still thinking about your material. You can show that you are talking about what is still fresh in your mind. For instance, if your topic concerns obstacles to communication, look for examples currently in the news:

- the problems of welfare recipients trying to fill out long bureaucratic questionnaires;
- problems of communication at an important international conference;
- objections by women's groups to language used by men in talking about women.

EXERCISE 1

Prepare a brief talk in which you explain a *difficult subject* to a group that has little relevant background and needs all the help you can give. For instance,

- explain a difficult concept in the natural sciences to a group of seventh or eighth graders;
- explain an important part of our system of government to a group of recent immigrants who want to become citizens;

- explain a new approach to teaching high school mathematics or theoretical science to a group of parents who had their own schooling many years ago;
- explain a movement in contemporary art that might appear new or strange to outsiders.

Prepare a brief talk on one of the following topics: threatened open spaces, pollution, traffic safety, street violence, educational opportunity, or integration vs. segregation. Throughout, relate your speech closely to the *current* situation and the *local* scene. Draw on local newspapers and similar sources for recent material of local interest.

EXERCISE 2

Prepare a brief talk in which you bring your audience up to date on developments in a part of the world that you have studied or read about. Make sure you study ample *background material* for your talk. Talk about a country or a region in which you have a special interest.

EXERCISE 3

Study the way an eloquent speaker sways and inspires listeners.

In times of crisis, the spoken word often plays a decisive role. The eloquence of a leader can inspire powerful feelings of loyalty and common purpose. It can make people challenge ideas and institutions. The eloquence of a trial lawyer can mean the difference between freedom and prison for the accused. The following excerpts will give you a chance to study the way an eloquent speaker can help shape the course of events.

O2

THE POWER OF WORDS

Study the way an eloquent speaker builds morale.

One of the oldest uses of the spoken word is to fire up the courage or determination of people at war. A famous example is the funeral oration of Pericles, delivered in honor of Athenian soldiers who died in the war against Sparta. This speech was given 2,400 years ago and is reported to us by a Greek historian of that time. The following excerpt is a eulogy to the city of Athens and the empire it had built. The speaker praises the institutions and customs of his native city. He tries to show that those who died fighting for Athens died for a country deserving of their love and sacrifice.

Study the passage carefully and then answer the questions that follow it.

O2a

The Eulogy

Let me say that our system of government does not copy the institutions of our neighbors. It is more the case of our being a model to others than of our imitating anyone else. Our constitution is called a democracy because power is in the hands not of a minority but of the whole people. When it is a question of settling private disputes, everyone is equal before the law; when it is a question of putting one person before another in positions of public responsibility, what counts is not membership of a particular class but the actual ability that the person possesses. No one, so long as he has it in him to be of service to the state, is kept in political obscurity because of poverty. And, just as our political life is free and open, so is our day-to-day life in our relations with each other. We do not get into a state with our next-door neighbor if he enjoys himself in his own way, nor do we give him the kind of black looks that, though they do no real harm, still do hurt people's feelings. We are free and tolerant in our private lives; but in public affairs we keep to the law. This is because it commands our deep respect.

We give our obedience to those whom we put in positions of authority, and we obey the laws themselves, especially those that are for the protection of the oppressed, and those unwritten laws that it is an acknowledged shame to break.

And here is another point. When our work is over, we are in a position to enjoy all kinds of recreation for our spirits. There are various kinds of contests and sacrifices regularly throughout the year; in our own homes we find a beauty and a good taste that delight us every day and that drive away our cares. Then the greatness of our city brings it about that all the good things from all the world flow into us, so that to us it seems just as natural to enjoy foreign goods as our own local products.

Then there is a great difference between us and our opponents in our attitude toward military security. Here are some examples: Our city is open to the world, and we have no periodical deportations in order to prevent people observing or finding out secrets that might be of military advantage to the enemy. This is because we rely, not on secret weapons, but on our own real courage and loyalty. There is a difference, too, in our educational systems. The Spartans, from their earliest boyhood, are submitted to the most laborious training in courage. We pass our lives without all these restrictions, and yet are just as ready to face the same dangers as they are. . . . There are certain advantages, I think, in our way of meeting danger voluntarily, with an easy mind, instead of with a laborious training, with natural rather than with state-induced courage. We do not have to spend our time practicing to meet sufferings that are still in the future. When they are actually upon us, we show ourselves just as brave as these others who are always in strict training. This is one point in which, I think, our city deserves to be admired. There are also others:

Our love of what is beautiful does not lead to extravagance. Our love of the things of the mind does not make us soft. We regard wealth as something to be properly used, rather than as something to boast about. As for poverty, no one need be ashamed to admit it: the real shame is in not taking practical measures to escape from it. Here each individual is interested not only in his own affairs but in the affairs of the state as well: even those who are mostly occupied with their own business are extremely well-informed on general politics. This is a peculiarity of ours; we do not say that people who take no interest in politics mind their own business; we say that they have no business here at all. We Athenians, in our own persons, take our decisions on policy or submit them to proper discussions: for we do not think that there is an incompatibility between words and deeds. The worst thing is to rush into action before the consequences have been properly debated. And this is another point where we differ from other people. We are capable at the same time of taking risks and of estimating them beforehand. Others are brave out of ignorance; and, when they stop to think, they begin to fear. But the person who is truly brave knows the meaning of what is sweet in life and of what is terrible and then goes out undeterred to meet what is to come. . . . Taking everything together, then, I declare that our city is an education to Greece. Each single one of our citizens, in all the manifold aspects of life, is able to show himself the rightful lord and owner of his own person, and do this, moreover, with exceptional grace and exceptional versatility. And to show that this is no empty boasting for the present occasion, but real tangible fact, you have only to consider the power that our city possesses and that has been won by those very qualities that I have mentioned. Athens, alone of the states we know, comes to her testing time in a greatness that surpasses what was imagined of her. In her case, and in her case alone, no invading enemy is ashamed at being defeated, and no subject can complain of being governed by people unfit for their responsibilities. Mighty indeed are the marks and monuments of our empire that we have left. Future ages will wonder at us, as the present age wonders at us now.

1. Early in this speech, Pericles refers to Athens as a "free country." Are there parts of this excerpt that sound as though they could have been taken from a speech made by an American about the United States? Show all similarities or parallels.

2. Are there parts that you would *not* expect in a patriotic speech by an American? Show the differences in detail.

3. Prepare an *outline* of this speech. What are the major points or major areas covered by the speaker?

4. One observer of the American scene claimed that "Americans have been shy at expressing their deepest convictions and have been verbally cynical

**FOLLOW-UP
QUESTIONS**

about Fourth of July oratory. Yet devotion to the American way has been none the less passionate." How shy or how open are Americans today about expressing patriotic feelings? What form does the expression of their patriotic sentiments take—what *style* does it follow? Use evidence from such sources as editorials, letters to the editor, political speeches, and the like.

5. Practice reading a portion of this speech out loud. (Your teacher may ask you to memorize your selection.) Read or recite it with the right gestures and tone of voice.

EXERCISE 1

The attitude of Americans toward their country has ranged from praise of everything American to strong criticism of our practices and institutions. Select an area or feature of the American way of life about which you have strong positive feelings. Prepare a speech in which you *praise or defend* it before an audience.

EXERCISE 2

When an ideal picture is contrasted with inadequate reality, disillusionment sets in. A famous example of protest against deceptive ideals is the Fourth of July speech made in 1852 by Frederick Douglass, the former slave who escaped to the North and became one of the leaders in the struggle for the abolition of slavery in America. What kind of speech would a modern Frederick Douglass prepare for the Fourth of July? Prepare a speech that protests against a failure of American reality to live up to its ideals, or that expresses dissent from one of the ideals traditionally celebrated by Fourth of July speakers.

EXERCISE 3

In recent years, many Americans have rediscovered their roots in the past. They have studied the history of their families, or of their racial or ethnic group, or of their political or religious affiliations. Prepare a talk about your own roots.

O2b
The Political Speech

Study the way an eloquent speaker mobilizes support.

Throughout recorded history, the political speech has been a major weapon in the battle for people's minds. An eloquent speaker can sway an audience and change the loyalties of a crowd. Antony's speech in Shakespeare's *Julius Caesar* is a famous demonstration of the power of the spoken word. The time is immediately after the assassination of Caesar. Brutus, the leader of the conspirators, and Antony, the slain dictator's friend, both speak to the citizens of Rome.

Compare and contrast the way they try to bring the citizens over to their side. Then answer the questions that follow the selection.

(Your teacher may ask you and your classmates to team up for a staging of this scene from the play.)

EXCERPT 1:

Brutus: Romans, countrymen, and lovers, hear me for my cause, *friends*
and be silent, that you may hear. Believe me for mine honor, and have respect to mine honor, that you may believe. Censure me in your wisdom, and awake your senses, that you may the better judge. If there be any in this assembly, any dear friend of Caesar's, to him I say that Brutus' love to Caesar was no less than his. If then that friend demand why Brutus rose against Caesar, this is my answer: Not that I loved Caesar less, but that I loved Rome more. Had you rather Caesar were living, and die all slaves, than that Caesar were dead, to live all free men? As Caesar loved me, I weep for him; as he was fortunate, I rejoice at it; as he was valiant, I honor him; but, as he was ambitious, I slew him. There is tears, for his love; joy, for his fortune; honor, for his valor; and death, for his ambition. Who is here so base, that would be a bondman? If any, speak; for him have I offended. Who is here so rude, that would not be a Roman? If any, speak; for him have I offended. Who is here so vile, that will not love his country? If any, speak; for him have I offended. I pause for a reply.

All: None, Brutus, none!

Brutus: Then none have I offended. I have done no more to Caesar than you shall do to Brutus. The question of his death is enrolled in the Capitol; his glory not extenuated, wherein he was worthy, nor his offenses enforced, for which he suffered death.

   (Enter Mark Antony, with Caesar's body.)

   Here comes his body, mourned by Mark Antony, who, though he had no hand in his death, shall receive the benefit of his dying, a place in the commonwealth, as which of you shall not? With this I depart, that, as I slew my best lover for the good of *best friend*
Rome, I have the same dagger for myself, when it shall please my country to need my death.

All: Live, Brutus! Live, live!

EXCERPT 2:

Antony: Friends, Romans, countrymen, lend me your ears;
  I come to bury Caesar, not to praise him.
  The evil that men do lives after them,
  The good is oft interrèd with their bones; *buried*
  So let it be with Caesar. The noble Brutus

most serious	Hath told you Caesar was ambitious.
	If it were so, it was a grievous fault,
	And grievously hath Caesar answered it.
	Here, under leave of Brutus and the rest
	(For Brutus is an honorable man,
	So are they all, all honorable men),
	Come I to speak in Caesar's funeral.
	He was my friend, faithful and just to me;
	But Brutus says he was ambitious,
	And Brutus is an honorable man.
	He hath brought many captives home to Rome,
	Whose ransoms did the general coffers fill;
	Did this in Caesar seem ambitious?
	When that the poor have cried, Caesar hath wept;
	Ambition should be made of sterner stuff.
	Yet Brutus says he was ambitious;
	And Brutus is an honorable man.
Roman festival	You all did see that on the Lupercal
three times	I thrice presented him a kingly crown,
	Which he did thrice refuse. Was this ambition?
	Yet Brutus says he was ambitious;
	And sure he is an honorable man.
	I speak not to disprove what Brutus spoke,
	But here I am to speak what I do know.
	You all did love him once, not without cause;
holds you back	What cause withholds you then to mourn for him?
	O judgment, thou art fled to brutish beasts,
	And men have lost their reason! Bear with me;
	My heart is in the coffin there with Caesar,
	And I must pause till it come back to me.

I think   *First Plebeian:* Methinks there is much reason in his
    sayings.
Second Plebeian: If thou consider rightly of the matter,
    Caesar has had great wrong.
Third Plebeian: Has he, masters?
    I fear there will a worse come in his place.
Fourth Plebeian: Marked ye his words? He would not
    take the crown,
    Therefore 'tis certain he was not ambitious.

dearly pay for it   *First Plebeian:* If it be found so, some will dear abide it.
Second Plebeian: Poor soul, his eyes are red as fire with weeping.
Third Plebeian: There's not a nobler man in Rome than Antony.
Fourth Plebeian: Now mark him, he begins again to
    speak.
Antony: But yesterday the word of Caesar might

Have stood against the world; now lies he there,
And none so poor to do him reverence.   *as to show him respect*
O masters! If I were disposed to stir
Your hearts and minds to mutiny and rage,
I should do Brutus wrong and Cassius wrong,
Who, you all know, are honorable men.
I will not do them wrong; I rather choose
To wrong the dead, to wrong myself and you,
Than I will wrong such honorable men.
But here's a parchment with the seal of Caesar;
I found it in his closet; 'tis his will.
Let but the commons hear this testament,   *common people*
Which, pardon me, I do not mean to read,
And they would go and kiss dead Caesar's wounds,
And dip their napkins in his sacred blood;   *handkerchiefs*
Yea, beg a hair of him for memory,
And dying, mention it within their wills,
Bequeathing it as a rich legacy   *leaving it*
Unto their issue.   *their children*

Fourth Plebeian: We'll hear the will; read it, Mark
    Antony.

All: The will, the will! We will hear Caesar's will! . . .

Antony: You will compel me then to read the will?
    Then make a ring about the corpse of Caesar,
    And let me show you him that made the will.
    Shall I descend? And will you give me leave?   *permission*

All: Come down.

Second Plebeian: Descend.   *(Antony comes down.)*

Antony: If you have tears, prepare to shed them now.
    You all do know this mantle, I remember   *cloak*
    The first time ever Caesar put it on:
    'Twas on a summer's evening, in his tent,
    That day he overcame the Nervii.
    Look, in this place ran Cassius' dagger through;
    See what a rent the envious Casca made;
    Through this the well-belovèd Brutus stabbed,
    And as he plucked his cursèd steel away,
    Mark how the blood of Caesar followed it,
    As rushing out of doors, to be resolved   *to know for sure*
    If Brutus so unkindly knocked, or no;
    For Brutus, as you know, was Caesar's angel.
    Judge, O you gods, how dearly Caesar loved him!
    This was the most unkindest cut of all;
    For when the noble Caesar saw him stab,
    Ingratitude, more strong than traitors' arms,

Quite vanquished him. Then burst his mighty heart;
And, in his mantle muffling up his face,
Even at the base of Pompey's statue
(Which all the while ran blood) great Caesar fell.
O, what a fall was there, my countrymen!
Then I, and you, and all of us fell down,
Whilst bloody treason flourished over us.
O, now you weep, and I perceive you feel

the force of   The dint of pity: these are gracious drops.
Kind souls, what weep you when you but behold

garment   Our Caesar's vesture wounded? Look you here,
disfigured . . . by   Here is himself, marred as you see with traitors.

First Plebeian: O piteous spectacle!
Second Plebeian: O noble Caesar! . . .
All: Revenge! About! Seek! Burn! Fire! Kill! Slay!
Let not a traitor live! . . .
Antony: Good friends, sweet friends, let me not stir you
up
To such a sudden flood of mutiny.
They that have done this deed are honorable.

grievances   What private griefs they have, alas, I know not,
That made them do it. They are wise and honorable,
And will, no doubt, with reasons answer you.
I come not, friends, to steal away your hearts;
I am no orator, as Brutus is;
But (as you know me all) a plain blunt man
That love my friend, and that they know full well
That gave me public leave to speak of him.
For I have neither wit, nor words, nor worth,
Action, nor utterance, nor the power of speech
To stir men's blood; I only speak right on.
I tell you that which you yourselves do know,
Show you sweet Caesar's wounds, poor poor dumb mouths,
And bid them speak for me. But were I Brutus,
And Brutus Antony, there were an Antony
Would ruffle up your spirits, and put a tongue
In every wound of Caesar that should move
The stones of Rome to rise and mutiny.
All: We'll mutiny.
First Plebeian: We'll burn the house of Brutus.
Third Plebeian: Away, then! Come, seek the conspirators! . . .
Antony: Why, friends, you go to do you know not what:
Wherein hath Caesar thus deserved your loves?
Alas, you know not; I must tell you then:
You have forgot the will I told you of.

All: Most true, the will! Let's stay and hear the will.

Antony: Here is the will, and under Caesar's seal.

  To every Roman citizen he gives,

  To every several man, seventy-five drachmas. . . .

  Moreover, he hath left you all his walks,

  His private arbors, and new-planted orchards,

  On this side Tiber; he hath left them you,

  And to your heirs forever: common pleasures,

  To walk abroad and recreate yourselves.

  Here was a Caesar! When comes such another?

First Plebeian: Never, never! Come, away, away!

  We'll burn his body in the holy place,

  And with the brands fire the traitors' houses. . . .

FOLLOW-UP QUESTIONS

1. What motives or standards does Brutus appeal to? Describe and evaluate his speech.
2. What motives or standards does Antony appeal to? Could a contemporary speaker use some of the same appeals, adapting them to our own contemporary setting and issues?
3. In what *order* does Antony proceed? Could this order be changed, or is it part of his strategy?
4. Would you call Antony a "demagogue"? Where and how do you draw the line between demagoguery and legitimate persuasion? Can you use current examples to clarify the point?
5. Assume that after Antony's speech Brutus had had an opportunity for *rebuttal.* Prepare a short speech in which you think of yourself as Brutus speaking a second time, trying to undo the damage already done.

EXERCISE 1

  Have you ever felt that something you believed in represented a *lost cause?* Prepare a speech in which you try your best to get a favorable hearing for an unpopular or unfashionable point of view. For instance, you might try to advocate:

- church membership to young people indifferent to religion;
- extended foreign aid to an audience of middle-class Americans;
- nonviolence to a group committed to militant action;
- censorship of reporting of violence to a group of media people.

EXERCISE 2

  In your study of history, have you ever wondered what would have happened if eloquent people had intervened at the right time in order to avert disaster? Imagine yourself present at one of history's *lost opportunities.* Prepare the kind of speech that you think might have helped prevent the worst. For instance, you might imagine yourself speaking to

- the British Parliament shortly before the final break between Great Britain and the American colonies;
- German writers and journalists shortly before World War II;
- a group of Japanese leaders shortly before Pearl Harbor.

(Study the relevant sections of a history textbook or similar source in order to familiarize yourself with the historical situation.)

O2c
The Plea for Justice

Study the way a speaker's eloquence affects our determination of guilt and innocence.

In a courtroom, a speaker's power to persuade has grave consequences. For the accused, much is at stake. But much is also at stake for a society that aims at justice for its citizens. How much depends on the eloquence and skill of the people speaking for the prosecution or for the defense?

Study the courtroom scene recorded on the magazine page reprinted with this section. (Arrange to reenact the scene in your classroom.) Answer the questions that follow it.

• • • • • • • • • • • • • • • • • • •

SUSAN B. ANTHONY

An account of the proceedings of her trial on the charge of illegal voting in the presidential election, 1872

Judge Hunt (ordering the defendant to stand up): Has the prisoner anything to say why sentence shall not be pronounced?

Miss Anthony: Yes, your honor, I have many things to say; for in your ordered verdict of guilty, you have trampled under foot every vital principle of our government. My natural rights, my civil rights, my political rights, my judicial rights, are all alike ignored. Robbed of the fundamental privilege of citizenship, I am degraded from the status of a citizen to that of a subject; and not only myself individually, but all of my sex, are, by your honor's verdict, doomed to political subjection under this, so-called, form of government.

Judge Hunt: The Court cannot listen to a rehearsal of arguments the prisoner's counsel has already consumed three hours in presenting.

Miss Anthony: May it please your honor, I am not arguing the question, but simply stating the reasons why sentence cannot, in justice, be pronounced against me. Your denial of my citizen's right to vote is the denial of my right of consent as one of the governed, the denial of my right of representation as one of the taxed, the denial of my right to a trial by a jury of my peers as an offender against law; therefore, the denial of my sacred rights to life, liberty, property and—

Judge Hunt: The Court cannot allow the prisoner to go on.

Miss Anthony: But your honor will not deny me this one and only poor privilege of protest against this high-handed outrage upon my citizen's rights. May it please the Court to remember that since the day of my arrest last November, this is the first time that either myself or any person of my disfranchised class has been allowed a word of defense before judge or jury—

Judge Hunt: The prisoner must sit down—the Court cannot allow it.

Miss Anthony: All of my prosecutors—from the eighth-ward corner grocery politician who entered the complaint, to the United States Marshal, Commissioner, District Attorney, District Judge, your honor on the bench—not one is my peer, but each and all are my political sovereigns; and had your honor submitted my case to the jury, as was clearly your duty, even then I should have had just cause of protest, for not one of those men was my peer; but, native or foreign born, white or black, rich or poor, educated or ignorant, awake or asleep, sober or drunk, each and every man of them was my political superior; hence, in no sense, my peer. Even, under such circumstances, a commoner of England, tried before a jury of Lords, would have far less cause to complain than should I, a woman, tried before a jury of men. Even my counsel, the Hon. Henry R. Selden, who has argued my cause so ably, so earnestly, so unanswerably before your honor, is my political sovereign. Precisely as no disfranchised person is entitled to sit upon a jury, and no woman is entitled to the franchise, so none but a regularly admitted lawyer is allowed to practice in the courts, and no woman can gain admission to the bar—hence, jury, judge, counsel, must all be of the superior class.

Judge Hunt: The Court must insist—the prisoner has been tried according to the established forms of law.

Miss Anthony: Yes, your honor, but by forms of law all made by men, interpreted by men, administered by men, in favor of men, and against women; and hence, your honor's ordered verdict of guilty, against a United States citizen for the exercise of *"that citizen's right to vote,"* simply because that citizen was a woman and not a man. But, yesterday, the same man-made forms of law declared it a crime punishable with $1,000 fine and six months'

imprisonment, for you, or me or any of us, to give a cup of cold water, a crust of bread or a night's shelter to a panting fugitive as he was tracking his way to Canada. And every man or woman in whose veins coursed a drop of human sympathy violated that wicked law, reckless of consequences, and was justified in so doing. As then, the slaves who got their freedom must take it over, or under or through the unjust forms of law; precisely so, now, must women, to get their right to a voice in this government, take it; and I have taken mine and mean to take it at every possible opportunity.

Judge Hunt: The Court orders the prisoner to sit down. It will not allow another word.

Miss Anthony: When I was brought before your honor for trial, I hoped for a broad and liberal interpretation of the Constitution and its recent amendments, that should declare all United States citizens under its protecting aegis—that should declare equality of rights the national guarantee to all persons born or naturalized in the United States. But failing to get this justice—failing, even, to get a trial by a jury *not* of my peers—I ask not leniency at your hands—but rather the full rigors of the law.

Judge Hunt: The Court must insist—(Here the prisoner sat down.)

Judge Hunt: The prisoner will stand up. (Here Miss Anthony arose again.) The sentence of the Court is that you pay a fine of $100 and the costs of the prosecution.

Miss Anthony: May it please your honor, I shall never pay a dollar of your unjust penalty. All the stock in trade I possess is a $10,000 debt, incurred by publishing my paper—*The Revolution*—four years ago, the sole object of which was to educate all women to do precisely as I have done—rebel against your man-made, unjust, unconstitutional forms of law that tax, fine, imprison and hang women, while they deny them the right of representation in the government; and I shall work on with might and main to pay every dollar of that honest debt, but not a penny shall go to this unjust claim. And I shall earnestly and persistently continue to urge all women to the practical recognition of the old revolutionary maxim, that "Resistance to tyranny is obedience to God."

—from *Intellectual Digest*

FOLLOW-UP QUESTIONS

1. Quote several phrases used by the defendant that would have an especially eloquent ring for American ears.
2. In your own words, restate the two or three most convincing or most striking arguments used by the defendant.
3. Could you reconstruct some of the arguments that you think were used by our great-grandfathers when they *denied* women the right to vote?
4. If you were a modern Susan B. Anthony, what would be the most important single issue, or the most important single example of injustice, that you would concentrate on? Prepare a brief talk in which you present your "plea for justice" to an audience of male judges, lawyers, and legislators.

EXERCISE 1

It is sometimes claimed that minority groups cannot expect to obtain equal justice in our courts. We are also sometimes told that juries are likely to be prejudiced against certain groups. Prepare a brief speech in which you try to counsel a group of prospective jurors against the dangers of prejudice.

EXERCISE 2

Lawyers sometimes complain that a client's case has been "tried in the newspapers." During the last year or so, do you recall a court case that has been exceptionally fully reported in the newspapers? From the published accounts, what conclusion did you reach concerning the probable guilt or innocence of the accused? Prepare a talk in which you support your conclusion as effectively as you can. Your classmates will sit as a jury called to judge the effectiveness or persuasiveness of your presentation.

(If you can find a classmate interested in taking the opposite side, you may be able to reenact in your classroom part of the courtroom drama.)

EXERCISE 3

Study a famous court case in which someone widely considered innocent was found guilty. You might choose the case of Dreyfus, Sacco and Vanzetti, or a more recent, widely reported example. If possible, study *more than one* account of the trial. Do you find yourself siding with the prosecution or the defense? Prepare a brief speech in which you sum up the case for the side you choose.

O3
PARTICIPATING IN DISCUSSION

Participate in responsible discussion on serious issues.

What does it take to make possible fruitful discussion on serious issues? Remember the following basic principles:

THE RIGHT TO BE HEARD: Whether in a club meeting or in the state legislature, we allow proponents of *different* proposals to present their views. We invite *discussion* before we take a vote. The speaker has to be able to get a *fair hearing*. No serious discussion is possible when opponents are shouted down. People do not get a fair hearing if they are discredited in advance by ugly rumors or intimidated by threats.

AN OPEN MIND: Educated people have to be able to say: "I was wrong. I have changed my mind." This is what happened in some of the great parliamentary debates of nineteenth-century England: On some of the great issues of the day, we find people changing their minds. In the great debates on the people's right to vote or on the limitation of child labor, we find people crossing the line, following their own consciences.

Assuming that the conditions are right for fruitful discussion, how do you hold your own? Remember advice like the following to help your own contribution come through clearly and effectively:

(1) State your main point (or points) clearly and forcefully. Do not simply survey the evidence without making it clear what the evidence proves. State your point forcefully at the beginning, and *restate* it at the end. If several other positions have become identified in the course of the discussion, you may want to show how your position *differs* and why.

(2) Use striking supporting material. Try to use the kind of statistics and the kind of testimony from authorities that people will remember *after* other speakers have had their say.

(3) Protect yourself against damaging counterattacks. When you make a hasty generalization, a skillful opponent can deflate it by citing one important exception. When you question someone's patriotism, a skillful opponent may arouse against you the audience's sense of fair play. When you act superior to the views of others, a skillful opponent can make you seem arrogant.

(4) Look for weaknesses in the position of your opponents. Look for evidence of obvious *slanting*—the omission of important facts. Look for attempts to evade the issue—show that evidence or testimony is not really relevant to the point being discussed.

(5) Do not lose your self-control. When you engage in personal abuse, you are likely to arouse the sympathy of the audience for the underdog. The more heated a discussion becomes, the more tempted you will be to make exaggerated statements. Even in the heat of debate, try not to say things that you will regret later.

Oral Language

EXERCISE 1

How good are you at participating in the kind of *informal discussion* that gives people a chance to state, to rethink, and to develop their views? Prepare to participate in an informal discussion of the points raised in the following passage. (Your teacher or your class may decide to base the discussion on a different passage of their own choice.) After the discussion, take stock of how much actual give-and-take took place. Did people listen to each other? Was anything accomplished?

There is, of course, nothing wrong with dating as such. It is, or ought to be, the natural way for young people of opposite sexes to get to know each other. What is wrong about it today is the aura of frantic compulsion and the rushing of the season. Girls who have their "sweet sixteen parties" or, a few years later, their "coming out" debuts actually have been "out" for six years, and there is no longer any real occasion to be festive.

In line with the hothouse approach to making children grow up, summer resorts encourage parents to have their children, and certainly their teen-agers, attend night clubs until the early morning hours. Other resorts, carrying the trend a little further, advertise teen-age night clubs as a novelty. As a result of this stress on early "maturing," dating becomes a forced, not a natural, activity for adolescents.

Margaret Mead, the anthropologist, said in an article for the Associated Press: "Instead of letting boys and girls go their separate ways in late childhood and adolescence, we are forcing them to practice, not how to be individuals, but how to be spouses and parents; catapulting them into premature, half-baked adulthood before they have a chance to grow up as individuals."—Grace and Fred M. Hechinger, *Teen-age Tyranny*

EXERCISE 2

Have you ever participated in a *formal debate,* with one or more speakers on each side taking opposed views on a clearly defined issue and with opportunity for rebuttal as well as for the original presentation of the conflicting views? Prepare to participate in a debate on one of the following propositions:

1. Political ideas or social ideologies should be kept out of a high school student's education.
2. Minorities are asking for too much and advancing too fast.
3. Property rights should come after human rights.
4. There should be no censorship of any kind to limit the freedom of literature and the arts.
5. The volunteer army should be abolished in favor of a military draft.
6. The danger of nuclear power plants outweighs their usefulness.
7. Experimenting on lab animals is immoral.

FOR FURTHER STUDY

SPEECHES IN LITERATURE

A person can learn much about the speaker's craft by reenacting some of the speeches or sermons that are part of our imaginative literature. The following list provides a brief sampling of possibilities. You may want to memorize a short excerpted passage or prepare for a reading of a longer selection.

- Henry V's speech before the battle of Agincourt (Shakespeare, *Henry V,* Act IV, Scene 3);
- Richard III's wooing of Anne (Shakespeare, *Richard III,* Act I, Scene 2);
- a soliloquy or monologue by Hamlet, Macbeth, or Lady Macbeth;
- Othello's account of his courtship (*Othello,* Act I, Scene 3);
- one of Romeo's or Juliet's speeches in *Romeo and Juliet;*
- Major's speech in Chapter 1 of George Orwell's *Animal Farm;*
- Satan's speech to his defeated legions in the opening pages of Milton's *Paradise Lost;*
- a speech from a play or novel you have recently read.

Chapter 7

Resources
Special Helps for Writers

R1
WRITING
BUSINESS LETTERS

Know how to write an effective business letter.

When we write a business letter, we want to show that what we have to say matters to us. We want the letter to make a good impression when it arrives.

R1a
Form and Style

Use a conventional format and an effective style.

Whenever you can, type your letter. If your letter is written by hand, make sure your handwriting is easy to read. Use blue or black ink. For a typed letter, use standard typing paper. (Use onion-skin paper only for carbon copies.) Use unruled white paper for handwritten letters—not paper from a notebook. Avoid unusual abbreviations and other shortcuts. Do a letter over when smudges or erasures would cause it to make a poor first impression.

Remember:

(1) Follow a conventional format.   Study the following elements of a conventional business letter. Study these elements at work in the two full-page model business letters that accompany this section on pages 438 and 439:

HEADING AND OPENING PART

(1) RETURN ADDRESS: Write your return address at the top of the page, toward the right. On printed business stationery, the return address is usually part of the printed **letterhead.**

(2) DATE: Type the date directly under your address. With a printed letterhead, drop down several spaces and put the date on the right side.

(3) INSIDE ADDRESS: Drop down four or five spaces and put the address of the person or firm you are writing to. Put it in the conventional three- or four-line block, flush left:

```
Dr. Sybil Ericson
3897 N. Central Avenue
Chicago, Illinois  60603
```

④ GREETING:
(Salutation)

Put the greeting flush left, followed by a colon: "Dear Dr. Ericson:" Some people continue to use the traditional *Mrs.* or *Miss.* Others prefer the new *Ms.* for either. Sometimes you will write to an office or a firm without knowing the name of the person in charge. Here are some possible greetings that you may use in such a case:

Ladies and Gentlemen:	Dear Madam:
Gentlemen:	Dear Sir:
Ladies:	Dear Madam or Sir:

Here are two examples for the opening portion of two typical business letters. The first is from an individual who has typed the return address. The second, on the following page, is from an organization that uses a printed letterhead:

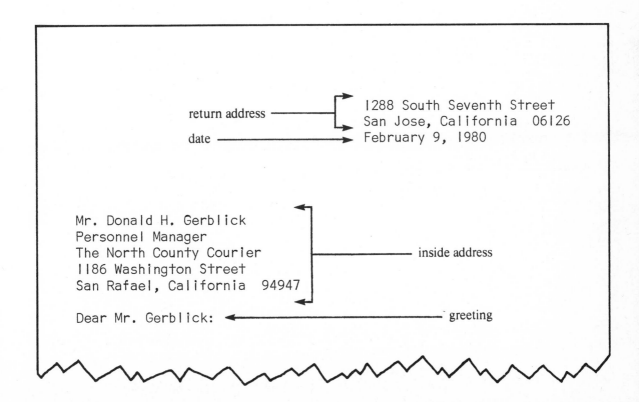

letterhead ——

INSTITUTE FOR BUSINESS WRITING

438 South Fulton Street
Grand Rapids, Michigan 49502

June 14, 1981

Mrs. Phyllis Quiroz
1382 South Park Boulevard
North Syracuse, New York 13212

Dear Mrs. Quiroz:

BODY OF
THE LETTER

⑤ SPACING: Single-space each paragraph of a typed letter. Use double-spacing between paragraphs.

⑥ INDENTATION: Many modern business letters now use a **block format.** Each paragraph starts flush left—it is not indented. But many people still prefer indented paragraphs, as in other kinds of writing. Whichever format you choose—block or indented—use it consistently throughout your letter.

⑦ MARGINS: Allow about a one-inch margin on both the left and right sides of the page.

CONCLUDING
PART

⑧ **CLOSING:** The concluding greeting is called the **complimentary closing.** Use "Sincerely," or "Sincerely yours," (note the comma at the end of the greeting).

⑨ **SIGNATURE:** Type or print your name below your signature. A representative of a firm or group will often include a title or a position below the name.

⑩ **NOTATIONS:** Initials in the left bottom corner are usually those of the writer, followed by those of the typist. Other notations may follow. Sometimes a letter you receive carries a note like "cc: Gloria Miller." This means that a carbon copy has gone to someone else who should know what was in the letter. "Encl." means that something has been enclosed with the letter. A price list or a poster may have been sent along.

Here is an example of the concluding part of a letter:

Sincerely yours,

Sylvia Gomez

Sylvia Gomez
Treasurer

SG:lbd
cc: Frank Chute
Encl.

A MODERN BUSINESS LETTER—Indented Format

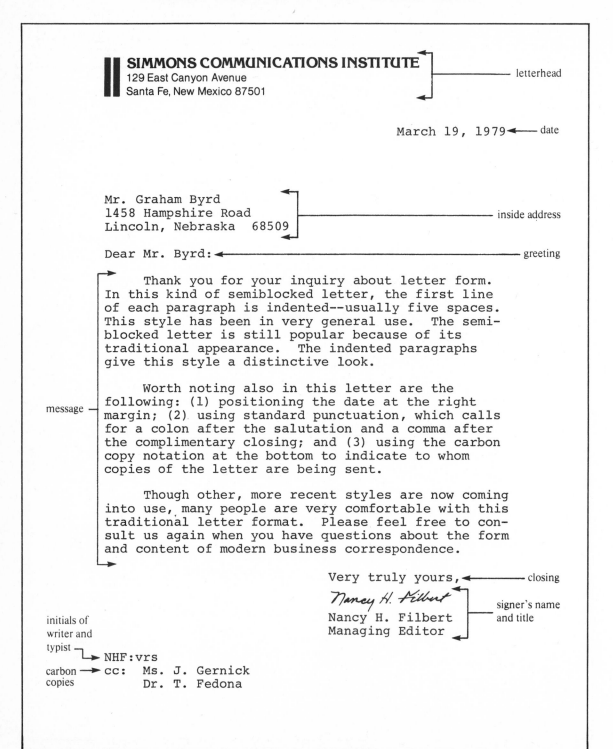

SIMMONS COMMUNICATIONS INSTITUTE
129 East Canyon Avenue
Santa Fe, New Mexico 87501

— letterhead

March 19, 1979 ◄— date

Mr. Graham Byrd
1458 Hampshire Road
Lincoln, Nebraska 68509

— inside address

Dear Mr. Byrd: ◄——————————————— greeting

message —

  Thank you for your inquiry about letter form.
In this kind of semiblocked letter, the first line
of each paragraph is indented--usually five spaces.
This style has been in very general use. The semiblocked letter is still popular because of its
traditional appearance. The indented paragraphs
give this style a distinctive look.

  Worth noting also in this letter are the
following: (1) positioning the date at the right
margin; (2) using standard punctuation, which calls
for a colon after the salutation and a comma after
the complimentary closing; and (3) using the carbon
copy notation at the bottom to indicate to whom
copies of the letter are being sent.

  Though other, more recent styles are now coming
into use, many people are very comfortable with this
traditional letter format. Please feel free to consult us again when you have questions about the form
and content of modern business correspondence.

Very truly yours, ◄—— closing

Nancy H. Filbert

Nancy H. Filbert
Managing Editor

— signer's name
and title

initials of
writer and
typist —┗► NHF:vrs
carbon —► cc: Ms. J. Gernick
copies   Dr. T. Fedona

A MODERN BUSINESS LETTER—Block Format

BUSINESS SERVICES INSTITUTE
1798 South 27 Street
Sacramento, California 95825

March 7, 1980

Ms. Frances Roeburn
Verran Business College
1200 Clinton Street
Charlotte, North Carolina 28202

SUBJECT: Kinds of Business Correspondence ◄——————— subject line

Dear Frances:

Not all business letters deal exclusively with impersonal business matters. Many business letters deal with the personal relations that are an important part of modern business life. For instance, a letter may congratulate someone on a promotion or on a successfully completed project.

Other letters may thank a business associate for some special assistance. They may carry informal invitations or the like. They may express regret for an unfortunate situation or explain an unfavorable decision.

Even letters that deal mainly with impersonal business matters often have a personal or human touch. A letter to someone who is personally known to the writer may conclude with a reference to a recent visit, to a recent sports event of interest to both, or the like. If the two people involved know each other well enough, they may use first names in both the greeting and the final signature.

Sincerely,

Rita F. Chandler

Rita F. Chandler
Associate Director

RFC: nn

postscript
(last-minute
addition)

PS: Short friendly or personal notes are of course often handwritten. They may not include the more formal parts of a letter: ◄◄┘ the inside address or the typed name and title of sender.

(2) Aim at a businesslike but friendly and positive tone. The main purpose of a business letter is to give clear and complete information. Tell the readers clearly what they need to know in order to understand the situation or to act on a request. To deal with business matters smoothly and effectively, however, you also have to use the right tone. In business as in other aspects of everyday life, much depends on how people feel they are being treated. A widely used guide to *Business English and Communication*[1] gives the following advice on how to maintain a friendly and positive tone:

- It costs nothing in money or time to be courteous and friendly when answering someone else's letter.
- Expressing anger is a luxury that business people cannot afford because it interferes with good relations.
- Patience in answering questions can be one of your most valuable assets.
- Few people understand that what they write or say may *imply* criticism. Study the following illustrations and learn how to avoid hinting at carelessness, negligence, or dishonesty.

NEGATIVE: You are not entitled to the 2 percent discount because you did not pay within 10 days. (*What are you trying to do, cheat us?*)

POSITIVE: You probably did not notice that your check was dated July 1 and that by then the discount period had expired. (*You are such a busy person that this minor slip is understandable.*)

NEGATIVE: We expect immediate delivery of this order. (*You've been pretty slack in the past, but this time we're demanding immediate service.*)

POSITIVE: Help us make a big sale of your merchandise by shipping this order immediately. (*You're noted for superior service, and you'll be helping us to sell your own merchandise.*)

ENVELOPE

(11) **RETURN ADDRESS:** Put your complete return address on the envelope in the left-hand corner.

(12) **RECEIVER:** Put the receiver's address on the right half of the envelope, about halfway down. Use the conventional block format. Check names and addresses here and in the letter itself carefully. Make sure there are no misspellings or mistakes.

---

[1]Marie M. Stewart and others, *Business English and Communication,* 5th ed. (New York: McGraw-Hill, 1978).

Here is a sample envelope:

```
Sheila Keilson
158 Rand Boulevard
Azusa, California  91702
```

```
                        Mrs. Eloise Benoit
                        Head, Public Relations
                        Hobby Services, Inc.
                        4378 Greatfield Drive
                        Northfield, Minnesota  55507
```

NOTE: Check for conventional punctuation. Check the following especially:

- Put a comma between *city and state:* Tacoma, Washington
- Put a comma between *title and office* when they appear on the same line: Manager, Products Division
- Put periods after *Mr., Ms., Mrs.* (but not *Miss*), *M.D.*
- Put a comma between *day and year* if the day follows the month: April 17, 1983 (but 17 April 1983).

Study the sample letters here and on the two following pages. Choose one or more of these as a model for a practice letter. Prepare the letter and the envelope, using real or fictitious names and addresses.

EXERCISE 1

1. A request for information or materials:

```
Dear Ms. Parker:

Last week you gave a set of records, "Typing to
Music," to the people who attended your press
conference on new discoveries in self-instruc-
tion typewriting.  Unfortunately, I was not
able to be at that conference, but I understand
that it was quite successful.
```

Several of our employees are brushing up on
their typewriting, and I have an idea that records such as the ones you introduced would be
very beneficial to them. At least, I would like
to listen to the records and prepare a decrip-
tion of them for our personnel bulletin. Would
you be able to give me a set?

I will be grateful if you can arrange to send
me these records.

Sincerely,

2. An invitation to participate in a program:

Dear Mr. Ramirez:

Your very interesting article in the August issue
of Young World magazine prompted me to write you.

Our Vocational Interests Club is having its annual
Career Night on Thursday, November 18. Our members
(we expect about 80 people in all) have expressed
a particular interest in hearing a lively talk on
"Better Letters." We are especially interested in
what employees can do to help employers with communication problems. Our program calls for a 30-
minute presentation from the speaker.

Would you be able to address our group on November
18? You can build your speech along the same lines
as your article, if you wish. Probably you know
that this night is the highlight of our year's
meetings, and we would be pleased to have you as
our guest speaker.

I hope you can accept this invitation, Mr. Ramirez.
If you can, I will write you again giving you all
the details--time, place, and complete program plans.

Sincerely,

3. A letter of refusal, rejection, or regret:

Dear Mr. Barton:

     Thank you for giving me an opportunity to read your manuscript, "Safari to Shangri-La." I have shared the manuscript with several assistants on the editorial staff, and they all found it enjoyable.

     Unfortunately, we find that our readers can take only two or three adventure stories each year; and our files are bulging with at least a dozen good adventure articles awaiting publication. I do not think it fair to you to keep your manuscript when we have no idea if and when we can use it. Therefore, I am returning the manuscript with the hope that you can sell it elsewhere.

               Sincerely,

4. A letter of thanks or appreciation:

Dear Connie:

     I just finished reading the new My Turn to Talk, prepared from papers written by students in senior English during the past year. I am glad you remembered to include me in your mailing list. The way the student writers responded to the challenge is impressive. My special favorites were the article on "Growing Up Italian Style" and the "Short Guide to Ethnic Cooking."

     Please congratulate all those who helped put the publication together. Keep up the good work.

              Sincerely,

    Collect some recent business letters addressed to you or to your family or friends. Bring them to class for discussion.

EXERCISE 2

R1b

The Letter of Application

Know how to write an effective letter of application.

One of the most important kinds of letters people write is the letter of application. When you apply for a job, try to include in your letter things that would show the following:

- you are familiar with the job or the area;
- you have had some previous experience;
- you have skills or training that would help;
- you would like the work;
- you would try to adjust to the employer's requirements concerning time, place, and the like;
- you would make every effort to appear for a personal interview.

Here is a summary of the instructions for writing the letter, as adapted from *Business English Essentials* (Gregg):

(1) Address your letter to a specific person in the organization if it is possible to obtain his or her name.

(2) Start with a summary of your special qualifications. This type of beginning gives the prospective employer an immediate indication of your ability and training. If these qualifications seem to be what is needed, the employer will read further.

(3) In the body of the letter, offer support for the statements made in the opening paragraph. Emphasize the highlights of your educational background and experience that are related to the job. You may also indicate why you would like to be employed by the firm to which you are applying.

(4) List references. You may need to supply the names, titles, and addresses of **references,** leaving to the interested employer the task of obtaining the desired information about your character, training, experience, and work habits.

Before using a person's name as a reference, request permission to do so. This permission may be obtained in person, by telephone, or by a letter. (Enclose a return envelope or postcard with a letter.)

(5) Prepare a written summary of your qualifications. This summary—called a **résumé,** a *data sheet,* or a *personal record*— usually includes a statement of your education, your employment record (experience), a list of references, and other useful data. You may use a résumé to accompany a letter of application, to present to an employer at an interview, or to assist you in filling out an employment application form.

Study the following model letter. Then write an imaginary letter of application for a job that you think you may be interested in in the future. Include qualifications that by then you hope to have.

1517 Fairlane Avenue
Northville, Michigan 48167
September 5, 1980

Mr. Louis B. Mendoza
Timely Fashions, Inc.
110 Wentworth Street
Detroit, Michigan 48208

Dear Mr. Mendoza:

Your advertisement in the Sunday, September 4, issue
of The Detroit News for an assistant to your fashion
coordinator describes just the sort of position for which
my training and experience have prepared me.

Two jobs in retail fashion shops and evening courses
at the Merchandising Institute have qualified me to work
for a top-level clothing house like Timely Fashions.

As a member of Hall's College Fashion Board, I helped
select the styles shown in their College Shop and also
modeled during their "Back-to-School" weeks. Also, working
for the sportswear buyer at Franklin's helped me learn a
great deal about fashion trends.

You will find additional information about my qualifications in the enclosed resume. On Thursday and Friday,
September 15 and 16, I shall be in Detroit and would appreciate your granting me an interview during that time.

Sincerely yours,

Pat T. Lorne

Enclosure

—instructions and letter adapted from *Business English Essentials* (Gregg)

Résumé

Pat T. Lorne
1517 Fairlane Avenue
Northville, Michigan 48167
Telephone: (313) 237-1710

POSITION SOUGHT: Assistant in merchandising.

EXPERIENCE: Franklin Shops, Wayne, Michigan. August, 19--, to present. Assistant to buyer of sportswear. Supervisor: Mrs. Janice Davidson. Duties included comparison shopping, producing bulletins for members of staff, and helping in the preparation of advertisements.

Hall's Department Store, Wayne, Michigan. August and September, 19--. Member of College Fashion Board. Supervisor: Mr. B. G. Thomas.

The Fashion Center, Northville, Michigan. Part time, 19-- and 19--. Salesclerk in the Junior Shop. Supervisor: Barbara Jameson.

EDUCATION: Merchandising Institute, Wayne, Michigan. Completed one year of evening school courses in Textiles, Retailing, and Fashion Trends in June, 19--.

Ellis College, Wayne, Michigan. Awarded certificate upon completion of one-year business program in June, 19--. Shorthand--120 w.p.m.; typing--65 w.p.m.

Memorial High School, Northville, Michigan. Graduated with honors in June, 19--, upon completion of college preparatory course.

REFERENCES: Dr. Marion J. Downes, Head, Department of Office Education, Ellis College, Wayne, Michigan 48184

Mr. Francis Graves, 819 East Scott Road, Northville, Michigan 48167

Ms. Estelle Lincoln, 63 Oakwood Terrace, Northville, Michigan 48167

—adapted from Henderson-Voiles, *Business English Essentials* (5th Ed.)

Know how to use a library.

An effective user of the library knows how to look for information and how to use the information to advantage. Knowing how to use a library begins with learning how to use the card catalogue.

Know how to use the card catalogue.

The card catalogue is the central inventory of the books in the library. Each book is listed on several cards: one alphabetized by author, one by title, and one by subject. If you were interested in books on Puritans, you would look for the *subject cards* under this heading.

The **call numbers** help you or the librarian find books on the shelves. Nonfiction or *factual* books are arranged numerically rather than alphabetically.

Two numbering systems are used:

• The **Dewey decimal system** is one classification system. Dewey classified nonfiction into ten major categories and assigned numbers as follows:

000–099 General reference works: dictionaries, encyclopedias, etc. These are almost always kept apart from the other nonfiction books.
100–199 Philosophy, psychology, ethics
200–299 Religion (including mythology)
300–399 Social sciences: immigration, economics, government, education, folklore
400–499 Language
500–599 Pure sciences: physics, chemistry, botany, etc.

Within these hundreds, groups of ten form subdivisions of the large area. For instance, 970–979 is North American history; 980–989 is South American history. Each digit within these groups of ten subdivides further: For instance, 972 covers the history of Mexico; 973 the history of the United States. A decimal added after these three numbers helps divide American history into periods: Colonial history is 973.2. A book dealing with the French and Indian wars during colonial times may be classified as 973.26.

• The **Library of Congress system** divides books into categories identified by letters of the alphabet. It then uses additional letters and numerals to subdivide each main category.

On the following page are the letters used by the Library of Congress classification system:

A	General Works	M	Music
B	Philosophy, Religion	N	Fine Arts
C	History	P	Language and Literature
D	History and Topography (except America)	Q	Science
		R	Medicine
E	America (general)— U.S. (general)	S	Agriculture (plant and animal industry)
F	United States (local) and America (except U.S.)	T	Technology
		U	Military Science
G	Geography—Anthropology	V	Naval Science
H	Social Sciences	Z	Bibliography and Library Science
J	Political Science		

More specific categories are shown by a second letter after the first. Here are some specific categories under the general category of Language and Literature:

PA Classical languages and literature
PC Romance languages
PD Germanic languages
PE English

Numbers further subdivide the specific categories. The complete call number usually appears on three lines at the upper left-hand corner of the catalogue card. It consists of the pair of letters followed by a series of numbers, the year of publication, and an author, or book, number. The author, or book, number consists of the first letter of the author's last name followed by a number. Study the following sample card:

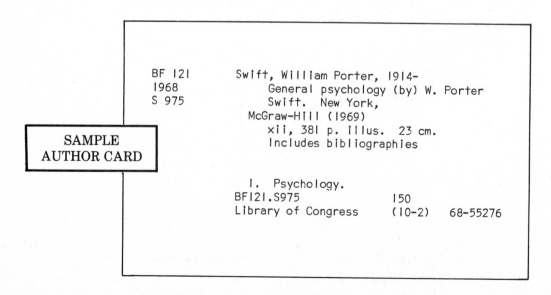

```
SAMPLE
AUTHOR CARD
```

```
BF 121        Swift, William Porter, 1914-
1968              General psychology (by) W. Porter
S 975         Swift.   New York,
          McGraw-Hill (1969)
                  xii, 381 p. illus.  23 cm.
              Includes bibliographies


              I.  Psychology.
          BF121.S975                150
          Library of Congress       (10-2)   68-55276
```

Know how to use guides to articles in periodicals.

Magazines of all kinds, since they are published daily, weekly, or monthly, are usually the best sources of current information. To update your information on any topic, consult one of the following indexes to periodicals:

- *Readers' Guide to Periodical Literature*—Supplements are issued monthly and eventually bound into volumes covering a two-year period. About 110 periodicals are indexed. Each article indexed is referred to by author and by subject.
- *The Social Sciences and Humanities Index* (formerly *International Index to Periodicals*)—This index is organized like the *Readers' Guide*, but it also covers non-American periodicals.
- *New York Times Index*—This index covers the contents of the last edition of each day's *Times,* America's most comprehensive newspaper. The index goes back to 1913. In many libraries, *The New York Times* is kept on microfilm.

The most widely used and most generally useful of these indexes is the *Readers' Guide*. The most recent issues of the *Readers' Guide* appear in booklet form. Back issues are hardbound in volumes covering two years. If you are looking for articles on Puritans, locate that entry in the alphabetical listing of subjects in the *Readers' Guide*. There you will find the titles and authors of articles dealing with the subject.

Entries give the following information: article title (without quotation marks); magazine (often abbreviated—key is found in the front of *Guide*); volume; pages; date of issue.

Sample subject entry:

POSTAGE stamps
    Natural world of the post office; natural his-
    tory theme on stamps.   A. Ross.   ii   Natur
    Hist 77:28-31 Ja '68

Sample author entry:

ROSS, Arnold
    Natural world of the post office. Natur Hist
    77:28-31 Ja '68

Know how to make use of reference books.

A large library has a wealth of general and specialized reference books:

ENCYCLOPEDIAS: Encyclopedias are attempts to summarize all of the world's knowledge between the covers of a few volumes. Although they cannot provide you with exhaustive current information, they can serve as jumping-off points for your research.

The information contained in reliable encyclopedias is assembled from various sources. Brief articles on relatively unimportant topics may be written by editors on the staff of the encyclopedia. On the other hand, an article on a major historical figure or scientific subject will generally be quite substantial and will be signed with the initials of the authority who wrote it. In some volume of the encyclopedia (usually at the beginning of volume one), there will be a list of each contributor's full name and title.

In addition to providing the researcher with an overview of a topic, a good encyclopedia usually provides an extensive bibliography at the end of each signed article. This bibliography can serve as a guide at the beginning of your research. Checking the books listed there helps you to begin your research.

The best-known multivolume encyclopedias are:

- *Encyclopaedia Britannica*—Kept current with an annual volume, *Britannica Book of the Year*
- *Encyclopedia Americana*—Kept current with an annual volume, *The Americana Annual*

SPECIALIZED REFERENCE BOOKS: In research, the need for specialized information arises frequently. There is a specialized reference book for almost every area of study. The following is but a partial list, containing books that you probably need most often.

BIOGRAPHY

- *Current Biography*—This is probably the best source of information on well-known people, containing extensive biographies on eminent contemporary Americans. About 300 to 400 are added each year.
- *Webster's Biographical Dictionary*—This work contains more than 40,000 biographical entries of famous people of all times and nationalities.
- *World Biography*—This book contains about 15,000 biographical sketches of living persons throughout the world, with special emphasis upon Americans and Europeans.

GEOGRAPHIC INFORMATION

- *The Columbia Lippincott Gazetteer of the World*—This reference work contains about 130,000 entries on virtually every geographical place name of any importance in the world.
- *Webster's Geographical Dictionary*—This is an alphabetical listing of about 40,000 place names throughout the world.

LANGUAGE STUDY

- *Roget's International Thesaurus*—A dictionary of synonyms grouped under subject headings.
- *Webster's Dictionary of Synonyms*—This work lists synonyms and antonyms in a dictionary format. It clearly distinguishes shades of meaning.

STATISTICS

- *The World Almanac*—This and other general almanacs are store-houses of general information.
- *Statistical Abstract of the United States*—This work contains a wealth of statistical information on all phases of American life.

NOTE: Since there are so many reference books, the need for a reference book on reference books is obvious. One of the most convenient to use is *How and Where to Look It Up* by Robert W. Murphy (McGraw-Hill). In addition to listing thousands of reference works under appropriate topics, the book contains advice on researching a topic.

Know how to draw on supplementary library resources.

R2d

Other Library Resources

Here are sources of material available in most libraries:

(1) **Newspapers**—The most logical source of up-to-date information is the daily or weekly newspaper. Most high schools subscribe to the local papers, the Sunday edition of *The New York Times,* and the *Christian Science Monitor.* Today's or this week's copy can usually be found hanging on a rack in the library. There is an index for *The New York Times,* often found in large libraries. The *Christian Science Monitor* is indexed, and therefore the copies are apt to be stored for a few years at least.

A very useful paper is *Facts on File,* a weekly summary of world news indexed by topic and person for the year. One index covers January to September. A supplement is issued for the remaining three months.

(2) **Current Magazines**—For material on subjects of current interest, go to the open racks of magazines and look in the current issues. Periodicals such as *Time, Newsweek,* and *U.S. News and World Report* tell about events almost as they happen. Others such as *The Nation, Harper's,* and *The Atlantic* offer commentary on current events but also treat topics of more long-range concern. Depending upon the nature of the subject, you might look into specialized magazines such as *Science News* or *Psychology Today.*

(3) **The vertical file**—Use the vertical file to locate miscellaneous printed material. The vertical file is an informal collection of pamphlets, newspaper clippings, and other forms of printed material that cannot be conveniently arranged on a shelf. It is stored in manila envelopes or folders and alphabetized in the manner of letter files in a business office.

(4) **Microfilm**—Newspapers, magazines, and books are now often stored in miniature form. You can read them by using a special viewer. Find out what material your library has available in this special form.

(5) **Interlibrary loan**—Some high school libraries belong to an association that exchanges books and other material from one library to another. If you know of a book, magazine, paper, or filmstrip that would help you in your research but that is not in your library, your librarian may be able to borrow it from another institution.

EXERCISE 1

Turn to the card catalogue of your library for answers to the following questions:

1. Are there any *subject cards* that would help you find books on one of the following?

   - Egyptian pyramids or other aspects of ancient Egyptian civilization;
   - Armenian history, culture, or religion;
   - the Maya or Inca civilizations of Central and South America;
   - Polynesian culture and history.

   Prepare a brief report on how many and what kinds of books are listed in the card catalogue.

2. How many books are listed by one of the following *authors:* John Dewey, Margaret Mead, Rachel Carson, Isaac Asimov, Loren Eiseley? Write down the title and the date of first publication of at least three books by your author.

3. Which of the following books are listed alphabetically by *title?* (Remember that words like *the* and *a* are ignored in alphabetizing titles.)

   - *Black Elk Speaks*
   - *The Overloaded Ark*
   - *Coming of Age in America*
   - *Children of Crisis*
   - *The Joys of Yiddish*
   - *The Uses of Enchantment*
   - *A Good Man Is Hard to Find*

In one or more recent volumes of the *Readers' Guide,* find at least three articles on one of the following subjects. Write out all information the *Guide* gives about each article—spell out the full name of the magazine, and the like.

EXERCISE 2

- drinking water—desalinization, purification, and the like;
- solar energy;
- antique cars;
- damming our wild rivers;
- country singers and country music.

What's in an encyclopedia? Report briefly on the information you can find on one of the following topics:

EXERCISE 3

- the early history of the Mormons;
- orthodox and reform Judaism;
- the Amish;
- the Penitentes of New Mexico;
- Greek Orthodox Christianity.

Find a biographical dictionary. Report on its treatment of one of the following:

EXERCISE 4

- W. E. B. DuBois;
- Malcolm X;
- Booker T. Washington;
- Martin Luther King;
- Harriet Tubman.

Make full use of the information provided in a good dictionary.

R3

USING A DICTIONARY

Dictionaries are important reference tools. Not only is a dictionary useful in checking the spelling, pronunciation, and meanings of a word, but it is also helpful in establishing the meanings of words during their history. The following are very comprehensive **unabridged** dictionaries:

- *Webster's Third New International Dictionary of the English Language* (Merriam-Webster)
- *Funk and Wagnalls New Standard Dictionary of the English Language*
- *The Random House Dictionary of the English Language*
- *The Oxford English Dictionary* (13 volumes)—This dictionary will be found only in larger libraries. It defines words historically, offering illustrations of meanings during various periods. *The Shorter Oxford English Dictionary* is based on the O.E.D.

Several of the best-known desk dictionaries are abridged versions of more comprehensive dictionaries. Authoritative collegiate dictionaries include:

Webster's New Collegiate Dictionary (Merriam-Webster)
The American Heritage Dictionary
Webster's New World Dictionary of the American Language
The Random House Dictionary, College Edition
Funk and Wagnalls Standard College Dictionary

Dictionaries intended especially for high school students are the following:

Webster's New Students Dictionary
Thorndike Barnhart Advanced Dictionary
Macmillan Dictionary

A dictionary offers the following information about every entry:

(1) **Spelling**—Some words have *more than one* correct spelling. Example: *grey* or *gray*. The plural of *ski* is given as "*skis* or *ski* also *skiis*," meaning that *ski* or *skis* is equally common but that *skiis* is less often used. Different spellings may be listed as separate entries.

(2) **Pronunciation**—There is *no one standard system* for representing sounds. Each major dictionary uses its own way of indicating English pronunciation. The symbols used are explained, with examples, at the beginning of the book, and usually at the bottom of every page. Pronunciation is often indicated in parentheses, as follows:

grav·i·ta·tion (grav'ətā'shən)

kin·der·gar·ten (kin'dər gärt'ən, ·gärd'ən)

pas·sage (pas'ij)

NOTE: In some dictionaries, the stress marks (accents) come *after* the stressed syllable: **gra·vy** (grā'vē). In others, they come *before* the stressed syllable: **gra·vy** \'grā-vē\.

(3) **Part of speech**—The grammatical status of a word usually appears in abbreviated form after its pronunciation: n. (noun); v. or vb. (verb); v.t. (transitive verb); v.i. (intransitive verb); adj. (adjective); adv. (adverb); conj. (conjunction or connective); prep. (preposition); pron. (pronoun); interj. (interjection—words like *Ah* and *Oh*). Often a word is used in more than one way.

KINDS OF DICTIONARY INFORMATION

pil·grim (pil′grim, -grəm), *n.* **1.** a person who journeys, esp. a long distance, to some sacred place as an act of devotion. **2.** a traveler or wanderer. **3.** *(cap.)* one of the Pilgrim Fathers. [early ME *pilegrim, pelegrim*; c. OFris *pilegrim*, MLG *pelegrim*, OHG *piligrim*, Icel *pīlagrīmr*, all < ML *pelegrīnus*, dissimilated var. of L *peregrīnus* alien < *peregrē* abroad = *per-* PER- + *-egr-* (comb. form of *ager* field; see ACRE) + *-e* adv. suffix] **—Syn. 2.** wayfarer, sojourner.

Alternate pronunciation
Capitalization style
Synonym list

Pil·sen (pil′zən), *n.* a city in Bohemia, in W Czechoslovakia. 141,736 (1963). Czech, **Plzeň.**

Geographical entry (location, population and date, foreign name)

pin (pin), *n., v.,* **pinned, pin·ning.** —*n.* **1.** a short, slender piece of metal with a point at one end and a head at the other, for fastening things together. **2.** a small, slender, often pointed piece of wood, metal, etc., used to fasten, support, or attach things. **3.** any of various forms of fasteners, ornaments, or badges consisting essentially or partly of a pointed or penetrating wire or shaft (often used in combination): *a fraternity pin; a tiepin.* **4.** a short metal rod, as a linchpin, driven through the holes of adjacent parts, as a hub and an axle, to keep them together. **5.** a short cylindrical rod or tube, as a wristpin or crankpin, joining two parts so as to permit them to move in one plane relative to each other. **6.** the part of a cylindrical key stem that enters a lock. **7.** a clothespin. **8.** a hairpin. **9.** See **rolling pin.** **10.** a peg, nail, or stud marking the center of a target. **11.** *Bowling.* one of the rounded wooden clubs set up as the target in tenpins, duckpins, etc. **12.** *Golf.* the flagstaff that identifies a hole. **13.** Usually, **pins.** *Informal.* the legs. **14.** *Music.* peg (def. 2). **15.** *Wrestling.* a fall. **16.** *Naut.* See **belaying pin.** **17.** a very small amount; a trifle. —*v.t.* **18.** to fasten or attach with or as with a pin or pins. **19.** to hold fast in a spot or position. **20.** to give one's fraternity pin to (a girl) as a pledge of one's fondness or attachment. **21.** *Wrestling.* to obtain a fall over one's opponent. **22. pin down, a.** to bind or hold to a course of action, a promise, etc. **b.** to define with clarity and precision: *to pin down a vague intuition.* **23. pin something on someone,** *Slang.* to blame someone for something on the basis of real or manufactured evidence. [ME *pinne,* OE *pinn* peg; c. D *pin,* G *Pinne,* Icel *pinni;* ? akin to MIr *benn* (for *bend*), now *beann* peak, steeple, gable, etc.]

Verb forms (past tense and past participle; present participle)
Cross reference to multiple-word entry
Usage label
Cross reference to one word entry
Idiomatic phrase

pin·y (pī′nē), *adj.,* **pin·i·er, pin·i·est. 1.** abounding in, covered with, or consisting of pine trees. **2.** pertaining to or suggestive of pine trees: *a piny fragrance.* Also, **piney.**

Adjective forms (comparative, superlative)
Example phrase

Pi·rith·o·üs (pī rith′ō əs), *n.* *Class. Myth.* a prince of the Lapithae and friend of Theseus, in whose company he attempted to abduct Persephone from Hades.

Mythological entry

pk, *pl.* **pks.** (in dry measure) peck.

Abbreviation

plan (plan), *n., v.,* **planned, plan·ning.** —*n.* **1.** a method of action or procedure. **2.** a design or scheme of arrangement: *an elaborate plan for seating guests.* **3.** a project or definite purpose: *plans for the future.* **4.** a drawing made to scale to represent the top view or a horizontal section of a structure or a machine. **5.** a map or diagram: *a plan of the dock area.* **6.** (in perspective drawing) one of several planes in front of a represented object, and perpendicular to the line between the object and the eye. —*v.t.* **7.** to arrange or project a plan or scheme for (any work, enterprise, or proceeding): *to plan a new recreation center; to plan one's vacation.* **8.** to draw or make a plan of, as a building. —*v.i.* **9.** to make a plan: *to plan for one's retirement.* [< F: plane, plan, groundwork, scheme < L *plān(us)* level *planum* level ground. See PLANE¹, PLAIN¹] **—Syn. 1.** plot, formula, system. PLAN, PROJECT, DESIGN, SCHEME imply a formulated method of doing something. PLAN refers to any method of thinking out acts and purposes beforehand: *What are your plans for today?* A PROJECT is a proposed or tentative plan, often elaborate or extensive: *an irrigation project.* DESIGN suggests art, dexterity, or craft (sometimes evil and selfish) in the elaboration and execution of a plan, and often tends to emphasize the purpose in view: *a disturbance brought about by design.* A SCHEME is apt to be either a speculative, possibly impractical, plan, or a selfish or dishonest one: *a scheme to swindle someone.*

Parts of speech
Consecutive definition numbers
Word History
Synonym study
Example in synonym study

—from *The Random House Dictionary, College Edition*

(4) **Changing forms**

• *Plurals:* If the plural of a word is unusual, it will be listed after the letters *pl.* Example: "*moose* (mōōs) n. pl. moose."

• *Past tense and participles:* If a verb is regular, that is, if it adds *–ed* for its past tense and past participle *(walk, walked, had walked, walking),* these forms are usually not listed. If it is irregular, the dictionary gives the variations; for example, "*take* (tāk), v., *took, taken, taking.*" Sometimes there is more than one past tense; for example, "*hang* (hang) v. *hung* or (esp. for capital punishment and suicide) *hanged; hanging.*"

• *Comparative or superlative:* No forms are given for adjectives and adverbs that are regularly compared *(small, smaller, smallest,* or *hostile, more hostile, most hostile).* However, if the adjective or adverb is irregular, the comparative and superlative are given in the dictionary; for example, "*little, less, least.*"

• *Other forms:* Adjectives and adverbs that follow logically from nouns in spelling and meaning may be put at the end of the noun entry. For example, if you look for the word *sarcastically,* you may find *sarcasm* as an entry. At the end of that entry may be *sarcastic* and *sarcastically.* Nouns directly formed from an adjective may be put at the end of the adjective entry. For example, under the entry *inseparable,* we find *inseparability* and *inseparableness,* as well as the adverb *inseparably.* Some words beginning with *in–* or *un–* and having a negative meaning are alphabetically included in the entries. Others whose meanings are directly opposite to their root words are listed in columns either under *in–* and *un–* or at the bottom of several pages of *in–* or *un–* words.

(5) **Definition**—Most words have several meanings and, when used with other words, become expressions with still other meanings. The word *take* used as a transitive verb may have nineteen numbered definitions; as an intransitive verb, eight more. Then there are expressions using *take* as a part of a familiar **idiom,** such as *take account of, take heart, take place,* etc. A definition with several meanings may give the oldest one first—the original sense of the word—and then others chronologically. Or it may give the most common meaning first.

(6) **Status labels**—Be alert for italicized words or abbreviations before definitions. Some of the common ones are:

OBS.	Obsolete. Has not been standard usage for at least 200 years.
ARCHAIC	Old-fashioned. Sometimes used now but not current modern usage.

SLANG	Extremely informal. Not acceptable for serious speech or writing.
SUBSTAND. or NONSTAND.	Not acceptable in standard English.
DIAL.	Dialect. Regional (sometimes with part of country given).
POETIC or LITERARY	Not used in ordinary conversation or writing.
COLLOQ.	Informal, everyday speech and writing.

(7) **Etymology**—Dictionaries give the derivation of words —they tell us where words came from and how they grew. The entry for *eerie* in *Webster's New Collegiate Dictionary* adds in square brackets: [ME *eri,* fr OE *earg* cowardly, wretched]. ME stands for *Middle English,* fr means *from,* and OE is *Old English.* An Old English word *earg* evolved into a Middle English word *eri* and then into our modern word *eerie.* Along with spelling change came meaning change, since the word no longer has the meaning of *cowardly.*

(8) **Synonyms and antonyms**—At the end of an entry you may find the abbreviation *Syn.* For example, after the word *center* we find "*Syn. 1. See middle.*" This means that *middle* is like *center* in some, but not necessarily all, of its meanings. After *Syn.* there may be the abbreviation *Ant.* An antonym is a word that means the opposite or almost the opposite of the entry. For example, in the entry *large* we find "*Ant. 1. small.*"

(9) **Additional information**—In the main part of the collegiate-sized dictionary are often found trademarks, biographical names, mythical characters, historical events, geographical names, medical terms, and scientific names of plants and animals. Some of these, however, may appear with separate kinds of information at the front or back of the book. First and most important, there is always information on that particular dictionary and how to use it. There may be as well:

- a guide to punctuation
- abbreviations (sometimes included in main part)
- signs and symbols (mathematics, music, etc.)
- proofreaders' marks
- biographical names
- geographical names
- given names (with meanings)
- colleges and universities with locations
- weights and measures

EXERCISE 1

Look up the following words. Check spelling, pronunciation, word class (how used in a sentence), other forms (like the plural of nouns), meaning, and history. Note especially if there is more than one way to spell, pronounce, or use the word.

1. formidable
2. program
3. antenna
4. Halloween
5. articulate
6. arithmetic
7. bayou
8. data
9. itinerary
10. alphabet

EXERCISE 2

Check a desk dictionary for the answers to the following:

1. *Pronunciation:* What do you learn about the pronunciation of *St. Louis, Worcestershire, New Orleans, San Jose, Prague?*
2. *Grammatical Information:* What are the plurals of *phenomenon, species, stimulus, index, analysis?*
3. *Word History:* What is the meaning and history of each of the following: *disparage, Sinn Fein, insomnia, concord, gargoyle?*
4. *Encyclopedic Information:* How much do you learn about each of the following: Mary Stuart, Montezuma, Annapurna, Jonas E. Salk, Mount Olympus?
5. *New Words:* Does your dictionary include all of the following: video tape, zip code, sun belt, microwave, android?

R4
TAKING TESTS

Make sure that tests show what you know and what you can do.

Tests are everywhere in today's world. The more you know about them, the better you will be able to handle them in a businesslike way. Remember the following advice:

(1) Read instructions or directions carefully. What exactly are you asked to do? Look for the key words in the directions you are given. For instance, are you asked to *list, outline,* or *summarize?* Are you asked to restate someone else's opinion, or to state your own? Are you asked to find a word with the *same* meaning (synonym) or one with the *opposite* meaning (antonym)?

(2) Budget your time. Often a test shows how much time you should spend on each part. Do not allow any part or any item on a test to use up *too much* time. Do not become flustered by something difficult or confusing. Move on—return to the difficult item or the difficult part later if you have the time.

(3) Use common sense about guessing. Some tests encourage guessing. If only *right* answers are counted for test results, even

wild guessing cannot hurt. If a test states, "Wrong answers will be penalized," wild guessing is not advisable.

(4) Make some notes before answering essay questions. Even though you may be under time pressure, pause to think before you begin to answer any essay question. While you are thinking, jot down a few key ideas. Take a moment to put those ideas in some logical or chronological order. Prepare a rough working outline.

(5) Allow time to proofread essay tests. A comma where a period should be, a misspelled word, a "their" for a "there"—these may seem to be small things. But little errors like these make the writer appear careless or badly prepared. Take a minute or so before you hand in a test, and correct any errors you may find.

Know the different ways tests measure your knowledge of vocabulary.

Tests of vocabulary occur in batteries of tests from kindergarten through the graduate schools of universities. They are used in tests that are given to applicants for many kinds of jobs. In almost all intelligence tests, the verbal part of the test measures vocabulary. The most common tests used by colleges and universities for admission purposes include measures of the applicants' vocabulary.

The *Scholastic Aptitude Test,* published by the College Entrance Examination Board, is widely used by colleges and universities in selecting the freshman class from the group of applicants. This test is commonly called the "S-A-T" and is frequently written as SAT. The SAT in recent years has used three kinds of test items to measure vocabulary. These sections are called: Antonyms, Analogies, and Sentence Completion. The verbal part of the SAT also measures reading comprehension. It gives from five to seven reading passages, with five questions for each.

Be prepared to handle the following kinds of test items:

(1) SYNONYMS

The most common vocabulary tests ask you to find **synonyms.** For a test word, you select the word that is closest to it in meaning. In each of the following examples, the answer has been circled:

1. *conflagration*	(a. fire)	b. obedience	c. patriotism	d. penitence
2. *lethargic*	a. ignorant	(b. listless)	c. plebeian	d. supernatural
3. *censure*	a. complain	b. eliminate	c. irritate	(d. rebuke)

② ANTONYMS

Vocabulary tests often ask you to find **antonyms.** An antonym test makes you look for a word with the *opposite* meaning. The Antonyms section of the SAT has directions like the following:

> *DIRECTIONS: In each test item, there is a word in capital letters followed by five answer choices. From these five choices select the one whose meaning is opposite to the meaning of the word in capital letters.*

In each of the following sample test items, the correct answer has been circled:

A EXPEDIENT	B PROLIFIC
(1) ambitious	(1) blustering
(2) compassionate	(2) colorful
(3) complex	(3) impetuous
(4) impractical	(4) triumphant
(5) slow	(5) unproductive
C OBSEQUIOUS	D GREGARIOUS
(1) disrespectful	(1) colossal
(2) fashionable	(2) dangerous
(3) observant	(3) expensive
(4) secretive	(4) friendly
(5) servile	(5) unsociable

In item B, the word *prolific* means fruitful or productive. The only word opposite in meaning to *prolific* is *unproductive.* In item C, the word *obsequious* means fawning or attentive in a servile manner. A person who is not obsequious would be one who shows no respect. An antonym of obsequious then can be *disrespectful.*

NOTE: Often the author of antonym items will include a synonym along with the answer choices. In item C, *servile* is a synonym for *obsequious.* In item D, *friendly* is often considered a synonym for *gregarious.* In an antonym test, however, these synonyms are *wrong* answers.

③ ANALOGIES

Two things are "analogous" if they are built the same way or work the same way. The Analogies section of the SAT has directions like those shown on the following page:

DIRECTIONS: Each test item contains a pair of words in capital letters. Try to establish a relationship between these two words. Then from the five answer choices select the pair of words whose relationship to each other is the same as that between the two words in capital letters.

In each of the following sample items, the correct answer has been circled:

E ONLOOKER : SPECTATOR : :	F EYE : VISUAL : :
(1) band : parade	(1) blind : deaf
(2) football : soccer	(2) (ear : auditory)
(3) player : fan	(3) glasses : spectacles
(4) (skill : dexterity)	(4) mouth : nose
(5) telescope : binoculars	(5) see : look
G OAK : TREE : :	H SWAM : SWAMP : :
(1) elm : maple	(1) damp : dam
(2) leaves : branches	(2) (dim : dime)
(3) strong : sturdy	(3) marsh : water
(4) (violet : flower)	(4) paddle : boat
(5) wood : board	(5) walk : land

- In sample E, you need words that are related to each other in the same way that *onlooker* and *spectator* are related. Since *onlooker* and *spectator* mean the same thing, the correct answer must also be a pair of synonyms. The only pair of synonyms is *skill* and *dexterity*.

- In sample F, the word *eye* is an organ of the body, and *visual* describes something that the eye can sense. The correct answer then must be an organ of the body and a word describing something that that organ can sense. An *ear* is an organ of the body, and *auditory* means something we can hear.

- In sample G, *oak* is a kind of *tree*. The only pair of words with a similar relationship is *violet : flower*. A violet is a kind of flower.

- In sample H, the word *swamp* is the same word as *swam* with only one letter added. Notice how the test includes some false leads. Although *damp* is the same as *dam* with a *-p* added. these words are not in the right order. Or you might think the relationship of the capital words is this: some things swam in the swamp. A similar relationship may be: some things *walked* on *land*. This answer choice is not correct, because the tense is wrong for *walk*. The correct answer to H is *dim : dime,* because the second word adds only a final *-e* to the first word.

④ SENTENCE COMPLETION

This kind of test item asks you to find the choices that would best fill the blank spaces in a sentence. Some of the wrong choices will make nonsense of a sentence. Others will fit—but badly. The right choices will fit into the context of the sentence, with the right shades of meaning.

The directions for the Sentence Completion section of the SAT are similar to the following:

> *DIRECTIONS: In each of the following sentences, one or two words are missing. Select the answer that fits the sentence best.*

In the following examples, the right choices have been circled:

J   Many _____ steps had to be planned and carried out in order to _____ the new project.
   (1) complex . . . . tolerate
   (2) indefinite . . . . nullify
   (3) preliminary . . . . initiate
   (4) simple . . . . terminate
   (5) unexpected . . . . define

K   Because the resulting fumes were highly _____ , steps were taken immediately for the _____ of the experiments.
   (1) expensive . . . . hiding
   (2) gaseous . . . . ratification
   (3) toxic . . . . termination
   (4) visible . . . . subtraction
   (5) explosive . . . . increase

L   The pilot _____ guided the ship through the _____ waters.
   (1) alone . . . . ocean
   (2) cleverly . . . . quiet
   (3) gingerly . . . . treacherous
   (4) slowly . . . . endless
   (5) truculently . . . . strange

M   We could barely hear the soloists because the hall had poor

   _____ .
   (1) acoustics
   (2) flooring
   (3) implementation
   (4) managers
   (5) instruments

Study the clues that guide us to these correct answers:

- Item J tests your knowledge of the meaning of *preliminary* and *initiate*. *Preliminary* means "leading up to" and *initiate* means "begin." It makes sense that some steps, required to lead up to the start of a new project, need to be planned and carried out.

- Item K requires you to know that *toxic* means "poisonous" and *termination* means "ending." We are likely to stop something that results in poisonous fumes. In the other answer choices, at least one of the two words does not fit. In (1), fumes are not likely to be expensive. In (2) and (4), it makes no sense to *ratify* or to *subtract* experiments.

- Item L has only one pair of words that go together to make sense of the sentence. *Gingerly* means very cautiously, and *treacherous* means untrustworthy. If a ship is sailing in unreliable waters, the pilot should be very cautious in guiding the ship.

- In item M, the word *acoustics* stands for the architectural qualities that determine how good the sound is in an auditorium. When the acoustics are bad, the audience cannot hear well.

I. SYNONYMS

SAMPLE TEST A

In each test item, there is a word in capital letters followed by five answer choices. From these five choices select the one whose meaning is most nearly like the meaning of the word in capitals. Write the letter of your choice in the space next to the item number.

____ 1. AMORPHOUS
    A excessive
    B exuberant
    C prodigious
    D shapeless
    E sympathetic

____ 2. COSMIC
    A chronic
    B cosmetic
    C incidental
    D universal
    E urban

____ 3. INVINCIBLE
    A hypercritical
    B hypocritical
    C panchromatic
    D synthetic
    E unconquerable

____ 4. ORTHOGRAPHY
    A eulogy
    B geography
    C handwriting
    D perpendicularity
    E spelling

____ 5. MAGNIFY
    A citify
    B correct
    C decrease
    D increase
    E restore

____ 6. CULPRIT
    A criminal
    B danger
    C doctrine
    D politician
    E victim

_____ 7. INNOCUOUS
   A consecutive
   B frequent
   C harmless
   D incomplete
   E temporary

_____ 8. SOLICITUDE
   A care
   B cost
   C market
   D silence
   E solitude

_____ 9. PARAPHRASE
   A report
   B exaggerate
   C hypothesize
   D restatement
   E sentence

_____ 10. INNATE
   A commence
   B inborn
   C interrogate
   D mediate
   E separate

II. ANTONYMS

In each test item, there is a word in capital letters followed by five answer choices. From these five choices select the one whose meaning is most nearly opposite in meaning to the word in capital letters. Write the letter of your choice in the space next to the number of the item.

_____ 1. CONSECRATE
   A conceal
   B desecrate
   C nourish
   D obey
   E repent

_____ 2. MALEFACTOR
   A benefactor
   B evildoer
   C femininity
   D puerility
   E virility

_____ 3. PATRICIAN
   A childish
   B conjugal
   C motherly
   D plebeian
   E spartan

_____ 4. INFINITE
   A abject
   B limited
   C noisy
   D terse
   E verbal

_____ 5. RIGIDLY
   A loosely
   B accidentally
   C correctly
   D fortunately
   E legally

_____ 6. OVERT
   A alienate
   B content
   C open
   D secret
   E underneath

_____ 7. INGENUOUS
    A contemptuous
    B ignorant
    C odious
    D simple
    E deceitful

_____ 8. CONSEQUENCE
    A cause
    B consecutive
    C magnificence
    D procedure
    E result

_____ 9. INFALLIBLE
    A audible
    B imperfect
    C springy
    D temporal
    E upright

_____ 10. TRAVAIL
    A labor
    B mutiny
    C quiet
    D relaxation
    E trouble

III. ANALOGIES

Each test item contains a pair of words in capital letters. Try to establish a relationship between these two words. Then select from the five answer choices the pair of words whose relationship to each other is the same as that of the two words in capital letters. Write the letter of your choice in the space next to the number of the item.

_____ 1. CENSURE : REBUKE : :
    A blame : wrong
    B cause : effect
    C colossal : gigantic
    D people : animals
    E simple : complex

_____ 2. CEDE : SEED : :
    A concede : succeed
    B give : grow
    C land : plant
    D law : farming
    E paws : pause

_____ 3. SKY : SKIES : :
    A eye : ice
    B half : halves
    C sly : slice
    D star : planets
    E why : wise

_____ 4. ANTHROPOLOGY : GEOLOGY : :
- A   archeology : geography
- B   history : science
- C   man : earth
- D   philanthropy : pyromania
- E   psychology : autonomy

_____ 5. FIRM : STUBBORN : :
- A   wrath : suffering
- B   brat : lad
- C   mule : donkey
- D   Napoleon : Waterloo
- E   resolved : obstinate

_____ 6. HYPOTHESIZE : GUESS : :
- A   conceptualize : think
- B   estimate : error
- C   Pythagoras : Ulysses
- D   theorize : know
- E   theory : practice

_____ 7. TORY : WHIG : :
- A   English : American
- B   king : queen
- C   lawyer : politician
- D   Republican : Democrat
- E   torso : head

_____ 8. MUNCH : EAT : :
- A   apple : pie
- B   drink : thirst
- C   hear : listen
- D   odor : smell
- E   yell : shout

_____ 9. HADDOCK : FISH : :
- A   general : specific
- B   net : line
- C   tortoise : hare
- D   whale : porpoise
- E   wrench : tool

_____ 10. DOG : CANINE : :
- A   cat : feline
- B   cow : bull
- C   donkey : horse
- D   man : feminine
- E   poodle : spaniel

IV. SENTENCE COMPLETION

In each of the following sentences, one or two words are missing. From the five answer choices select the one that fits the sentence best. Write the letter of your choice in the space next to the number of the item.

1. Although our nation had fought for freedom against _____ , many justified slavery as a _____ institution.
   A odds . . . . jealous
   B tyranny . . . . benevolent
   C serfdom . . . . tyrannical
   D slavery . . . . subversive
   E witchcraft . . . . superstitious

2. We found it difficult to understand why the wealthy old bachelor was reluctant to help his _____ relatives.
   A dubious
   B anonymous
   C indigent
   D affluent
   E indifferent

3. It was a massive _____ , not an ordinary greed, that compelled her to burn the will.
   A dog
   B fear
   C ghost
   D hatred
   E rapacity

4. The delay was not mere _____ but truly _____ .
   A days . . . . weeks
   B headache . . . . disease
   C hesitation . . . . procrastination
   D accident . . . . deliberate
   E reluctance . . . . dislike

5. She had criticized many of the girls, but when she _____ Annette, Annette _____ right back.
   A bothered . . . . considered
   B called . . . . screamed
   C ignored . . . . hurried
   D deplored . . . . denied
   E insulted . . . . jeered

_____ 6. A threat of rejection makes some people _____ , but others _____ and become again like little dependent children.

    A happy . . . . cry
    B hungry . . . . eat
    C lovable . . . . hide
    D militant . . . . regress
    E successful . . . . fail

_____ 7. While the _____ goal is to feed the starving children, the long-range aim is to help people assume _____ for their own food supply.

    A apparent . . . . farmlands
    B imagined . . . . struggles
    C immediate . . . . responsibility
    D leader's . . . . chores
    E real . . . . requirements

_____ 8. Questioned _____ without sleep, the suspect fell into a kind of _____ .

    A accusingly . . . . slump
    B automatically . . . . dream
    C deliberately . . . . fantasy
    D incessantly . . . . stupor
    E sometimes . . . . trench

_____ 9. Amid an atmosphere of _____ concern, the committee is still _____ the reports.

    A great . . . . vacillating
    B little . . . . writing
    C mounting . . . . analyzing
    D no . . . . studying
    E some . . . . rejecting

_____ 10. The speaker's _____ convinced the entire audience of the _____ of the deceased senator.

    A eulogy . . . . importance
    B sarcasm . . . . friendliness
    C metaphors . . . . wealth
    D repetition . . . . dullness
    E truthfulness . . . . falseness

R4b

Tests of Written English

Know how tests measure your command of English.

Many different tests help measure the student's ability to write standard English. These tests have names such as _Test of English Usage, Test of English Grammar, Test of Language Expression, Test_ *of Mechanics of English,* and the like. The correct answer on such tests is the choice that is right for formal written English. Things to be marked wrong or incorrect include problems of usage and mechanics, such as the following:

- informal or slang words;
- lack of agreement between subject and verb;
- nonstandard forms of verbs;
- nonstandard comparative or superlative forms;
- vague use of pronoun;
- wrong form of pronoun;
- double negatives;
- sentence fragments;
- wrong use of comma;
- problems with capitalization;
- wrong use of the apostrophe.

In senior high schools, these tests are usually included in a battery of achievement tests, which also measure reading and mathematics. Among the most widely used achievement tests are the *California Achievement Tests* (now called "CAT" by many users), the *Comprehensive Tests of Basic Skills* (CTBS), the *Metropolitan Achievement Tests* (often called "Metro"), and the *Stanford Test of Academic Skills* (TASK). In colleges, tests of English usage and the mechanics of written composition are often administered to entering students to aid in placing them in appropriate English classes.

The best way to find out if students have writing ability is to ask them to write an essay. Such tests are called essay tests. Multiple-choice tests are designed to measure some of the skills that are part of writing ability. The following is a sampling of test questions that you may be asked to answer.

① PARAGRAPH REVISION

This kind of test asks students to check a paragraph for usage problems or errors in mechanics. Portions of sentences in these paragraphs are underlined and numbered. The student is asked to mark each numbered phrase as follows:

U for usage problem
P for punctuation error
C for capitalization error
NE for no error

Read the example on the following page:

Europeans, <u>who travel to Nepal,</u> often describe the cultural
₁

and natural life of <u>the himalayan valleys</u> as ''reminiscent
₂

<u>of the swiss</u> <u>Alps.''</u> Similarities of the two areas in their flora, rock
₃   ₄

formations, <u>and architecture</u> <u>is remarkable</u>. In the highland pastures of
₅   ₆

both, the summer huts stand on carpets of <u>unusual, mountain flowers</u>.
₇

At lower altitudes, winding paths lead from rock-fenced meadows

to villages of gabled roofs and well-tended gardens.

In answering test items of this type, remember that you are looking for a punctuation error, a capitalization error, or inappropriate usage. All sentences should be written in formal standard English.

Here are the answers for the sample paragraph:

• In item 1 there is a restrictive relative clause. Only those Europeans who travel to Nepal can compare it with Switzerland. There should be *no* commas. The answer is *P*.

• In item 2, the Himalayas is the name of a chain of mountains. As a proper name, it should be capitalized, and so should an adjective derived from it. The answer to 2 is *C*.

• In item 3, the word *Swiss* is part of a proper name and should be capitalized. The answer to 3 is *C*.

• In item 4, a period comes before the quotation mark. There is no punctuation error. Since *Alps* is part of the name of the mountains, it is correctly capitalized. The answer is *NE*—no error.

• In item 5, a comma follows the second noun in a series of three. None of the words need capitalization. There is no usage problem. The answer is *NE*.

• In item 6, the period is the correct punctuation for the end of the sentence. Neither of the words need capitalization. But the subject of the sentence is *similarities,* a plural noun. The verb should agree in number with the subject. The verb *is* should be changed to *are.* The answer is *U*.

• In item 7, there should be no comma between *unusual* and *mountain,* because these words are not interchangeable adjectives. The answer is *P*.

② BEST-SENTENCE TESTS

One type of item that is used to measure writing ability lists three or four sentences, each saying roughly the same thing. The student is then asked to choose the sentence that is the best expression of that idea. Often the best choice is the most direct statement: brief and clear, with an active verb, with no dangling or misplaced modifiers, and with no confusing shifts. Look at the following four sample items and try to choose the *best* sentence for each item:

---

8 A Grandmother asked about the baby's new teeth, how was Jimmy's schoolwork, and for a recipe for fudge.

  B Grandmother asked about the baby's new teeth, about Jimmy's schoolwork, and for a recipe for fudge.

  C Grandmother asked about the baby's new teeth, Jimmy's schoolwork, and she wanted a recipe for fudge.

9 F If you want to pass, all assignments should be turned in on time.

  G To pass the course, all assignments should be turned in by you on time.

  H If you want to pass, you should turn in all assignments on time.

10 K In our school, if he or she wishes to, a teacher may assign homework.

  L If a teacher wishes to assign homework, he or she may do so in our school.

  M In our school, teachers who wish to assign homework may do so.

11 A My parents influenced my selection of a career.

  B In selecting a career, my parents influenced me.

  C My selection of a career was due in part to influence of my parents.

Answers:

• In item 8, choices A and C lack parallel structure. In B the three prepositional phrases are parallel: *about* . . . , and *for* . . . . The answer is B.

• In item 9, choices F and G shift from active to passive. Only H is consistent: The subject *you* appears in both parts of the sentence. The answer is H.

• In item 10, both K and L are awkward, partly because sentence parts do not appear in their most natural order. Sentence M is more direct and smoother than the other sentences. The answer is M.

• In item 11, sentence B has a misplaced verbal. (The parents were selecting a career?) The active verb in A makes it more direct and less awkward than C. The answer is A.

③ SENTENCE REVISION

Some tests ask the student to look for a problem—punctuation, capitalization, or usage—in two or three parts of a single sentence. Parts of the sentence are underlined and numbered. The student is asked to label the problem, if any, in each numbered section. The student marks:

P for a punctuation error
C for a capitalization error
U for a usage problem
NE for no error

Try to find the problem in each underlined phrase of the following sentences. If there is no error, mark *NE* on your worksheet.

It <u>didn't use to</u> bother her when <u>uncle Joe</u> asked her, "Mary, want a
　　　12　　　　　　　　　　　　　13

<u>stogy</u>"?
　14

Nobody tried to prevent <u>him from driving</u>, although all knew <u>he had</u>
　　　　　　　　　　　　15　　　　　　　　　　　　　　　16

several <u>drinks'</u>.
　　　　17

Answers:
• In item 12 *didn't use to* is not acceptable in formal English. The phrase should be *used not to*.) The answer is *U*.

• In item 13, *uncle* should be capitalized as part of the person's name. The answer is *C*.

• In item 14, there are two punctuation marks: a question mark and quotation marks. Because the direct quotation is a question, the question mark should come *before* the quotation marks. The answer is *P*.

• In item 15, *from* is the right preposition to use with *prevent*. The answer is *NE*.

• In item 16, the man drank several drinks *before* "nobody tried to prevent him from driving." The verb should be in the more *distant* past (past perfect): *he had had.* The answer is *U*.

• In item 17, the apostrophe in *drinks* is incorrect. The word *drinks* in this sentence is an ordinary plural, not a possessive. The answer is *P*.

④ COMPLETION TESTS

One widely used test of language expression provides paragraphs with several blanks. For each numbered blank, the student is given four choices. The student picks the choice that fits best. Sometimes the four choices are different forms of the same word. For other blanks, the student must select the right relative pronoun, or the right comparative or superlative form of an adjective or adverb, or the right word to fit the context of the sentence. The following paragraph is an example of this kind of test. Read the entire paragraph first and then go back to answer the sample items.

Shyness often results from a feeling of _____18_____ and a fear of taking risks. It prevents us from realizing our full potential and enjoying the _____19_____ of other people. Some persons are _____20_____ as adults than they were as children. Some others, who were shy children, are not _____21_____ adults. The saddest people are _____22_____ who are shy all their lives.

18	A	claustrophobia		19	F	company
	B	emotion			G	homes
	C	happiness			H	openness
	D	inferiority			J	writing
20	K	shyer		21	A	bold
	L	more shyer			B	gregarious
	M	most shy			C	shy
	N	mostly shy			D	strong
22	F	them				
	G	those				
	H	them there				
	J	those there				

Answers:

• This entire paragraph deals with shyness, and the first sentence states a cause. *Emotion* or *happiness* does not cause shyness. The author includes *claustrophobia* as a false lead: *-phobia* means *fear,* and you might choose it to go along with the other *fear* in the sentence. The right answer is *inferiority.*

• Because shy persons do not mix well with others, they miss out on enjoying others' *company.* The answer to item 19 is *company.*

• Item 20 asks only for the correct comparative form of *shy.* The answer to item 20 is *shyer.* (Another correct spelling for this word is *shier.*)

• In item 21, the only answer choice that fits the sense of the sentence is *shy.*

• In item 22, a demonstrative pronoun is needed after the linking verb *are,* which refers to *people. Them* would be nonstandard, and the choices with *there* do not fit. The answer is *those.*

(5) MISSING TRANSITIONS

Some tests include a paragraph with numbered blanks to be filled by the right transitional expression. The missing link may be a coordinating connective, for instance, or an adverbial connective. For each blank the student selects the best word from the four choices. Read the following paragraph and select the best transition word for each numbered blank from the lists of four choices below the paragraph.

She asked her father for a raise in her allowance, ____23____ he was watching the game on TV ____24____ he seemed not to hear her. ____25____, he pulled out a five-dollar bill and handed it to her; ____26____, she was able to go to the movies with her friend.

23 A and
    B besides
    C but
    D moreover

24 F and
    G because
    H in fact
    J therefore

25 K Furthermore
    L However
    M Indeed
    N Instead

26 A consequently
    B still
    C whereas
    D while

Answers:

- For the blank in item 23, a connective is needed to show contrast. The answer is *but*.

- Item 24 needs a connective to link two clauses on an equal footing. The answer is *and*.

- Item 25 needs an adverbial connective that prepares us for a contrast with the previous statement. The answer is *However*.

- Item 26 needs an adverbial connective that prepares us for the result. The answer is *consequently*.

(6) PARAGRAPH ORGANIZATION

Below are examples of test items that test your ability to develop a paragraph. Each item has a list of four sentences, numbered from one through four. You are asked to order these sentences to make the best paragraph.

---

27 1 The starter's pistol cracked, and the women's mile-relay competitors broke from the blocks.

     2 The public address system boomed, "Winner, Brooklyn Atoms; time 3:47.5; a new American record."

     3 Brenda Nichols and Cheryl Toussaint lengthened it even farther, winning by 40 yards.

     4 Gail Fitzgerald of the blue-clad Brooklyn Atoms seized the baton from teammate Michele McMillan and established a clear lead.

       A 1–4–3–2
       B 2–1–3–4
       C 2–1–4–3
       D 3–4–1–2

28 1 She replied, "More willpower than I."

     2 Helen had a fault that she decided to correct.

     3 She said to her friend, Ted, "My New Year's resolution is to stop correcting others."

     4 Ted said, "If you can stick to a resolution, you have more willpower than me."

       F 2–3–4–1
       G 3–4–1–2
       H 4–1–2–3
       J 4–3–2–1

Answers:

• Item 27 is a paragraph about a race. We need to put the sentences in the right chronological order. It is logical that the first sentence would involve the *starter's pistol*. The paragraph would then go on to the lead being *established* and then *lengthened*. Finally, the loudspeaker would announce the *winner*. The answer is A.

• Item 28 is a humorous paragraph about someone's making a New Year's resolution. Because sentences 1 and 3 start with *She,* the person's name should appear in an earlier sentence. Sentence 2 names *Helen* and would make a good start. Sentence 4 makes a good reply to 3. Sentence 1 corrects sentence 4. The answer is F.

**SAMPLE
TEST B**

I. ACCIDENT REPORT

Read the accident report completely. Then go back and reread it carefully. When you come to a numbered, underlined section, look at the four answer choices whose number corresponds to that of the underlined section. Decide which of the four answers is the best choice. If you think that the underlined material is correct as it exists in the passage, mark the letter for "No Change." If you think that one of the three other answers is the best choice, mark the letter of that choice. Write your choice in the space next to the number of the item.

ACCIDENT REPORT

This is a report of a car accident in <u>Carlton on January</u> 20, 1979.
₁
The time was 3:30 p.m. There <u>were nobody</u> hurt. I was driving my
₂
1973 Javelin with license number 369JTJ. I was going east on

<u>Main street</u> when I <u>decide to park</u> in front of the Sears store. There
₃   ₄

was only one parking space left. <u>Because</u> there were cars behind
₅

me, I tried to move forward into the space instead of backing into

it. I misjudged the clearance on the <u>right, and my</u> front right fen-
₆

der struck the front left fender of a 1969 <u>ford pickup truck,</u> license
₇

number 1B23415.

I <u>look everywhere</u> for the truck's owner but <u>couldn't not</u> find
₈   ₉

him. My estimate of the damage to the truck is about \$200, and

my estimate of the damage to my car is about \$300. I <u>send</u> this re-
₁₀

port to the Carlton Police Department and to the National Farmers

Insurance Company.

___ 1. A Carlton, on January
     B Carlton Friday January
     C Carlton during
     D No Change

___ 2. A were no one
     B wasn't nobody
     C was nobody
     D No Change

___ 3. A Main Street
     B a main Street
     C the Main street
     D No Change

___ 4. A was deciding to park
     B decided to park
     C make a decision to park
     D No Change

___ 5. A Although
     B Because of
     C Moreover
     D No Change

___ 6. A right: and my
     B right. And so my
     C right, therefore my
     D No Change

___ 7. A Ford Pickup truck
     B Ford pickup truck
     C ford Pickup Truck
     D No Change

___ 8. A look high and low
     B looked
     C look in the stores
     D No Change

___ 9. A couldn't nowhere
     B couldn't not at all
     C could not
     D No Change

___ 10. A sended
     B did sent
     C am sending
     D No Change

II. APPLICATION LETTER

The letter that follows was written in application for a position
advertised in a newspaper. Read it completely. Then go back and
reread it carefully. When you come to a numbered, underlined section, look at the four answer choices whose number corresponds to
that of the underlined section. Decide which of the four answers is
the best choice. If you think that the underlined material is correct
as it exists in the passage, mark the letter for "No Change." If you
think that one of the three other answers is the best choice, mark
the letter of that choice. Write your choice in the space next to the
number of the item.

244 West Wilson Street
Dorton, PA 19642
August 17, 1980

Box 225
Dorton Daily News

Dear Mr. Roberts:

Please consider <u>me, an applicant</u> for the position <u>mention in your</u>
₁   ₂
advertisement in the Dorton Daily News of August 17. I am 21

years old and a graduate of <u>Dorton high school</u> in the class of
₃

1976.

I have also <u>received a AS</u> degree from Milton County Community
₄

College in 1978, where I <u>studied drafting and</u> electronics.
₅

For <u>the passed two</u> years I have been employed in <u>the shops, of</u>
₆   ₇

Collins Electric Co.

I can refer you for information about my <u>ability's and</u> character
₈

to Jean Collins at <u>Collins Electric to</u> Dr. Megan King at Milton
₉

Community, and to Reverend Carter of the Dorton Baptist Church.

I <u>sure would like to</u> come for a personal interview at your con-
₁₀

venience.

Very truly yours,

___ 1   A   myself to be an applicant   ___ 2   A   mentioned in your
        B   me, an applicant,   B   mentioning in your
        C   me an applicant   C   mentioned in you
        D   No Change   D   No Change

___ 3   A   Dorton High School   ___ 4   A   won a A.S.
        B   Dorton high   B   received an A.S.
        C   Dorton Hi   C   graduated an A.S.
        D   No Change   D   No Change

___ 5   A   studied, drafting   ___ 6   A   the past two
        B   studied drafting,   B   two past
        C   studied: drafting   C   two passed
        D   No Change   D   No Change

__7 A the shops were is
     B the shops of
     C the shops, of the
     D No Change

__ 8 A abilities and
      B ability's, and
      C abilities. And
      D No Change

__9 A Collins Electric Co. to
     B Collins electric company, to
     C Collins Electric, to
     D No Change

__10 A insist that I
      B want to
      C should be glad to
      D No Change

III. PARAGRAPH ORGANIZATION

Each following item has a list of four numbered sentences. Read the sentences and decide which sentence order makes the best paragraph. If you find that order among the answers, mark the letter of that choice in the space next to the number of the item.

_____ 1. 1 It could carry three or four sledders at one time.
          2 When I was a child, we sledded on almost anything.
          3 My favorite vehicle was my Flexible Flyer, which could be steered—in a fashion.
          4 We used cafeteria trays, empty barrels, the hood of an old Hudson, and the seat of our pants.
             A 2–3–1–4
             B 2–4–3–1
             C 3–1–4–2
             D 3–4–2–1

_____ 2. 1 She has also answered pleas of several families who have sought her help in locating a loved one.
          2 Doris Tidler is a psychic.
          3 She is able to see beyond the scope of her knowledge and experiences.
          4 In the past decade she has cooperated with many police departments to help locate missing persons.
             A 2–3–4–1
             B 2–4–3–1
             C 4–1–3–2
             D 4–1–2–3

_____ 3. 1 If uranium is found of good quality and in large amounts, full-scale mining and milling are begun.
          2 Drilling rigs are used at promising sites to sample rock layers beneath and to check for natural radiation.
          3 Uranium, the source of nuclear power, can be found in small amounts in many kinds of rock.

    4 Finding deposits large enough to mine is a big challenge.

       A 1–2–3–4
       B 1–2–4–3
       C 3–2–1–4
       D 3–4–2–1

____ 4. 1 In these warm waters they mate and, in the following year's visit, give birth, after which they begin the long journey northward toward their feeding grounds.

    2 They feed for four summer months in the frigid waters of the Arctic seas.

    3 Then, in October, they leave for the 6,000-mile trip southward to the warm lagoons of Baja California.

    4 The annual migration of the California gray whales is one of the longest undertaken by mammals.

       A 1–2–3–4
       B 2–1–3–4
       C 4–1–2–3
       D 4–2–3–1

____ 5. 1 The kitchen provides ideal conditions for raising some house plants.

    2 In addition, kitchen lights are on for long hours, and artificial light helps plants grow.

    3 Moreover, it is always easy to water plants from the nearby sink.

    4 Adequate humidity comes from the steam during cooking and from running water.

       A 1–2–3–4
       B 1–4–3–2
       C 4–2–3–1
       D 4–3–2–1

____ 6. 1 In 1780 General Gates suffered a bitter defeat at the Battle of Camden.

    2 Two years after he lost his command, a congressional committee was organized to investigate him, but the investigation was canceled before it ever took place.

    3 Forgotten, Gates died in New York City in 1806.

    4 He was removed from his post of commander of his army and replaced by Nathanael Greene.

       A 1–2–4–3
       B 1–3–2–4
       C 1–4–2–3
       D 3–4–2–1

____ 7. 1 The latter is a round cut with 58 facets precisely formed to enhance diamonds' high refraction.

2 The value of a diamond is determined, in part, by its cut.

3 Cut refers to the quality of polishing and shape of the finished diamond.

4 The four common shapes are pear, emerald, marquise, and brilliant.

    A 2–1–4–3
    B 2–3–4–1
    C 3–1–2–4
    D 3–4–2–1

_____ 8. 1 With ax on his shoulder, our tracker set off for help, for long jungle miles lay ahead.

2 I fell asleep watching the small lizards patrol the walls for insects.

3 A problem arose soon after—our jeep refused to start.

4 At first light, a crash of birdsong announced the new day.

    A 1–2–3–4
    B 2–4–3–1
    C 3–1–2–4
    D 4–3–1–2

_____ 9. 1 He gained reelection as governor with a plurality of nearly a million votes.

2 In 1930 Roosevelt won the most brilliant victory in the history of the state of New York.

3 A month later he invited Ed Flynn to the Governor's Mansion.

4 In the library after dinner, he said, "Eddie, I believe I can be nominated for the Presidency in 1932."

    A 2–1–3–4
    B 2–3–1–4
    C 3–4–2–1
    D 4–2–1–3

_____ 10. 1 Also refer to sample filled-in returns in the Appendix of this TAX GUIDE.

2 Acquaint yourself thoroughly with the IRS forms before attempting to fill them in.

3 The Appendix is specifically designed as a step-by-step guide to help you prepare your return.

4 In addition, it may include last minute tax information that may affect your return.

    A 2–1–3–4
    B 2–4–1–3
    C 3–2–1–4
    D 3–4–2–1

ILLUSTRATION CREDITS

ACKNOWLEDGMENTS

Harry M. Caudill and The Atlantic Monthly Company for permission to reprint an excerpt from "Farming and Mining" by Harry M. Caudill. Copyright © 1973, by The Atlantic Monthly Company, Boston, Massachusetts. Reprinted with permission.

The Dial Press for permission to reprint an excerpt from "Puritans of the Orient" by Jade Snow Wong, excerpted from the book *The Immigrant Experience,* edited by Thomas C. Wheeler. Copyright © 1971 by The Dial Press. Used by permission of The Dial Press.

California State University, San Jose, Department of English for permission to reprint the poems "Batman" by Candy Fleming, and "Honey" by Paula Truesdell, from *The Reed,* 1967.

Dean A. Cervenka for permission to reprint "Success Story" by Dean A. Cervenka which appeared in *Since You Asked Me* (Purdue University).

Harper's Magazine for permission to reprint an excerpt from "Cheating," by Immy Humes. Copyright © 1973 by Harper's Magazine. All rights reserved. Reprinted from the September 1973 issue by special permission.

Lois Phillips Hudson for permission to reprint an excerpt from "Springtime in the Rockies" by Lois Phillips Hudson, which appeared in *The Reporter.*

Little, Brown and Company in association with the Atlantic Monthly Press for permission to reprint an excerpt from "The Magnificence of Age" from *The Craft and The Calling* by Catherine Drinker Bowen. Copyright 1953, © 1969 by Catherine Drinker Bowen. Originally appeared in *Harper's.*

Macmillan, Inc. for permission to reprint an excerpt from *The Rise of the Unmeltable Ethnics* by Michael Novak. Copyright © 1971, 1972 by Michael

Novak; and entries from *The Macmillan Dictionary*, William D. Halsey, Editorial Director, copyright © 1973, Macmillan Publishing Company, Inc.

G. & C. Merriam for permission to reprint the entry *nice* from *Webster's New Students Dictionary*, © 1974 by G. & C. Merriam Co.; the entry *fluorescent*, and the synonymies for the entry *long* from *Webster's Seventh New Collegiate Dictionary*, © 1976 by G. & C. Merriam Co.

Casey Miller and Kate Swift for permission to reprint the riddle "One Small Step for Genkind" by Casey Miller and Kate Swift.

William Morrow & Company, Inc. for permission to reprint an excerpt from *Teen-Age Tyranny* by Grace and Fred M. Hechinger. Copyright © 1962, 1963 by Grace Hechinger and Fred M. Hechinger. Reprinted by permission of William Morrow & Company.

Harold Ober Associates, Inc. for permission to reprint an excerpt from "Who Am I?" by Marya Mannes. Copyright © 1968 by Marya Mannes. Reprinted by permission of Harold Ober Associates, Inc.

Oxford University Press for permission to reprint the dictionary entries of *economy-size, cope, Frisbee, brainwashing,* and *cat*, from *A Supplement to the Oxford English Dictionary*, volume 1, A–G. Copyright © Oxford University Press 1972. Reprinted by permission of Oxford University Press.

Random House, Inc. for permission to reprint an excerpt from *Born Free,* by Joy Adamson. Copyright © 1960, by Joy Adamson. Reprinted by permission of Pantheon Books, a Division of Random House, Inc.

St. Martin's Press, Inc. for permission to reprint an excerpt from *Red Roses for Me* by Sean O'Casey. Copyright © 1965 by St. Martin's Press. Reprinted by permission of St. Martin's Press.

Saturday Review World for permission to reprint "Who Killed Benny Paret?" by Norman Cousins (May 5, 1962 issue), and an excerpt from "What's Wrong with Objectivity" by Herbert Bruckner (October 11, 1969 issue). Both reprinted from *Saturday Review*.

Scott, Foresman and Company for permission to reprint the synonymies for the dictionary entry *roam* from the *Thorndike-Barnhart High School Dictionary* by E. L. Thorndike and Clarence L. Barnhart. Copyright © 1968 by Scott, Foresman and Company. Reprinted by permission.

Simon and Schuster for permission to reprint an excerpt from *The Decline of the Wasp* by Peter Schrag. Copyright © 1970, 1971 by Peter Schrag. Reprinted by permission of Simon & Schuster, a Division of Gulf and Western.

INDEX

Numerals in italic indicate illustrations. Charts are identified in the Index.

or events, 178–182

to inform (generalizations),
 198–200

to interpret and evaluate
 (criticism and research),
 231–235, 237–249

to persuade, 222–226

to provide firsthand
 experience
 (autobiography), 189–191

Pyles, Thomas, 12

Question mark

at end of long question, 375

to end sentence needing
 reply, 374

and polite requests, 375

and position with final
 quotation mark, 401

Questions

auxiliaries in, 90

exception to rules for
 forming, 90

inverted verb form in, 89

transformed from
 statements, 88–90

use of *be* and *do* in, 89, 90

use of question words in,
 90

Question words

in noun clauses, 385

to signal question
 transformations, 90

Quotation

block quotations, *252–254,*
 402

capitalization of first word,
 402

colon to introduce, 401

credit tag, 401

direct quotation, 400–401

ellipsis points to show
 omission, 402

examples of correct use in
 research paper, *252–255*

how to footnote, 249

indirect, 404

as part of theme
 conclusion, 169

of poetry and dialogue, 402

quotation within quotation,
 402

quoted words and phrases,
 404–405

short, without comma, 401

square brackets to show
 addition, 402

use in critical paper, 235

use in research paper, 238

Quotation marks

for excerpted words or
 phrases, 401, 404–405

with direct quotations,
 400–401

overuse, with slang terms,
 405

for parts of publications
 (chapter and article
 titles, etc.), 405

and position of other
 punctuation marks, 401

single quotation marks,
 402

for technical words and
 terms, 405

q.v., meaning of, 249

Rau, Santha Rama, 168

*Readers' Guide to Periodical
 Literature,* definition
 and sample entries, 449

Red Roses for Me, 331

Redundancy

in sentence construction,
 306–307

in word choice, 40

Reference, shifts in, 310

Reference materials

card catalogue, 447–448

dictionaries, 453–457

encyclopedias, 450

*How and Where to Look It
 Up,* 451

interlibrary loan
 association, 352

magazines and newspapers,
 451

periodical indexes (*Readers'
 Guide,* etc.), 449

specialized reference books
 (biography, geography,
 etc.), 350–351

vertical file and microfilm,
 352

Reflexive pronouns, avoiding
 nonstandard forms, 273

regardless vs. *irregardless,*
 276

Relative clauses

and agreement, 298

function of, 104, 385

introduced by *that,* 386

misplaced as modifier, 304

omission of relative
 pronoun in, 105

position in sentence,
 104–105, 304

punctuation of, 105,
 385–386

relative pronoun to
 introduce, 104–105, 385

restrictive vs.
 nonrestrictive, 385–386

Relative pronouns

and effect on complete
 sentence, 368

to introduce relative
 clause, 104–105, 385

Requests

imperative verb in, 90

review of (chart), 91

subject deleted in, 90

subject "understood" in, 91,
 368, 369, 375, 377

2 3 4 5 6 7 8 9 10 DODO 88 87 86 85 84 83 82 81 80

HANDBOOK KEY